**SPRINGER PUBLISHING**

W0006968

GET THE MOST FROM YOUR BOOK

 **SPRINGER PUBLISHING CONNECT**™

VOUCHER CODE:

8CFM41N0

Online Access

Your print purchase of *Social Work Child Welfare Practice: A Culturally Responsive Applied Approach,* includes **online access via Springer Publishing Connect**™ to increase accessibility, portability, and searchability.

Insert the code at http://connect.springerpub.com/content/book/978-0-8261-5285-5 or scan the QR code and insert the voucher code today!

Having trouble? Contact our customer service department at cs@springerpub.com

Instructor Resource Access for Adopters

Let us do some of the heavy lifting to create an engaging classroom experience with a variety of instructor resources included in most textbooks SUCH AS:

INSTRUCTOR MANUAL

POWERPOINTS

TEST BANK

Visit **https://connect.springerpub.com/** and look for the **"Show Supplementary"** button on your **book homepage** to see what is available to instructors! First time using Springer Publishing Connect?

Email **textbook@springerpub.com** to create an account and start unlocking valuable resources.

Social Work Child Welfare Practice

Giesela Grumbach, PhD, LCSW, PEL (IL), is the Chair of the Department of Social Work at Governors State University. Her work experience spans 35 years working in schools and in medical and legal settings, as well as private practice. Dr. Grumbach provided counseling services for parents seeking reunification with their children as a subcontractor of child welfare agencies and has provided court testimony for clients seeking family reunification due to involvement in the child welfare system. Additionally, she provided clinical supervision to child welfare professionals seeking licensure postgraduation from an accredited MSW program through an Illinois Department of Children and Family Services (IDCFS) and Governors State University partnership. Dr. Grumbach is a coauthor of *Critical Service Learning Toolkit: Social Work Strategies for Promoting Healthy Youth Development*, published in 2018. This book provides guidance for addressing social-emotional learning standards paired with critical service learning as a tool for elevating youth voices in a variety of settings. She recently coauthored a book with JoDee Keller, *School Social Work: A Skills-Based Competency Approach* (2022), published by Springer Publishing. Dr. Grumbach is the past president of the National Association of Social Workers, Illinois Chapter (2005–2007). She continues to engage in professional associations through the NASW and the Council on Social Work Education (as a reviewer of MSW minority fellowship applicants).

JoDee Keller, PhD, LICSW (WA), is Professor Emerita of Social Work at Pacific Lutheran University, where she taught for 34 years. Dr. Keller has explored comparative child welfare, examining child welfare practices in both European and Caribbean countries. Dr. Keller has conducted research on child abuse prevention and help-seeking behavior as it relates to ethnic diversity and income status, as well as exploring supports and barriers for parents who are seeking assistance with parenting. She has taught BSW-level child welfare courses, with content on resources and risks for children globally and comparative child welfare approaches. Other research interests and publications have included public housing, focusing on children and families; family engagement in schools; parenting education; and school social work. She also has been the faculty liaison for students completing internships in various child welfare settings, both public and private. Most recently, Dr. Keller coauthored a book with Giesela Grumbach entitled *School Social Work: A Skills-Based Competency Approach* (2022), published by Springer Publishing. She maintains her involvement with NASW; the Council on Social Work Education, where she is a reaccreditation site visitor; a local school district; and a Washington State Educational Service District, where she is a member of a multidisciplinary team providing professional training for applicants seeking school certification.

Yolanda Jordan, MSW, LCSW, is a highly seasoned practitioner with over 32 years in child welfare service. Ms. Jordan has worked in various positions within child welfare, including case management, clinical services, and the juvenile court. She also has been a supervisor and manager for foster care placement teams. Ms. Jordan received a departmental award, Outstanding Child Welfare Administrator, and recognition from NASW-IL-Calumet District (Emerging Leader Award, Social Worker of the Year). She is a licensed clinical social worker and private practitioner serving children, families, and couples. Ms. Jordan is currently a Program Manager for Cook County Agency Performance in Illinois, where she manages supervisors, provides direction for clinical competency, community and interagency relationship building, professional development, and program improvement through measurable outcomes. Ms. Jordan uses her skills as a licensed clinical social worker and trained labor relations and mediation/conflict resolution professional to enhance her work in child welfare. In addition, Ms. Jordan also served the profession through her role as the Co-Chair of the Social Work Licensure and Disciplinary Board through the Illinois Department of Financial Professional Regulation. She is also a past president of the National Association of Social Workers, Illinois Chapter (2010–2013).

Social Work Child Welfare Practice

A Culturally Responsive Applied Approach

Giesela Grumbach, PhD, LCSW, PEL (IL)

JoDee Keller, PhD, LICSW (WA)

Yolanda Jordan, MSW, LCSW

 SPRINGER PUBLISHING

Springer Publishing Company, LLC
902 Carnegie Center/Suite 140, Princeton, NJ 08540
www.springerpub.com
connect.springerpub.com

Acquisitions Editor: Mindy Okura-Marszycki
Compositor: Amnet
Production Editor: Joseph Stubenrauch

ISBN: 978-0-8261-5284-8
ebook ISBN: 978-0-8261-5285-5
DOI: 10.1891/9780826152855

SUPPLEMENTS:

 A robust set of instructor resources designed to supplement this text is located at **http://connect.springerpub.com/content/book/978-0-8261-5285-5.** Qualifying instructors may request access by emailing **textbook@springerpub.com.**

Instructor Materials:
LMS Common Cartridge With All Instructor Resources ISBN: 978-0-8261-5282-4
Instructor Manual ISBN: 978-0-8261-5286-2
Instructor Test Bank ISBN: 978-0-8261-5287-9
Instructor PowerPoint Presentations ISBN: 978-0-8261-5288-6
Instructor Sample Syllabus ISBN: 978-0-8261-5289-3

Student Material:
Child and Family Team Meeting PowerPoint Presentation for Video 2 ISBN: 978-0-8261-5281-7
Video Transcripts ISBN: 978-0-8261-5269-5

24 25 26 27 / 5 4 3 2 1

Library of Congress Cataloging-in-Publication Data
Names: Grumbach, Giesela, author. | Keller, JoDee, author. | Jordan, Yolanda, author.
Title: Social work child welfare practice : a culturally responsive applied
  approach / Giesela Grumbach, JoDee Keller, Yolanda Jordan.
Description: New York, NY : Springer Publishing Company, [2025] | Includes
  bibliographical references and index.
Identifiers: LCCN 2024000258 (print) | LCCN 2024000259 (ebook) | ISBN
  9780826152848 (paperback) | ISBN 9780826152855 (ebook)
Subjects: MESH: Child Welfare | Social Work | United States
Classification: LCC HV713 (print) | LCC HV713 (ebook) | NLM WA 320 AA1 |
  DDC 362.7--dc23/eng/20240202
LC record available at https://lccn.loc.gov/2024000258
LC ebook record available at https://lccn.loc.gov/2024000259

Contact sales@springerpub.com to receive discount rates on bulk purchases

Printed in the United States of America.

This textbook is dedicated to the children, youth,
and families served by the child welfare system.
This textbook is also dedicated to the tireless social justice,
antiracist warriors on the frontlines of the child welfare profession every day.

Contents

**SECTION IV. VISIONS FOR TRANSFORMATION OF THE CHILD
WELFARE SYSTEM: PUTTING CHILDREN AND FAMILIES FIRST**

Contributors

Verónica Rodríguez Bailey, MSW, LICSW, Workforce Development, Director of Student Services, Year Up Puget Sound, Seattle Central College, Seattle, Washington

Sara Castillo, Graduate Student in Child Development, Erikson Institute, Chicago, Illinois

Arely Cerda, Graduate Student in Child Development, Erikson Institute, Chicago, Illinois

Cassandra McKay-Jackson, PhD, MSSW, LCSW, Associate Dean for Academic Affairs and Student Services, Associate Professor, Jane Addams College of Social Work, University of Illinois at Chicago, Chicago, Illinois

David A. Simpson, PhD, MSSA, LCSW, Assistant Professor, College of Social Work and Criminal Justice, Florida Atlantic University, Boca Raton, Florida

Eric Velasco, Graduate Student in Child Development, Erikson Institute, Chicago, Illinois

Child welfare professionals are in high demand and are essential to addressing child safety. Choosing a career in child welfare involves critical self-reflection, honesty, and a commitment to serving children and families from a culturally humble position. We are excited to offer this child welfare textbook for students who want to learn as much as possible about the field before entering it.

Child abuse and neglect continue to be pervasive problems, cutting across all demographics. Moving forward, child welfare professionals will be needed to work with families in many aspects, including strengthening parenting skills, preventing child abuse and neglect, and identifying alternative homes for children unable to live with their biological families.

In addition, there have been calls for the increasing professionalization of workers in the child welfare system to decrease turnover and promote quality services. Child welfare professionals have a unique skill set to meet the ever-changing needs of children and families while contributing to shaping policies and practices. In a highly diverse society, appreciation of difference, acceptance of cultural complexities, and recognition of the systemic hindrances that affect families are critical to effective child welfare practice.

GOALS OF THIS TEXT

The authors are two scholar-practitioners and one child welfare practitioner/ administrator. Guest authors are practitioners in clinical specialties, one scholar/ administrator, and several students concerned with the field of child welfare. This textbook was *intentionally designed* to include voices from the field (i.e., child welfare professionals), clinically focused practitioners, and scholars. It enriches the theory-to-practice stance needed to enhance student learning. "It is imperative that students in professional programs be able to put into practice what they have learned in the classroom" (Wren & Wren, 2009, p. 258). One of the *goals of this textbook* is to bridge theoretical content to real-world contexts. As students read through the content, they are prompted to apply what they learn and reflect on how the content relates to their future work.

Critically important to this textbook is to present the reality of child welfare. In so doing, the authors acknowledge system flaws, recognize the need to address systemic oppression, decolonize policies/practices, and implement antiracist/anti-oppressive interventions. The authors further petition readers to *reimagine* a changed system and focus on human-centered, equity-centered, liberatory, and humanizing approaches to working with children and families during their most vulnerable states.

INSTRUCTOR RESOURCES

Included with this textbook are an instructor manual, sample syllabus, test bank, and PowerPoint slides. Additional resources are incorporated in each chapter, including discussion questions, case scenarios, reflection boxes, and other activities. A few video resources have also been provided to illustrate child welfare practice such as conducting home visits and facilitating family team meetings.

INTENDED AUDIENCE

This textbook will primarily be used in child welfare courses taught as part of BSW and MSW programs. It may also be used in courses offered in sociology, psychology, human services, public health, or education. The primary audience is students considering a career in child welfare.

The social work profession is a growing field, with *child welfare* being one of the leading settings for practice. The "Profile of the Social Work Workforce" (Salsberg et al., 2017) examined areas where social workers are employed and found that 41% of bachelor-level social workers are employed in individual and family services, which is a broad category that would include *child welfare*. The "Results of the Nationwide Survey of 2018 Social Work Graduates" (Salsberg et al., 2019), a survey of recent MSW graduates, found that 34.8% of MSW graduates were employed in fields *serving children and families*.

CONTENTS

This textbook is divided into four sections delineating the history of child welfare, child welfare practice, special topics in child welfare, and ways to transform the system.

This book gives students solid background information on child abuse and neglect and current federal policies guiding practice. Additionally, it covers the many roles practitioners play in child welfare. The authors stress the importance of relationships in working with children and families, including significant content on engaging with families, building rapport, conducting home visits, and maintaining quality connections.

The book includes content on the types of abuse and neglect, including current research on risk and protective factors. It reviews the processes from reporting through investigating, as well as all of the possible outcomes, including supportive services for families, removal from the home, relative or foster placement, group homes, family reunification, termination of parental rights, adoption, and aging out of the foster care system. Additionally, there is content on working with diverse and specialized populations within the child welfare system.

The book includes two chapters covering trauma-informed practices. One focuses on the trauma experienced by children in the system as well as their families. Signs of trauma, the importance of considering trauma, and trauma-informed care and practice strategies are reviewed. Another chapter focuses on the vicarious trauma experienced by child welfare professionals. The field needs strong, skilled, ethical, and experienced professionals. The secondary trauma of repeatedly seeing the most vulnerable members of society being harmed or at risk of harm can negatively impact the well-being of the practitioners, potentially leading to impaired practice or leaving the field altogether. By attending to signs of secondary trauma and incorporating supportive supervision and intentional self-care strategies, practitioners can maintain their commitment to this critical field of practice, have higher job satisfaction, and continue to provide quality care to clients.

This text focuses on decolonizing content and seeks to infuse socially just and antiracist practices and cultural humility. It emphasizes the role of culture in understanding families. It addresses social justice issues that permeate the child welfare field, including poverty, racial disproportionality, discrimination experienced by LGBTQ+ youth and adults, and treatment of immigrant and mixed-status families.

DISTINGUISHING FEATURES

This textbook incorporates several unique features. Many chapters contain case scenarios and reflection boxes to promote the application of best practices in child welfare to contextualize the information presented in the chapter. Also included are figures, tables, and various active learning activities such as reflection/discussion questions, chapter summaries, and resources.

This textbook embraces decolonizing and antiracist practices in alignment with core social work values and standards. The child welfare system has historically perpetuated differential treatment based on gender, sexual orientation, social class/poverty, race/ethnicity, ability, language, and immigration status. The text highlights this historical context to promote an understanding of the need for policy change and system transformation. In addition, this textbook offers students guidance in determining their career goals, preventing burnout, and engaging in self-care strategies to increase employee satisfaction.

While many books make strong contributions to the study of child welfare, this text combines several unique elements that focus on practitioners in child welfare and their skill development. The text emphasizes the foundational knowledge and skills essential for effective practice. Additionally, unique to this textbook is how child welfare intersects with other systems. One chapter focuses on child welfare and the school setting for supporting youth in foster care. Another chapter is dedicated to special topics, including military families, teen parents, immigrant families, exploited/trafficked/missing children, runaway children/youth, and inequities associated with substance use.

The blend of practitioner-focused and culturally responsive interventions provides an innovative educational approach to learning. The textbook reviews interventions that promote critical thinking about disproportionality, challenge linguistic and racial biases that impact children and families, and promote diversity, equity, and inclusion through cultural humility.

The authors include content on specific practices in child welfare (e.g., home visits, family team meetings, supervised parent–child visits, reading and understanding social and cultural cues, and worker safety) that are missing from many texts. The practitioner-focused content stresses relationship-building and reviews engagement strategies for working with families in crisis.

This textbook acknowledges the many critiques of the system (such as the upEND movement, family policing, and oversurveillance of low-income families and families of color) due to implicit bias, differential treatment, children being re-traumatized by separation from their families, and the overrepresentation of vulnerable families. Conversely, the authors call on their readers to critically weigh the pros and cons of these critiques. The textbook concludes with possible strategies for transforming the system. One must be able to critically examine all factors related to child welfare to make a difference. Some of these strategies include human and equity-centered and liberatory approaches to community engagement and sustainable practices.

Giesela Grumbach
JoDee Keller
Yolanda Jordan

REFERENCES

Salsberg, E., Quigley, L., Mehfoud, N., Acquaviva, K., Wyche, K., & Sliwa, S. (2017). *Profile of the social work workforce.* The George Washington University Health Workforce Institute and School of Nursing. https://www.socialworkers.org/LinkClick.aspx?fileticket=wCttjrHq0gE%3d&portalid=0

Salsberg, E., Quigley, L., Richwine, C., Sliwa, S., Acquaviva, K., & Wyche, K. (2019). *From social work education to social work practice.* The George Washington University Health Workforce Institute and School of Nursing. https://www.socialworkers.org/LinkClick.aspx?fileticket=eLsquD1s2qI%3d&portalid=0

Wren, J., & Wren, B. (2009). Enhancing learning by integrating theory to practice. *International Journal of Teaching and Learning in Higher Education, 21*(2), 258–265. https://files.eric.ed.gov/fulltext/EJ899313.pdf

Acknowledgments

The authors would like to acknowledge the contributions of current child welfare practitioners for their timely and relevant feedback. We are grateful for the support we had throughout the development of this textbook. Moreover, we appreciate the case scenarios from the field shared by practitioners, illuminating practice in child welfare. In addition, the textbook was enriched by the practitioner reviews of each chapter and those who helped us by editing.

We thank (in alphabetical order): Kyle Biedron, Don Brown, Linda Campos-Moreira, Barbara Darling, Jalance Foxworth (illustrations), Stephanie Gulledge, Kelly King-Holliday, Jennifer Parsons, Kerri Pedrick, Megan Scott, Kristen Smith, Monique Smith, Amy Vujaklija, Chandra Wallace, and Misha Wofford. For assistance in creating the ecomap and genogram in Chapter 6, we thank two MSW graduates (2023), Dorolyn Peters and Kenosha Robinson. We appreciate their creativity, willingness to contribute to this project, and passion for placing children and families first.

Our sincerest gratitude goes to Hope Halliburton, television/media director, for her extraordinary talent, time, and spirit of collaboration. She is passionate about her work and giving back to others through community engagement. She works at major studio venues and is a freelance director.

We are especially grateful for the contributions of guest authors who are scholars and practitioners. These authors offered their specialized insights related to child welfare, trauma (David Simpson), secondary trauma (Veronica Rodríguez Bailey), and schools (Cassandra McKay-Jackson, Sarah Castillo, Arely Cerda, and Eric Velasco).

List of Videos

Video content, available to all purchasers of this text at http://connect.springerpub.com/content/book/978-0-8261-5285-5/chapter/ch00 or via the QR code, supplement the content and can serve as additional resources for several chapters. Each video provides real-world examples and applications for child welfare professionals.

Video 1. New Worker Home Visit

Video 2. Child and Family Team Meeting
(*see also: Child and Family Team Meeting PowerPoint available at http://connect.springerpub.com/content/book/978-0-8261-5285-5*)

Video 3. Adult Transition Planning

Resources

All purchasers of this text have access to the following resources at http://connect .springerpub.com/content/book/978-0-8261-5285-5:

- **Three videos** to supplement the text. This content focuses on real-world applications for child welfare professionals.
- **Child and Family Team Meeting PowerPoint** to accompany Video 2.
- **Video Transcripts**

INSTRUCTOR RESOURCES

 A robust set of instructor resources designed to supplement this text is located at http://connect.springerpub.com/content/book/978-0-8261-5285-5. Qualifying instructors may request access by emailing textbook@springerpub.com.

- **LMS Common Cartridge–All Instructor Resources**
- **Instructor Manual** that includes the following:
  - Chapter summaries
  - Learning objectives
  - Chapter discussion questions
  - Suggested responses
  - Activities for the classroom
- **Instructor Test Bank** with more than 60 short-answer questions with guided responses
- **Instructor PowerPoint Presentations**
- **Instructor Sample Syllabus** containing:
  - Course description
  - Course overview
  - Student competencies
  - Course expectations and assignments
  - Grading rubrics
  - Recommended schedule

Visit http://connect.springerpub.com/content/book/978-0-8261-5285-5 and look for the **"Show Supplementary"** button on the **book homepage**.

Child Welfare History and Services

1

Overview and History of Abuse and Responses to Abuse and Neglect in Child Welfare Practice

Though many tout family values and assert the importance of children as representing society's future, reports of child abuse and neglect and what may seem like inadequate responses to these reports are all too common in the news. At the same time, those who critique the child welfare system suggest that its mission is not child protection but family surveillance and control. What contributes to these apparent contradictions in values? What can social workers, particularly those in child welfare settings, do to address this important social problem of child abuse and neglect while ensuring that children and families are treated justly? What can we, as a society, do to support children and youth more effectively and to truly put children and families first? How can we broaden our perspectives to recognize that families come in many forms, each operating with its own values and traditions, so that we respect and honor all families? How have our views of childhood and appropriate treatment of children evolved over time?

LEARNING OBJECTIVES

By the end of the chapter, you will be able to:

- Articulate changing perspectives on child development throughout history.
- Describe different cultural understandings of childhood.
- Identify practices related to child well-being that emerged in the past two centuries.
- Identify key events in history in response to abuse and neglect.
- Understand the effects of systemic racism and colonialism on the child welfare system.

INTRODUCTION

Children may be viewed as society's greatest resource, providing a sense of hope for the future. Childhood is often portrayed as a magical time for growing, developing, exploring, and expanding one's potential. Childhood also can be seen as a period of vulnerability, as the potential threats in children's physical and social environments can place them at risk. While not all risks and potential harm can be avoided, ideally all children will feel valued, supported, and protected.

Child welfare can be a rewarding, demanding, and intense field of practice: rewarding because of the potential to have a positive impact on some of the most vulnerable members of society; demanding because of the hard work involved and the level of professionalism required; intense because of the sometimes life-and-death decisions and public scrutiny of those in the field. Child welfare social work is complex and challenging. Ethical and evidence-based decisions need to be made in a timely manner, and must consider a multitude of factors. Like all social work practice, it requires a foundation of knowledge, values, and skills.

To understand the current child welfare system, it is important to know the context of this system. This includes the history of the treatment of children and beliefs about the child, as well as informal and then more formal attempts to ensure safe, nurturing environments for all children. This chapter examines different views of childhood, including how the understanding of the child and this stage of the life cycle have changed over time as well as the ways in which the child may be celebrated. The reader is introduced to various cultural practices and beliefs about the birth process, childhood, and parenting. Early responses to child abuse and neglect are discussed, along with milestones in the history of child welfare. Finally, the chapter reviews historical and current contributions to child welfare from communities of color and explores some of the ways racism, colonialism, classism, and sexism have permeated the child welfare system.

HISTORICAL PERSPECTIVE ON THE TREATMENT OF CHILDREN

Child maltreatment, including physical, sexual, and emotional abuse and neglect, has been a significant social issue throughout history. In ancient history around the globe, children were abandoned, beaten, or even sacrificed including in Greek, Semitic, Roman, Egyptian, and Aztec societies (French, 2002; Rundin, 2004). Infanticide occurred for a range of reasons, often economic and/or gender-related, within many different cultures. Murder by neglect (Grey, 2011) or abandonment and exposure occurred worldwide in various forms and eras. Parents were able to sell their children into slavery. However, those aspects of child treatment must be balanced with other views: excavations of some very early burial sites in Egypt suggest that infants were granted personhood, as demonstrated by the care taken with the burial and the items left with the infant's body (Metcalfe, 2021); hieroglyphic and burial evidence indicates that ancient Egyptians treasured and valued their children (French, 2002). In Greece, though, where infanticide was practiced, infants were not considered legal persons until their formal acceptance into the family, which could be a week or so after birth; thus, they would be buried without any special rites or practices (French, 2002). French further notes that Greek and Roman children were an important part of the family but were not the center of family life. Children were less valued in Sparta, which was more militaristic than in other Greek city-states. In Mesopotamia, based on evidence from burials, there is no evidence of children being valued (French, 2002).

In the Middle Ages, children born with apparent disabilities may have been viewed by some as harbingers of evil, possibly representing a union between the mother and a demon; others, however, were more compassionate toward children with disabilities. Within some cultures and religious traditions, children were viewed as requiring severe discipline to help them grow up to be contributing members of society. The saying "Spare the rod and spoil the child" derives from the book of Proverbs in the Christian Bible (New Oxford Annotated Bible, 2001). In many patriarchal societies, children historically were viewed as property. Parents might apprentice out children as young as 5 years of age. Some children came to the British colonies in North America as indentured servants, forming a critical part of the labor force, along with the slaves who were also brought against their will. In fact, over half of the people coming to the colonies south of New England in the 18th century were indentured servants, most of whom were under 19 years of age (Mason, 1994). And, of course, children born into slavery, comprising approximately 20% of children in the Colonies by the late 1700s, could be separated from their parents at any time (Mason, 1994). While these practices would be horrifying in the present day, many were not considered abusive in the era in which they were practiced.

Though perspectives on children's rights have changed and laws have been passed banning child maltreatment and child labor, children continue to be abused and neglected. At the same time, children have been treasured and viewed as a family's and society's hope for the future. Children embody both the hopes and fears of their parents and caregivers—hopes for the future and what they can contribute to society, and fears for their safety and about their possible detriment to society (Boustran & Stratton, 2016). As hope for the future, children require nurturing and support. Fears for their safety require protection and precautions. And parents who have fears for what their child could grow up to be might be inclined to administer harsh punishment.

Overview and History of Abuse and Neglect

In order to understand the context of child abuse, it is important to first explore various perspectives on children and childhood, how these perspectives have changed over time, and how they vary across cultures. Historically, children may have been viewed as miniature adults without understanding their unique needs. Also, while it might be easy to assume that children develop in the same way across cultures and throughout history, that is not the case. All children go through developmental stages, but not necessarily in the same way across cultures, nor with the same meanings. Additionally, the idea of what constitutes abuse has changed over time as perspectives on children have changed.

Historical and Cross-Cultural Views of Childhood

History plays a role in how children and childhood are understood, and we can identify how views of childhood have changed over time. For example, one change most prevalent in industrialized societies is lengthening childhood, maintaining dependency and delaying entry into adult roles. In addition to the effects of the historical era, culture plays a role in child development.

Development takes place in social, cultural, and biological contexts and is best understood within those contexts (Albert & Trommsdorff, 2014). Human development and culture are in constant interaction, each affecting the other (Albert & Trommsdorff, 2014), and as everyone is unique and culture is constantly changing, the process is dynamic. Though all children (and adults) continue to develop across the life span through somewhat similar stages, there are differences in meaning and in development itself, best understood through the lens of culture. Fleer (2015) notes the importance of a cultural–historical model of child development, considering both culture and the historical era, as each by itself gives an incomplete and potentially inaccurate picture. She further states that while development may be viewed as a biological process, any understanding of child development must include non biological dimensions such as values, beliefs, and traditions and a recognition of the reciprocal relationship between each child and their environment. This suggests that while there are some common aspects of child development, there are unique meanings attached to each stage of the process. Lancy (2015), noting the extended period of development for humans compared to the rest of the animal world, suggests that children can contribute to the family's work at earlier ages than typically occurs in Western industrialized countries. He notes circumstances where children have needed to step in and step up, assuming responsibilities beyond what might be considered typical. Historically, children have assumed roles and responsibilities beyond what would be considered appropriate in the present era, including working, caring for younger siblings, and performing demanding household chores.

Albert and Trommsdorff (2014) assert that the same or similar life events can be defined as normative or non normative, depending upon cultural understandings. Cultural differences exist around the meaning of childhood—in some cultures, this phase of development leads directly to adulthood without transitions, so children are raised to be prepared to assume adult roles. In some cultures, children are viewed as a part of heaven and God, needing to be free from any adult responsibilities, whereas in other cultures, children are viewed as economic resources. In some cultures, children are raised to be independent beings, while in others, they are raised to be more interdependent.

The roles of parents/caregivers also vary across cultures and time. "Usually, caregivers' child-rearing goals and practices are part of the general goal to foster the development of qualities and attitudes which are needed to fulfill certain roles in the society successfully, or more specifically, in their relevant social subgroup" (Albert & Trommsdorff, 2014, p. 9). Albert and Trommsdorff further note that when parenting behaviors are consistent with general cultural values, children are more likely to feel accepted and, in turn, accept those parental expectations. This suggests some challenges in families where parents have immigrated and have one set of beliefs and values while their children are surrounded by peers who have another. Additionally, "adults do not parent in isolation, but always do so in a social and cultural context" (Bornstein et al., 2011, p. 214). An awareness of culture, which helps people to make meaning of their experiences, and in turn, shapes behaviors and beliefs, is critical in understanding parenting.

CULTURAL PERSPECTIVES ON BIRTH: CELEBRATIONS OF THE CHILD

Childbirth presents just one example of cultural differences as well as similarities. Childbirth is one of the most celebrated life experiences, and while it is a biological event, it also is socially constructed (Ohaja & Anyim, 2021) with its own unique meanings. In the United States, people often hold baby showers for the expectant parent(s) to celebrate the upcoming birth and provide needed supplies. Childbirth itself has become increasingly medicalized in the United States, ostensibly as a way of reducing infant and child mortality, though some parents are moving away from that model, utilizing midwives, doulas, and home births. Still, prenatal care is viewed as being a necessity, with the recognition that the time before birth is critical to the healthy development of the infant and the well-being of the birthing parent. It should be noted that people in many countries, even Western industrialized nations, have always viewed birth as a natural process as opposed to an illness or medical event.

The United States, as well as other countries, is increasingly diverse in terms of ethnic makeup, and there are many different customs and traditions surrounding the birth process brought by immigrants and refugees from around the world. For example, in some Latin American countries, *la cuarentena* is practiced. This involves a 40-day quarantine of the new mother. Latina mothers may continue this practice (Waugh, 2011) after they immigrate to the

United States. Essentially, this period of time allows for the mother's recovery following the birth, as the human body is viewed as being open after the birth process, needing to close to protect the mother's health (Waugh, 2011). The mother may require the support of the extended family during this time, and if women are not allowed to practice la cuarentena, they may be at greater risk for postpartum depression (Waugh, 2011).

Those of Turkish heritage may make a special drink called *Lohusa Serbeti*. This is a drink made from Lohusa sugar that is pink in color, with additional spices, including cinnamon and cloves. This drink is first given to the mother in the hospital to help bring in her milk, but it also is given to others in the family to celebrate the birth. Interestingly, the Lohusa period is also considered to be 40 days, and during that time, the mother and baby do not leave home (Karahan et al., 2017).

Immigrants from Bali may bring the custom of *nyambutin*, where the infant's feet are only allowed to touch the ground for the first time when the infant has reached the age of 3 months (Rousseau, 2017). Younger babies are considered too holy to touch the ground. Additionally, the child's spirit is not considered fully attached to the child until 3 months following birth, a belief growing out of a Balinese form of Hinduism. Mothers and other female relatives are generally responsible for keeping the infant's feet off the ground, but other relatives and friends also may assist (Rousseau, 2017). In the nyambutin or nyabutan ceremony, the parents are first purified; then, thanks are given to the spirits for protecting the baby. The baby's hair from birth is considered unclean and is cut off. The infant's feet are then allowed to touch the ground for the first time, and the infant is named.

In some parts of Nigeria, Omugwo is practiced. This involves care for the new mother for a period of 40 days or sometimes up to 6 months. Essentially, the birth is celebrated by the entire community. The custom truly represents the adage, "It takes a village to raise a child." The new father may be dusted with baby powder. The mother and infant are cared for by the maternal or paternal grandmother or another relative if the grandmothers are unavailable (Ohaja & Anyim, 2021). These supportive family members also cook and clean, allowing the mother time to recuperate from the birth.

There are countless other examples of birth traditions related to culture, religion, or even one's own family unit. However, there are interesting parallels among traditions, including a period of rest and recovery and sometimes seclusion for the mother and baby (Lancy & Grove, 2011), naming ceremonies, practices with the umbilical cord, and cutting the baby's hair. Some of the customs are in support of practical considerations—the isolation and support of the mother and infant promote a time of recovery and bonding for mother and infant as well as minimizing infant exposure to diseases (Lancy & Grove, 2011); naming traditions encourage ties to the family, religious community, and geographic region. Other traditions facilitate connection to culture and family. The presence of many traditions and rituals underscores the fact that birth is one of the community's most significant life events and that the new child is embraced as a family and community member.

CULTURAL MEANINGS OF CHILD REARING/PARENTING

While the child may be viewed as a special gift to be treated with the utmost care, ideas on parenting continue to evolve and vary widely. What is considered "good parenting" also has changed over time. In the United States, an early book on parenting, *The Care and Feeding of Children*, written by Luther Holt, a pediatrician, in 1894, recommended a "scientific" approach to childrearing, including such practices as strict feeding schedules, not responding to crying, and not cuddling one's baby. In 1928, behavioral psychologist John Watson wrote *Psychological Care of Infant and Child*. Similar to Holt, Watson recommended strict schedules for feeding and sleeping. While it may seem surprising, many parents followed these "scientific" approaches to parenting, even when it was difficult, because it was what experts recommended.

Benjamin Spock's first book came out in 1946, just following the end of World War II. In contrast to the earlier parenting books, he encouraged mothers to trust their instincts and to move away from strict feeding and toilet training schedules, instead responding to the unique needs of their infants. He, also, was a pediatrician, and his books provided a dramatic reversal of the advice given to parents previously. He had a profound influence and changed parenting practices in the United States.

In Nazi Germany, a physician, Johanna Haarer, wrote *The German Mother and her First Child*, published in 1934. In this book, she recommended strict, unemotional parenting (Kratzer, 2019). Parents were advised to only touch their child for feeding and bathing and to ignore their crying. Children were viewed as beings whose wills needed to be broken (Kratzer, 2019). Her books remained in use into the 1960s. This is just one example of the ways in which parenting can be influenced by prevailing views and societal pressures.

Parenting itself is framed within the context of culture. Lu (2016) argues that culture provides the context through which parenting meanings are constructed and argued. She notes differences in approaches to parenting depending upon prevailing cultural values. Cultural contrasts that may emerge in parenting styles and approaches include independence versus interdependence, individualism versus the collective, permissiveness versus discipline, and autonomy versus respect and honor. Culture is dynamic and ever-changing and is expressed in different ways at different times by different individuals. It is transmitted from generation to generation and is modified in the process. Culture is created across the life span in the context of families and communities (Bjorklund et al., 2002, p. 276).

Changes to Views of Childhood

The past 200 years have seen significant changes in the way childhood is viewed. The context of childhood has changed, particularly in Western cultures. Beginning in the 1800s, the period of childhood was increasingly recognized as distinct from adulthood. This distinction was accompanied by the need to protect children from the risks and demands of adulthood. Contributing to changing views of the child were the works of various philosophers. John Locke (1632–1704) and Jean-Jacques Rousseau (1712–1778), among others, presented differing views of childhood (Ryan, 2008). Locke held that the human mind is a *tabula rasa* or blank slate, though humans are born with the ability to receive and manipulate new content. Rousseau rejected the prevailing Christian idea of "original sin" and presented the view that humans are good in their natural state but can be corrupted through institutions. "By the late eighteenth century, the generative tension between the conditioned child and the authentic child (as cut by Locke and Rousseau) helped open a new vista upon childhood" (Ryan, 2008, p. 570). These philosophers and those who followed into the 20th century have contributed to changing perspectives on childhood.

This evolving understanding of childhood continues with the relatively recent discussion of the adolescent brain. Also, the period from birth to adulthood has extended, as has the life span as a whole, leading to the inclusion of additional stages of development. By the mid-1900s, the recognition of the rights of children came into focus, in contrast to the historical view of children as property.

Within industrialized nations, some of the changes over the past century in the ways children and childhood have been understood include:

- *The medicalization of childbirth:* While pregnant women have increasing knowledge of pregnancy and birth, the norm is that they are under the care of a medical provider. The goal is to reduce infant and maternal mortality, and that has happened. However, due to historical and ongoing oppression, inequities in infant mortality rates continue in the United States, with Black, Native Hawaiian/Pacific Islander, and American Indian and Alaska Native (AIAN) rates being significantly higher than those in Asian, White, and Latinx communities. There are geographical differences as well, with higher rates of infant mortality in southern states (Ely & Driscoll, 2020).

- *Child labor laws excluding children from paid work:* In the late 1800s and early 1900s, large numbers of children worked in factories. Addressing child labor was a goal of the Progressive Era movement and one of the aims of the child-saving movement. Various attempts were made to pass legislation regulating child labor. Some states passed laws, but these often were not enforced. Federal legislation was passed in 1916 and 1919, but these laws were ruled unconstitutional. The Fair Labor Amendment was passed by Congress in 1924 but was not ratified by enough states to become law. Finally, the Great Depression and its accompanying widespread unemployment brought about an interest in limiting child labor. As a result, the Fair Labor Standards Act (FLSA) was signed into law in 1938. In part, the law prohibited oppressive child labor, although farm labor was excluded. Though this exclusion was intended to support the family farm, migrant farm workers' children continue to perform hazardous agricultural work, including exposure to toxic chemicals found in fertilizers, pesticides, and herbicides.

- *Compulsory education:* Coinciding with the Progressive Era, emphases were on banning child labor and keeping children and youth in school. The value of education was increasingly recognized. If children were no longer working in factories, it became important for them to have productive activities that could contribute to their lifelong well-being. The responsibility for public education is delegated to the states, and individual states have passed compulsory education laws, at varying times, from as early as the Massachusetts Bay Colony in 1642 (later as a state, passing the first compulsory education law in 1852) to Mississippi, in 1918 (Katz, 1976). However, the mechanisms for enforcement were not in place until the 1930s, when it became increasingly important to have an educated workforce (Katz, 1976).

- *More money spent on children:* Previously, children were viewed as an economic asset, additional help on the farm. As the median age and life expectancy increased in the United States, children became a smaller segment of the population and were viewed as less of an economic asset and more of an economic liability. Rather than talking about the contributions of the child to the family income (laborers on the family farm, working in the factory after completing eighth grade), the focus is on the cost to raise a child from birth to age 18, with that cost rising each year. There is more emphasis on active parenting and providing children with resources and opportunities to enhance their development. As a result, children and youth have become a marketing niche with specialized products, activities, and clothing.

- *Development of child welfare as a field:* The need for child protection represents another change over the past two centuries, described further in the following.

- *Emphasis on the "rights of the child":* Increasingly, with the recognition of childhood as a unique stage of development, the considerations of the child have received increasing attention, even globally, with the United Nations (UN) Convention of the Rights of the Child (CRC; UN, 1989). Though the CRC was unanimously ratified by the General Assembly of the UN, it has never been ratified in Congress. However, in the United States, children are recognized in their own right and not as a "subperson over whom the parent has an absolute possessory interest" (Cornell Law School, n.d., para. 1). Because the emphasis on individual rights is primarily a Western concept, it is important to recognize other perspectives. For example, Indigenous cultures often incorporate a relational worldview emphasizing spirit and spirituality; the emphasis may be on the sense of community, and respect for the individual grows out of that.

Perspectives on the Family: Privilege Versus Antiracist Views

Families may take many different forms; no specific form should be considered the standard. There are many ways to raise and nurture children. However, the nuclear family has been held up as the ideal in the United States for the past half-century (Brooks, 2020) or longer, even though this model has never truly been the norm (Coontz, 2016). Yet many people continue to view the nuclear family as the aspirational model, inaccurately seeing it as the dominant family form during an earlier era when times may have seemed less complicated—even though this "ideal" never was the dominant type of family (Coontz, 2016). Many myths exist about the benefits of a nuclear family, mostly denigrating single parents or never married parents. There is no evidence that being raised by a single parent increases the likelihood of dysfunction in the family or in children; even family poverty is explained by systemic economic factors more so than family structure (Coontz, 2016).

This privileged status given to the nuclear family may undermine children from other family contexts. Indirectly, the nuclear family, as the ideal, has privileged the upper class, who have the resources to create many of the supports of the extended family, while lower-income families do not. Historically, it is apparent that the extended family has often played a role in the informal support provided for dependent children. Collective child-rearing has been the norm throughout much of history (Coontz, 2021). In fact, over time, grandparents and, to a lesser extent, other extended family members of all cultures have played a significant role in supporting children (Bjorklund et al., 2002). Extended families provide resilience and exemplify the saying that it takes a village to raise a child, as there are many role models for the developing child (Brooks, 2020). Brooks also makes the point that for much of human history, across the globe, extended family included not just blood relatives but other important associations made by choice.

In particular, the privileging of the nuclear family has harmed families of color, especially Native American and African American families, who have become significantly overrepresented in the child welfare system. Among Native Americans, "It was common and desirable for extended family members . . . to participate in the upbringing of children. However, non-Indians maligned this cherished aspect of Indian life as out of step with modern American family standards" (Jacobs, 2013, p. 147). Extended family, fictive kin, and community have historically played an important role in the care and nurturing of children, but rather than viewing these additional supports as strengths, the child welfare system may have treated families as deficient or unstable if they were not the traditional nuclear family. Essentially, though, children and youth need a strong network of support and a family that is not demeaned or viewed as being less valuable.

Reflection Box 1.1

1. What initially comes to mind when you think of the term "family"?
2. How do you define family?
3. In what ways do you think some family forms are superior to others for raising children? Why or why not?
4. How might your personal experiences in a family affect your approach to working with children and families in a child welfare setting?
5. How might you become aware of these experiences so that they do not become a form of implicit bias?
6. How do you see the idealization of the nuclear family as having an impact on the field of child welfare?

HISTORY OF RESPONSES TO ABUSE AND NEGLECT: EARLY APPROACHES TO SERVICES

Prior to the 1830s, there were few orphanages in the United States. Widows and orphans were considered part of the worthy poor, so families and communities generally provided care for them. Additionally, indenturing or apprenticing allowed children to live in private homes if their parents were unable to care for them. However, with increased immigration and urbanization, unsupervised and impoverished children were more visible, with less community support. Orphanages began to be more prevalent, largely under religious auspices. Other approaches emerged for the care of children in need.

Orphan Trains: Charles Loring Brace

Charles Loring Brace was a Protestant minister and founder of the New York Children's Aid Society in 1853. He was concerned about the plight of low-income children in New York and other urban communities and authored *The Best Method of Disposing of Our Pauper and Vagrant Children* (1859). He is best known for the orphan train movement, whereby children were removed from New York and other eastern cities and sent by train to midwestern and western states, Canada, and Mexico (Adoption History Project, n.d.). Brace's intent was to remove children from what he saw as neglectful circumstances, either being abandoned or orphaned or living with parents who were not adequately caring for them, and moving them to what he may have viewed as more stable families, who, in turn, might benefit from child labor. In actuality, most of these children came from poor Catholic families, many of whom were immigrants, in crowded urban environments, and they were sent by train to be placed with Anglo-Protestant families in rural communities and small towns. As most of the children were Catholic, some viewed Brace's work as more like child stealing than child saving. This led to an increase in sectarian orphanages, with 322 infant asylums and orphanages serving more than 70,000 children by 1910 (Adoption History Project, n.d.). The orphan trains continued until the 1930s, and it is estimated that 200,000 children were placed with new families during the roughly 80 years of this program. During the 1900s, the Children's Bureau played a role in phasing out orphan trains and moving toward orphanages, foster care, and more permanency for children. The orphan train movement stopped in 1930 for a variety of other reasons, including a decreased need for farm labor in the Midwest, a greater emphasis by social service agencies on keeping struggling families intact, the beginnings of welfare programs to help with financial supports for children, child labor restrictions, and programs to help immigrants find housing and employment (Warren, 1998).

Boarding Schools: Ethnocide

Child abuse can occur at an individual/family level but also at an institutional level. The Native American boarding schools represent institutionalized child abuse, disrupting traditional support systems and creating trauma passed on from one generation to the next, which may then contribute to the perpetuation of abuse and neglect. In 1819, the U.S. Congress passed the Indian Civilization Act, authorizing funds for benevolent organizations to educate Native American children (U.S. Department of the Interior [DOI], 2021). Though some at the time may have viewed this as a way of supporting Indigenous populations through assimilation, this began the process of destroying Native American culture and assimilating children and youth into European American culture. Between 1819 and 1969, hundreds of thousands of children and youth were removed from their homes and placed in boarding schools run or funded by the U.S. government (National Native American Boarding School Healing Coalition, n.d.; DOI, 2021). The first such school was Carlisle School in Pennsylvania.

In the 150-year span between 1819 and 1969, there were 408 federal boarding schools across 37 states or territories, including 21 in Alaska and seven in Hawaii (DOI, 2022). These schools were generally located at a distance from the reservation, and the intent was to remove the children from the cultural and linguistic influences of their Native American nations. Attendance was mandated by the U.S. government, regardless of whether parents gave consent. Approximately 50% of these schools received some support in the form of funding, personnel, or infrastructure from a religious organization (Newland, 2022). Children as young as 3 years of age were removed from their families, who were forbidden to visit. Children and youth were forced to cut their hair and were punished for not speaking English or not using their English names; they were forced to complete military-style drills (DOI, 2022). The overall goal was broad assimilation into the dominant culture. Authorities expressed concerns about the ways that Native American children were being raised and were especially critical of Indian mothers (Jacobs, 2013). Beyond assimilation, a secondary goal was to decrease the strength and influence of Indigenous groups, a practice that had a significant disruptive effect on family life and normalized the separation of Indigenous children from their families (Jacobs, 2013).

Many youths succumbed to influenza, tuberculosis, measles, and other diseases while residing in the boarding schools. Many parents refused to allow their children to be taken to boarding school and fought for their rights in court. However, thousands of children and youth were removed from their homes, never returning to their families, and experiencing physical, sexual, cultural, and spiritual abuse. By the 1920s, more people began to question the methods used in boarding schools. However, the schools continued for many years. Alaska Natives and Native Hawaiian children were also subjected to similar removal and forced assimilation methods.

In the 1950s and 1960s, with the relocation and termination policy, many Native Americans were relocated to urban areas. Essentially, this federal government policy sought to relocate Native Americans, then terminate tribal recognition (National Library of Medicine, n.d.). In urban environments, Native Americans faced increased challenges and adjustments, but without the support of extended family and community (Stanford Medicine, n.d.). The limited support and increasing visibility to social service agencies significantly increased Indigenous children in state child welfare systems (Jacobs, 2013).

Due to the removal of such large numbers of children from Indigenous families, multiple generations did not learn how to parent within their cultural context, thereby laying the groundwork for the adoption of Native children by White families, which occurred with great frequency into the 1960s and 1970s under what became known as the Indian Adoption Project (IAP), a joint venture between the Bureau of Indian Affairs (BIA) and the Child Welfare League of America (CWLA) (Jacobs, 2013). Between 1958 and 1967, CWLA cooperated with the BIA, under a federal contract, to facilitate an experiment, primarily in the New England states, in which 395 Indian children were removed from their tribes and cultures for adoption by non-Indian families. CWLA channeled federal funds first to its oldest and most established private agencies to arrange the adoptions, though public child welfare agencies also became involved. Exactly 395 adoptions of Indian children were completed and studied during this 10-year period, with the numbers peaking in 1967. Apart from the children included in this experiment, White adoption of Indian children continued into the 1960s, with approximately 650 children being removed from their families and tribes (Sciamanna, n.d.). In 2001, Shay Bilchuk, then CWLA president, apologized for this profoundly detrimental practice (Tribal Law and Policy Institute, 2011).

During the same time as the IAP, state child welfare departments removed disproportionately higher numbers of Native American children from their families. The Association for American Indian Affairs (AAIA) gathered data from various states across the country and discovered that in states with large Native American populations, 25% to 35% of those children had been removed and placed in adoptive families, foster families, or institutions (Jacobs, 2013). Many social workers played an active role in this process due in part to the misapplication of White middle-class understandings of family environments. Poverty may also have played a role, as it was viewed as a moral failing of the individual family (Jacobs, 2013) rather than as a systemic issue. Jacobs (2013) cites an example of children removed from their families because they had no indoor plumbing. Workers also applied stereotypes of alcoholism among Native Americans when there was no evidence of such (Jacobs, 2013). The continued removal of Native children led Indigenous nations to develop their own child welfare agencies and compelled activists to push for the adoption of the Indian Child Welfare Act (ICWA), passed in 1978 (Jacobs, 2013).

The removal of children and attempts at assimilation, along with other injustices, contributed to historical trauma. Indigenous historical trauma (IHT) has been characterized as being "*colonial* in origin, *collective* in impact, *cumulative* across adverse events, and (especially) *cross-generational* in transmission of risk and vulnerability" (Gone et al., 2019, p. 21), making historical trauma distinct from other forms of trauma. Native American children continue to be disproportionately involved in the child welfare system, even with ICWA and Indigenous nations having their own child welfare systems. The issues related to boarding schools and adoptions have not received the acknowledgment or attention they are due, perhaps because of the trauma, pain, and sense of shame involved in these activities; many may not want to relive or revisit these experiences (Jacobs, 2013). Learning about Indigenous history and the boarding schools can cause anger, hurt, shame, and many other emotions. While noting the IHT, it also is important to recognize resilience; trauma is only part of the story. In 2021, the Senate proposed a bill to establish the Truth and Healing Commission on Indian Boarding School Policies in the United States. This bill has been referred to the Committee on Indian Affairs. Deb Haaland, Secretary of the Interior under President Biden, has requested an investigation into the federal Indian boarding school system.

Child Saving Movement

Before the Civil War, orphanages were generally small, usually run by women, and religiously oriented. Following the Civil War, orphanages grew in size and were often under the administration of men, as women were pursuing other issues such as suffrage. At the same time, with the changing views of childhood and the recognition of the importance of this stage, ideas about ways to help children were evolving.

The period between 1865 and 1900 marked a dramatic transition in the United States, moving from an agrarian to a more industrialized society with increasing affluence and income disparities (McNally, 1981). Population growth was dramatic, with a demographic population shift, as well as geographic redistribution and the beginning of suburbs. Immigrants were often blamed for urban poverty (McNally, 1981). The progressive movement emerged at this time, focusing on social ills. Middle-class women became more vocal about addressing those ills (McNally, 1981). The child-saving movement arose during this same period. The primary emphasis of the child-saving movement was the development of the juvenile court system, though the accompanying problems of child labor and lack of compulsory education were also raised (McNally, 1981). Ultimately, child savers held the perspective that children should not be treated as adults. Although initially the child-saving movement, and particularly the adoption of children from lower-income immigrants by middle-class parents, led to competing values during the Progressive Era, eventually support came out on the side of birth parents (Davies, 2017). In the early 1900s, with increasing awareness of the child's need to remain within an intact family whenever possible, there was a shift in the original goals of child saving toward the provision of resources to families so children could remain with them, reducing the need for orphanages or institutions (Davies, 2017). As an example, a report following the attempt to rehouse children who lost their fathers in the Monongah, West Virginia, Mining Disaster of 1907, in which over 400 men died, recommended that "Wherever it is possible, mothers will be encouraged to keep their children, with the assistance of relatives and the proceeds of life insurance policies and the relief measures" (Davies, 2017, p. 160).

Mary Ellen Wilson: American Society for the Prevention of Cruelty to Animals

The story of Mary Ellen Wilson illustrates the lack of a comprehensive child abuse reporting system and the role that concerned individuals can play in assisting children experiencing abuse and bringing about systemic changes to benefit children more broadly. This story is significant as it set in motion a more formal system to report and intervene in abuse and neglect cases. Mary Ellen Wilson was born in 1864 in New York City. Shortly after her birth, her father died, and her mother was unable to take care of her. As was the custom at that time, her mother boarded her out with another woman. However, her birth mother fell behind in payments, and Mary Ellen was then turned over to the Department of Charities, who placed her with yet another family. The new foster mother, Mary McCormack Connolly, badly mistreated Mary Ellen. Neighbors were aware of the mistreatment and asked a mission worker, Etta Wheeler, if she could help the child. New York, at that time, did have a law permitting the state to remove children who were neglected by their caregivers. However, authorities chose not to intervene. Wheeler came upon Henry Bergh, founder of the American Society for the Prevention of Cruelty to

Animals (ASPCA). Ultimately, a New York SPCA investigator confirmed the alle-gations. As a result, Bergh filed cruelty charges and contacted *The New York Times*, resulting in reporters attending court hearings. Since no child welfare agency would come to Mary Ellen's aid, an agency to help animals took the lead. They argued that Mary Ellen was part of the animal kingdom and, therefore, they had the right to intervene on her behalf. She was removed from her foster mother. This case highlighted the necessity for more agencies and services to assist children. In 1875, the New York Society for the Prevention of Cruelty to Children (NYSPCC) was founded, the world's first child protection agency (NYSPCC, n.d.). This agency is in existence today, providing prevention, counseling, educational, and legal services.

White House Conferences on Children

The first White House Conference on Children was convened by President Theodore Roosevelt in January 1909. These conferences were held approxi-mately every 10 years and focused on a theme that was relevant to the decade in which each occurred (U.S. Department of Health, Education, and Welfare [HEW, now known as the Department of Health and Human Services], 1967). The last such conference was held in 1970. The first conference came in response to the growth in institutionalized care of children that characterized the later years of the 19th century (HEW, 1967). Concerns arose from a number of differ-ent sources. The National Child Labor Committee was more broadly concerned with children's welfare (Stretch, 1970). James West, a child adoptee who grew up to be an attorney and friend of Roosevelt, was one of the planners of the White House Conference (Jambor, 1958).

The novelist and then editor of the *Delineator* magazine, Theodore Dreiser, was motivated by the need to rescue children from institutionalized care and place them in a family environment. At the *Delineator*, he began a Child Rescue Campaign with the slogan: "For the Child that Needs a Home and the Home that Needs a Child" (Jambor, 1958). While originally seeking to place children with middle-class families, Dreiser had a change of heart and later argued that outside organizations should not have sole discretion about mothers' abilities to care for their children, as this allows for unnecessary intrusion on homes and families and puts excessive power in the hands of the few.

The general timing of the White House Conference and broader interest in children was not surprising, as there was increasing recognition of the need for the federal government to be involved in the welfare of the nation's residents (Jambor, 1958). The conference concluded that home life is superior to institutional life, recommending that children should remain with "worthy parents or deserv-ing mothers" (Stretch, 1970, p. 369), urging adoption whenever possible and pro-moting quality foster care. Institutions, when they are the best or only available option, should be organized in smaller cottages with qualified staff and with states monitoring quality (HEW, 1967). The emphasis placed on keeping the child in the home environment when appropriate and possible, and the belief that poverty should not be a reason for removal, led to the movement for mothers' pensions (Stretch, 1970). Other recommendations of the conference included the creation of a federal children's bureau and a voluntary national agency engaged in child welfare, resulting in the CWLA in 1920.

By 1935, most states had mothers' pensions in place, and this became the foundation for the Aid to Dependent Children (ADC) provision of the Social Security Act of 1935. Though orphanages were viewed less favorably than a family environment, it was not until the 1950s that the number of children living in foster homes exceeded the number living in orphanages or other institutional settings (Adoption History Project, n.d.-b).

The second White House Conference on Standards of Child Welfare was held in 1919, at the end of the Great War (World War I), and was concerned with how to give every child an opportunity in a peaceful world. It was called at the urging of Julia Lathrop, a social worker, then Chief of the Children's Bureau (HEW, 1967). Before the conference, 1918 was proclaimed The Children's Year to highlight the importance of preserving childhood during a national crisis. In 1919, following the war, President Wilson noted that besides the care of veterans of the Great War, there was no duty more patriotic than protecting children, who made up one third of the population at that time. The Conference concluded with recommendations regarding the health of mothers and children, child labor, and children with special needs. Subsequent conferences were organized around themes consistent with the historical era, as seen in Table 1.1

TABLE 1.1 WHITE HOUSE CONFERENCES ON CHILDREN

YEAR	PRESIDENT	THEME	CONTEXT	ISSUES
1930	Hoover	Child and Health Protection	Great Depression, child welfare workers overwhelmed by poverty	Focus on social and environmental factors affecting children, compulsory education, rights of children with disabilities; Children's Charter (19 statements of what children need)
1940	Franklin Delano Roosevelt	Children in a Democracy	Prior to U.S. involvement in World War II	Include all children, not just those facing poverty; prepare children to grow up to participate in a democracy; ensure adequate wage for breadwinner

(continued)

TABLE 1.1 WHITE HOUSE CONFERENCES ON CHILDREN (*continued*)

YEAR	PRESIDENT	THEME	CONTEXT	ISSUES
1950	Truman	Midcentury Conference on Children	Post World War II, "Baby Boom"	Emotional and spiritual qualities for responsible citizenship; physical, emotional, and social conditions for optimal development; 10% of participants were under 21 years of age

Source: Adapted from U.S. Department of Health, Education, and Welfare. (1967). *The story of the White House Conferences on Children and Youth.* Social and Rehabilitation Service, Children's Bureau. https://files.eric.ed.gov/fulltext/ED078896.pdf

Julia Lathrop: Children's Bureau

Prior to the establishment of the Children's Bureau, the reformers of Hull House advocated for child labor laws, the establishment of juvenile courts, and interventions to protect abused and neglected children (Child Welfare Information Gateway, n.d.-a). In fact, the first two chiefs of the Children's Bureau, Julia Lathrop and Grace Abbott, were former residents of Hull House. The Children's Bureau was the first federal agency tasked with the well-being of children. Lillian Wald of the Henry Street Settlement and Florence Kelley of Hull House are credited with having the idea for this agency as early as 1903. They secured a meeting with then-President Roosevelt, who was supportive. Following the first White House Conference on the Care of Dependent Children in 1909, Roosevelt wrote a letter to Congress endorsing the establishment of a federal children's bureau (Child Welfare Information Gateway, n.d.-a).

President Taft signed the act creating the Children's Bureau into law in 1912. Julia Lathrop, the first chief of the Children's Bureau, was committed to supporting the well-being of children. She studied maternal and infant health, the birth rate, child labor, orphanages, juvenile courts, and accidents and diseases of children, and she developed child welfare services (Child Welfare Information Gateway, n.d.-a). Lathrop promoted the use of research in assessing infant and maternal mortality as well as other issues relevant to child well-being. The first study of infant mortality began in 1913 in Johnstown, Pennsylvania. These studies and resulting interventions contributed to the 24% decline in infant mortality between 1915 and 1921 (Child Welfare Information Gateway, n.d.-a). The Bureau published booklets on Prenatal Care and Infant Care to distribute findings to the public.

In 1918, the Bureau promoted the first Children's Year with the theme of *Saving 100,000 Babies.* As this was during the First World War, parents were encouraged to protect their children as part of their patriotic duty; this included keeping their children in school and out of the workforce, promoting their children's health, and monitoring their weight and growth (Child Welfare Information Gateway, n.d.-a).

The Children's Bureau continues to exist and provides several services in support of child welfare, including funding to support research on effective interventions. Lathrop's recommendations for infant and maternal health helped to create the foundation for the Sheppard-Towner Act.

Sheppard-Towner Act

The legislation leading to the Sheppard-Towner Act was first introduced in 1918 by Representative Jeanette Rankin of Montana, the first woman in Congress. Interestingly, she was elected to Congress in 1916, 4 years before women had the right to vote. After Rankin left Congress in 1919, the legislation was sponsored by Senator Sheppard of Texas and Representative Towner of Iowa (U.S. House of Representatives, n.d.). The Act was signed into law in 1921 by President Warren Harding. The Sheppard-Towner Act intended to address high mortality rates among mothers and infants and provided $1 million annually for state programs, with a special emphasis on prenatal and infant care facilities in rural states (U.S. House of Representatives, n.d.). Sheppard-Towner was administered by the Children's Bureau. This Act was controversial because it was a first step toward a federal government role in welfare-related issues; it was not renewed by Congress in 1929. In addition to the controversy over the role of government, there was the debate over which federal agency should administer such programs, the male-dominated Public Health Service or the female-dominated Children's Bureau (Child Welfare Information Gateway, n.d.-a).

Child Welfare League of America: 1920

One of the recommendations of the first White House Conference on Children was the establishment of a permanent organization that would focus on standards to implement the other conference recommendations. In late 1920, the CWLA was established. Its original purposes were to study child welfare to improve methods and develop quality standards, assist social welfare agencies, and promote community planning to better serve children (Social Welfare History Archives [SWHA], 2013). The organization continued to promote foster care over institutional placement of dependent children and was involved in the development of child protective services as well as federal legislation related to child abuse and neglect (SWHA, 2013). The CWLA continues its work today; it has published a journal since 1922, sponsors an annual national conference, provides training in a wide range of areas relevant to child well-being, is engaged in legislative and advocacy work, and partners with a number of member organizations in the United States and Canada (CWLA, n.d.).

The 1920s and 1930s produced a growing emphasis on child welfare. Wilma Walker began teaching at the University of Chicago School of Social Service Administration in 1928, and in 1937 she published *Child Welfare Case Records*, which became a major text for those students going into child welfare social work (National Association of Social Workers [NASW] Foundation, n.d.-b).

C. Henry Kempe: Battered-Child Syndrome: (*Journal of the American Medical Association*)

Following World War II during the 1940s and 1950s, physicians in the United States and the United Kingdom began to notice discrepancies between parents' explanations of injuries and the physical appearance of those injuries in young children. Up to the early 1960s, emergency department physicians observed that some child injuries did not correspond with parent descriptions. Seeing this pattern, C. Henry Kempe, a radiologist, coined the term battered-child syndrome in an article with the same title that he co-authored in 1962 for the *Journal of the American Medical Association* (*JAMA*). This article served to increase public awareness of child abuse in both the United States and the United Kingdom. As physicians became more aware of abuse, others, including social workers, teachers, and the general public, were expected to share this responsibility for protecting children. "Child abuse became a social and political problem, as well as a medical one" (Crane, 2015, p. 768). The increased awareness of physical abuse led to more states strengthening services for children and was the impetus, a decade later, for the passage of the Child Abuse Prevention and Treatment Act of 1974 (CAPTA). Kempe's article exhorted physicians to investigate when the injuries did not match the descriptions. The x-rays might, for example, show evidence of several incidents of abuse over time because of the nature of children's bone growth. However, physicians were initially reluctant to recognize this (Crane, 2015). At the time, the approach of Dr. Kempe and other physicians was a radical departure from the customary practice in that they considered the child as the patient rather than the parents (Crane, 2015). A few decades later, pediatricians more widely accepted the approach common in present practice, where the child is viewed as the patient. Physicians valued privacy but increasingly recognized how secrecy around family issues could be detrimental in the case of child abuse (Table 1.2).

TABLE 1.2 KEY EVENTS IN CHILD WELFARE HISTORY

DATE	EVENT	SIGNIFICANCE
1819	Indian Civilization Act	Funding for boarding schools for Native American children
1854	First Orphan Train arrived in Michigan and continued into the 1930s	Precursor of foster care system; i.e., out-of-home care that is not an orphanage; removal of mostly Catholic immigrant children from northeastern cities, sending to mostly Protestant rural families in the Midwest
1974	Mary Ellen Wilson referred to NY Society for the Prevention of Cruelty to Animals	Illustrated lack of services for abused and neglected children; led to establishment of NY Society for the Prevention of Cruelty to Children

(continued)

TABLE 1.2 KEY EVENTS IN CHILD WELFARE HISTORY (*continued*)

DATE	EVENT	SIGNIFICANCE
1909	First White House Conference on Children	Raised awareness of needs facing children; led to establishment of the Children's Bureau
1912	Establishment of Children's Bureau	First federal agency dedicated to the well-being of children; utilization of data and research in decision-making
1920	Child Welfare League of America founded	Coalition of public and private child welfare agencies dedicated to advocacy and enhancing positive outcomes for vulnerable children, youth, and families
1921	Sheppard-Towner Act	Funding for pre- and neonatal care; beginning of federal role in providing welfare services until 1929
1962	Publication of "The Battered-Child Syndrome"	Increased awareness in medical community of physical indicators of child abuse

VOICES OF PEOPLE OF COLOR IN CHILD WELFARE HISTORY

Diverse communities have been a part of the history of the United States from the beginning of the Colonial era in the North American continent up through the present day. Obviously, Indigenous populations existed with established systems of political structure and care for dependent persons. People of African heritage have been present since the early 1600s (Hannah-Jones, 2019). Over its history, the United States has become increasingly diverse, with many different racial and ethnic groups. The voices of people of color are often absent in telling the history of child welfare.

African American Voices

Before developing a formal government child welfare system, African American children in need were cared for in their communities. Hodges (2001) asserts that there are themes running through the African American history of child and family well-being, beginning with relying on older women in slave communities for support and care. These themes also include mutual aid, contributions of the church and religion, and the impetus to improve oneself and support one's community with an eye to the future. African American children were historically excluded from child welfare services, whether private or public, and those in need had to typically rely on an older woman in the community or volunteers in the African American settlements (Hodges, 2001). In the 20th century, when child welfare services became more professionalized, African American children were often excluded from public, private, and sectarian childcare institutions (Hodges, 2001). As a result of this exclusion, other institutions had to provide care for children in need, including churches (orphanages, clothing, food) and women's clubs (support for orphanages and kindergartens; Hodges, 2001).

It is important to note that African Americans were largely residents of the rural South prior to the 20th century (Sabbath, 2001; Wilkerson, 2010), though people of African heritage lived throughout the colonies and, later, states. Initially, the colonies developed housing patterns for those African Americans who were not enslaved, whereby no more than one African heritage family would live on a residential block. This was intended to keep the Black population from coordinating revolts or uprisings against slavery (Sabbath, 2001). These restrictions were gradually relaxed, particularly in the northern cities, up until the period before the Civil War, when the push to maintain the system of slavery in the South led to wholesale restrictions and the dehumanizing of all African Americans (Sabbath, 2001). By 1860, the separation of races was deeply ingrained in U.S. life.

Philadelphia was one city that always had a Black population, and the number of African Americans rose significantly following the beginning of the Great Migration. The Great Migration (1910–1970) marked the largest movement of people in America. Approximately 6 million African Americans fled southern states and Jim Crow policies in aspiration of opportunities for employment, better quality of life, and greater liberties. The impetus was to escape the oppression and racialized violence of the South to seek freedom in northern, midwestern, and western states. The Great Migration led to the establishment of the Armstrong Association of Philadelphia (established in 1907) and the Women's Christian Alliance (WCA, founded in 1919). The WCA grew out of a group of women led by Melissa Thompson Coppin, a physician, who were members of the African Methodist Episcopal Church in Philadelphia. The WCA sought to provide safe housing and care for working women migrating from the South, including mothers who were homeless. The WCA expanded into foster care work in 1921. Coppin's sister, Syrene Elizabeth Thompson Benjamin, came to help with the work of the WCA. In 1927, she founded her own agency, the Bureau for Colored Children (Sabbath, 2001). Though she died a short time later, the Bureau grew to become the "largest African American-operated child welfare agency in Philadelphia in the 1930s" (Sabbath, 2001, p. 26), providing foster care, shelter, and a residential program.

Ada S. McKinley founded the South Side Settlement House (SSSH) in Chicago in 1926. In addition to a range of other services in support of family and community life, the Infant Welfare Station operated at the SSSH from 1926 to 1934. This program was established to address infant mortality; services included weighing infants, developing diets, and providing milk if needed (Lee & Dieser, 2020; Mosely, 1939). The SSSH also developed a Children's Leisure Time Service, providing summer vacation programs for children and youth (Mosely, 1939).

The National Association of Colored Women's Clubs (NACWC) was incorporated in 1904 in St. Louis with a mission that included, among other objectives:

"To protect the rights of women and youth; To raise the standard and quality of life in home and family" (NACWC, n. d., para 2). The organization's goals were broad, generally focusing on the well-being of women and children.

Later in the 20th century, other organizations were established, such as the National Association of Black Social Workers (NABSW), in 1968, which was founded by a group of Black social workers who had attended the National Conference on Social Welfare meeting in San Francisco (NABSW, 1968) and who were concerned with the lack of responsiveness to issues affecting the Black community. In 1972, the NABSW issued a statement against transracial adoption. The organization further developed its views, issuing a position statement in 1994, *Preserving African American Families,* that stressed the importance of reunification with birth families, relative placement, removing barriers to adoption by African American parents, and promoting culturally relevant agency practices (NABSW, 2003).

The Black Administrators in Child Welfare, Inc. (BACW) was formed in 1971 and incorporated in 1975. Its mission is to address the need for specialized services for Black children and their families as well as advocate for increased representation of BACW. The BACW also provides a support network for administrators; some states have organized local chapters that remain active.

Disproportionality in the child welfare system has been a concern since the late 20th century, though efforts to address it have not been adequate. While the overrepresentation of African American children may have decreased slightly in recent years, disproportionality is still a significant issue (Gourdine, 2019). Racism and poverty are two factors often cited as reasons for this disproportionality. Poverty should not be a sufficient reason for removing children from their homes and may be linked to other variables, such as parental stress, lack of childcare, substance abuse, parental incarceration, or community violence, that can contribute to child neglect (Gourdine, 2019). Further, structural racism which limits opportunities and implicit bias which contributes to negative judgments about parenting, are factors in the failure to achieve equitable treatment of Black children and families in the child welfare system (Gourdine, 2019).

Native American Voices

Though there are and were numerous Indigenous groups in North America, each with their own language, culture, and traditions, some common themes run through Native American care for children. Historically, cultural traditions, laws, and practices were the foundation for childcare systems. Children were typically viewed as gifts from the creator, and the parents and community were responsible for raising and nurturing their children. When children needed care, the extended family or others in the community stepped in. The arrival of Europeans disrupted this system, and the continued influx of Europeans, as well as the establishment of the United States with laws and policies affecting Native communities, further undermined traditional systems of childcare and child welfare.

While not denying the lingering effects of the abuses of boarding schools, it is important to also note the resilience of Native American families and of social workers of Native heritage. Ada Deer (1935–2023), from Wisconsin, was a member of the Menominee nation. She was indirectly involved in child well-being through her work in the public schools, and later taught at the University of Wisconsin School of Social Work and led the BIA. Ronald Lewis (1942–2019) was the first Native American to earn a PhD in social work and became known as the *Father of Indian Social Work*. Lewis's work contributed to the development of the ICWA (NASW Foundation, n.d.-a). He also was instrumental in promoting culturally appropriate services for Native Americans and was an activist, participating in the occupation of Alcatraz in the late 1960s and the standoff at Wounded Knee in 1973, two monumental events in the history of Native American rights (NASW Foundation, n.d.-a).

The National Indian Child Welfare Association (NICWA), based in Portland, Oregon, was founded in 1987 as a regional organization but broadened its emphasis to have a national focus in 1992 (NICWA, n.d.). Its mission, broadly, is to support the well-being of American Indian and Alaska Native (AIAN) children. The Indigenous and Tribal Social Work Educators' Association (ITSWEA) was established in the 1990s and was formerly known as the AIAN Social Work Educators' Association.

For the first time in the history of the United States, a Native American, Deb Haaland, was appointed by President Joseph Biden as the Secretary of the Interior, the cabinet department that oversees the BIA. In June 2021, Secretary Haaland announced the creation of the Federal Indian Boarding School Initiative to investigate the legacy of federal policies related to the history of boarding schools in the United States (U.S. Department of Interior [DOI], 2021). Secretary Haaland has noted the destructive nature of the boarding schools on history, culture, and family and child well-being, stating that this system has contributed to the crossgenerational transmission of trauma (DOI, 2022). As a result of the recommendations in the initial report, Secretary Haaland announced a year-long tour, *The Road to Healing*, across the United States, where she would be visiting survivors of the boarding schools, allowing them to tell their stories to promote healing, and create a vision for moving forward (DOI, 2022). These historical relations between the U.S. government and Native Americans hold particular relevance for child welfare practice today. Secretary Haaland's appointment to a cabinet position is an important but long overdue step toward healing, reconciliation, and elevating the voices of Indigenous populations.

Latinx Voices

Though Latinx families historically have been underrepresented in the child welfare system, more recently there has been an increase in these families in the system (Rodriguez-JenKins & Ortega, 2021). Additionally, though the Latinx community may be underrepresented in the child welfare system overall, they are overrepresented in states with large Latinx populations (Rodriguez-JenKins & Ortega, 2021). Latinx is a broad category, and depending upon the country of origin, members may have widely varying trauma histories, cultural traditions, and current stressors (Rodriguez-JenKins & Ortega, 2021). Professionals working with these families may be unfamiliar with Latinx culture and language. "The philosophical differences between the often collectivist and family-oriented Latino worldview and the individualist, child-focused nature of the child welfare system creates a disconnect between the needs and engagement expectations of Latino families" (Rodriguez-JenKins & Ortega, 2021, p. 4). Research utilized in child welfare decisions is often based on White middle-class children; caseworkers may misunderstand or misapply this research when assessing risk in Latinx families. It is important to understand the culturally congruent way to deal with depression, interpersonal violence (IPV), and other issues. Also, there may be legitimate fears around help-seeking. Latinx immigrant families are less likely to access supportive services, such as referrals to Spanish-speaking professionals, and are more likely to experience linguistic and cultural barriers to services (Lanesskog et al., 2020). Latinx immigrant families are less likely to come into contact with the child welfare system, but if they do, they are more likely to experience challenges in accessing the services needed to keep their families together. Additionally, they may experience fears of deportation and losing children when encountering the system (Lanesskog et al., 2020).

Individuals with limited English proficiency are guaranteed services in their language as a civil right (Sulieman, 2003). Because Latinx families are coming into increasing contact with child welfare agencies, particularly those families facing poverty, marginalization, and stress, including those related to immigration status (Sulieman, 2003), it is important to address issues relevant to working with these families. Latinx children currently are the fastest growing child population in the United States and may be more likely to be in a two-parent and larger family than the population as a whole (Sulieman, 2003). Language is an important aspect of culture but may not have received adequate attention in the provision of services historically (Sulieman, 2003).

Asian American and Pacific Islander Voices

Similar to challenges with other immigrant families, Asian American immigrants need to adapt to a new culture and norms. They may not be sure about the child welfare system or about seeking help and receiving services (Lee & Lee, 2002). Those from low-income families face the same increased risk of neglect reports as other low-income families (Lee & Lee, 2002). Pelczarski and Kemp (2006) note that similar to Latinx families, Asian Americans and Pacific Islanders encompass many different groups with wide-ranging cultural traditions. Though Asian Americans and Pacific Islanders are underrepresented in the child welfare population, there are considerable differences between different population groups, with those experiencing greater poverty more likely to be involved with the child welfare system. Additionally, some cultural traditions may be misunderstood by those reporting or investigating child abuse, leading to potentially disruptive and traumatic situations for families. As a broad population, though, they remain at the margins of the child welfare system, and there is considerably less research on this population than on others.

Racism and Colonialist Practices Permeating the Child Welfare System

The child welfare system historically has demonstrated practices that have privileged White middle-class families and disadvantaged other populations. This is apparent when considering the orphan trains, boarding schools, disproportionate separation of Black and Indigenous children from their families, and transracial and international adoption. The privileging of the nuclear family also has contributed to negative judgments about more collective cultures with varied family forms and parenting styles. This has led to increased disruption of families of color. For example, while there was a growing emphasis on safeguarding parental rights, this did not extend to Native American families, where significant numbers of children were adopted by White families (Jacobs, 2013). The issue of disproportionality in child welfare continues to be a concern, as African American children are more likely than their White counterparts to be in the child welfare system, from reporting to screening to being separated from family to termination of parental rights. Disproportionality refers to "the overrepresentation or underrepresentation of a racial or ethnic group compared with its percentage in the total population," and disparity means "the unequal outcomes of one racial or ethnic group compared with outcomes for another racial or ethnic group" (Child Welfare Information Gateway, 2021, p. 2).

More recently, there have been calls for the abolition of the child welfare system as it currently exists, suggesting that it is more about family regulation and family policing rather than child welfare and well-being (Gottlieb, 2021). Because of the many judgments that are made about which environments are safe for children, child welfare may be rife with implicit and explicit bias. For example, drug use and child accidents are two types of events that lead to widely varying outcomes for children and families depending on race (Gottlieb, 2021). This disparate treatment of children by race has lasting consequences for individual children, families, and society. The trauma of family break-up followed by placement, sometimes in multiple foster families, has a negative effect on child development and may leave children less equipped to navigate adult demands. Some have referred to the foster care-to-prison pipeline (Gottlieb, 2021), as children/youth who have experienced foster care are significantly more likely to enter the criminal justice system as juveniles and/or adults than other youth and young adults

(Goetz, 2020). This raises important questions about how child welfare programs and services can be implemented to more effectively meet the needs of children and youth as well as their families.

The Pendulum of Child Safety and Family Preservation

"The history of child welfare in the United States can be characterized by a continuous thematic shift between family preservation and child safety" (Child Welfare Information Gateway, n.d.-b, para. 1). Early in the country's history, women and children were seen as property. As has been seen, increased recognition of children's needs and rights led to more intervention within families. Often, White middle-class standards were applied to families, resulting in the removal of children from families that did not meet those standards. As time passed, awareness of the disruptive effects of a child's removal increased. Additionally, concerns about government intervention in family life grew. This pendulum between child safety and family autonomy has swung back and forth (see Figure 1.1).

The current emphasis is on *child safety* as a priority while acknowledging the importance of *family preservation*. In other words, if a child's safety cannot be ensured in a family environment, the decision is generally made to remove them and place them in a safe environment. At the same time, increased recognition of the trauma of separation has led to more caution and thoughtfulness in making

Figure 1.1 Pendulum of Child Safety and Family Preservation

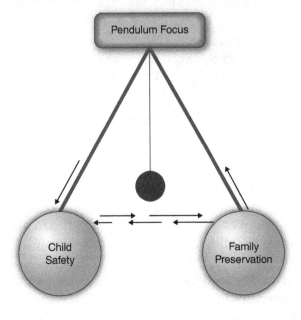

such an impactful decision as removing a child from their home. Even those children who are abused or neglected are attached to their families and experience trauma when removed. The decision to remove children from their families comes with the understanding that there are significant costs to the child and family. These costs must be weighed against the benefits to the child, such as ensuring their safety, nurturing, and healthy development.

When placed, the first priority is placement with a relative if this is deemed to be safe, as this reduces the trauma and ideally places the child in a more familiar environment. Also, permanency and stability are recognized as essential to the child's long-term well-being. Thus, a plan for family reunification or another stable long-term solution is put in place. As the data show, though, disproportionality has not been sufficiently addressed, with increased numbers of Black and AIAN children experiencing the trauma of removal from their families. More work must be done to ensure child safety while preserving the family unit.

Reflection Box 1.2

1. Do you agree or disagree with the premise that the child welfare system, as it currently exists, more accurately represents family monitoring and family policing? Support your answer.

2. What are your thoughts about the abolition of the child welfare system as it currently exists?

3. What might the ideal child welfare system look like?

4. What preventive services might reduce the need for more drastic child welfare interventions in families, such as the removal of children?

5. When children need to be removed because of imminent threats to their safety, how could this experience be less traumatic for the child and family?

CHAPTER SUMMARY

From ancient human history through the present day, children have been viewed in very different ways: as property, as gifts, as economic resources, and as a source of pride and honor. The way that children and childhood are understood leads to different approaches to childrearing. The historical era also plays a role in childrearing beliefs and practices. The makeup of the family has been changing as well, with smaller families, increased mobility, greater emphasis on the nuclear family, and less contact with extended family. However, historically, extended family and community have provided support for members in times of need. In less individualized and more collective-oriented cultures, the extended family and fictive kin often still play an important role in providing material and emotional support. The privileging of the nuclear family and the White middle-class view of "appropriate parenting" may disadvantage children and families of color when encountering the child welfare system.

Historically, there has been an evolution of responses to child abuse and neglect, including those events that raised awareness of the needs of children, such as the case of Mary Ellen Wilson in the 1870s and Dr. Kempe's article on the battered-child syndrome in the 1960s. In terms of addressing the needs of children, there have been misguided and culturally and class-based attempts at interventions, such as boarding schools and orphan trains. There also were activities such as the White House Conferences on Children and the formation of the Children's Bureau, which sought to address such issues as maternal and infant health and to gather and utilize data in making decisions. Disproportionality and disparity of outcomes continue to plague the child welfare system.

DISCUSSION QUESTIONS

1. How might understanding historical views of childhood give you insight into the current views and practices of childrearing in the present day?
2. Were you surprised by any of the information about the history of child welfare services in the United States? If so, which information or events?
3. Why is it important to include voices of people of color in discussing child welfare needs and services?
4. How does the current child welfare system reflect a Western orientation?
5. How might you decolonize or de-westernize approaches to child welfare?

RESOURCE

The Children's Bureau Video Series
https://www.childwelfare.gov/more-tools-resources/resources-from-childrens-bureau/cb-videos/

 A robust set of instructor resources designed to supplement this text is located at http://connect.springerpub.com/content/book/978-0-8261-5285-5. Qualifying instructors may request access by emailing textbook@springerpub.com.

REFERENCES

The Adoption History Project. (n.d.). *Orphan Trains*. University of Oregon. https://darkwing.uoregon.edu/~adoption/topics/orphan.html

Albert, I., & Trommsdorff, G. (2014). The role of culture in social development over the lifespan: An interpersonal relations approach. *Online Readings in Psychology and Culture, 6*(2), 1–28. https://doi.org/10.9707/2307-0919.1057

Bjorklund, D. F., Younger, J. L., & Pellegrini, A. D. (2002). The evolution of parenting and evolutionary approaches to childrearing. In M. H. Bornstein (Ed.), *Handbook of parenting volume 2: Biology and ecology of parenting* (2nd ed., pp. 3–30). Lawrence Erlbaum Associates.

Bornstein, M. H., Putnick, D. L., & Lansford, J. E. (2011). Parenting attributions and attitudes in cross-cultural perspective. *Parenting: Science and Practice, 11*, 214–237. https://doi.org/10.1080/15295192.2011.585568

Boustran, R., & Stratton, K. (2016). Children and violence in Jewish and Christian traditions. *Journal of Religion and Violence, 4*(3), 305–316. https://doi.org/10.5840/jrv2016121334

Brooks, D. (2020). The nuclear family was a mistake. *The Atlantic.* www.theatlantic.com/magazine/archive/2020/03/the-nuclear-family-was-a-mistake/605536/

Child Welfare Information Gateway. (n.d.-a). *Children's bureau timeline.* U.S. Department of Health and Human Services, Administration for Children and Families.

Child Welfare Information Gateway. (n.d.-b). *Concept and history of permanency in U.S. Child Welfare.* U.S. Department of Health and Human Services, Administration for Children and Families, Children's Bureau. https://www.childwelfare.gov/topics/permanency/overview/history/

Child Welfare Information Gateway. (2021). *Child welfare practice to address racial disproportionality and disparity.* U.S. Department of Health and Human Services, Administration for Children and Families, Children's Bureau. https://www.childwelfare.gov/pubs/issue-briefs/racial-disproportionality/

Child Welfare League of America. (n.d.). *Child Welfare League of America.* https://www.cwla.org.

Coontz, S. (2016). *The way we never were: American families and the nostalgia trap.* (Revised & updated edition). Basic Books. (Original work published 1992)

Coontz, S. (2021). Family values, social reciprocity, and Christianity. In J. M. Kohlhaas & M. M. Doyle Roche (Eds.), *Human families: Identities, relationships, and responsibilities: College Theology Society Annual Volume 66.* Orbis Books.

Cornell Law School. (n.d.). *Children's rights.* https://www.law.cornell.edu/wex/Children's_Rights

Crane, J. (2015). 'The bones tell the story the child is too young or too frightened to tell': The Battered Child Syndrome in post-war Britain and America. *Social History of Medicine, 28*(4), 767–788. https://www.ncbi.nlm.nih.gov/pmc/articles/PMC4623854/

Davies, J. (2017). Women's agency, adoption, and class in Theodore Dreiser's "Delineator" and "Jennie Gerhardt." *Studies in American Naturalism, 12*(2), 141–170. https://doi.org/10.1353/SAN.2017.0009

Ely, D. M., & Driscoll, A. K. (2020). Infant mortality in the United States, 2018: Data from the period linked birth/infant death file. *National Vital Statistics Reports, 69*(7). https://www.cdc.gov/nchs/data/nvsr/nvsr69/NVSR-69-7-508.pdf

Fleer, M. (2015). A cultural historical view of child development: Key concepts for going beyond a universal view of the child. *Asia-Pacific Journal of Research in Early Childhood Education, 9*(1), 19–37. https://doi.org/10.17206/apjrece.2015.9.1.19

French, V. (2002). History of parenting: The ancient Mediterranean world. In M. H. Bornstein (Ed.), *Handbook of parenting volume 2: Biology and ecology of parenting* (2nd ed., pp. 345–376). Lawrence Erlbaum Associates.

Goetz, S. L. (2020). From removal to incarceration: How the modern child welfare system and its unintended consequences catalyzed the foster care-to-prison pipeline. *University of Maryland Law Journal of Race, Religion, Gender & Class, 20*(2), 289–305. https://digitalcommons.law.umaryland.edu/rrgc/vol20/iss2/6/

Gone, J. P., Hartman, W. E., Pomerville, A., Wendt, D. C., Klem, S. H., & Burage, R. L. (2019). The impact of historical trauma on health outcomes for Indigenous populations in the USA and Canada: A systematic review. *American Psychologist, 74*(1), 20–35. https://dx.doi.org/10.1037/amp0000338

Gottlieb, C. (2021, March 17). Black families are outraged about family separation within the U.S. it's time to listen to them. *Time Magazine.* https://time.com/5946929/child-welfare-black-families/

Gourdine, R. M. (2019). We treat everybody the same: Race equity in child welfare. *Social Work in Public Health, 34*(1), 75–85. https://doi.org/10.1080/19371918.2018.1562400

Grey, D. J. R. (2011). Gender, religion, and infanticide in colonial India, 1870–1906. *Victorian Review, 37*(2), 107–120. https://doi.org/10.1353/vcr.2011.0043

Hannah-Jones, N. (2019). The 1619 project. *New York Times Magazine.* https://www.nytimes.com/interactive/2019/08/14/magazine/1619-america-slavery.html

Hodges, V. (2001). Historical development of African American child welfare services. In I. B. Carlton-LaNey (Ed.), *African American leadership: An empowerment tradition in social welfare history.* (pp. 203–213). NASW Press.

Jacobs, M. D. (2013). Remembering the "forgotten child": The American Indian child welfare crisis of the 1960s and 1970s. *American Indian Quarterly, 37*(1–2), 136–159. https://doi.org/10.1353/aiq.2013.0014

Jambor, H. A. (1958). Theodore Dreiser, the "Delineator" magazine, and dependent children: A background note on the calling of the 1909 White House conference. *Social Service Review, 32*(1), 33–40. https://doi.org/10.1086/640392

Karahan, N., Aydın, R., Güven, D. Y., Benli, A. R., & Kalkan, N. B. (2017). Traditional health practices concerning pregnancy, birth, and the postpartum period of women giving birth in the hospital. *Southern Clinics of Istanbul Eurasia, 28*(3), 190–198. https://doi.org/10.14744/scie.2017.33042

Katz, M. S. (1976). A history of compulsory education laws. *Phi Delta Kappan.* https://files.eric.ed.gov/fulltext/ED119389.pdf

Kratzer, A. (2019). Harsh Nazi parenting guidelines may still affect German children of today. *ScientificAmerican.*https://www.scientificamerican.com/article/harsh-nazi-parenting-guidelines-may-still-affect-german-children-of-today1/

Lancy, D. F. (2015). Children as a reserve labor force. *Current Anthropology, 56*(4), 545–568. https://doi.org/10.1086/682286

Lancy, D. F., & Grove, M. A. (2011). Being noticed: Middle childhood in cross-cultural perspective. *Human Nature, 22,* 281–302. https://doi.org/10.1007/s12110-011-9117-5

Lanesskog, D., Muñoz, J., & Castillo, K. (2020). Language is not enough: Institutional supports for Spanish speaking client-worker engagement in child welfare. *Journal of Public Child Welfare, 14*(4), 435–457. https://doi.org/10.1080/15548732.2019.1621235

Lee, J., & Lee, L. (2002). *Crossing the divide: Asian American families and the child welfare system.* Coalition for Asian American Children and Families. https://files.eric.ed.gov/fulltext/ED464163.pdf

Lee, K. J., & Dieser, R. B. (2020). Ada S. McKinley: A hidden history of African American Settlement House in Chicago. *Leisure Sciences.* https://doi.org/10.1080/01490400.2020.1830904

Lu, X. (2016). Ideological contestation over parenting styles: Dr. Spock vs. Amy Chua. *China Media Research, 12*(1), 25–34.

Mason, M. A. (1994). *From father's property to children's rights: The history of child custody in the United States.* Columbia University Press.

McNally, R. B. (1981). *Nearly a century later: The Child Savers—Child advocates and the juvenile justice system.* U.S. Department of Justice. Office of Justice Programs (OJP). https://www.ojp.gov/ncjrs/virtual-library/abstracts/nearly-century-later-child-savers-child-advocates-and-juvenile

Metcalfe, T. (2021). Earliest modern female human infant burial found in Europe. *National Geographic.* https://www.nationalgeographic.com/history/article/earliest-modern-female-human-infant-burial-found-europe

Mosely, D. S. (1939). *The South Side Settlement House, Chicago, Illinois: A study of the development of and needs met by a Negro settlement house* [Master's thesis, Loyola University of Chicago]. Loyola eCommons. https://ecommons.luc.edu/cgi/viewcontent.cgi?article=4655&context=luc_theses

National Association of Black Social Workers. (1968). *Harambee: 30 years of unity.* https://cdn.ymaws.com/www.nabsw.org/resource/resmgr/position_statements_papers/nabsw_30_years_of_unity_-_ou.pdf

National Association of Black Social Workers. (1972). *Position statement on transracial adoptions.* https://cdn.ymaws.com/www.nabsw.org/resource/resmgr/position_statements_papers/nabsw_trans-racial_adoption_.pdf

National Association of Black Social Workers. (2003). *Preserving families of African ancestry*. https://cdn.ymaws.com/www.nabsw.org/resource/resmgr/position_statements_papers/preserving_families_of_afric.pdf

National Association of Colored Women's Clubs. (n.d.). *Our mission*. https://www.nacwc.com/mission

National Association of Social Workers Foundation. (n.d.-a). *Social work pioneers—Ronald Lewis*. NASW Pioneers Biography Index. https://www.naswfoundation.org/Our-Work/NASW-Social-Work-Pioneers/NASW-Social-Workers-Pioneers-Bio-Index/id/556

National Association of Social Workers Foundation. (n.d.-b). *Social work Pioneers—Wilma Walker*. NASW Pioneers Biography Index. https://www.naswfoundation.org/Our-Work/NASW-Social-Workers-Pioneers/NASW-Social-Workers-Pioneers-Listing.aspx?id=497

National Indian Child Welfare Association. (n.d.). *About NICWA*. https://www.nicwa.org/about/

National Library of Medicine. (n.d.). *Native Voices, 1953: Congress seeks to abolish tribes, relocate American Indians*. National Institute of Health, U.S. Department of Health and Human Services. https://www.nlm.nih.gov/nativevoices/timeline/488.html

National Native American Boarding School Healing Coalition. (n.d.). *U S Indian Boarding School History*. https://boardingschoolhealing.org/education/us-indian-boarding-school-history/

Newland, B. (2022). *Federal Indian boarding school initiative investigative report*. https://www.bia.gov/sites/default/files/dup/inline-files/bsi_investigative_report_may_2022_508.pdf?utm_medium=email&utm_source=govdelivery

New Oxford Annotated Bible. (2001). *Proverbs 13:24* (New Revised Standard Version). Oxford University Press.

New York Society for the Prevention of Cruelty to Children. (n.d.). *About us*. https://nyspcc.org/about-nyspcc/

Ohaja, M., & Anyim, C. (2021). Rituals and embodied cultural practices at the beginning of life: African perspectives. *Religions, 12*(11), 1024. https://doi.org/10.3390/rel12111024

Pelczarski, Y., & Kemp, S. P. (2006). Patterns of child maltreatment referrals among Asian and Pacific Islander families. *Child Welfare, 85*, 5–31. https://www.jstor.org/stable/45398749

Rodriguez-JenKins, J., & Ortega, D. M. (2021). Different contexts, different outcomes: Early childhood parenting context for Latina mothers vulnerable to child welfare involvement. *Child & Youth Services, 42*(1), 3–23. https://doi.org/10.1080/0145935X.2020.1792770

Rousseau, B. (2017). In Bali, babies are believed too holy to touch the earth. *The New York Times*. https://www.nytimes.com/2017/02/18/world/asia/bali-indonesia-babies-nyambutin.html

Rundin, J. S. (2004). Pozo Moro, child sacrifice, and the Greek legendary tradition. *Journal of Biblical Literature, 123*(3), 425–447. https://doi.org/10.2307/3268041

Ryan, P. (2008). How new is the "new" social study of childhood? The myth of a paradigm shift. *The Journal of Interdisciplinary History, 38*(4), 553–576. https://doi.org/10.1162/jinh.2008.38.4.553

Sabbath, T. F. (2001). African Americans and social work in Philadelphia, Pennsylvania 1900–1930. In I. B. Carlton-LaNey (Ed.), *African American leadership: An empowerment tradition in social welfare history* (pp. 17–33). NASW Press.

Sciamanna, J. (n.d.). *100 Years of CWLA: Moment in history*. https://www.cwla.org/100yearsofcwla-moment-from-history/

Social Welfare History Archives. (2013). *History of the Child Welfare League of America: 1919–1977*. https://socialwelfare.library.vcu.edu/programs/child-welfarechild-labor/child-welfare-league-history-1919-1977/

Stanford Medicine, Ethnogeriatrics. (n.d.). *1953 to 1969: Policy of termination and relocation*. https://geriatrics.stanford.edu/ethnomed/american_indian/learning_activities/learning_1/termination_relocation.html

Stretch, J. J. (1970). The rights of children emerge: Historical notes on the first White House Conference on Children. *Child Welfare, 49*(7), 365–372.

Sulieman, L. P. (2003). Beyond cultural competence: Language access and Latino civil rights. *Child Welfare, 82*(20), 185–200.

Tribal Law and Policy Institute. (2011). *Apology from Child Welfare League of America*. https://tlpi.wordpress.com/2011/08/11/apology-from-child-welfare-league-of-america/

United Nations. (1989). *Convention on the rights of the child*. https://www.unicef.org/child-rights-convention/convention-text#

U.S. Department of Health, Education, and Welfare. (1967). *The story of the White House Conferences on Children and Youth.* Social and Rehabilitation Service, Children's Bureau. https://files.eric.ed.gov/fulltext/ED078896.pdf

U.S. Department of the Interior. (2021). *Press release: Secretary Haaland announces Federal Indian Boarding School Initiative.* https://www.doi.gov/pressreleases/secretary-haaland-announces-federal-indian-boarding-school-initiative

U.S. Department of the Interior. (2022). *Press release: Department of the Interior releases investigative report, outlines next steps in Federal Indian Boarding School Initiative.* https://www.doi.gov/pressreleases/department-interior-releases-investigative-report-outlines-next-steps-federal-indian

U.S. House of Representatives. (n.d.). *Historical highlights: The Sheppard-Towner Maternity and Infancy Act.* https://history.house.gov/Historical-Highlights/1901-1950/The-Sheppard–Towner-Maternity-and-Infancy-Act/

Warren, A. (1998). The orphan trains. *The Washington Post.* https://www.washingtonpost.com/wp-srv/national/horizon/nov98/orphan.htm

Waugh, L. J. (2011). Beliefs associated with Mexican immigrant families' practice of la cuarentena during postpartum recovery. *Journal of Obstetric, Gynecologic & Neonatal Nursing, 40*(6), 732–741. https://doi.org/10.1111/j.1552-6909.2011.01298.x

Wilkerson, I. (2010). *The warmth of other suns: The epic story of America's great migration.* Random House.

2   Types of Abuse and Neglect in Child Welfare Practice

Jane Addams, Grace Abbott, Julia Lathrop, Mildred Arnold, and other early pioneers championed children's rights. Social workers and other child welfare professionals are responsible for protecting our children. This chapter serves as a reminder of the need to continue the fight against the abuse and neglect children suffer at the hands of those who should care for them, protect them, and love them unconditionally.

LEARNING OBJECTIVES

By the end of the chapter, you will be able to:

- Identify what constitutes abuse and neglect.
- Identify the types of abuse.
- Demonstrate an understanding of the context in which abuse occurs.
- Review the limbic system and its connection to trauma.
- Demonstrate an understanding of the impact of childhood maltreatment on the brain structure.
- Discuss the significance of risk and protective factors related to child abuse and neglect.

INTRODUCTION

Child abuse is a horrible reality, and it has been presumably since the beginning of time. Rules for the treatment of children came under the paternalistic and the regnant rule of law. The sophistry of humanity produced laws intended to protect children but instead fell short. English common law viewed women and children as the property of men (i.e., of their husbands and fathers, respectively). These views continued in the actions of American colonists into the 16th and 17th centuries.

The case of Mary Ellen Wilson detailed the suffering of abused children in the early 1870s. Mary Ellen was an abused orphan who was repeatedly beaten by her caregivers. At the time, there was no formal agency to protect children. Sadly, the American Society for the Prevention of Cruelty to Animals (ASPCA) was formed in 1866 before establishing the New York Society for the Prevention of Cruelty to Children (NYSPCC) in 1875. Despite the establishment of the NYSPCC, there was no national response to child abuse until C. Henry Kempe and colleagues broadened our view of its occurrence. Child abuse and neglect received greater attention in America after C. Henry Kempe and colleagues began writing about it in the *Journal of the American Medical Association* (*JAMA*, 1962). At that time, they published an article entitled "The Battered-Child Syndrome" (1962). Kempe was a radiologist who began noticing fractures and other injuries to children and detected a pattern of unexplained injuries.

The federal government sought to address the issue of child abuse and neglect, though these efforts were rudimentary at the beginning. Policymakers at the highest levels of government influence society's policy focus depending on the administration's priorities. In essence, administrations may either amplify or ignore important issues such as child abuse/neglect, depending on their political frame and polity. For instance, while New Deal liberals had searched for solutions to social problems, the Nixon, Reagan, and George H. W. Bush administrations did not focus on the issue of childhood abuse and neglect and, in fact, downplayed it. According to Carter (2011), Nixon, Reagan, and Bush's foci were on their political ideology of getting tough on crime.

By the latter part of the 20th century, the United States recognized child abuse and neglect as a social problem. A social problem has four components: (a) It affects many people, (b) in negative ways, (c) is something believed to be correctable, (d) through collective social action. When a social problem is identified in society, it beckons social change. In the United States, protecting children from harm was enacted through the provision of the Child Abuse Prevention and Treatment Act (CAPTA, P.L. 93–247) of 1974. Heightened attention to social problems creates opportunities for change. With this new legislation, professionals became mandated reporters, and statewide systems for reporting and investigating child abuse allegations were born.

This chapter reviews the types of child abuse and neglect and the multiple factors thought to influence childhood abuse and neglect. In addition, the chapter reviews the connection of trauma to the limbic system, the impact of childhood maltreatment on the brain structure, and the significance of risk and protective factors related to child abuse and neglect.

A REVIEW OF CHILD ABUSE AND NEGLECT

Both federal and state laws define child abuse and neglect. States have the discretion to use civil and criminal statutes in defining child abuse and neglect. The Child Welfare Information Gateway (2019) provides civil definitions to determine how and when child welfare agencies will intervene at the state level. CAPTA defines child abuse and neglect as "any recent act or failure to act on the part of a parent or caregiver, which results in death, serious physical or emotional harm, sexual abuse or exploitation, or an act or failure to act [that] presents an imminent risk of serious harm" ("CAPTA Reauthorization Act of 2010," 2010, p. 31).

Neglect is viewed as an act of omission and accounts for over three quarters of confirmed cases in the United States (Child Welfare Information Gateway, 2019). Through the U.S. Department of Health and Human Services (HHS) Administration for Children and Families (ACF), the Children's Bureau published the 29th edition of the Child Maltreatment Report in 2020 using data from 2018. The Child Maltreatment Report collects data from the National Child Abuse and Neglect Data System (NCANDS), "a voluntary national data collection and analysis program of state child abuse and neglect information" (Milner, 2020, para. 9). All 50 states, the District of Columbia, and the Commonwealth of Puerto Rico contribute to this data collection program.

Nationally 678,000 children were determined to be victims in 2018 out of 3,534,000 children who were the subject of an investigation (Milner, 2020). "In total, 60.8% of victims were neglected, 10.7% were physically abused, and 7.0% were sexually abused. More than 15% were victims of two or more maltreatment types" (Milner, 2020, para. 4). These data show that children enter the system primarily due to neglect, not physical abuse (Milner, 2020). It is also important to note that child abuse/neglect is no *respecter of persons*—it happens everywhere in the nation and across all income levels, ethnicities, and religious affiliations. It is also important to note that the severity, frequency, onset, and types of abuse create lifelong effects for child survivors of abuse into adulthood.

Health Consequences and Brain Neurobiology

There are negative consequences of child abuse and neglect. Notably, experiencing child maltreatment can have health complications associated with a reduced life expectancy (Teicher & Samson, 2016) due to adult onset of inflammation, ischemic heart disease, cancer, and shortened telomeres. Telomeres, which form the ends of chromosomes, progressively shorten with age and are associated with increased disease incidence. In essence, telomere shortening limits stem cells' function, regeneration, and organ maintenance. Also, chronic and perceived psychological stress contributes to early-onset age-related disease progression. The harmful effects of child abuse and neglect on the developing child sometimes can, unfortunately, endure across an individual's life span.

Another long-term effect is how child maltreatment impacts the brain or one's neurobiology. Teicher and Samson (2016) completed a literature review to detail the most salient discoveries related to research on potential neurobiological consequences of childhood exposure to abuse and neglect. They write that among survivors of childhood maltreatment, there is a higher prevalence of depression, anxiety, suicidality, and other disorders (such as substance use, eating disorders, and personality disorders), diminished cognitive functioning, and even more severe forms of mental illness like psychosis.

While previous research has shown that some brain areas are affected, more recent research reveals "substantial alterations in connectivity and network architecture" (Teicher & Samson, 2016, p. 241). The impact of repeated abuse impacts the limbic system (see Figure 2.1). The limbic system is complex, so we highlight the four main components that relate to behavior. Emotions are also complex and may be identified in more ways than those listed in the following:

1. *Hippocampi*: There is one located on each hemisphere of the brain. They help humans consolidate information; are responsible for short-term, long-term, and spatial memory; and influence neural plasticity in the brain. Abuse may affect memory and spatial memory.

Figure 2.1 The Limbic System

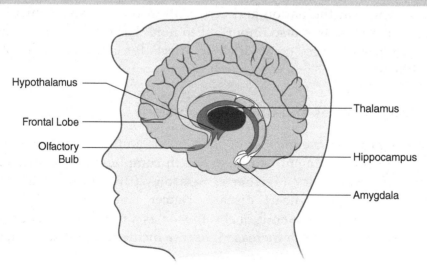

Source: Illustration by Jalance Foxworth

2. *Amygdala*: One of two nuclei located within the temporal lobes in the cerebrum. The amygdala activates emotional responses and helps with decision-making and memory. Abuse can interfere with memory, especially since strong emotional components may endure and be associated with more aggression, irritability, loss of control of emotions, and deficits in recognizing emotions. Moreover, the amygdala is responsible for rapidly assessing sensory stimuli for possible threats (Fields, 2019) and recognizing fear.

3. *Hypothalamus*: It controls the hormone system in the body; it also controls appetite, sexual behavior, and emotional responses and regulates body temperature. The hypothalamus also controls the body's response to stress. If impaired, it can lead to aggressive behavior, feeling stressed, fatigue, and other symptoms of overstimulation. Differences in the hypothalamus have been associated with mental health problems like depression, bipolar disorder, and schizophrenia.

4. *Thalamus*: Two of them function as a sensory relay station (hearing, seeing, touching, and tasting).

Jedd and colleagues note that "fronto-limbic" circuitry is affected by early trauma. "Converging evidence suggests that maltreatment leads to an altered processing of emotions and social stimuli" (Jedd et al., 2015, p. 2). They also emphasize that altered emotion processing following maltreatment has implications for neural differences located in the limbic system. In fact, children who have been abused process facial expressions differently than children who have not been abused. Additionally, changes to the hippocampus may be responsible for intrusive memories and flashbacks for people who develop symptoms of post-traumatic stress (Corcoran & Walsh, 2016).

Adverse childhood experiences (ACEs) greatly impact the developing child into adulthood with cognitive, emotional, mental, and health-related consequences (Nelson et al., 2020). Abuse affects the entire system, and symptoms may include uncontrolled emotions, olfactory and memory impairments, and abnormally high or low sexual behavior (or drive later in life). The good news is that research on brain plasticity—the brain's ability to change and remain malleable with repeated stimulation—provides hope for survivors of child abuse and neglect.

Teicher and Samson (2016) note the relatively nascent inquiry into the potential impact of childhood maltreatment on brain structure. Child maltreatment is being studied in varied ways. One systematic review synthesized noninstitutionalized child maltreatment across the life span. Carr and colleagues (2020) examined thousands of previously published systematic reviews and meta-analyses, and after a reduction process (i.e., eliminating studies according to their set criteria), the researchers were left with 111 studies. Carr and colleagues found significant associations between child maltreatment and physical health, mental health, and psychological adjustment. They documented six critical findings regarding child maltreatment:

1. It is associated with a wide range of *health problems* (e.g., pro-inflammatory states associated with compromised immune systems).

2. It produces significant abnormalities in the structure of the brain and how it functions, which may be associated with *mental health problems.*

3. It is associated with *mental health problems* in *adolescence and adulthood.*

4. It is associated with a wide range of negative outcomes throughout the life span (including psychosocial and relational stress, difficulties managing sexual urges, and other impulses). These challenges create adjustment problems in school, work, and overall life satisfaction.

5. It is associated with *more adverse outcomes* when the maltreatment was *severe and multiple forms* of maltreatment were experienced by the survivor.

6. It is associated in ways *similar to the abuse experienced.* For example, if maltreatment was in the form of physical abuse, the outcome was aggression; if the form of abuse was sexual, sexuality problems ensued, and if the abuse was emotional, severe mental health problems were indicated.

Abuse does not happen for just that moment; it affects people throughout their lives in many ways. McElvaney (2011) reminds readers in *Unbroken Spirit: Abby's Story* that the abuse and neglect children experience may be denied (in thoughts or utterances), but the body does not forget; the body remembers. Child maltreatment profoundly affects children's entire system (body, mind, and soul). When people have not healed, the cycle of abuse can continue to their children and subsequent generations.

The next section in this chapter provides a review of the types of abuse (physical, sexual, and emotional forms of abuse). One shared characteristic of abuse across types is that it exerts power and control over children. The World Health Organization (WHO, 2020) states the harm abuse does to children under the age of 18 results in "actual or potential harm to the *child's health, survival, development or dignity* in the context of a relationship of responsibility, trust or power" (para. 2). Children deserve to grow up in nurturing environments with the developmental support and unconditional love they need throughout their childhood.

Physical Abuse

Physical abuse takes many forms, including beatings, shaking, scalding, burns, fractures, punching, biting, and other forms of physical harm or injury to children. Martinkevich and colleagues (2020) emphasize the need to understand the child's age and developmental level in assessing non accidental injuries (NAIs). It is important for the child to be examined thoroughly (i.e., the child's entire body) by healthcare professionals. This team of researchers, orthopedic specialists, and public health professionals detail ways that healthcare providers can detect specific signs of abuse, especially during times of crisis (such as in a pandemic when the incidence and prevalence of child abuse are expected to be elevated and underreported). Martinkevich and colleagues (2020) highlight the importance of removing barriers that "hamper reporting" (p. 528). They begin with a description of skin manifestations.

Skin manifestations are common non accidental injuries, including bruises, bite marks, and thermal injuries. *Bruises* are the most common type of skin manifestation, and they leave a mark. NAI bruises are clustered in protected areas like the torso, ears, and neck (TEN). In the torso region, bruises are commonly located on the chest, abdomen, back, buttocks, genitourinary region, and hips. Although abdominal bruising is rare, it warrants investigation (Martinkevich et al., 2020). *Bite marks* should create a suspicion of abuse and are considered to be dangerous. Odontologists can be especially helpful in identifying the perpetrator. They are highly skilled professionals who study inter canine distance in order to distinguish between bite marks left by adult humans and bite marks by animals. Martinkevich and colleagues also indicate that *thermal injuries* due to abuse occur either by contact or immersion. Many victims are under the age of three. Immersion in scalding hot tap water is common. When burn injuries are inflicted, they cover a "wider and deeper surface area, and tend to include … the back, buttocks, perineum, and lower extremities with symmetrical and clear demarcation lines as compared with accidental burn injuries" (Martinkevich et al., 2020, p. 529). Healthcare professionals can detect distinct and symmetrical lines of demarcation.

Physical abuse also includes fractures and other radiological red flags such as multiple rib fractures, intracranial lesions, and abusive head trauma(s). Multiple fractures must be taken seriously and may sometimes present with respiratory compromise or on a skeletal survey where suspicion of non accidental injuries have occurred (Martinkevich et al., 2020). Martinkevich and colleagues warn healthcare professionals about multiple fractures—especially those detected through radiology—which are red flags warranting a report to child protection agencies.

Multiple fractures (to the rib, posteriorly located) have a predictive association with abuse. "Intracranial hemorrhages may also be suggestive of AHT [abusive head trauma] but are common after accidents" (Martinkevich et al., 2020, p. 529). According to Martinkevich and colleagues, severe forms of AHT are a leading cause of death in children under the age of 2 years. Healthcare professionals must consider all findings and the child's history at diagnosis. Predicting head trauma and distinguishing it from other plausible causes is sometimes difficult. More recently, clearer clinical predictions and decision rules have been developed to rule out other reasons for head injuries. Tools like the Pittsburgh Infant Brain Injury Score (PIBIS) help to determine when head CTs are needed. According to Martinkevich and colleagues (2020), the "Pediatric Brain Injury Research Network's (PediBIRN) and Predicting Abusive Head Trauma (PredAHT) have been developed to differentiate between AHT and other reasons for a validated intracranial injury and have a high sensitivity and PPV [positive predictive value] for AHT" (p. 531).

All social workers play an essential role in identifying and reporting child abuse. For abuse that is not identified by medical personnel, there are sometimes subtle signs that warrant attention. Signs of physical abuse of children are often discovered when the narrative is explored. When a child's explanation for the bruises, swelling, marks, or other injuries does not match the pattern of injury, this may be an important sign of abuse that should not be overlooked. Also, if the child's explanation appears to be prescriptive, oversimplified, or does not honestly answer the questions asked, the child may be providing a rehearsed response or a prescriptive answer.

When children are physically abused, they may experience an array of competing emotions. Children may even internalize the harm perpetrated against them and believe they are at fault for their mistreatment. These feelings of self-doubt undermine their sense of agency, self-worth, and help-seeking. Social workers should be vigilant for signs where children begin to withdraw from the activities they used to enjoy. Other signs may include the child becoming angry, aggressive, hostile, and overly active. In school, abused children may also display absenteeism, avoidant behaviors like not wanting to go home, running away behaviors, resistance toward authority figures, self-harm, hostility, and parasuicidal behavior, thoughts, and attempts. Warning signs must be taken seriously enough to warrant investigation but are not definitive indications that abuse is indeed occurring. Social professionals are mandated to report suspicion of abuse, but when making a call to the child protection hotline, they should do so in a responsible manner, with knowledge of the signs, symptoms, frequency, duration, severity, onset, and context of the abuse. Child welfare professionals in investigations have the authority and training to assess whether abuse is indicated and should do so in accordance with their governing agency's guidelines. Child welfare professionals must know their state's child protective services (CPS) policies on physical abuse (i.e., how it is defined and assessed for risk and determination of whether it has occurred).

Child Abuse: Serious Harm and Death

Child welfare professionals depend on the documentation of medical doctors, especially in the case of children suffering broken bones, head injuries, and even death. In the event of a child's death, the child welfare worker will consult with a forensic team, including the medical examiner. It is also important to note that these types of investigations last longer since there are multiple systems involved; that is, police, medical examiner(s), child welfare administrator(s), and medical doctors. In the case of child survivors, it may also be necessary for CPS to conduct forensic interviews to minimize the child's exposure to retraumatization from repeating their account of the abuse.

Child welfare professionals are susceptible to secondary trauma and must take steps to prevent burnout and vicarious harm. It is critical for supervisors and administrators to be in attunement with their workers to provide timely support, collaboration, and supervision for workers who experience child deaths and other harsh conditions in the field.

Case Scenario: The Case of Josh Davis (Pseudonym)

Ms. Davis was a 25-year-old single mother of two children, ages 3 and 5, with a live-in boyfriend who was not the father of her children. Ms. Davis worked long hours in a warehouse overnight. She left for work one night, leaving her children in her boyfriend's care. The younger male child (Josh) was not fully potty trained. He soiled himself, and the boyfriend, David, became very angry, hitting him in the chest and whipping him with a belt.

Ms. Davis returned home from work, checked in on the children, and found that Josh was unresponsive, blue, and cold to the touch. Immediately, she called 911 and attempted CPR. The ambulance arrived and took Josh to the hospital, where he was pronounced dead on arrival (DOA). The hospital authorities noticed suspicious old and new bruising. The injuries did not match the mother's explanation that the minor fell down the stairs. The hospital contacted child protective services.

A child protective services professional interviewed the mother and her boyfriend. After assessing the home and evaluating the 5-year-old child, it was determined that a safety plan needed to be developed for the child who was left in the home until further evaluation was completed. This was done before protective custody was taken. The local police were working in collaboration with the child protective team. During the police interrogation, it was discovered that the boyfriend had a history of punching Josh in the chest. Ms. Davis tried to deny this and downplay this critical incident month before. David admitted to punching Josh in the chest because he wanted to make a man out of him. Clearly, David was frustrated and did not understand child development or how to care for a 3-year-old. Because of the old bruising and the mother's inability to protect Josh over time, CPS asked the court to grant them temporary custody of the other child. The court denied this request until a safety assessment was completed.

FACTS

Let's review what is known so far about Ms. Davis and David:

- Ms. Davis did notice bruises on Josh prior to his death.
- Ms. Davis did notice that Josh would cling to her when David was around.
- Ms. Davis was on probation at work and did not want to risk losing her job.
- Ms. Davis was the primary source of income.
- The 5-year-old did not have bruises nor reported being hit by David.

(continued)

Case Scenario: The Case of Josh Davis (Pseudonym) (*continued*)

- David had no child-rearing experience or children himself.
- Ms. Davis and David were in a relationship for approximately 5 months.

DISCUSSION QUESTIONS

1. What could the mother have done to protect Josh from this fatal abuse?
2. Why do you think the mother was in denial about the abuse?
3. Why is it important for parents to have an understanding of child development?
4. What might the child welfare administrator do to support the child protection professional in this scenario since it resulted in death?
5. What kind of support should be provided to the sibling of the deceased child?
6. What kind of trauma might the sibling of the deceased child have experienced?
7. What are the steps that should be taken during the investigation process (i.e., forensic interview):
   a. What would be important for them to know?
   b. Who should they interview?
   c. What valuable information might family members, neighbors, or significant others be able to provide?
8. What types of documentation/reports would be of value in this investigation process?
   a. For the children
   b. For the mother
   c. For the boyfriend

Sexual Abuse

The Child Welfare Information Gateway, based on CAPTA, defines abuse/neglect as any act or failure to act to avoid the imminent risk of serious harm to children. CAPTA considers the exploitation of children for the purpose of sexual conduct (explicit or otherwise) and the depiction of sexual conduct to be abuse. This definition includes rape, sexual abuse by caregivers or friends or relatives, molestation, prostitution, other forms of sexual exploitation, and incest with children. Sexual abuse of children is defined differently by each state.

Many states provide a distinct definition, while other states link their definition of sexual abuse with their overall definition of abuse. Connecticut has the most concise definition of sexual abuse, and Missouri, New Jersey, New York, Rhode Island, South Carolina, South Dakota, Virgin Islands, and Wyoming intertwine their definition with their overarching definition of child abuse. Other states provide distinct and comprehensive definitions of sexual abuse.

One noted difference is how age is defined in state codes. For instance, Arkansas defines sexual abuse by a person's age denoting minor age perpetration (i.e., sexual abuse may be committed by a person aged 14 or older to a person younger than age 18 who is not their spouse). In essence, in the state of Arkansas, a 14-year-old may be determined to be a sexual abuser. Other states may view this as sexually reactive behavior, recognizing that the perpetrator is a child victim in need of services/treatment. Some states treat youth perpetrators in the juvenile court system; however, they receive intensive treatment and are separated from other youth. Their behavior is often monitored to ensure the safety of other children (through a safety plan).

Reflection Box 2.1

The Child Welfare Information Gateway provides a link to search each state's statutes about child abuse and neglect: https://www.childwelfare .gov/topics/systemwide/laws-policies/state/
    Select two states. Compare and contrast their definitions of:

- Physical abuse
- Sexual abuse
- Neglect

Next, answer the following questions and discuss them in small groups.

1. Which two states did you choose? Why?
2. What were the greatest differences between states?
3. Were you surprised by anything you discovered?
4. What differences and similarities do you see based on the type of abuse?
5. Based on Arkansas' definition of sexual abuse by age, what implications does this have for minor-aged children?
6. Do state definitions adequately define abuse and neglect?

What specific gaps need to be addressed in the state statutes?
Report key points in your discussion to the entire class.

Interview Procedures for Child Sexual Abuse

Child welfare professionals should understand how to approach the investigation of sexual abuse. They need to know when to conduct a victim-sensitive interview (VSI) which is forensic in nature (i.e., the state's attorney and law enforcement officials are unobtrusively present for these interviews within local advocacy centers) and conducted by a trained interviewer. A child will also be given a medical exam to assess for the level of sexual trauma (i.e., penetration, fondling, genital bruising, or other forms of sexual abuse).

Emotional Abuse

The definition of emotional abuse will not be presented state by state: "Almost all states, the District of Columbia, American Samoa, Guam, the Northern Mariana Islands, Puerto Rico, and the Virgin Islands include emotional maltreatment as a part of their definitions of abuse or neglect" (Child Welfare Information Gateway, 2019, p. 3). Many states provide a specific definition of emotional abuse and denote non accidental injury, psychological injury, and impact on the child's emotional stability. Specifically, they cite observable and substantial changes in the child's behavior, emotional response, or cognition, internalizing behaviors like anxiety, depression, and withdrawal, and even externalizing behaviors like aggression. Some definitions refer to the child's developmental appropriateness in their ability to function. Some states require the diagnosis of a mental health expert or physician to substantiate the claim of abuse. Delaware notes very specific language around the emotional abuse of a child: "chronic or recurring incidents of ridiculing, demeaning, making derogatory remarks, or cursing" (Child Welfare Information Gateway, 2019, p. 21). Two states, Georgia and Washington, do not mention or acknowledge a formal policy around emotional abuse in their statutes.

Common Signs of Abuse

The Washington State Department of Children, Youth & Families (2022) indicates the following as possible signs of child abuse or neglect—as noticed—in the *child*: a display of sudden changes in behavior or school performance; lack of medical attention; learning difficulties not attributable to specific physical or psychological reasons; hypervigilance; lack of supervision; being overly compliant, passive, or withdrawn; or demonstrating a desire not to go home and even to arrive early and stay late at school activities.

Parents present concerns when they show little concern for their child's well-being, demonstrate a lack of empathy, or express views of the child as worthless, bad, or a burden. Parents who signal concerns of possible abuse also deny or blame the child for problems they have and hold the child to a higher level of performance than the child's abilities; they may even look to the child for care, attention, and to satisfy their emotional needs. Further, parents may also request that others treat the child in a harsh and punishing manner (e.g., asking teachers or caregivers to use harsh physical discipline if the child misbehaves). When able to observe the parent and child together, it is a good idea to watch how the parent and child interact with one another. It is especially telling with young children if they wince at a raised arm or stop or shrink back in the abusive parent's presence. A child who protests when it is time to go home may be another signal of possible abuse.

Child Neglect (Medical, Educational, Material)

As defined by CAPTA earlier in the chapter, neglect occurs when a parent or caregiver who is responsible for the child fails to act on the child's behalf to protect them from serious harm or death. According to the Child Welfare Information Gateway (2019), nearly all states provide a definition of child abuse and neglect in their state statute. More specifically, neglect may include the failure of the parent or caregiver to provide food, clothing, shelter, medical care, supervision, or the abandonment of children. As many as 24 states include failure to educate their child as a form of neglect. Seven states consider the lack of medical care or failing to provide treatment or mental health care as possible medical neglect; and five states define medical neglect as "the withholding of medical treatment or nutrition from disabled children with life-threatening conditions" (Child Welfare Information Gateway, 2019, p. 3). Some states use drug-specific language to acknowledge other forms of neglect. Several states include terminology in their definitions of neglect (permitting a child to enter or remain in any structure or vehicle in which *volatile, toxic, or flammable chemicals* are found or equipment is possessed by any person for the purposes of *manufacturing a dangerous drug*). Others include definitions acknowledging abuse that occurs prenatally when the fetus is exposed to drugs or other illicit substances, medication obtained without a prescription, or dangerous chemicals during the production of methamphetamines, as well as fetal alcohol syndrome or fetal alcohol effects. Colorado also considers homelessness, running away behaviors, and when the child is beyond the control of their parent, guardian, or legal custodian as neglect and dictates the need for services (Colorado Revised Statutes, 2022). Whatever the type of neglect children experience, the fact remains that neglect has a high prevalence rate when compared to other types of child maltreatment (Sedlak et al., 2010; Stoltenborgh et al., 2015).

Mulder and colleagues (2018) conducted a meta-analytic review of risk factors for child neglect. They examined the literature and reported that a total of 315 effect sizes were extracted from 36 primary studies and classified into 24 risk domains (mostly at the parental level). According to Mulder and colleagues (2018) multiple risk factors are present in cases of child neglect. The strongest predictors of child neglect "can be found in parental characteristics" (p. 205). Parents who are stressed, psychiatrically challenged, and underresourced are considered next in consideration of contextual factors.

CONTEXTS OF THOSE WHO ABUSE CHILDREN

The recognition of abuse and neglect also ushered in the need to understand those who abuse or exploit the vulnerability of infants and minor-age children. The etiology of child maltreatment is complex and multidimensional (Carr et al., 2020) and can be understood as epiphenomenal at best. To contextualize this discussion, it is necessary to consider the role stress plays in parenting.

Parenting stress can also be a contextual factor through which abuse and neglect occur. Parental experience of stress plays a big part in managing households and interacting with children (either in positive or negative ways). "Parenting stress results from the parent's evaluation that the demands of the parenting role are exceeding his or her coping abilities" (Miragoli et al., 2018, p. 2). Miragoli and colleagues assert that parents' social–cognitive capacities influence parenting practices. According to Miragoli and colleagues (2018), the social information processing (SIP) model views parenting behavior as a series of cognitive stages:

- In *stage 1*, parents interpret their children's behavior (this could be positive or negative).

- In *stage 2*, parents then utilize the information they have available to them (from what they know and from their own life experiences).

- In *stage 3*, parents select their disciplinary response and monitor the child's behavior.

- In *stage 4*, the likelihood of abuse may be heightened if parents make inaccurate perceptions, use biased interpretations, fail to integrate information, or inadequately monitor their disciplinary actions.

How parents interpret their child's behavior and perceive their child influences their parental actions and stress level. Moreover, parental stress may lead to misinterpretations of the child's actions. Children's behavior may signal a specific need but may be interpreted as misbehavior by a parent experiencing life stressors. In these cases, the stressed parent does not consider the behavior from a child-centered perspective. The research shows that parents who abuse children display faulty thinking about their children's actions. In essence, abusive parents attribute negative child behavior as intentional (i.e., internal cause), interpret information in more hostile ways, and view their child's behavior as stressful (Ball Cooper et al., 2018; Larkin et al., 2021; Miragoli et al., 2018). Furthermore, the lack of knowledge about child development contributes to the misinterpretation of children's behavior. In addition, parents who were raised without adequate parenting may repeat the cycle of poor parenting practices.

Parental Psychiatric Considerations

Understanding parental well-being and managing psychiatric illness is significant in supporting families and children. The literature has identified parental mental health problems as a risk factor for child maltreatment. Childhood abuse has lasting effects and may be attributable to adult mental health problems such as depression, anxiety disorders, eating disorders, sexual dysfunction, personality disorders, dissociative disorder, substance use disorders, traumatic disorders (Read et al., 2018), and schizophrenia, and parents with these disorders are three times more likely to be reported to child protection services (Hefti et al., 2020). Parental psychiatric problems strongly predict child neglect (Mulder et al., 2018). Some parents with mental disorders lack support, do not exhibit strong help-seeking behaviors, and at times have alienated their support system (extended family and friends). Hefti and colleagues indicate that parents need support to develop the skills to cope with their mental health problems to bolster their child's protection. It is important to note that there are parents with mental disorders and substance use problems who can protect and ensure their children's safety. Some parents engage in protective parenting by creating a care plan for their children and shielding them from their more dysfunctional behaviors or conditions (e.g., drug use or an acute mental crisis).

Further, environmental surroundings such as hoarding and unsanitary homes may give rise to the neglect of children in the care of their parents. Parents who hoard may suffer from a paralyzing form of depression. The environment of the home plays a critical role in ensuring the safety of children and assessing parental mental health. The environment is important to assessing child safety: knowing what the home looks like, how the children are living, their sleeping arrangements, and if there are additional people living in the home. Any of these factors may pose a safety risk for children and exacerbate the mental health challenges of the parental unit. Environmental safety may be enhanced by social and programmatic support, medication maintenance, counseling, and substance use treatment. Parent coaches have been used by some agencies to augment parental knowledge through mentoring and practical demonstrations of parenting tasks to enhance safety in the child's environment.

Intimate Partner Violence

Intimate partner violence (IPV) has a pernicious effect on the family. Children were once thought to be silent witnesses to intimate partner violence. The truth is, when one parent is battered by their partner, even if it is done out of the visual range of the child, the child may hear the violence erupting and may intuit emotional changes such as a rise in their parents' stress levels (especially the one who is battered). They may also experience varying degrees of care due to the ability of the abused parent to stay attuned to their needs while nursing their own injuries, bruises, shame, fear, and humiliation. In child welfare, the goal is to protect the child from abuse and neglect, but who does the system hold accountable when one parent is being abused as well? Ballou (2017), a legal scholar, wrote about the failure of our nation's civil system to properly address this accountability issue: "Perhaps the most glaring flaw in our civil system exists in our nation's tendency to punish mothers who are victims of domestic violence for 'failing to protect' their children" (Ballou, 2017, p. 357). This is akin to blaming the victim.

According to Ballou, the legal system often provides battered women with little legal recourse against spousal abuse [sic]. Ballou suggests that victims of domestic violence need more flexibility, protection through legal means (i.e., orders of protection), and adequate police response in accordance with the National Council on Juvenile and Family Court Judges Guidebook. In addition, further training may be needed for those who handle such cases to mitigate any latent biases against women. It is critical for child welfare workers to understand the context of IPV while also assessing the safety and welfare of children. Tutty and Nixon (2020) note the importance of avoiding a deficit model of mothering due to IPV and suggest "a number of authors refute the perception that abused mothers are generally helpless, incompetent, or aggressive parents" (p. 2). When a woman is entangled in a violent intimate relationship, her action may be to protect the child(ren) by placating their partner, sending the child(ren) to a neighbor's or relative's home, or ending the relationship (as a longer-term strategy). "For others, though, remaining with the abuser is the preferred strategy because they fear for their own children's physical safety if they were to separate" (Tutty & Nixon, 2020, p. 2). Child welfare workers must have a good understanding of IPV and how to assess the safety of the child and parent and the worker's safety when visiting. In addition, child welfare agencies must consider viable options to support parents who are victimized and unable to protect themselves or their children.

RISK FACTORS AND CONTEXT

Dubowitz and Bennett (2007) define the risk factors for child abuse in multidimensional terms—not determined based on one particular cause or circumstance. Risk factors may include but are not limited to parental depression, intimate partner violence, a child's disability status/medical susceptibility, and societal factors such as poverty and living in dangerous neighborhoods (Dubowitz & Bennett, 2007). Nonetheless, Dubowitz and Bennett warn against bias toward low-income families. It is important to note that poverty as a risk factor is not prescriptive for all families living in poverty and should be considered based on multiple contexts and a just assessment of parental ability to maintain child safety. It is critical to see each child, parent, or family in the fullness of their humanity rather than as a stereotypical trope based on preconceived notions about impoverished families and families of color.

Child's Disability/Medical Condition

Kendall-Tackett and colleagues (2005) note the lack of protection for children with disabilities and report that Oregon was one of the first states to address this social problem. Out-of-home placements are sometimes difficult to find, depending on the nature and severity of the disability. Kendall-Tackett and colleagues (2005) also note the difficulty with high caseloads, budget cuts, staff turnover, and the stress of the system in general, making it difficult to manage these over-lapping systems in the care of children. Coordinating with multiple systems like families, schools, foster families/agencies, clinics, and mental health centers, to name a few, is necessary for enhanced care options for children with disabilities.

Some tasks for child welfare agencies would be (a) the early identification of the disability status of children who enter the child welfare system (Kendall-Tackett et al., 2005), (b) consideration of the criteria needed to assess fully whether or not a child has a disability (sans official documentation) and the type of disability related to maltreatment risk (Kendall-Tackett et al., 2005), (c) provision of additional training for child welfare professionals on screening for disability, and (d) analysis of the onset and severity of the disability and when the abuse began (Kendall-Tackett et al., 2005).

Societal Factors

Societal factors like poverty, homelessness, joblessness, and violence contribute to the demise of child safety. All poor families, unemployed parents, and those living in violence-ridden communities are not automatically assumed to be abusive; however, these societal factors can serve as contributing stressors for child maltreatment. The 1919 White House Conference on Children (U.S. Department of Health, Education, and Welfare [HEW], 1967) emphasized parents' need for employment and a livable wage to support the family. This is a recommendation that has never been fulfilled.

"All too often, we know that neglect is closely tied to poverty and therefore requires us to pinpoint our focus on strengthening communities to meet the basic needs of families to increase their capacity to care for their children in safe and loving homes" (Milner, 2020, para. 13). Milner, the Associate Commissioner of the Children's Bureau, highlights the need to develop more intensive interventions to address poverty and other root causes of neglect. He further asserts that addressing poverty requires prevention efforts focused on the root causes of neglect. Providing more intensive interventions is the best way to avoid the trauma of children experiencing familial disruption.

PROTECTIVE FACTORS

Protective factors are defined as characteristics associated with a lower likelihood of negative outcomes or reduction in the impact of risk. The Child Welfare Information Gateway (2020, March) lists several protective factors to prevent child abuse and neglect (see Figure 2.2).

- *Nurturing and attachment*: Children's early attachment and bonding experiences influence their overall development. Children learn to trust that their needs

Figure 2.2 Protective Factors

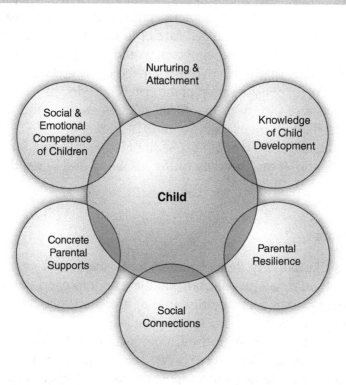

Source: Adapted from Child Welfare Information Gateway. (2020). *Protective factors to promote well-being and prevent child abuse and neglect.* https://www.childwelfare.gov/topics/preventing/promoting/protectfactors/

will be met when parents are caring and nurturing. Parental care and nurturing provide love, acceptance, positive guidance, and protection.

- *Knowledge of how to parent with an understanding of child and youth development:* Children fare better when "parents provide respectful communication and listening, consistent rules and expectations, and safe opportunities that promote independence" (para. 6). When children are provided with a supportive environment, they can perform better in school. Parents play a critical role in fostering psychological adjustment and overall child well-being.

- *Parental resilience:* Children fare better when parents can cope with the vicissitudes of life, such as "family history of abuse or neglect, health problems, marital conflict, or domestic or community violence—financial stressors, such as unemployment, poverty, and homelessness" (para. 7). When parents are resilient, they display an ability to bounce back from adversity. The authors understand that in instances of intimate partner violence, bouncing back from adversity is a complicated matter and requires a keen understanding of domestic violence and appropriate interventions for the abused parent and child.

- *Social connections*: Children fare better when their parents are supported. Parents and caregivers who have a strong support system find it easier to care for themselves. Supportive family, friends, and neighbors can provide a sympathetic ear and offer advice or other means of direct support.

- *Concrete support for parents*: Children are better off when parents have access to the community resources they require. Parents may need help identifying what resources they need to prevent unintended abuse or child maltreatment. For instance, the United Way provides a free, confidential hotline to connect the public with food, employment, crisis support, and health and housing assistance resources.

- *Social and emotional competence of children*: Children's social and emotional development benefits when parents can model it for them. Children learn to express their feelings, convey emotions, practice self-regulation, and become adept at making friends.

Risk factors identified by Rijbroek and colleagues (2019) include three main clusters in their review of the literature. First, at the *child level*, a child who has an easy temperament, positive coping skills, good intellectual ability, and self-esteem possesses protective factors on an individual level. Second, at the *parental level*, protective factors for the child occur when parents have self-esteem, an internal locus of control, understanding, acceptance of care, and cooperation with a professional. Other parental abilities, such as having a secure attachment with their child, stability within the home, knowledge of child development, enhanced parental empathy and support, and good communication in the family, also serve as protective factors. Third, the *environmental level may* be protective when family and friends provide the social support needed to buffer the effects of stress. Friendships with peers can provide valuable support to parents experiencing stress. Social support increases personal well-being and bolsters parents' abilities to withstand some of the vicissitudes of life.

Reflection Box 2.2

In groups of four, select a book to review from the list provided. Each book focuses on child abuse or cultural variations that may impact how the case is viewed (For example, *The Spirit Catches You and You Fall Down*). Prepare a 30 to 45-minute PowerPoint presentation.

1. *Introduction*
2. *Summary of the entire book*

(continued)

Reflection Box 2.2 (*continued*)

3. *Analysis* of the book in relation to:
   a. family dynamics
   b. family income and access to resources
   c. untreated mental illness or substance use
   d. intimate partner violence
   e. child welfare
   f. social work interventions at the micro, mezzo, and macro levels

4. *Recommendation*: Indicate why you would or would not recommend this to social workers or child welfare workers to read.

5. *Implications for social justice*: Identify and explain dimensions of social justice and their implications for prevention and intervention.

6. *Conclusion*: Give your main take-aways for the book and use one quote (each group member) to support that take-away.

Provide students with a list of books (see the following examples and add to the list):

- *A Child Called It: One Child's Courage to Survive*
- *Damaged: The Heartbreaking True Story of a Forgotten Child*
- *Spilled Milk: Based on a True Story*
- *A Boy Who was Raised as a Dog: And Other Stories from a Child Psychiatrist's Notebook—What Traumatized Children can Teach us About Loss, Love, and Healing*
- *The Spirit Catches You and You Fall Down*
- *The Body Keeps the Score: Brain, Mind, and Body in the Healing of Trauma*
- *Unbroken Spirit: Abby's story*

CHAPTER SUMMARY

This chapter focused on defining child abuse and neglect, including distinguishing among different states' definitions, and explored the health and neurobiological consequences of experiencing maltreatment. It also discussed what physicians look for in determining if a health concern is the result of abuse and neglect. The authors provided a review of the characteristics and contexts of those who abuse children. They showed that child protection professionals provide invaluable assessments to ensure the safety of vulnerable children nationwide. The child welfare system helps bolster family support when possible and may provide families with needed referrals for intensive interventions or case management.

DISCUSSION QUESTIONS

1. What is cultural empathy, and how might it be used in child welfare?
2. What signs of abuse are red flags, and how can you avoid missing the signs of abuse?
3. Discuss the potential risk factors that jeopardize a child's safety.
4. Discuss possible protective factors and how to bolster those in families.
5. What areas would you target for social justice reform in child welfare practice?

RESOURCES

National Responsible Fatherhood Clearinghouse
https://www.fatherhood.gov/?gclid=EAIaIQobChMI__3MlbbB9wIVBylMCh1YmgK
    _EAAYAyAAEgIwHvD_BwE

New York Society for the Prevention of Cruelty to Children (NY SPCC)
https://nyspcc.org

The Child Welfare Information Gateway
https://www.childwelfare.gov/

The Child Welfare Information Gateway—State Statutes Search
https://www.childwelfare.gov/topics/systemwide/laws-policies/state/

 SPRINGER PUBLISHING
CONNECT™ | A robust set of instructor resources designed to supplement this text is located at **http://connect.springerpub.com/content/book/978-0-8261-5285-5.** Qualifying instructors may request access by emailing **textbook@springerpub.com.**

REFERENCES

Ball Cooper, E., Abate, A., Airrington, M. D., Taylor, L., & Venta, A. C. (2018). When and how do race/ethnicity relate to dysfunctional discipline practices? *Journal of Child & Family Studies, 27,* 966–978. https://doi.org/10.1007/s10826-017-0931-1

Ballou, K. (2017). Failure to protect: Our civil system's chronic punishment of victims of domestic violence. *Notre Dame Journal of Law, Ethics & Public Policy, 31,* 355. https://scholarship.law.nd.edu/ndjlepp/vol31/iss2/4/?utm_source=scholarship.law.nd.ed

CAPTA, S. Rep. No. 111-378 (2010). https://www.govinfo.gov/content/pkg/CRPT-111srpt378/pdf/CRPT-111srpt378.pdf

Carr, A., Duff, H., & Craddock, F. (2020). A systematic review of reviews of the outcome of noninstitutional child maltreatment. *Trauma, Violence, & Abuse, 21*(4), 828–843. https://doi.org/10.1177/1524838018801334

Carter, D. A., (2011). *President Bill Clinton, African Americans, and the politics of race and class* (Doctoral dissertation, University of Memphis). University of Memphis Digital Commons. https://digitalcommons.memphis.edu/etd/201

Child Welfare Information Gateway. (2019). *What is child abuse and neglect? Recognizing the signs and symptoms.* U.S. Department of Health and Human Services, Children's Bureau. https://www.childwelfare.gov/pubPDFs/whatiscan.pdf

Child Welfare Information Gateway. (2020). *Protective factors to promote well-being and prevent child abuse and neglect.* https://www.childwelfare.gov/topics/preventing/promoting/protectfactors/

Colorado Revised Statutes. (2022). *Colorado Revised Statutes 2018. Title 19: Children's Code. §§ 19-1-103; 19-3-102.* https://leg.colorado.gov/sites/default/files/images/olls/crs2018-title-19.pdf

Corcoran, J., & Walsh, J. (2016). *Clinical assessment and diagnosis in social work practice* (3rd ed.). Oxford University Press.

Dubowitz, H., & Bennett, S. (2007). Physical abuse and neglect of children. *The Lancet, 369*(9576), 1891–1899. https://doi.org/10.1016/S0140-6736(07)60856-3

Fields, R. D. (2019). The roots of human aggression: Experiments in humans and animals have started to identify how violent behaviors begin in the brain. *Scientific American, 320*(5), 65. https://www.ncbi.nlm.nih.gov/pmc/articles/PMC8284101/pdf/nihms-1711578.pdf

Hefti, S., Pérez, T., Fürstenau, U., Rhiner, B., Swenson, C. C., & Schmid, M. (2020). Multisystemic therapy for child abuse and neglect: Do parents show improvement in parental mental health problems and parental stress? *Journal of Marital and Family Therapy, 46*(1), 95–109. https://doi.org/10.1111/jmft.12367

Jedd, K., Hunt, R. H., Cicchetti, D., Hunt, E., Cowell, R. A., Rogosch, F. A., Toth, S. L., & Thomas, K. M. (2015). Long-term consequences of childhood maltreatment: Altered amygdala functional connectivity. *Development and Psychopathology, 27*(4 Pt. 2), 1577–1589. https://doi.org/10.1017/S0954579415000954

Kempe, C. H., Silverman, F. N., Steele, B. F., Droegemueller, W., & Silver, H. K. (1962). The Battered-Child Syndrome. *Journal of the American Medical Association, 181*(1), 17–24. https://doi.org/10.1001/jama.1962.03050270019004

Kendall-Tackett, K., Lyon, T., Taliaferro, G., & Little, L. (2005). Why child maltreatment researchers should include children's disability status in their maltreatment studies. *Child Abuse & Neglect, 29*(2), 147–151. https://doi.org/10.1016/j.chiabu.2004.09.002

Larkin, F., Hayiou-Thomas, M. E., Arshad, Z., Leonard, M., Williams, F. J., Katseniou, N., Malouta, R. N., Marshall, C. R. P., Diamantopoulou, M., Tang, E., Mani, S. & Meins, E. (2021). Mind-mindedness and stress in parents of children with developmental disorders. *Journal of Autism and Developmental Disorders, 51*(2), 600–612. https://doi.org/10.1007/s10803-020-04570-9

Martinkevich, P., Larsen, L. L., Græsholt-Knudsen, T., Hesthaven, G., Hellfritzsch, M. B., Petersen, K. K., Bjarne, M. M., & Rölfing, J. D. (2020). Physical child abuse demands increased awareness during health and socioeconomic crises like COVID-19: A review and education material. *Acta Orthopaedica, 91*(5), 527–533. https://doi.org/10.1080/17453674.2020.1782012

McElvaney, J. (2011). *Spirit unbroken: Abby's story.* AuthorHouse Publisher.

Milner, J. (2020). *Child abuse, neglect data released* [Press release]. Administration for Children and Families, U.S. Department of Health & Human Services. https://www.acf.hhs.gov/media/press/2020/2020/child-abuse-neglect-data-released

Miragoli, S., Balzarotti, S., Camisasca, E., & Di Blasio, P. (2018). Parents' perception of child behavior, parenting stress, and child abuse potential: Individual and partner influences. *Child Abuse & Neglect, 84*, 146–156. https://doi.org/10.1016/j.chiabu.2018.07.034

Mulder, T. M., Kuiper, K. C., van der Put, C. E., Stams, G. J. J., & Assink, M. (2018). Risk factors for child neglect: A meta-analytic review. *Child Abuse & Neglect, 77*, 198–210. https://doi.org/10.1016/j.chiabu.2018.01.006

Nelson, C. A., Bhutta, Z. A., Burke Harris, N., Danese, A., & Samara, M. (2020). Toxic stress and PTSD in children: Adversity in childhood is linked to mental and physical health throughout life. *BMJ, 371*, 1–9. https://doi.org/10.1136/bmj.m3048

Read, J., Harper, D., Tucker, I., & Kennedy, A. (2018). Do adult mental health services identify child abuse and neglect? A systematic review. *International Journal of Mental Health Nursing, 27*(1), 7–19. https://doi.org/10.1111/inm.12369

Rijbroek, B., Strating, M. M., Konijn, H. W., & Huijsman, R. (2019). Child protection cases, one size fits all? Cluster analyses of risk and protective factors. *Child Abuse & Neglect, 95*, 104068. https://doi.org/10.1016/j.chiabu.2019.104068

Sedlak, A. J., Mettenburg, J., Basena, M., Peta, I., McPherson, K., Greene, A., & Li, S. (2010). *Fourth national incidence study of child abuse and neglect (NIS-4): Report to Congress.* U.S. Department of Health and Human Services. https://cap.law.harvard.edu/wp-content/uploads/2015/07/sedlaknis.pdf

Stoltenborgh, M., Bakermans-Kranenburg, M. J., Alink, L. R., & van IJzendoorn, M. H. (2015). The prevalence of child maltreatment across the globe: Review of a series of meta-analyses. *Child Abuse Review, 24*(1), 37–50. https://doi.org/10.1002/car.2353

Teicher, M. H., & Samson, J. A. (2016). Annual research review: Enduring neurobiological effects of childhood abuse and neglect. *The Journal of Child Psychology and Psychiatry, 57*(3), 241–266. https://doi.org/10.1111/jcpp.12507

Tutty, L. M., & Nixon, K. (2020). Mothers abused by intimate partners: Comparisons of those with children placed by child protective services and those without. *Children & Youth Services Review, 115*, 105090. https://doi.org/10.1016/j.childyouth.2020.105090

U.S. Department of Health, Education, and Welfare. (1967). *The story of the White House conferences on children and youth.* Social and Rehabilitation Service, Children's Bureau. https://files.eric.ed.gov/fulltext/ED078896.pdf

Washington State Department of Children, Youth & Families. (2022). *Report child abuse or neglect.* https://www.dcyf.wa.gov/safety/what-is-abuse

World Health Organization. (2020). *Child maltreatment (Fact sheet).* https://www.who.int/news-room/fact-sheets/detail/child-maltreatment

3

Careers in Child Welfare

All professions represent an institutional way of organizing and controlling an occupation (Parker & Doel, 2013). Parker and Doel assert their functionalist understandings of professions, believing them to have a distinct knowledge base and practice methods, ethics specific to the profession, and a role in maintaining social order. The child welfare profession is highly regulated. As a profession, child welfare provides standards of care through its operational procedures and safeguards and seeks to honor the law related to child protection.

LEARNING OBJECTIVES

By the end of the chapter, you will be able to:

- Consider the various roles and responsibilities within child welfare.
- Understand the mission and goals of the child welfare system.
- Explore the fit between your passion and the positions offered within the child welfare system.
- Understand the connection between policy and practice.
- Understand the importance of the juvenile court process.

INTRODUCTION

Various positions in child welfare play a role in keeping children safe. It takes a team to ensure that the most vulnerable populations receive the support and services they need to strengthen their families and promote loving, safe environments for their children. In child welfare, social workers utilize core social work principles to support families and help to create healthy environments for families to thrive. When this is not possible, child welfare professionals are responsible for ensuring that every child has a nurturing and safe home with family members or a foster family that bolsters their healthy development. A secure placement may also be provided through subsidized guardianship or adoption. Yet there are still youth in care who are not able to find a forever family. The child welfare system supports these youth with services to assist them with transitioning into adulthood in the healthiest ways possible. Older youth in care are provided with support to help them maximize their educational goals through college or obtain their chosen vocational training to pursue careers in various areas. Older youth in care prefer to find jobs and work while learning to live independently with the ultimate goal of supporting themselves in their own housing. In some situations, youth are impacted by medical, mental health, and developmental concerns that influence their ability to be maintained in a home environment. In these circumstances, child welfare professionals work with various government programs that provide resources for youth to access adult transition services, including a focus on independent living skills. Whenever possible, the goal is to find a permanent home for youth in care, regardless of medical complexities or disabilities, by providing as much support as possible to families to ensure they have the resources to manage the youth in their homes, assisting them to thrive.

FOCUS OF CHILD WELFARE

In the field of child welfare, it is essential to be trauma-informed and understand the impact involvement in the child welfare system has on children and families. Abuse and neglect can cause trauma, but further trauma is caused when children are separated from their families. Children's sense of time is different than it is for adults. One month of being separated from their family could feel much longer to them, increasing their trauma and anxiety. Children's most critical relationships are interrupted when they enter the child welfare system. The children and youth are left to process the trauma of the disconnection while at the same time being placed in foster homes with families with whom they are not familiar. Child welfare professionals must understand trauma and how it manifests in the child's behavioral responses. The trauma may ultimately lead to mental health issues and behavioral concerns, which must be addressed strategically to reduce further interruption in developmental and emotional growth.

It is also critical to understand how trauma impacts parental responses. When parents respond negatively, child welfare professionals must contextualize the negative feedback they receive from parents. For instance, when the child welfare professional imposes a strict timeline for services, which clashes with the parent's work schedule, parents may protest adamantly! Hourly workers have little flexibility in their work schedule and face dire consequences for missing work related to job stability and financial security. Another example of a negative interface occurs

Figure 3.1 Social Worker Link to Community and Family

when parents displace their anger on the child welfare system and minimize their own role in the removal of their child(ren) from their care. The worker represents the demise of the family system, which parents resent. The reality of child welfare is that it is multisystemic. For the child welfare professional or social worker, collaboration with various community providers, private child welfare agencies, and public systems are necessary for supporting families and keeping children safe. Many families become involved with the child welfare system due to lacking access to needed resources. Services are either absent, underdeveloped, or financially out of reach. The lack of private insurance or federally funded insurance to support necessary interventions for the many needs of children and families can also be a barrier. This lack of access gives rise to heightened and urgent needs and vulnerabilities of children and families. Due to these needs and lack of community resources, the incidents of abuse and neglect among children are intensified. Child welfare professionals serve an important role in connecting families to community resources and collaborating with child welfare agencies (see Figure 3.1).

CHILD WELFARE CAREERS

Social workers who choose careers in child welfare are dedicated to community services and advocating for those in need. There are six core social work values that social workers keep in mind when working with children, families, and the community: (a) service, (b) social justice, (c) dignity and worth of the person, (d) importance of human relationships, (e) integrity, and (f) competence (National Association of

Social Workers [NASW], 2021). Utilizing these principles allows child welfare professionals to remain vigilant and non judgmental. Empowering individuals to live their best lives and to thrive as human beings is the key to serving families in child welfare. When we engage and empower families, the success rate of keeping families together increases. Children placed out of the home return to their families at an accelerated rate when we provide the support they need and empower parents to make healthy choices for their children and families. The NASW values outline key standards for service that can be applied to the child welfare system.

1. *Service*—Social workers are called to address social problems in helping relationships. Social workers in child welfare should place service to others above their own self-interest. Child welfare professionals should strengthen their knowledge of child development, family systems, and community resources.

2. *Social justice*—When applied to the child welfare profession, social justice means challenging the status quo, advocating for policy changes, fighting for the rights of oppressed children and families, and empowering families to advocate for fair treatment.

3. *Dignity and worth of the person*—Just as social workers respect the dignity and worth of all persons, child welfare professionals should also understand the importance of this value. Professionals should engage parents, children, and families with respect and understanding. Child welfare professionals should attempt to honor the parents' right to self-determination by respecting their voices. Despite adhering to agency policies, child welfare professionals must understand how to balance their dual responsibilities of supporting families while complying with child safety.

4. *Importance of human relationships*—Social workers recognize the centrality of human relationships. Child welfare professionals should engage family systems to promote, maintain, and restore family functioning. Establishing positive helping relationships as partners with parents whenever possible is vital to working effectively with parents, children, extended family members, and other stakeholders. It is also important to support family relationships throughout the process.

5. *Integrity*—Social workers are called to practice ethically, act honestly, and engage in personal and professional self-care. Child welfare professionals must also engage in professional decorum in the representation of their agency. Integrity also means addressing any impairments the professional may have so they do not impede the ability to provide quality services.

6. *Competence*—Social workers practice within their areas of competence and develop their level of expertise. Child welfare professionals must also continue training in understanding family systems and diversity, engagement, assessment, and knowledge of evidence-based interventions.

Although these principles are social work-related, child welfare workers may find them helpful as they develop their own professionalism and practice. A few examples of how these values may be integrated within the work of the child welfare professional are displayed in Table 3.1.

It takes commitment, compassion, and dedication to navigate the field of child welfare. Remaining trauma focused and aware of its impact may help child welfare workers manage difficult family situations in the field. Child welfare is a rewarding career for those called to protect children and keep them safe. The field helps to meet the needs of some of the most vulnerable members of society and can be a meaningful career choice. At the same time, it is a challenging field of practice.

The field of child welfare engenders blame. There are a lot of misunderstandings about the field that fuels how society views the system, families, and child welfare workers. Not only is the job challenging, but child welfare workers do not always have support from the general public. Moreover, blame flows system wide and from every direction—judges, media outlets, the public, legislators, and the child welfare system itself. Blame can place a tremendous responsibility and burden on workers within the system. The child welfare system must find ways to support and motivate its workers and provide continuing professional development and safeguards to prevent high turnover.

High turnover in child welfare is common. Working with children and families dealing with various life stressors can be overwhelming. Child welfare workers may experience the stress of working in complex situations with families. The complexities and chaotic nature of the family system may impede the progression of services and the likelihood of family reunification. Child welfare workers must reflect on difficult cases and structural challenges within the system as they learn to navigate the most complicated family situations. Workers must be careful not to place unrealistic expectations on themselves or the families they work with and must learn to balance responsibility. Responsibility is reciprocal; it is essential to understand that responsibility for change belongs to the parents/family and worker.

The child welfare worker's professional identity may be challenged at times. Child welfare professionals often make difficult decisions that do not always garner public support in the media. Consequently, workers may feel crushed under the weight of the decisions they are compelled to make, which may compromise their confidence as a professional. Supervisors and managers need to be consistent in their supervision; they should work to retain child welfare staff through support, training, and assistance with managing stress and setting appropriate boundaries. Staff turnover can also impact the outcomes for children and families. When a family encounters multiple case managers due to staff turnover, it can cause a delay in service provision and cause an overall delay in returning youth home or providing permanency through foster care.

TABLE 3.1 PRACTICAL APPLICATION OF SOCIAL WORK VALUES TO CHILD WELFARE

EXAMPLE	SOCIAL WORK CORE VALUES	APPLICATION TO CHILD WELFARE
A caseworker has recently been assigned three new cases on top of an already heightened caseload. The caseworker is feeling overwhelmed after receiving a call from the foster parent who is having difficulty with a child placed in their home. The foster parent would like for the caseworker to meet with them.	**Service**—Social workers are called to address social problems in helping relationships. Social workers should place service to others above their own self-interest.	*Cultivating relationships and providing support are paramount in the field of child welfare. It is important to return calls, provide support, and address concerns in a timely and effective manner. It is also important to find the balance between self-care and serving others to ensure healthy working relationships.*
A father of a youth in care has reached out to the case manager in an effort to set up visitation with his child, who is in foster care with a maternal relative. The father is concerned that he is not being offered the resources and visitation afforded to the mother, and he would like an opportunity to work toward the return of the child to his care.	**Social Justice**—This is defined as challenging social injustice, advocating for policy changes, and fighting for the rights of the oppressed.	*A part of the work of a child welfare professional is to advocate for the children and families that they serve to ensure their input is garnered and respected. When we encounter parents who are concerned that their voices are not being heard, it is important to join with them to advocate for fair treatment when it appears their rights are being violated.*
A mother had her children removed due to substance use and allegations of neglect. Children and families are impacted by various social problems that can contribute to abuse and/or neglect. Substance use/abuse, mental illness, and developmental concerns can impede the progress of family reunification. It is important that families are treated with respect even when we are not in agreement with their lifestyles.	**Dignity and worth of the person**—Social workers must respect the dignity and worth of all persons. This means engaging children and families with empathy and respect. It also includes allowing them to fully participate in determining their path as they work toward family reunification.	*Regardless of our own beliefs, it is important to treat everyone that we encounter with dignity and respect. Although we may not agree with the lifestyle or behaviors of the families that we encounter, it is important that they are treated fairly and that child welfare professionals are providing them with the services that they need while ensuring the safety of children.*

Value	Scenario	Application
Importance of human relationships—Social workers recognize the centrality of human relationships.	The biological parents reach out to the supervisor because they do not believe that the child welfare worker is willing to work with them to reunify their family. The problem has been poor communication between the parents and the worker.	*Establishing helping relationships as partners is key to working effectively with parents, children, extended family, and stakeholders. When child welfare workers join with families, it strengthens the relationship and reinforces trust.*
Integrity—Social workers are called to practice ethically, act honestly, and engage in personal and professional self-care. Child welfare professionals must also engage in professional decorum in the representation of their agency. This also means addressing any impairments the professional may have so that it does not impede their ability to provide quality services.	A complaint is made to the child welfare department about a specific worker who has been unresponsive to a parent. The children were recently removed from the parent's care. The parent has been calling the newly assigned case worker for visitation and has not been able to reach the worker, leaving the parent feeling helpless. Further, the parent is anxious to see their children and is concerned for their well-being.	*When this value is applied in child welfare, workers should address the specific needs of parents from a person-in-environment perspective. This includes understanding the traumatic consequences of their involvement in the child welfare system. It is important for child welfare workers to practice professionalism by adhering to agency policy. It is also a matter of professionalism to respond to clients/parents in a timely manner.*
Competence—Social workers practice in their area of competence while developing their expertise.	A foster parent has expressed concerns about renewing their foster care license and contacted their case worker to ask additional questions. This is out of the purview of the case worker's expertise.	*Learning the child welfare system and being aware of one's area of practice and competence level is important. Families should be able to count on their case manager to route them to the correct division when questions and concerns arise that are out of the area of expertise of the case manager. This is a part of building credibility and establishing trusting relationships.*

OVERVIEW OF CHILD WELFARE REPORTING PROCESSES

Child welfare reporting processes may vary from state to state. Each state has its own central registry for child maltreatment. A registry is a central database that collects information on all child abuse and neglect reports. Updating this registry is a critical process in child protection services because it allows the system to keep track of vital information regarding historical child abuse and neglect cases. In addition, this central registry helps to vet adults who work with and care for youth. For instance, those seeking employment working with children often undergo background checks through the criminal legal system and the child abuse and neglect system, where the central registry database is used.

In this section, the authors provide an overview of customary child welfare reporting procedures and the roles of child welfare professionals. Reporting processes include screening calls, conducting investigations of child abuse and neglect, and supporting families through material resources and other referrals.

Child welfare reporting starts with the suspicion of child abuse and neglect. A call is made to a child abuse hotline by either a mandated reporter or a concerned individual. The information is provided to the screener, who determines how the information should be processed. Suppose it is determined that the information received does not meet the criteria for an investigation. In that case, the information is referred to a child welfare services (CWS) worker who will assess the family for services and make community referrals to provide support to the family. If the call meets the criteria for an investigation, the report is referred to the investigation's unit. If a case is already opened, the information in the new allegation may be considered "information only" and is given to the current case manager so the concerns can be assessed and addressed (see Figure 3.2). If the information provided meets the criteria for an investigation, there could be a few different outcomes. If there is no indication of abuse or neglect, the investigation is considered "unfounded or unsubstantiated," and the investigation is completed and closed. If it is determined that there is an indication of abuse or neglect, depending on the level of risk and safety to the child, the following decisions may be made:

1. The family could be referred to *intact family services*, where a case manager is assigned to link them to community services to address the safety and parenting concerns. The family case is monitored for at least 6 months and assessed for closure once the family is stabilized and there are no longer safety issues for the children involved.

2. The child(ren) *may be removed* if deemed necessary and placed with either a relative or a foster family. They are assigned to a case manager who works with the family by providing reunification services to the parents, addressing the reasons that the family came to the attention of the child welfare system. Children in care are also assessed for services so that support can be put in place to address any emotional, developmental, and educational concerns.

Figure 3.2 Child Welfare Reporting

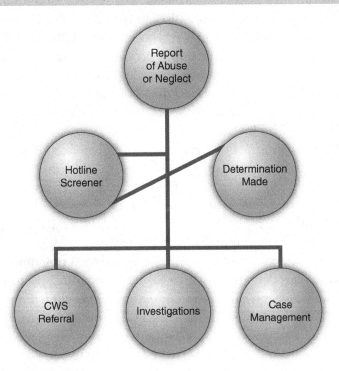

3. Another possibility may be *providing supportive services* to families experiencing an acute crisis that threatens the functioning of the family system in a way that may injure or harm the child. For instance, the sudden death of a parent may create financial and housing disruptions, which may impact the risk or safety of the child(ren) in the home.

In the case of intact family services, families have been assessed for minimal risk and safety concerns. They are engaged in various supportive services to address the reasons for referral to the child welfare system. In some states, intact family services may be voluntary. But suppose the level of safety and risk is of great concern, and a family refuses to cooperate with the intact family services worker. In that case, a court order may be sought to mandate the family's compliance.

In the case of placement services, the goal is always to preserve families while ensuring the safety of the child(ren). Therefore, when children are removed from their biological parents, relative care is sought to provide continuity of care through kinship connections. Optimally, placing a child with relatives provides a sense of familiarity and comfort to children separated from their parents. When relative placement is not viable, foster care placements are pursued for children coming into child protective custody.

Service referrals are a preventive measure to support children and families needing resources to sustain and stabilize their family system. Some states refer to this as family preservation services or other alternative names. Family preservation is important because it is the least intrusive intervention with families while simultaneously strengthening child safety and family functioning. Ensuring the safety of children requires *critical decision-making*, as illustrated in the decision tree (see Figure 3.3). Beyond the screening process, the Child Welfare Information Gateway (2020) thoroughly describes the decision-making process as it relates to investigations. If cases meet the definition of further inquiry, an investigation ensues. During the investigation phase, there are several options regarding the outcome for families. The level of risk to children determines whether they may stay home with their parents or be removed and placed in relative or foster care. If there appears to be abuse or neglect and the risk of future maltreatment to the child is high, a court petition may be filed to consider removing the child from their parent's home to a safe environment. When there is a low risk to a child's safety, the family may be referred for voluntary intact family services. The case is generally closed if there is minimal risk to the child.

When children are removed from the home, several outcomes can be considered. The child is placed with a relative foster parent, and reunification services are provided. This decision offers the family and child clinical interventions and tools to support reunification so children can safely return home. In the event that the child(ren) cannot be returned home safely and they are placed with a relative, there may be an opportunity for the relative to take guardianship of the child(ren). When children are placed with relatives or foster parents and the biological parents do not work toward reunification in a reasonable timeframe as identified by the state statute, the court may move to terminate parental rights. At that time, the relative or foster parent may have the opportunity to proceed to adoption or permanent guardianship. There are circumstances in which youth in the foster care system are not placed in an adoptive home or prefer not to be adopted. These are generally older youth in care, and they are provided with adult transition services to prepare them for independent living once they transition out of the foster care system. Foster care programs in some states provide support for employment and educational opportunities for this population. In circumstances where youth in care have psychiatric or developmental needs, additional assessments are conducted, and recommendations are made for specialized services. In these cases, the youth can be linked to supportive services and specialized living environments for adults as they transition out of the system.

Placement Options

The placement of children within the foster care system should be done with great care and consideration. The trauma of being removed from family and familiar environments can be overwhelming, and child welfare professionals are responsible for identifying the least restrictive placement for children. Therefore, locating viable family or extended family members at the onset who will become

Figure 3.3 Flow Chart of the Decision-Making Process for Child Safety in the Child Welfare System (CWS)

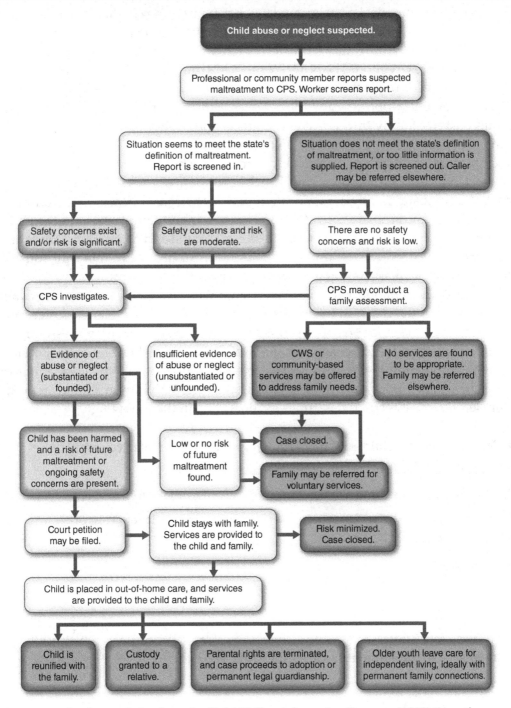

Source: Used with permission from the Child Welfare Information Gateway. (2020). *How the child welfare system works.* U.S. Department of Health and Human Services, Administration for Children and Families, Children's Bureau. https://www.childwelfare.gov/pubs/factsheets/cpswork/

kinship foster parents is crucial. This option may reduce the impact of prolonged trauma and provide children with the comfort of being in familiar environments and with family.

Specifically, families of color tend to operate from a *collectivist viewpoint* and rely on extended family for support. Historically, the National Association of Black Social Workers (NABSW, 2003) has been a fierce advocate for kinship care to promote family preservation. The NABSW espouses three central values in support of the cultural needs of Black families. First, kinship care honors the African tradition of caring for and supporting their loved ones. Kinship care is critical in preserving family history, family traditions, and cultural continuity. Second, when children cannot live with their parents, kinship care provides cultural and social growth and spiritual development (where applicable). Kinship ties help to keep the child connected to family (their own kin). Third, kinship care is a viable option that supports the child and family's reunification plan. "The consequences of government regulation of families and forced family separation are long-lasting. In the name of child protection, state-intervention destroys familial and community bonds and subjects families to extreme trauma" (Copeland, 2022, p. 2). In this way, kinship care can be viewed as a culturally responsive practice.

Other placement options can be considered when no viable relatives are available to care for the children being removed from their homes to enter foster care. Depending on the emotional and physical needs of the child(ren), it is essential to consider what kind of placement would best fit the needed level of care. Possible placements include therapeutic foster homes, group homes, and residential or transitional and independent living programs. The continuum of care may go from least to most restrictive settings as illustrated in the following:

1. Maintaining the child(ren) in a familiar environment (relative care);
2. Placing the child(ren) with extended family or friends;
3. Placing the child(ren) in foster care homes (unfamiliar environments);
4. Placing the child(ren) in a shelter setting (temporary placement); or
5. Placing the child(ren) in a formalized setting such as:
   a. Group homes;
   b. Transitional living programs (16 years and older) for education/ employment training;
   c. Independent living programs (working youth with a high school diploma);
   d. Residential treatment facilities (behavioral); and
   e. Skilled medical facilities (medical).

When children enter the foster care system, every effort is made by investigators to find family members that can provide a safe and nurturing environment for the child(ren). Suppose no relatives are available and a family friend or godparent is available. In that case, they can be considered as a placement resource for the child if they are able to provide a safe environment. If there are no relative placement options, the investigator and case manager try to locate a foster home.

Foster homes are a second option for placement consideration for children entering foster care. Foster homes are licensed, and foster parents receive training to prepare them for fostering. Every effort is made to ensure that siblings are placed together when possible. When children present with significant behavioral concerns or extensive medical issues, a more specialized level of placement may need to be considered. There are foster care options where foster parents are trained to care for behaviorally challenged and medically complex children. These higher-level foster homes can be specialized treatment and therapeutic foster homes. They utilize contracted specialized services, community support, theoretically sound approaches to behavior modification, family systems, and support. In addition, foster parents may be asked to take in children with medically complex situations and consult with medical providers.

When a child cannot be maintained in a home environment and requires a more therapeutic structured environment, a group home or a residential treatment facility may be considered depending upon the presenting behaviors. These types of placements are designed to be short-term structured behavioral health programs, providing mental health treatment in hopes of increasing the child's ability to utilize coping strategies and regulate behaviors. When children present with significant medical issues that require skilled nursing care, they may be placed in skilled nursing care facilities to meet their needs.

As youth age in the foster care system, their level of need changes. The type of support needed shifts to facilitate the development of youth in care into well-rounded, productive adults. Transitional living and independent living programs are placement options for adolescent youth. These types of placements offer educational, vocational, and emotional support while assisting the youth with developing and sustaining the independent living skills needed to maintain a stable and productive quality of life once they exit the foster care system. When adolescent youth are impacted with developmental delays and mental health concerns that impede their ability to care for themselves, adult services and housing options are sought to support this population upon their exit from the foster care system (see Figure 3.4).

Lee and colleagues (2013) indicate, "The main goal of the CPS investigation process is to gather information to assess risk and, thus, to develop a plan to remediate the abuse" (p. 635). In 2020, the United States received approximately 3.9 million referrals for child maltreatment (U.S. Department of Health & Human Services [DHHS], 2022) involving 7.1 million children. The first allegation is typically received at the state level through a child protective services hotline and screened to determine if further action is needed, as readers will discover in the following.

Figure 3.4 Child Placement Options

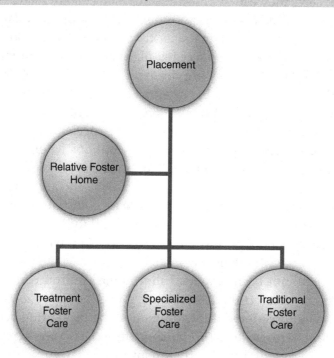

SPECIFIC CHILD WELFARE CAREERS

Child welfare is a broad area of practice, and there are many positions within the field. It is important to consider one's interests and skill set. Also, it is important to note that career interests may change over time. For some, determining their interests is a significant first step. In contrast, others may already understand where their interests lie and may be on the pathway to deciding on a career development plan.

Determining Career Interests and Skills in Child Welfare

To have a satisfying child welfare career, one must know one's interests to determine what role is a good fit. It may also assist in developing one's professional identity and in maintaining the motivation needed to work in such a demanding field. Aligning interests and skill sets is important for professional growth. The following section describes the roles of call center screener, investigator, intact family worker, placement permanency worker, support worker, and licensing worker. Working as a call center screener may be a good fit if one's skills are well-suited to dealing with crises and include a strong ability to engage people by phone. Suppose one is highly driven to protect children and able to manage emotions in the face of witnessing vulnerable children who have been harmed in unspeakable ways. In that case, their skill set in investigations is sorely needed. Investigators must also know how to manage multiple demands during an investigation, know how to dig deeper, and have keen assessment skills for determining risk and safety. For those who are interested in family preservation, working in intact family services or support services may be well suited to them. Detail-oriented individuals, who can assess organizational compliance and adequacy of foster home placements, may use their skills as licensing professionals.

Deciding on a Career Development Plan in Child Welfare

In addition to the skills and positions already mentioned, deciding on the best fit in the field of child welfare is a dynamic and ongoing process. For some, gaining experience in many child welfare positions fits their career trajectory. Diversity of experience is attractive to many workers who are committed to the well-being of children and families. Additionally, those interested in upper-level management may intentionally seek expertise in more than one position to get to know the inner workings of the entire organization. To map out a career plan:

- Outline career goals in child welfare.
- Consider 3- and 5-year plans.
- Determine what will give a sense of meaning and purpose in one's work life/ career.
- Determine the best pathway for reaching goals.
- Determine the type of professional development needed to attain these goals.
- Consider how each position fits one's life (e.g., schedule, availability, salary).
- Determine the things one likes the most and the least in the field of child welfare.

Lastly, it is essential to match one's personality type with the tasks and responsibilities of the position. Personality theories and tests are used to help people determine their career interests. For the best fit, one must understand one's reactions to typical child welfare situations, ability to bounce back, and ability to continue to meet the demands in a highly stressful field. The sense of fulfillment in the position is critical to consider. In the following section, the actual responsibilities of a variety of child welfare positions are described.

Call Center Screener

Reports of suspected child abuse or neglect are made to the child abuse hotline, available 24 hours per day, 7 days per week. The screener takes the call, and their role is to take the information provided and decide on how the situation will be handled. Depending on the information presented, responses can range from simply receiving the information to taking steps toward urgent and immediate intervention. Calls to the hotline may indicate a family in need of supportive services. These calls are referred to units that provide family preservation services to ensure the safety of children. Screeners are trained to make a determination based on the information they receive. The screener's job requires patience and a clear understanding of abuse and neglect allegations. The screener needs to document the report thoroughly and accurately because the initial report to the screener is an official document that can be used in court. The report should include the facts, describe the incident of harm that supports the allegations made, flow logically and clearly, and provide details of the current location of all subjects.

Screeners must be able to determine what kind of report they are taking, its severity, and how it should be addressed. Calls needing intervention are confirmed in writing and referred to the investigations unit after consultation with a supervisor. The supervisor sends the report to the investigations unit, where the case is assigned to an investigator to make a site visit and assess the allegations of abuse and neglect.

Federal and state statutes require certain professionals to be mandated reporters of suspected child abuse and neglect. This list includes but is not limited to professionals in the medical field, social workers, clergy members, educational providers, law enforcement, and members of the legal field. These statutes were created in an effort to keep children safe. Whenever there is a suspicion of child abuse or neglect, these professionals are required to make a report to the hotline. There are times when professionals are hesitant to make these calls due to being uncertain about what they perceive as abuse and neglect or the fear of compounding an already complex situation by making a report to a child protection system that they don't necessarily trust (Dombrowski et al., 2003). Anyone can report child abuse or neglect when it is suspected to ensure a child's safety. Anyone making a report in good faith is protected from liability or prosecution.

Abuse and neglect allegations are categorized by type and seriousness. The categorization determines the level of response needed and the kind of information that will need to be gathered. The following are examples of allegations that are made to the hotline regarding abuse:

- *Dependency* is an allegation usually made when the parent is mentally or medically incapacitated, deceased, or absent and unable to care for the child. In these instances, efforts are made to identify family members to care for the child. When this is not an option, the child enters the foster care system.

- *Physical abuse* is an allegation signifying that there is evidence that a child has been the victim of some type of abuse. The evidence can be in the form of cuts, welts, or bruises. Abuse allegations can be categorized as serious when a child suffers head injuries, broken bones, or fatal injuries from the abuse.

- *Sexual abuse* can take on many different forms, from exposing youth to pornographic material to touching a child or youth physically, all of which are harmful to a child's emotional and physical well-being.
- *Neglect* allegations indicate a variety of safety concerns due to a lack of care by the parent, causing the child to have unmet needs that could be crucial to their health and safety.

Investigator

The child protection investigator is the most critical role in child welfare. In this role, the investigator is charged with the responsibility of making sure that children are safe by reviewing all evidence gathered and completing all interviews and determining if a child is the victim of abuse or neglect. Investigators also need to determine the level of risk the child is experiencing and if the risk creates safety concerns that warrant the removal of the child from their home and family. Child welfare agencies develop policies and procedures to serve as a guide to assist the investigator in making decisions and ensure that they are reviewing every possible angle. Nonetheless, some child welfare workers perceive the reality of investigations differently. One study shows that participants reported that "department policies and workers' day-to-day realities do not align well" (Lee et al., 2013, p. 638). It is important to note the challenges within the child welfare system perceived by its workers. The day-to-day operations do not always account for every scenario outlined in policies, as human behavior can fluctuate unpredictably, creating emotionally volatile and contested situations in the field.

Various types of abuse and neglect allegations are investigated on a daily basis. Child maltreatment can range from neglect to the death of a child. Most systems categorize allegations by the seriousness of the injury. Children also go into the foster care system when there is a dependency allegation due to either the death of a parent or a parent's inability to care for a child, as stated previously.

Intact Family Worker

The intact family worker is responsible for monitoring and providing services to families after investigators have made the decision to leave children in the home with their parents. When an investigator determines that the abuse/neglect does not rise to a level of risk to the child, but the family could benefit from supportive services to keep children safe, they refer the case for intact family services. The intact worker initially engages the family on a weekly basis to assess the family's needs and make appropriate service referrals. The intact family worker continues to visit with the family monthly to continue assessing safety and stabilizing the family home. Keeping a family intact reduces the trauma of separating children from families while at the same time ensuring that needed support is in place to help families thrive.

It should be noted that in most states, intact services are voluntary, and families must agree to receive them. If a family declines services and safety concerns continue, it is generally best practice for the intact family worker to gather pertinent information and screen the case with the state's attorney's office to determine if safety concerns are high enough to consider taking custody of the children and placing them in foster care. If safety concerns are low, the families are generally provided with a list of resources to access when needed.

Placement/Permanency Worker

Placement workers are responsible for servicing families when children can no longer remain in the home and are brought into the foster care system. This role requires the worker to plan with biological families to address the concerns that caused the children to enter the foster care system. They begin by completing an assessment, utilizing information from investigation reports, and engaging the biological family through a child and family meeting. Recommendations are made for the types of services and support the biological family will need. The placement worker sits down with the biological family and develops a plan for service provision and a visitation plan between the parents and the children. In circumstances where siblings are placed in separate homes, plans are made for the siblings to visit as well.

The placement workers' tasks can be overwhelming due to the varying service needs of the children and families on their caseloads. For many placement workers, caseloads are often high, which creates a challenge for them. The initial goal for all families is for the child to return home to the parents whenever possible. After a youth is in foster care for 24 months, however, with no progress toward the goal of returning home, placement workers concurrently plan for other types of permanent living arrangements, such as adoption or guardianship. There are also cases where the child is older and has no interest in adoption or guardianship. The placement worker has to explore other types of placements that will provide the youth with adult living skills. These skills are developed in transitional, independent living programs and long-term relative or foster homes. In many states, youth who age out of the foster care system have the opportunity to pursue higher education at no cost, which further prepares them to care for themselves as adults.

There are also cases when the needs of a child cannot be met in a relative or foster home due to psychiatric and developmental concerns, so the child is placed in group homes or residential facilities for recommended treatment. In these cases, the placement worker is responsible for attending staff meetings and visiting the child consistently to assess and evaluate the child's progress in the treatment programs. While the child is in residential care, the placement worker should begin a plan to move the child into a less restrictive setting, such as a relative or foster home.

Relationships and engagement are vital for a placement worker. Placement workers need to collaborate with families so that they are in agreement with the recommended services. Strong relationships are critical to progress and successful reunification. Having child and family team meetings and checking in with parents consistently is paramount to successful outcomes.

Support Worker

Support workers help assist child welfare workers and investigators in the field. This position may have different titles and responsibilities that vary by state. It is important to know what your state offers. There are various types of support workers, including foster parent support specialists, case aides, and clerical support workers. In some states, such as Illinois, *foster parent support specialists* are current or former foster parents who work to provide support to the other foster parents and the agency staff.

Foster care support specialists also liaise between foster parents and the child welfare agency. They assist with locating foster parents and respite homes when children come into care. They are able to identify foster parents for youth who are hard to place. Foster care support specialists are trained child welfare employees who attend training sessions for new foster parents to meet and welcome them. When foster care support specialists collaborate with child welfare professionals, they can be a great resource and save time by locating needed foster homes and other services.

Case aides are support workers that assist child welfare workers with transporting the children and youth in care for parent/child visits and sibling visits. Case aides also monitor supervised visitations and complete case notes to inform caseworkers of the quality of the visit. They also assist with getting youth in care to scheduled appointments when needed.

Clerical support is available to assist with filing, completing data entry, and typing documents when needed. Overall, most child welfare agencies consist of various divisions. All divisions work together to ensure the safety of children and the preservation of families.

Licensing Worker

Licensing workers are responsible for recruiting, licensing, and monitoring foster homes. Generally, they assess the homes of potential foster parents by completing the procedural activities that include but are not limited to background checks on all individuals in the house. They also verify that potential foster parents complete the mandatory training. Licensing workers view the home to assess safety (confirming that the home is free from all observable hazards) and determine if there is enough room for children to be placed in the home. Licensing workers are resourceful and support placement workers, particularly when seeking placement for youth in care in a foster home. They also investigate complaints and concerns that may pose a safety issue for a child in the home. They follow up with foster parents for license renewals and additional training that may be needed to address any concerns that they may have.

Licensing workers are also responsible for licensing and monitoring day care centers and day care homes. They provide guidelines for obtaining a license to open a day care center or home and work with the applicants as they prepare their environments to care for children. The guidelines are focused on safety and ensuring that the proper equipment and paperwork are available and in order.

Reflection Box 3.1

GOODNESS OF FIT

Take a few minutes to reflect on your strengths, your interests in child welfare, and your passion for helping others. Based on this reflection answer the following questions:

1. If you had your choice, what would be the first role you would want to assume in the child welfare field?
2. What draws you to this role?
3. Describe your strengths, interests, and passions for a particular role in child welfare and state why the role is a good fit for you.
4. What would be the least desirable role for you in child welfare? Why?
5. What conditions do you need in order to stay committed to a career in child welfare?
6. How comfortable are you in articulating these desired conditions in a job interview?

It is important to continue to think about the goodness of fit between what you bring to the job and what the setting offers. This may change over time. It is important to always understand where your professional interests and strengths lie and in what setting you feel most fulfilled. Remember that no job is perfect, but finding the best match for yourself is critical.

PREPARING FOR AND GOING TO COURT

Going to court is an integral part of child welfare, and investigators, intact workers, and placement workers must be prepared with the appropriate documentation and prepared to testify. There are stages to the court process when children are removed from their parents. Children are placed in protective custody when it is no longer safe for them to remain in their homes. A *shelter care hearing*, also known as a *temporary custody hearing*, typically occurs within 24 hours (check state policy for specific information about the time frame for these hearings). At the initial court hearing, the investigator is present along with the family. The state's attorney presents the evidence used to determine that the home was unsafe and required the removal of children from the home. A *guardian ad litem* (GAL) who is present in court will represent the children's best interest. During this hearing, the judge decides whether there is probable cause and urgent and immediate necessity to remove the children. A determination is then made to give temporary custody to the state's child welfare system or agency. If the judge determines there was no probable cause, the children will return to the parents, and the case will be closed. In other instances, the judge may decide that although there was no probable cause, the family could benefit from services provided by the child welfare agency, so they have the option to send the children home under an order of protection. In this case, the family would be referred to an intact family worker for service referrals.

The next hearing is the *court family conference*. This hearing occurs approximately 55 days after the temporary custody hearing. At this time, the judge reviews the progress made by the parents to complete recommended services and provide a safe environment for the children. A review is conducted to determine what needs to be done for the children to return home safely. The *adjudicatory hearing (trial)* is the next hearing, held 90 to 120 days after the case opening. During this hearing, the judge reviews the evidence and determines if abuse, neglect, or dependency concerns exist. If the judge determines that there is not enough evidence, the child can be returned to the parents. If the judge determines that enough evidence exists, a *dispositional hearing* is held. If the judge believes the children can be returned home safely during this hearing, the children will be returned. If safety concerns still exist, guardianship of the children is given to the state's child welfare agency. At this point, the 24-month clock begins, and *permanency hearings* are held to monitor progress toward permanency goals and include updates on the parents' progress to have the children returned to their care. During these hearings, the children can be returned home based on decreased safety concerns and the parents' progress in services. If they are unable to return home, the parental rights can be terminated, and the children can be adopted or placed under guardianship, or the children may be old enough to go into an independent living program where they can learn adult living skills and eventually live on their own.

The 24-month clock addresses the need for children or youth in care to have a sense of permanency. If children cannot return safely to their parents, other permanency options must be considered to avoid children/youth languishing within the child welfare system. This safeguard was first established with the Adoption and Safe Families Act (ASFA) of 1997 to prevent children and youth in care from remaining in foster care indefinitely. The purpose was to improve children's safety and promote adoption and other permanent homes for children in care. ASFA provides authorized adoption incentive payments to state child welfare agencies that promote adoptions (beyond the average rate of adoptions).

SPECIALIZED SERVICES

Drug Court/Early Childhood Court

There are specialized services in juvenile court that provide support to families in hopes of improving outcomes. Some states have drug courts for families in which substance abuse is the primary reason for the family's involvement in the child welfare system. This type of court has resources such as assessments and intensive substance abuse treatment to support families in reunification. Early childhood court focuses on children who enter the foster care system under the age of 5 years. This specialty focuses on the developmental needs of children to reduce the level of trauma by working diligently with the family to increase the likelihood of family reunification. The court closely monitors child and family team meetings, court hearings, visitation, and case management to ensure consistent progress is made to reunify young children with their families in shorter time frames.

Child and Worker Safety

Child welfare professionals' and social workers' primary goal is to keep children physically and emotionally safe. When child protection workers visit a family's home after a hotline call is received, they are constantly assessing the children's safety in many different ways. Children are removed from their home environments when it is no longer safe to remain with their families. The initial plan is always to return children to their families, but only when the home environment is safe.

In addition to child safety, there has been increased concern about the safety of child welfare professionals as they go out into the field working to protect children. Occasionally, child welfare professionals have encountered threatening situations while visiting homes where there are allegations of abuse and neglect. In some cases, child welfare professionals have been assaulted and even killed in the line of duty as they make efforts to assess the safety of children.

Child welfare agencies must commit to improving worker safety (i.e., protocol, training, supervision, and debriefing) if they want to maintain their workforce and avoid high levels of employee turnover. Kim and Hopkins (2015) found that when workers perceive the workplace as unsafe, it lowers their commitment to the agency. Child welfare professionals' safety is of paramount importance. Working in highly volatile situations places strain on the worker. Heightened frustrations can increase the probability of risk to one's safety. It is important not to overestimate or underestimate the level of risk to one's safety when interfacing with clients.

The only way to maintain child safety is to maintain worker safety. Child welfare professionals who conduct home visits must remain vigilant of their surroundings at all times and be able to quickly assess the climate. Safe practices include engaging in worker safety from the start and are contingent on state policies. Workers benefit when safety precautions are in place. For instance, some workers go out with an agency partner or law enforcement official when removing a child from the home. All child welfare organizations have an onus to educate their staff on personal safety in the field. Supervisors can do their part by assisting with planning the home visit (especially for new workers) and being aware when removal visits are made. Clinical supervisors should also be responsible for training and supervising their workers in anticipation of any possible safety concerns. Child welfare professionals should:

1. *Consider the case in its entirety.* The child welfare professional should understand the full context in which the child resides in order to anticipate possible concerns for safely removing the child from the home. A broader understanding can be determined by checking the criminal background of individuals in the home, considering the reasons for the hotline call, learning the severity of prior domestic violence incidents, and knowing how many people are alleged to be in the home.

2. *Observe the environment carefully when conducting home visits.* Child welfare workers must understand that they are in an unfamiliar environment when conducting home visits. What is experienced from one home to the next or from one visit to the next cannot be taken for granted and must be assessed each time, including the size of the home and how many people reside there, crash there, or hang out there. What smells emanate from the home? What can be seen in the approach to the home (how many pairs of shoes and what kinds of shoes are at the door—adult or children's sizes)? It is important to trust one's instincts, especially regarding safety.

3. *Trust clinical inklings.* If the professional feels uneasy, they should trust their instincts and make sure to have adequate reinforcements (for their safety and the child's safety).

4. *Intentional positioning to avoid explosive confrontations.* The worker should consider how they are positioned in the home and make sure they have a clear route to an unobstructed exit (in case of an emergency). Law enforcement professionals also warn of the dangers of being in certain rooms. In kitchens,

there is easy access to knives, hot food, skillets, plates, glassware, or other blunt objects. Other dangerous rooms include bedrooms where guns may be stored or bathrooms where there is no way of escape.

5. *Watch one's back.* It may sound cliché, but it is essential to be aware of who is approaching at all times to avoid being cornered or ambushed. It is important to understand the climate of the communities when conducting home visits (police response time, neighborhood criminal activity, community violence, drug activities, and other factors).

6. *Context of community.* It is important to understand the makeup of a community, including how homogeneous a community may be, how open or closed it is, and how people from outside of the community may be perceived (whether in rural or urban settings).

Case Scenario: Personal Safety Is Paramount

A Black child welfare professional working in investigations is asked to conduct a home visit in an all White community known to harbor anti-Black sentiment and racist views. There are a lot of racialized tensions in this community, and symbols of the confederacy are prominently displayed in the town. The child welfare professional fears for their safety and wonders how they will be able to ensure the safety of the child. They need direction on how to proceed.

DISCUSSION QUESTIONS

1. What should the child welfare professional do first?
2. How might the child welfare professional advocate for themselves in this case?
3. What options can the supervisor provide to the child welfare professional?

After reading the scenario, discuss it in small groups to determine what strategies (if any) should be followed. Apply the six safety precautions supervisors should use when preparing child welfare professionals for home visits to this scenario.

Child welfare workers collaborate with many other professionals and should maintain good rapport with local law enforcement officers and other public and local officials and professionals. Establishing these relationships is vital to getting the resources and support workers need.

In addition, child welfare professionals may also consider the individual interface and try a few strategies for managing risk. Child welfare workers should use active listening skills and be aware of facial repose (i.e., the parent/guardian's resting face, tenseness, and other nonverbal cues that indicate possible stress). The child welfare worker has a professional obligation to convey to the parent/guardian their rights and what to expect when removing children from their care. This is a sensitive moment for the entire family, but the first priority is to expediently remove the child from the home to minimize any risk of harm.

Child welfare workers should continue to participate in supervision to discuss safety issues in the field. They should pursue professional development opportunities to learn the latest de-escalation techniques, understand current agency policies, and advocate for new ones where needed. It is also important to note locality-specific measures that may be used in rural and urban environments.

When child welfare workers receive the support they need in a respectful environment where children, families, parents, and workers are valued, it can boost worker morale. But even high morale does not ensure safety. The actual onus for worker safety should fall on the child welfare system. Scalera (1995) suggested strategies for child welfare systems related to worker safety. Then he noted the high incidence of violence against child welfare workers.

According to Scalera (1995), "Caseworkers, protective service investigators, and human care licensing inspectors routinely confront emotional and volatile family and client situations" (p. 341) that place them at risk for hostile encounters that can turn violent. Scalera developed a nine-point plan to improve worker safety:

1. *Mandating the Use of a Teamed Response* (or buddy system). The teamed response would be a great way for child protective workers to support each other in an ideal child welfare setting. However, many child welfare agencies struggle with maintaining the staffing levels required to create the use of a teamed response. In situations where it is critical to use a teamed response, child protective workers and case managers find ways to support one another by going out in teams.

2. *Creating a Worker Safety Manual.* Every child welfare program should have a worker safety manual. It is critical for child welfare staff to have access to such a manual that provides them with a blueprint to ensure that they are being safe when visiting and assessing families. Child welfare staff should be well-educated on ways to ensure safety.

3. *Requiring Compulsory Safety Training of Workers.* Many child welfare agencies make safety training a part of their orientation and training for new employees, with refreshers throughout the year. Safety training for child welfare staff has become critical. Over the past few years, there has been an increase in physical violence against child welfare staff as they go out into homes to assess the safety of children. Some states have equipped their staff with panic buttons and various tools to ensure safety when visiting and assessing children in homes.

4. *Advising Staff of Their Rights to Self-Defense*. Self-defense training has become a popular way to equip child welfare investigators and case managers with ways to defend themselves if needed. Many child welfare agencies have begun to offer self-defense classes as a part of training.

5. *Establishing a Worker Safety Committee*. Most child welfare agencies have health and safety committees within their organization. These committees meet regularly and consistently to promote health, wellness, and safety for employees. Having a committee to review these critical concerns allows employees to communicate their safety concerns to management.

6. *Establishing Protocols for Assisting and Supporting Staff Members Who Are Victims of Violence*. For risk management purposes, most child welfare agencies have safety protocols in place to guide staff in the event of an emergency. Child welfare staff encounter most of their safety concerns in the field. Therefore, child welfare agencies need to have specific protocols in place to support staff if they become victims of violence both physically and emotionally. Resources such as employee assistance programs (EAP) referrals, self–help literature, employer-promoted self-care, and time off are examples of assistance that can be provided.

7. *Developing Strategies for Effectively Providing Services to Clients in High-Crime Areas*. Some states have developed plans to have child welfare staff partner with local law enforcement and police social workers to navigate neighborhoods in high-crime areas. They also accompany child welfare workers to homes where the situation may escalate when there are anticipated threats of violence.

8. *Improving Communication Systems to Promote Worker Safety*. Most child welfare agencies develop communication protocols for staff in the office and the field. Many agencies have safety committees where employees can discuss safety concerns and make policy recommendations. Some child welfare agencies invest in mobile devices for their staff to ensure they can communicate and contact authorities in the event of an emergency.

9. *Filing Criminal Charges* (in the name of the agency) *Against Any Person Who Assaults or Threatens an Agency*. Agencies should ensure that they have legal representation in the event that they have to file criminal charges against any person who assaults or threatens the agency. They should also create a path to provide support for employees. Too often, threats are made against agencies and employees by angry family members when involvement in the child welfare system is warranted, and child welfare staff needs to know that they have this type of support.

When child welfare workers are onboarded, organizations can demonstrate their support by being transparent about the challenges of the job. This onboarding disclosure should be an integral part of their orientation and training. It is critical that new workers understand safety measures to ensure their and the child's safety.

Case Scenario: Lucy—A Worker's Perspective

Lucy has been a social worker working for her state's Department of Children, Youth, and Families (DCYF) for about 10 months. Lucy reflects that when she started working for the DCYF, she wanted to quit. She was overwhelmed with the amount of information to process, the specialized way of writing for the court, and her large caseload. Lucy was also highly disappointed in the way some workers would talk about the parents of children on their caseloads. Lucy decided to stay with it because she had a passion for protecting children and helping parents reunite with them. Lucy has had her own childhood struggles and knows sometimes people just need to be heard.

Lucy states it was difficult initially, but she had a great supervisor who helped her with the logistics and was patient as she learned the job. As Lucy began meeting the children and parents on her caseload, she took the time to listen to the parents' stories and assure them they were being heard. For example, Lucy had a teen parent who lost her baby at birth due to testing positive for drugs. Other workers and the teen's family members were saying she was too young to parent and shouldn't get her baby back, but Lucy got to know the teen and heard her story. Lucy stated that the teen really felt supported by her and knew that Lucy had her best interest at heart. The teen entered drug rehabilitation and completed all the necessary steps to get her baby returned to her care. Since this case, Lucy has been able to reunite six children with their parents. Lucy sees that providing empathetic listening has changed how parents respond; they then show more motivation. Lucy feels this has been one of the most rewarding jobs she has ever worked; she is happy she stayed with it and has been able to support families. She knows there will be more difficult times, but she is grateful to have a supportive and seasoned supervisor.

DISCUSSION QUESTIONS

The child welfare field sees significant staff turnover. Yet the work is critical for the well-being of children, youth, and families, and retaining dedicated employees is essential to providing quality services.

1. Thinking of the case of Lucy, what role does a seasoned and supportive supervisor play? What about the roles played by coworkers? How might negativity spread through the workplace?

2. Do you think new child welfare professionals enter the field passionate about children, only to find that the experience doesn't meet their expectations? If so, what can be done to better prepare new professionals for what they may encounter in the workplace?

(continued)

Case Scenario: Lucy—A Worker's Perspective (*continued*)

3. Knowing that child welfare professionals will be exposed to some extremely challenging and tragic experiences, how can they process these experiences in a way that allows them to work with their clients in an effective and empathetic manner?

4. Child welfare involvement is marked by identifying deficits. Yet, in social work practice, we talk about the importance of identifying and building on strengths. In review of the scenario, how was Lucy able to listen to her clients, suspend judgment, and build on strengths? In what ways did Lucy's ability to listen intently contribute to successful family reunification?

CHAPTER SUMMARY

In this chapter, the authors discuss the various roles in child welfare. Working in child welfare can be both rewarding and challenging due to the role that child welfare workers play in the lives of families. They intervene with families during the most sensitive times in their lives. Practice in the field of child welfare requires a commitment to keeping children safe and supporting families. The field of child welfare is vast, with many opportunities to promote safety, permanency, and well-being for children at risk of abuse and neglect. Exploring the various roles in this field provides an opportunity to identify the most suitable areas of practice for child welfare professionals. As discussed throughout this chapter, working in child welfare requires multiple skills to engage, assess, plan, and intervene with families toward reunification, which is the ultimate goal.

DISCUSSION QUESTIONS

1. What role in child welfare would you like to explore or learn more about?

2. How might child welfare professionals better understand families and their full context?

3. What are the primary roles of investigators, case managers, and placement specialists?

4. How should case supervisors prepare new workers so they understand safety concerns?

5. How does the NASW Code of Ethics inform child welfare practice (see Table 3.1)?

RESOURCES

Child Welfare Information Gateway
https://www.childwelfare.gov/topics/management/workforce/recruitment/

Social Work Degree Guide
https://www.socialworkdegreeguide.com/lists/5-in-demand-careers-in-social-work-in-child
-welfare/

Children's Home and Aid
https://www.childrenshomeandaid.org/careers/

Policy Issue: Child Welfare / NASW
https://www.socialworkers.org/Advocacy/Policy-Issues/Child-Welfare

 A robust set of instructor resources designed to supplement this text is located at http://connect.springerpub.com/content/book/978-0-8261-5285-5. Qualifying instructors may request access by emailing **textbook@springerpub.com.**

REFERENCES

Child Welfare Information Gateway. (2020). *How the child welfare system works.* U.S. Department of Health and Human Services, Administration for Children and Families, Children's Bureau. https://www.childwelfare.gov/pubs/factsheets/cpswork/

Copeland, V. (2022). Centering unacknowledged histories: Revisiting NABSW demands to repeal ASFA. *Journal of Public Child Welfare, 16*(1), 1–6. https://doi.org/10.1080/15548732.2021.1976349

Dombrowski, S. C., Ahia, C. E., & McQuillan, K. (2003). Protecting children through mandated child-abuse reporting. *The Educational Forum, 67*(2), 119–128. https://doi.org/10.1080/00131720308984549

Kim, H., & Hopkins, K. M. (2015). Child welfare workers' personal safety concerns and organizational commitment: The moderating role of social support. *Human Service Organizations: Management, Leadership & Governance, 39*(2), 101–115. https://doi.org/10.1080/23303131.2014.987413

Lee, S. J., Sobeck, J. L., Djelaj, V., & Agius, E. (2013). When practice and policy collide: Child welfare workers' perceptions of investigation processes. *Children and Youth Services Review, 35*(4), 634–641. https://doi.org/10.1016/j.childyouth.2013.01.004

National Association of Black Social Workers. (2003). *Preserving families of African ancestry.* https://cdn.ymaws.com/www.nabsw.org/resource/collection/0D2D2404-77EB-49B5-962E-7E6FADBF3D0D/Preserving_Families_of_African_Ancestry.pdf

National Association of Social Workers. (2021). *Read the code of ethics.* https://www.socialworkers.org/About/Ethics/Code-of-Ethics/Code-of-Ethics-English

Parker, J. & Doel, M. (2013). Professional social work and the professional social work identity. In J. Parker & M. Doel (Eds.), *Professional social work* (pp. 1–18). SAGE Publications.

Scalera, N. R. (1995). The critical need for specialized health and safety measures for child welfare workers. *Child Welfare, 74*(2), 337–350. https://www.jstor.org/stable/45399042

U.S. Department of Health & Human Services. (2022). *Child maltreatment 2020.* Administration for Children and Families, Children's Bureau. https://www.acf.hhs.gov/cb/data-research/child-maltreatment

4

Policies Affecting Child Welfare Practice

Many variables contribute to child well-being in its broadest sense, including socioeconomic status, parent/caregiver mental health, extended family and community support systems, parent relationships, and parental stress. The child welfare *system*, though, historically has focused reactively on child protection, even as there is continuing research into effective prevention programs such as parenting programs and early childhood education (Harden et al., 2020). Is our current focus on child protection too narrow? Is it time to rethink the structure and purpose of the child welfare system? How have child welfare policies contributed to this narrow conceptualization of child welfare? What factors have led to this approach to child welfare? What changes can we make moving forward?

LEARNING OBJECTIVES

By the end of the chapter, you will be able to:

- Identify key policies that affect the delivery of child welfare services.
- Discuss the effectiveness of specific policies as well as the unintended consequences.
- Demonstrate an understanding of the effects of specific policies on children and families of color.
- Describe and be able to critically analyze ways to develop more effective policies that are anti-racist and support diversity, equity, and inclusion.

INTRODUCTION

Social workers understand how policy informs practice and their role in advocating for equitable and just policies. Additionally, social workers realize that policies are often developed and enacted by people who are seeking to address a particular issue but may not be familiar with the day-to-day practice in the field. This is true in child welfare. It is important to recognize that policies often have unintended effects due to this lack of familiarity with the field, changing circumstances, and other factors. Additionally, policies can reinforce power imbalances, oppression, and racism. This chapter covers several of the primary policies and laws at the federal level that impact the field of child welfare. Some of these are general policies affecting children and families; others are enacted specifically to address abuse and neglect. The chapter reviews the policies, their historical context, and their effectiveness. Finally, the unintended consequences and the effects of systemic racism on communities of color are discussed as they pertain to child welfare.

GENERAL TRENDS IN CHILD WELFARE POLICY

During the early history of the United States, parental treatment of their children was largely regarded as the family's private business (Feely et al., 2020). In the post-Colonial era, children were viewed as the property of their fathers, often with the assumption that they required harsh discipline to promote obedience (Schreiber, 2011). As the country evolved with industrialization, urbanization, and increased mobility isolating families from their traditional support networks, the need to get dependent children off the streets and out of adult institutions was emphasized (Nelson, 2020), resulting in the development and gradual expansion of orphanages. Most children in orphanages were not truly orphans but might have come from single-parent or destitute families, had significant disabilities, or been neglected or mistreated (Schreiber, 2011). Foster care and adoption became more widely accepted as means to care for dependent, abandoned children (Nelson, 2020). During the Progressive Era, with increasing recognition of the special stage of childhood, two distinct approaches to nurturing children and promoting well-being became accepted: (a) adoption and (b) providing government assistance to birth families to address poverty and keep families together (Nelson, 2020).

The U.S. Congress established the Children's Bureau in 1912, creating a broad role for the federal government in child well-being (Harden et al., 2020). The Social Security Act (SSA), in 1935, strengthened and expanded this role with the creation of Aid to Dependent Children (ADC, later changed to Aid to Families with Dependent Children [AFDC], then replaced by Temporary Assistance to Needy Families [TANF]). The final quarter of the 20th century saw a narrowing of the focus on child well-being, conceptualized as child abuse and neglect, and the appropriate responses to these concerns. The country also saw punitive policies that disproportionately affected certain populations, particularly children and families of color (Harp & Bunting, 2020). As an example, there continues to be a range of responses to substance use during pregnancy, resulting in harsher treatment of Black mothers than White mothers who have used substances during pregnancy.

Child well-being is important; as a society, we are obligated to protect all children. Child welfare is costly but rarely receives much attention in policy debates (Berger & Slack, 2020). As the majority of families involved with the child welfare system are low income and often receive other governmental assistance, such as TANF, Supplemental Nutrition Assistance Program (SNAP), and Medicaid/State Children's Health Insurance Program (S-CHIP), it is curious that child welfare services are not given more attention in social policy debates (Berger & Slack, 2020). With the significant personal, family, and societal costs associated with child maltreatment, the economic costs of providing child welfare services, and the increasing body of evidence linking income with reports of child maltreatment, a greater discussion of child welfare policies focusing on prevention is warranted. Prevention is both more humane and cost-effective.

In terms of federal funding of child welfare programs, the six largest programs are the three which target children involved with the child welfare system: Title IV-E of the SSA, Title IV-B of the SSA, and the Child Abuse Prevention and Treatment Act (CAPTA). The three that serve children for reasons other than maltreatment are TANF, Social Services Block Grant (SSBG), and Medicaid (Haskins, 2020).

CHILD WELFARE POLICIES

The child welfare system is complex and complicated. Many policies contribute to various aspects of child maltreatment and intervention, including definitions of abuse and neglect and regulations surrounding foster care, adoption, rights of children, rights of parents, and understandings of family well-being. Each major policy is presented in chronological order. Only the more significant federal policies are covered, though it is important to recognize that policies exist at the state, local, and agency levels. Additionally, policies are reinforced or clarified through court rulings. Many of these have been at the state supreme court level, though the U.S. Supreme Court has also issued rulings. It is important for child welfare workers to be aware of the policies that guide their practice in the state and agency in which they work.

Children's Bureau: P.L. 62–116 (1912)

In 1912 (P.L. 62–116), Congress created the federal Children's Bureau, the first federal agency dedicated to the welfare of children, requiring it to

> investigate and report . . . upon all matters pertaining to the welfare
> of children and child life among all classes of our people, and shall
> especially investigate the questions of infant mortality, the birth rate,
> orphanages, juvenile courts, desertion, dangerous occupations, accidents
> and diseases of children, employment, legislation affecting children in
> the several States and Territories. (Children's Bureau, 1912)

Initially, the Children's Bureau set priorities and engaged in advocacy and education to address high infant mortality rates and child labor, achieving significant successes in both areas (Lieberman & Nelson, 2013).

The Children's Bureau is also important to social work history, as the early chiefs of the Bureau, Julia Lathrop and Grace Abbott, were influential in social work and worked with other social reformers at Hull House. In its early years, the Children's Bureau also had strong ties to social work education through its connections to the Chicago School of Civics and Philanthropy (later the University of Chicago Crown Family School of Social Work, Policy, and Practice).

Additionally, in the early 1930s, the leaders of the Children's Bureau played a critical role in ensuring that children's interests were included in the SSA (P.L. 74–271), specifically, the provisions under Child Welfare Services (originally in Title V, Part 3 of the act, later moved to Title IV-B). The SSA allocated funds:

> for the purpose of enabling the United States, through the Children's
> Bureau, to cooperate with State public welfare agencies in establishing,
> extending, and strengthening, especially in predominantly rural areas,
> public [child] welfare services . . . for the protection and care of homeless,
> dependent, and neglected children, and children in danger of becoming
> delinquent. (SSA, Title V, Part 3, § 521)

Social Security Act of 1935: P.L. 74–271

Because the SSA is comprehensive and is not strictly child welfare legislation, it may be overlooked when discussing child welfare policy. It is important in any discussion of child welfare for a number of reasons: (a) It created policies, services, and programs relevant to families and children that were intended to enhance child well-being. (b) It was the first major *federal* legislation to address needs of families, establishing the role of the federal government in family well-being, though with a limited definition of family. (c) Some legislation and modifications, described in the following, are *directly* applicable to child welfare.

The SSA was controversial at the time because some felt it was government overreach, and others opposed increased taxes on employers (National Archives, n.d.). The SSA of 1935 instituted the first federal grants to families. Services provided under Title IV and Title V provided funding to the states that administered the programs. Services focused on children in rural areas with more limited access to services and/or those children under Title IV, which provided ADC, explicitly set up to protect children by relieving single mothers of the responsibility of working (Congressional Research Service, 2022).

Title V provided grants for maternal and child welfare, including health services. Additionally, Part 3 of Title V provided funding "for the protection and care of homeless, dependent, and neglected children, and children in danger of becoming delinquent" (SSA, Title V, Part 3, § 521(a)). Title V Part 3 of the SSA was the first *federal* program focused on child welfare (Williams-Butler et al., 2020).

Context

The SSA was passed in the midst of the Great Depression in an attempt to broadly meet the needs created by the Depression. The Great Depression was global, experienced by people worldwide. In the United States, the Depression was the most serious crisis faced by the country since the Civil War. By 1933, the lowest point of the Depression, roughly 15 million Americans were unemployed, and nearly half of the country's banks had failed. As a result of poverty, hunger, food insecurity, and homelessness, breadlines and soup kitchens were prevalent. In an attempt to address the needs of many of the nation's residents, President Franklin Roosevelt was able to implement his New Deal legislation in stages, initially including several employment programs, followed by the SSA in 1935, which created specific social welfare programs. The SSA provided unemployment compensation, disability payments, pensions for older persons, and services that could broadly be considered child welfare, including maternal and child health services and what was termed "child welfare" in the form of the ADC. The ADC (later known as AFDC) program was included initially to assist states in continuing their mothers' aid laws (Gordon & Batlan, 2011). It was written and promoted by the then-current (Katherine Lenroot) and former (Grace Abbott) chiefs of the Children's Bureau, as most of the other provisions of the SSA addressed the needs of the *male breadwinner* (an antiquated term that is now viewed as sexist).

Effectiveness

In terms of the broad effects on child welfare, including child well-being, early reports note a significant decrease in maternal and infant mortality following the increased funding for maternal and child health services; these services included pediatric clinics, obstetric clinics, training for healthcare providers, and nutrition education (Daily, 1941). The ADC program allowed states to continue and increase spending on mothers' pensions, presumably allowing more children to remain with their birth families.

Unintended Consequences

The ADC program, specifically, promoted "gendered ideals of sexuality (i.e., it is socially unacceptable for women to have children out of wedlock) and as a result, targeted women and their children who were poor and Black" (Williams-Butler et al., 2020, p. 79), allowing states to deny assistance to some children from families that were determined to be *unsuitable*, in other words, often families of color. In the language of policy analysis, the use of the term *unintended consequences* is typical nomenclature. However, one could argue that some of these specific policies were intended as a way to control certain segments of the population. The ADC originally was intended to allow mothers to remain out of the paid workforce to care for their children, though this changed over time, partially in response to changing perceptions about ADC recipients. Children who were removed from the ADC rolls due to judgments about their mothers were then labeled *neglected*, beginning the pairing of neglect and poverty (Williams-Butler et al., 2020). It was not until the 1960s that unmarried *mothers* could receive what was renamed AFDC for their children. Policymakers, oblivious to concerns about social justice, racism, and sexism, often deemed mothers *unsuitable* if they were not married; they often felt pressured to give up their children and were told their children would be regarded as "bastards" and "illegitimate" if they kept them (Nelson, 2020). This essentially created a stratified family support system and a form of social control—in other words, widows with children receiving social insurance provisions (survivor benefits) under the SSA were viewed more favorably than those receiving ADC/AFDC, largely unmarried mothers (Testa & Kelly, 2020). Perspectives about these programs and their recipients grew out of traditionally sexist views of women as either *worthy or unworthy*, where widows were considered worthy, but never-married or divorced women were not (Lawrence-Webb, 1997).

In 1956 and 1962, amendments to the income provisions of the SSA included social services as ways of supporting families and addressing some of the challenges faced by families in poverty, but these services were discontinued after a few years (Testa & Kelly, 2020). In the 1960s, increasing numbers of families receiving AFDC and the changing racial demographic contributed to a more negative public perception. Recipients were largely women with children who had been deserted, divorced, or never married and were on the receiving end of an increasingly hostile narrative. Expanding welfare rolls were framed as supporting failed marriages and undermining rather than supporting the family. AFDC caseloads continued to grow, dramatically shifting from family preservation strategies to work incentive strategies and moving toward a more punitive approach (Testa & Kelly, 2020). The 1967 amendments threatened to cut off or reduce AFDC if mothers refused work or work training. The 1967 amendments to Title IV-A Foster Care expanded assistance to children who would have been eligible for AFDC during the month they were removed from their home, even if their parents had not applied for AFDC; it also created Title IV-B of the SSA so that child welfare funding (AFDC) would move from Title V.

Effects on Communities of Color

Racial oppression was a part of the SSA, including the ADC program, from the beginning because the federal government left it up to the states to implement their own restrictions on eligibility (Lawrence-Webb, 1997). States could expel those families they deemed *"immoral"* from their rolls. States implemented rules around *"man-in-the-house"* and *"illegitimate children."* Families of color were often initially excluded from receiving ADC, as they may have been judged to be *"unsuitable."* SSA Titles IV and V used "immorality, home suitability, illegitimacy" clauses to discriminate against Black families in certain states (Williams-Butler et al., 2020). Subjective judgments about the mother could determine that her children were not entitled to benefits (Lawrence-Webb, 1997).

The Flemming Rule: 1960

This rule, issued in 1960, is named for Dr. Arthur Flemming, who was Secretary of the Department of Health, Education, and Welfare (now Health and Human Services) under President Eisenhower. The rule was intended to reduce discrimination in Louisiana and other states that had expelled countless needy children from the ADC/AFDC rolls. Before this rule, most African American families in southern states did not receive ADC benefits because they were denied in an arbitrary and purposeful manner. In Louisiana, 23,000 children were removed from the rolls because they were deemed to be living in an unsuitable home environment (Lawrence-Webb, 1997). Expulsions happened without due process, the right to appeal, or any investigation of the welfare of the children.

The Flemming Rule provided due process if a family was denied services and required services for families determined to be *"unsuitable."* Secretary Flemming said that states could not deny benefits to children solely based on someone's judgment about the behavior of the adult they were living with (Lawrence-Webb, 1997). This led to a change in conversations about *"morality"* to conversations about *"neglect."* The Flemming Rule was formally codified into law under P.L. 87–31, which went further in providing states with funds to assist in the systematic and monetized removal of children from *"neglectful"* homes, thereby leading to unintended negative consequences for children of color. As a result, neglect was tied to needed support and services, leading to surveillance and increased removal of children from their homes. AFDC eligibility workers were not social workers, were not skilled at clinical interventions, were not educated in family dynamics or other underlying issues (Lawrence-Webb, 1997), and were not sensitive to different traditions or views of parenting. States were required to report children to the court system, beginning the criminalization (or what could feel like criminalization) of what was viewed as neglect. The combination of increased federal funds to place children in out-of-home care and negative attitudes toward families receiving public assistance became the foundation for redefining home suitability as neglect (Lawrence-Webb, 1997).

Over time the Flemming Rule evolved to require services to accompany cash assistance but framed welfare concerns as abuse or neglect rather than moral questions, resulting in an increase of children receiving services under the *"neglect"* category. Black families who were low income needed to engage with predominantly White child welfare and legal systems and could not opt out (Williams-Butler et al., 2020), establishing a process where families of color were most negatively impacted. One outcome was a dramatic increase in children in out-of-home care who were largely African American and Native American. By 1963, over 51% of children served by public agencies were receiving some type of foster care, and 81% were in care because their parents were unmarried, divorced, or separated (Lawrence-Webb, 1997). Secretary Flemming's intent was to protect children, but instead, the rule was applied in an oppressive manner and has had long-lasting effects on child welfare (Lawrence-Webb, 1997).

Temporary Assistance for Needy Families

TANF was part of the Personal Responsibility and Work Opportunity Reconciliation Act of 1996 (PRWORA) and replaced the AFDC program in the SSA. The PRWORA was part of the Contract with America, promoting a *conservative agenda* of tax cuts and welfare reform. PRWORA created a work requirement for mothers (similar to the 1967 AFDC amendments). It was more punitive and grew out of a negative attitude toward single mothers. TANF created a lifetime limit of 60 months for the parent, at which point benefits stop. Essentially, the federal government provides block grants to the states so that they can design programs that address one or more of the primary goals of TANF, including (a) providing assistance to needy families allowing children to be cared for in their own or in relatives' homes; (b) promoting job preparation, work, and marriage to end dependence of needy parents on the government; (c) preventing and reducing out-of-wedlock pregnancies, establishing numerical goals for reducing the incidence of these pregnancies; and (d) encouraging the formation and maintenance of two-parent families (U.S. Department of Health and Human Services [DHHS], 2019; TANF, n.d.).

The change from AFDC to TANF led to a decrease in children receiving benefits but had no impact on the number of children and youth in foster care (Testa & Kelly, 2020). Testa and Kelly (2020) note that the percentage of children living with one or both parents has remained at around 95% to 97% since the 1960s, and for the 3% to 5% who do not live with a parent, over 70% live with kin. Because of the focus on promoting self-sufficiency and employment of the adults, measures of the effectiveness of TANF have not examined other outcomes, including increased burdens on mothers moving into the workforce; that is, they have not considered what supports children need when mothers are required to work (Feely et al., 2020). Interestingly, in all but a few states, relatives who care for children eligible under TANF do not have the same lifetime limits or means tests as birth parents, though the rate of eligible families applying for these benefits is relatively low (Testa & Kelly, 2020).

Child Abuse Prevention and Treatment Act (1974): P.L. 93–247

The CAPTA is the foundational and most comprehensive federal legislation affecting responses to child abuse and neglect (Child Welfare Information Gateway, 2019a). Originally passed in 1974, it is the first major federal law to specifically address child abuse and neglect. It has been amended and reauthorized over 20 times in the nearly 50 years since it was passed, with the most recent reauthorization being the CAPTA Reauthorization Act of 2010 (P.L. 111–320). It was most recently amended through the Victims of Child Abuse Reauthorization Act of 2018 (P.L. 115–424). At this writing, there are bills in the U.S. House and Senate to reauthorize CAPTA again. The original purpose of CAPTA was to provide financial assistance for prevention, identification, and intervention with regard to child abuse and neglect (Child Welfare Information Gateway, 2019b). It was the first time the federal government had identified a basic understanding of maltreatment (Feely et al., 2020).

Major Provisions of the Act

CAPTA has several provisions to address child abuse and neglect, including:

a. Providing assistance to the states to develop child abuse and neglect prevention and identification programs;
b. Authorizing government research on prevention and treatment;
c. Creating the National Center on Child Abuse and Neglect within the U.S. Department of Health, Education, and Welfare (now the DHHS) with the following purposes:
   i. Administering grant programs,
   ii. Identifying areas for new research and demonstration projects, and
   iii. Collecting information on best practices for dissemination to states.
d. Creating the National Clearinghouse on Child Abuse and Neglect Information (now the Child Welfare Information Gateway); and
e. Establishing state and demonstration grants for training and innovation focused on prevention and intervention (Children's Bureau, 2023).

Context

CAPTA was signed into law by President Nixon in 1974. During the 1960s, the public became more aware of child abuse following the publication of "The Battered Child Syndrome" authored by Dr. C. Henry Kempe in the *Journal of the American Medical Association*. CAPTA required states to pass laws implementing mandated reporting for suspected abuse and neglect cases. The law provided guidelines to states regarding abuse and neglect but did not operationalize the definition of neglect, a definition that lacked clarity and did not include any reference to income disparities or differentiating between neglect and poverty (Williams-Butler et al., 2020).

Effectiveness

In many ways, CAPTA has been effective in raising public awareness about abuse and neglect and in spawning research and evidence-based interventions. All states have child welfare departments, procedures for identifying and investigating abuse and neglect, and mandated reporter laws. Physical and sexual abuse rates have declined significantly in the past three decades, but neglect has remained constant (Feely et al., 2021), suggesting no common understanding of what constitutes neglect.

Unintended Consequences

One outcome of CAPTA was narrowing the federal role in family life, emphasizing reporting and interventions with victims and perpetrators rather than family-focused programs and services (Harden et al., 2020). As a result, the legislation effectively ignored the complexity of child abuse and neglect and the range of systemic variables contributing to abuse and neglect. It wasn't until the 1990s that the federal government included Community-Based Child Abuse Prevention (CBCAP) funds to promote family-strengthening programs (Harden et al., 2020).

CAPTA focused primarily on physical abuse and used interventions to target it, which have successfully reduced abuse rates (Feely et al., 2020) but did not adequately address poverty factors which may be misinterpreted as neglect. Interventions have been primarily geared toward mental health rather than addressing poverty, resulting in families who may be charged with neglect being trapped in a system that is not designed to help them (Feely et al., 2020). Conditions external to the family are not considered under CAPTA (Feely et al., 2020).

Effects on Communities of Color

CAPTA provided some guidelines around definitions of abuse and neglect but failed to account for cultural considerations for child rearing or acknowledge that the cultural lens of the worker and family may differ (Williams-Butler et al., 2020), potentially affecting assessment and intervention. The legislation did not make any distinction between neglect and poverty, leaving that up to the discretion of the caseworker. This has led to a disproportionate overrepresentation of Black children in the system (Williams-Butler et al., 2020).

State Laws: Mandated Reporting

Mandated reporting laws were required under CAPTA. At least 47 of the states designate, by profession, who is required to report suspected child abuse and neglect; these tend to be professionals having frequent contact with children (Child Welfare Information Gateway, 2019c). The remaining states do not designate specific persons to report but simply require reporting by all persons suspecting abuse or neglect. Some states include language around institutional reporting of abuse or neglect; some discuss privileged communication; some include standards for reporting. Each state provides definitions of what constitutes specific types of abuse or neglect.

Reauthorizations

CAPTA has been reauthorized several times and amended through other legislation many times. Some of the changes are listed in the following.

1978 P.L. 95–266, CHILD ABUSE PREVENTION AND TREATMENT AND ADOPTION REFORM ACT OF 1978

This act created the U.S. Advisory Board on Child Abuse and Neglect. This Board reviews the nation's progress in meeting the expectations of CAPTA and makes recommendations to improve how the system addresses child abuse and neglect. The act facilitated the placement of children with special needs in permanent adoptive homes, seeking to reduce barriers to placement. Finally, it requires annual summaries of research on child abuse and neglect (Child Welfare Information Gateway, 2019b).

1984 P.L. 98–457, CHILD ABUSE AMENDMENTS OF 1984

Title II of this act promoted the adoption of children with special needs, particularly infants with life-threatening conditions. Title III focused on family violence and created a national clearinghouse on family violence prevention.

1996 P.L. 104–235, CHILD ABUSE PREVENTION AND TREATMENT ACT AMENDMENTS OF 1996

This act reorganized the Children's Bureau and created the Office on Child Abuse and Neglect. It also required states to develop expedited termination of parental rights when an infant has been abandoned or when the parent is responsible for a child's death or serious injury. It also recognized the rights of parents to follow their religious beliefs regarding medical care.

2003 P.L. 108–36, KEEPING CHILDREN AND FAMILIES SAFE ACT OF 2003

This legislation reauthorized and amended CAPTA through the fiscal year 2008. It also provided training for child protective services (CPS) workers on legal duties to protect the rights of families and children.

2018 P.L. 115–271, SUBSTANCE USE-DISORDER PREVENTION THAT PROMOTES OPIOID RECOVERY AND TREATMENT FOR PATIENTS AND COMMUNITIES ACT

This legislation focused primarily on the opioid epidemic and made some changes in CAPTA. Specifically, it authorized grants to states to assist a range of child welfare agencies; social services agencies; substance use disorder treatment agencies; mental health, medical, and public health facilities; and maternal and child health agencies to collaborate in developing, implementing, and monitoring Plans of Safe Care (POSC; Child Welfare Information Gateway, 2019b).

2019 P.L. 115–424, VICTIMS OF CHILD ABUSE ACT REAUTHORIZATION ACT OF 2018

People who made good-faith child abuse or neglect reports were provided immunity from prosecution. This law expanded immunity to include protection from civil and criminal liability for people making good-faith child abuse or neglect reports or providing other information or assistance, including medical information, as part of a report, investigation, or legal proceeding.

Indian Child Welfare Act (1978): P.L. 95–608

The general purpose of Indian Child Welfare Act (ICWA) was to establish standards and procedures for the placement of Native American children in foster and adoptive families. It is designed to both protect the rights of children and families and preserve the culture of American Indians and Alaska Natives (AIAN). The federal government provided definitions of who is considered a Native American child. The act recommended as best practice that judges clearly ask about Native American heritage at every hearing unless it has already been established (Williams et al., 2015).

Major Provisions of the Act

To address the welfare of AIAN children, ICWA created a number of provisions, including:

- Minimum standards for the removal of Native American children from their families;
- Requirements for foster or adoptive homes that reflect the culture with a preference for Native family environments for foster and/or adoptive placements;
- Assistance to tribes in support of child and family service programs;
- Tribal jurisdiction over Indian child custody proceedings if requested by the tribe, parent, or Indian "custodian";
- Funding to tribes, nonprofit off-reservation organizations, and multiservice centers to improve child welfare services to Native American children and families;

- Requiring state and federal courts to abide by tribal court decrees; and
- A standard of proof beyond a reasonable doubt for terminating Indian parents' parental rights. (Child Welfare Information Gateway, 2019b; 2021).

Context

Before ICWA, the long and painful history of separating Native children from families began with boarding schools and continued through the adoption of Native children by White families. The ICWA was enacted following 4 years of hearings and debates about the widespread removal of children from their homes (Fletcher, 2009). It was estimated that between 25% and 35% of Indian children were removed from their families, with 90% of them being placed in non-Native homes (Fletcher, 2009; Williams et al., 2015). Oftentimes, the removal of children did not follow any due process or protocols, was based on skimpy evidence, and provided minimal or no services or investigation to families. Removal seemed to be based on the broad and racist assumption that the reservation was not a good place for children (Fletcher, 2009).

Effectiveness

Limited data have been collected on outcomes or even compliance with the ICWA. When implemented as intended, Native families are better protected from the unnecessary removal of children. The rates of placement with non-Native families have decreased. Still, disproportionality continues, with Native children at much greater risk of removal from their families than White children. Additionally, the law has been under assault since it was first implemented, with continued lawsuits challenging aspects of the law (Association on American Indian Affairs, 2022). Renick (2018) suggests that the law is misunderstood and widely ignored.

Unintended Consequences

Minimal data have been collected on the outcomes of children and youth covered by the ICWA (Martin & Connelly, 2015), making it difficult to identify positive or negative outcomes. Compliance is a concern; with no federal oversight, it is up to the states to comply, and not all do. Also, some definitions in the legislation are subject to different interpretations by the states, such as what constitutes "active efforts" to keep families together (Williams et al., 2015). Barriers to compliance include challenges identifying eligible children, lack of training in the law for judges, social workers, and attorneys, and the rate at which some state courts act in pursuit of what is perceived as the best interests of the child without due consideration of the best interests of the tribe (Williams et al., 2015).

Effects on Communities of Color

The ICWA has raised awareness of the importance of matching children and placements regarding race, identity, and culture. Some state child welfare departments have become more engaged in culturally responsive assessment and intervention and in working more collaboratively with tribal child welfare agencies. However, given the disproportionate overrepresentation of Native children in the child welfare system and some of the intensive efforts needed to reunify families, not enough funding is allocated to meet the needs of these children (Williams et al., 2015), and more needs to be done to preserve families and their culture.

Case Scenario: When Policy Meets Practice: Across Cultures

Angela is an intern placed in an agency that contracts with the state child welfare agency to provide foster care services to children and youth in need of out-of-home placements. Angela has been assigned to work with two White families fostering Native American children. Angela has tried to be well briefed on the requirements of the ICWA. One family is fostering 2-year-old Jacob, a member of the Puyallup tribe. The plan is to return him to his parents. The biological parents have requested that the foster parents allow him to continue his Native traditions. However, the foster parents took him for a haircut, which directly countered the family's wishes and expectations. Angela was very upset when she learned this.

The second family has two young daughters, 9 months and 2 years of age. The mother has been in and out of substance abuse treatment for several years. After initial plans for reunification, the goal was changed to put the children up for adoption. Their father has moved out of the area and has had no contact or interest in the children. Their mother has not followed up with parenting classes and has missed supervised visits. The foster parents are interested in adopting the two girls. Angela is concerned because the foster parents are White, and she doesn't understand why there weren't more attempts made to find Native American foster and adoptive parents.

DISCUSSION QUESTIONS

1. With what you know about the ICWA, what do you think should have happened in each of these scenarios?

2. Do you think the biological family experienced the haircut as a micro-aggression?

3. What can an intern do to help the foster parents understand the importance of the child's traditions, customs, and culture?

(continued)

> ## Case Scenario: When Policy Meets Practice: Across Cultures (*continued*)
>
> 4. How prepared were the foster parents to receive children from another culture?
> 5. What other measures could the agency have taken to expand their Native American foster families?
> 6. What should the state child welfare agency have done to ensure compliance with the ICWA?

Adoption Assistance and Child Welfare Act of 1980 P.L. 96–272 (1980)

The purpose of the Adoption Assistance and Child Welfare Act (AACWA) was to create an adoption assistance program, strengthen foster care assistance for needy and dependent children, and improve programs for child welfare, social services, and the AFDC.

Major Provisions of the Act

The AACWA made several changes to existing laws. In effect, it de-prioritized the original purpose of the AFDC as providing income support to maintain children in the home of a parent or relative as an alternative to institutional or foster family care (Testa & Kelly, 2020). It required states to make adoption assistance payments to parents who adopt a child with special needs and are eligible for financial assistance. Also, it:

- Defined a child with special needs as one who cannot be returned to the parent's home with a special condition and necessitates assistance to be placed in an adoptive home.
- Required that states, to receive federal foster care-matching funds, make "reasonable efforts" to prevent the removal of children and return those who have been removed as quickly as possible.
- Required states to develop reunification and prevention programs for all children in foster care.
- Required states to place the child in the least restrictive setting close to the parent's home if that is deemed beneficial for the child.
- Required a review of the status of any child in any nonpermanent setting every 6 months to determine the best interest of the child, focused most heavily on returning the child home.

- Required the court to determine the child's future status, whether this is a return to parents, adoption, or continued foster care, within 18 months of the initial placement outside the home.

Context

Because of concerns about children, particularly those with special needs, remaining in foster care without the benefit of a stable family, this legislation sought to remove financial barriers to adoption by providing adoption assistance to those children and families who are eligible. The additional financial support helped more families be able to adopt and provide permanency. Other youth supports, including scholarships, vocational education, and tuition waivers, are available.

Child Abuse Prevention, Adoption, and Family Services Act of 1988: P.L. 100–294

This legislation created the Inter-Agency Task Force on Child Abuse and Neglect. It established a national data system to expand the types of data collected, including false or unsubstantiated cases and the number of deaths resulting from abuse and neglect. It expanded the Adoption Opportunities program with the goal of increasing the number of children of color placed in adoptive families.

Family Prevention and Support Services Act of 1993

The Family Preservation and Support Services Act (FPSSA) of 1993 revised Title IV-B of the SSA by adding support for states to develop services enhancing parent functioning, promoting family strengths, and implementing family preservation for those families in crisis (Harden et al., 2020). Funding was provided for states to develop more effective prevention strategies incorporating broad community input and planning. These funds were reauthorized under the Promoting Safe and Stable Families program and are largely designated for the purpose of preventing foster care placement (Harden et al., 2020).

Multi-Ethnic Placement Act (1994) P.L. 103–382

Multi-Ethnic Placement Act (MEPA) was enacted to prevent discrimination on the basis of race, color, and/or national origin when making foster or adoptive placements (as enacted by Title V, Part E, Subpart 1, of the Improving America's Schools Act of 1994). More specifically, MEPA sought to address concerns that the policies of race matching may delay the placement of African American children (McRoy, 2013). MEPA sought to facilitate the recruitment of adoptive families so that more children could be adopted (Nelson, 2020).

Major Provisions of the Act

This act prohibited state agencies and other entities receiving federal funding and involved in foster care or adoption from delaying, denying, or otherwise discriminating on the basis of the parent's or child's race, color, or national origin when making placement decisions. It prohibited state agencies and other entities receiving federal funds from denying any person the opportunity to become a foster or adoptive parent solely based on the race, color, or national origin of the parent or child. It required that states develop plans to recruit foster and adoptive families who reflect the racial and ethnic makeup of the state's population. It did allow an agency or entity to *consider* the cultural, ethnic, or racial background of a child as well as the capacity of adoptive or foster parents to meet the needs of a child from that background. It specifically did not affect the provisions of the ICWA. Additionally, failure to comply with this law became a violation of Title VI of the Civil Rights Act.

MEPA was amended in 1996 by the Interethnic Placement Provisions, which clarified language around the consideration of race, color, or natural origin and also required active recruitment of diverse foster and adoptive families.

Context

With the decline in available White babies due to increased use of birth control, access to abortion, and reduced stigma toward single parenthood, White couples looked to adopt children of other races and backgrounds. The Civil Rights Era of the 1960s saw an increase in transracial adoption. This was controversial at the time and remains so. Tensions existed between the belief that children will be more comfortable, adjust better, and understand their culture and identity better when placed in a family from a similar background and the view that the primary concern should be providing children with a stable, loving home environment regardless of parent and child "matching." The National Association of Black Social Workers (NABSW) issued a statement in 1972 in opposition to transracial adoption: "We fully recognize the phenomenon of transracial adoption as an expedient for white folk, not as an altruistic humane concern for Black children" (NABSW, 1972, p. 2).

Historically, African American children in the child welfare system were more likely to be offered foster care rather than adoptive services, resulting in them remaining in the system longer (McRoy & Griffin, 2012). Congress passed the MEPA in 1994 to address this disparity by stating that a child's race should not be a barrier to placement (McRoy & Griffin, 2012).

Effectiveness

Some say the goals of the MEPA and Interethnic Placement Provisions are contradictory and confusing and do not make sense in such a large and unwieldy system (NABSW, 2003). Additionally, the legislation has not met the goals of increasing adoptions of Black children or reducing their time in the foster care system. Black children continue to be adopted at lower rates than other racial and ethnic groups and remain in the system longer than their White counterparts (McRoy & Griffin, 2012). Black families seeking to adopt were discriminated against, further affecting the rate of adoption of Black children. A study of the first 25 years after MEPA found that the number of adoptions had increased overall, but transracial adoptions increased at a higher rate, and the proportion of transracial adoption of Black children increased (DHHS, 2020). The study further found that most states' plans for recruiting diverse foster and adoptive parents were ineffective and needed improvement (DHHS, 2020). Racial disparities continue to exist as Black children remain in foster care longer.

Effects on Communities of Color

While the intent may have been to increase the adoption of African American children, disproportionality remains a significant issue. Black children continue to be overrepresented at every stage of the child welfare process, including in foster care. The NABSW (2003), while stating its opposition to transracial adoption, has stressed that a primary emphasis is on preserving families of African ancestry. Their position parallels that of the ICWA, where it recommends: (a) stopping unnecessary out-of-home placements; (b) reunification of children with parents; (c) placing children of African ancestry with relatives or unrelated families of the same race and culture for adoption; (d) addressing the barriers that prevent or discourage persons of African ancestry from adopting; (e) promoting culturally relevant agency practices; and (f) emphasizing that transracial adoption of an African American child should only be considered after documented evidence of unsuccessful same race placements have been reviewed and supported by appropriate representatives of the African American community (NABSW, 2003, para. 3).

Adoption and Safe Families Act (1997) P.L. 105–89

The purpose of the Adoption and Safe Families Act (ASFA), which amended Title IV-E of the SSA, is to promote the adoption of children in foster care and to reduce the amount of time in foster care.

Major Provisions of the Act

It reauthorized the Family Preservation and Support Services program, renaming it the Promoting Safe and Stable Families program with the following additions:

- Extended categories of services to include time-limited reunification services and adoption promotion and support services;

- Defined "time-limited family reunification services" as those services provided to a child in out-of-home care and to the child's parents or primary caregiver with the purpose of facilitating safe and timely reunification (only during the 15-month period that begins on the date that the child is considered to have entered foster care), including the following:
    - Individual, group, and family counseling;
    - Inpatient, residential, or outpatient substance use treatment services;
    - Mental health services;
    - Assistance to address domestic violence;
    - Temporary childcare and therapeutic services for families, including crisis nurseries; and
    - Transportation to or from any of those services and activities.
- Ensured safety for abused and neglected children through the following:
    - Addressing health and safety concerns when a state determines placement;
    - Requiring the DHHS to report on the scope of substance use in the child welfare population and the outcomes of services provided to that population; and
    - Adding "safety of the child" to every step of the case plan and review process.
- Accelerated permanent placement of a child in foster care through the following:
    - Requiring states to initiate court proceedings to free a child for adoption after 15 of the most recent 22 months in foster care unless there is some type of exception; and
    - Allowing children to be freed for adoption more quickly in extreme cases.

The ASFA sought to increase the number of adoptions through (a) rewarding states that increase adoptions with incentive funds, (b) requiring states to use reasonable efforts to move children from foster care to permanent placements, (c) promoting adoptions of children with special needs by providing health coverage for these children once adopted, and (d) prohibiting states from delaying or denying placements of children based on the geographic location of the prospective adoptive families.

Additionally, the ASFA required states to document and report child-specific adoption efforts and increase accountability by (a) requiring the DHHS to set new outcome measures to monitor state performance, and (b) requiring states to document specific efforts to move children into adoptive placements. It clarified "reasonable efforts" through prioritizing children's health and safety and required states to specify when efforts to prevent foster placement or reunification of children were not required. Moreover, the ASFA required shorter time limits for making decisions about permanent placements for children by (a) requiring permanency hearings no later than 12 months after the date the child enters care and (b) requiring states to initiate termination of parental rights when the child has been in foster care for 15 of the previous 22 months unless the child is in the care of a relative or when severing the parent–child relationship is deemed to not be in the child's best interests.

Context

The ASFA came about in response to concerns about the large numbers of children and youth in foster care (Goetz, 2020) and the negative outcomes of "foster care drift," referring to the process whereby children were moved from one home to another without any plan for permanency. The two primary goals of the legislation were to (a) ensure child safety and (b) promote permanency for children through adoption or return to families. The legislation sought to reduce the number of children in foster care and to expedite either reunification or termination of parental rights.

Effectiveness

In terms of meeting the primary goals, adoptions have increased with the incentives paid to states that increase their number of adoptions. Additionally, the length of time that children are in care has declined (McRoy & Griffin, 2012). However, an artificially imposed time limit for the termination of parental rights has other consequences.

Unintended Consequences

Some have argued that the ASFA contributed heavily to the foster care-to prison-pipeline by traumatizing children and families (Goetz, 2020). Milner and Kelly (2021) assert that the link between addiction and trauma is overlooked in this legislation and that addiction treatment may not always fit within artificially imposed time constraints. Additionally, the ASFA reflects more punitive approaches to addiction rather than viewing it as a medical concern, and it also overlooks racism and other inequities in terms of access to services (Milner & Kelly, 2021). The law has led to quicker termination of parental rights, thereby severing the ties between children and their families. These artificial time limits on the termination of parental rights have been detrimental to many children and families (Dettlaff et al., 2020). By giving financial incentives to states for increasing the number of adoptions, family reunification may be less of a priority. As a result, adoption has become elevated over less intrusive permanency goals (Milner & Kelly, 2021).

Effects on Communities of Color

Because Black children are overrepresented in the child welfare system, including in foster care, parents of these children are more likely to have parental rights terminated, with the accompanying life-altering negative effects for both children and parents. This increased severing of family ties affects extended families and communities and systematically undermines the Black family (Dettlaff et al., 2021). Dettlaff and colleagues (2020) state that the effects on the community should not be overlooked, as significant numbers of people in the community have been touched by the child welfare system in a way that feels like an additional layer of surveillance and racism. The trauma of removal and separation can be transmitted generationally, and the negative outcomes associated with foster care are exacerbated for Black youth by institutional racism (Dettlaff et al., 2020).

Foster Care Independence Act of 1999

Youth who reach 18 without being adopted or returned to their families age out of the system. Without adult support and other protective factors, combined with multiple Adverse Childhood Experiences (ACEs), these youth face a host of challenges transitioning to adulthood, including increased likelihood of an abbreviated education trajectory, unstable employment, physical or behavioral health concerns, housing instability, and involvement with the criminal justice system. Congress recognized these challenges and passed the John H. Chafee Foster Care Independence Act.

This legislation is covered under Title IV-E of the SSA. It provides flexible funding that states can use for children aging out of foster care at 18, which would help them find employment or continue their education. Assistance could be provided to help youth obtain a high school diploma, vocational or college education, housing, job placement, education in substance abuse, smoking, pregnancy prevention, nutrition, and budgeting training. More recently, funding was provided to prevent homelessness when exiting the child welfare system. Yet youth exiting foster care continue to face a more difficult transition to adulthood than their peers (Social Security Administration, 1999).

Fostering Connections to Success and Increasing Adoptions Act of 2008

This legislation amended Parts B and E of Title IV of the SSA to connect and support relative caregivers, enhance outcomes for youth in foster care, enhance tribal access to IV-E foster and adoption funding, and enhance incentives for adoption. In essence, it expanded funding to states that chose to provide extended foster care support until age 21. The legislation:

- Created a path for kinship guardian assistance payments for youth in foster care;
- Required fingerprint background checks for kinship guardians before payment authorization;
- Amended the John H. Chafee Foster Care Independence Program so that youth leaving foster care for kinship care or adoption after age 16 can continue to receive services;

- Authorized grants to state, local, or tribal child welfare agencies for children in or at risk of foster care placement by having family group decision-making meetings, kinship navigator programs, efforts to find biological family members, and residential family treatment programs;
- Extended the Adoption Incentive Program and increased incentive payments for special needs and older child adoptions;
- Revised the adoption assistance program eligibility to separate it from the AFDC requirements; and
- Allowed states to extend Title IV-E assistance to youth remaining in foster care beyond age 18 and those adopted or released to kinship guardianship if they are in school, employed, engaged in employment-preparation activity, or unable to do so due to documented medical condition.

It is important to note that not all states have developed extended foster care options, though both federal- and state-funded options exist. By 2019, 26 states were approved by the DHHS to receive federal funding (U.S. Government Accountability Office [GAO], 2019). However, when including programs where states used their own funds for extended foster care, up to 48 states have some type of extended foster care (Child Welfare Information Gateway, 2022b). Most state-funded programs follow school and work guidelines similar to those receiving federal funds (Child Welfare Information Gateway, 2017). Programs vary from state to state but may include housing in college residence halls, apartments, employment training programs, and transitional living programs (GAO, 2019). Though extended foster care can be very beneficial for those youth who participate, the program is underutilized, as some youth decline services and others may not be informed about the available services.

Family First Prevention Services Act (2018)

The Family First Prevention Services Act (FFPSA) went into effect on October 1, 2019, and amended the SSA. This legislation allows significant reforms in the child welfare system over the next several years (Berger & Slack, 2020). It seeks to return Title IV-E to its original purpose of keeping children and youth in their homes rather than in foster care or institutions (Testa & Kelly, 2020). Title IV-E of the SSA funds the federal Foster Care Program with funds being annually appropriated. The FFPSA seeks to change the focus to prevent: (a) maltreatment of children and (b) unnecessary removal of children from their families (Children's Bureau, 2020). This Act allows for states to utilize federal funds under Title IV, Parts B and E, of the SSA to provide specific services to children and families to prevent foster care placement. It further provides the opportunity to implement evidence-supported interventions to keep children in their homes and to ensure that those in state care are in the least restrictive setting (Testa & Kelly, 2020). Berger and Slack (2020) note that the FFPSA of 2018 has transformed child welfare funding by allowing federal Title IV-E funds, previously used for partial federal reimbursement of foster care, adoption assistance, and kinship care, to be used for evidence-based prevention efforts.

Context

With increasing empirical knowledge that children and youth do best in families and the acknowledgment that evidence supporting the removal of children may be lacking, it has been important to find ways to provide children and youth at risk of moving into foster care with the types of support they need to remain in their families. The trauma experienced by children, youth, and caregivers brought about by the removal of children can be life-lasting and create risk factors for a range of physical and behavioral health concerns. Additionally, professionals in the field and the general public have become increasingly aware of the racially disproportionate removal of children, leading to calls to reduce unnecessary removal and provide intensive services to prevent removal.

Provisions of the Act

The act aims to re-envision child welfare by prioritizing the family, keeping children in their communities and schools, utilizing foster parents as resources to support families, addressing child and parent trauma, building capacity for community-based services readily accessible to families, and developing a stable and skilled child welfare workforce (Children's Bureau, 2020). Essentially, the law focuses on four specific types of prevention activities: in-home parenting programs, mental health services, substance abuse prevention and treatment, and kinship navigator services. The law gives states and tribes the ability to target their existing federal resources into an array of prevention and early intervention services to keep children safe, strengthen families, and reduce the need for foster care.

The legislation provides federal funds for evidence-based kinship navigator programs that link relative caregivers to a broad range of services and supports to help children remain safely with them. It requires states to document how their foster care licensing standards accommodate relative caregivers.

The legislation emphasizes the utilization of interventions supported by data. By incorporating an evidence-based practice (EBP) constraint on social services spending, Family First limits reimbursements to only those interventions that meet scientific evidence standards of promising, supported, or well-supported practices (Wilson et al., 2020). The FFPSA requires definitions of service delivery based on written descriptions that explain the practice protocol and how it is implemented. It also requires outcome measures that are reliable and valid and administered to all who receive the intervention. Under the FFPSA, a *promising* intervention must be subject to an independent systematic review that attests to the quality of the study design and execution. It requires some type of control, such as a placebo group, waitlist, or group not receiving the intervention, as well as an observed difference in outcomes that is both statistically and clinically significant. To be considered *supported*, the program, in addition to meeting the minimum criteria for promising, must also include at least one randomized controlled trial (RCT) carried out in a usual practice setting. If an RCT is not available, the intervention may be supported by a study using a rigorous quasi-experimental design. A *well-supported* designation requires an additional rigorous RCT (or a rigorous quasi-experimental research design) that replicates the first set of findings. Intervention effects must be maintained for at least 12 months past treatment (Testa & Kelly, 2020). By 2024, 50% of federal funds need to be spent on well-supported programs, though states and tribes can claim these federal dollars to conduct their own rigorous studies on effectiveness to hopefully identify more well-supported programs. States and tribes have discretion in determining which children are candidates for foster care or at imminent risk, allowing for variability in the programs that are funded. Under the legislation, eligible tribes are those with their own child welfare Title IV-E programs but not the much larger number of tribes that partner with state agencies under Title IV-E agreements (Testa & Kelly, 2020). These proposed federal requirements for data collection should be culturally responsive and inclusive of differences. This may require child welfare agencies to engage in participatory research models as well as to hire culturally diverse research experts.

The legislation also establishes requirements for placement in residential treatment programs and improves the quality and oversight of services. It allows federal reimbursement for care in certain residential treatment programs for children with emotional and behavioral challenges requiring specialized treatment. To qualify, a residential treatment facility must be accredited, use trauma-informed intervention models, and employ licensed or registered nurses and other clinical staff. The law recommends ongoing assessments to determine if children and youth are making progress and whether this restrictive setting continues to be warranted (Child Welfare Information Gateway, n.d.), compelling facilities to be more effective while recognizing that each child has unique needs. It also addresses the concern with youth remaining in institutions longer than they need to, recognizing that remaining in a psychiatric facility beyond medical necessity can be detrimental. Best practices include a discussion of discharge planning when the child/youth is admitted.

The FFPSA improves services to older youth by allowing states to offer services to youth who have aged out of foster care up to age 23, along with adding flexibility to the Education and Training Voucher (ETV) program. The 15-month time limit for foster care placement will be eliminated in the renamed "Time-Limited Family Reunification Services" program in Title IV-B. Children in foster care preparing to return home will have access to 15 months of family reunification services that begin on the date the child returns home (Sec. 50721). The federal FFPSA of 2018 also emphasizes the use of family foster homes over group homes. Except in certain situations, the federal government limits payments to 2 weeks for placements that are not family foster homes or approved residential treatment programs (Child Welfare Information Gateway, n.d.).

Effectiveness

Since this is relatively new legislation, being phased in over several years, the effectiveness is not yet known. Testa and Kelly (2020) note that this legislation does not focus on some of the contextual factors that may be related to abuse, including employment stability; lack of transportation; access to healthcare, food, and stable housing; lack of childcare; and food insecurity. While the act does focus on mental health and substance abuse, the list of resources can be contributing factors that affect one's medical health, mental health, substance use, and/or risk of abusing or neglecting one's child(ren). The interventions focus only on a subset of children at risk; that is, those children who have already come into contact with the child welfare system and are at imminent risk of placement. The focus is on maintaining children at home through intact family services. The legislation does not take a public health prevention approach that targets the community as a whole (Testa & Kelly, 2020). Thus, the intent is not to prevent child abuse but to prevent the secondary negative consequences associated with the removal of children; however, without addressing the contextual factors, the clinical interventions may not be as effective as they could be (Testa & Kelly, 2020).

Unintended Consequences

This legislation is not yet implemented on a wide enough scale or for enough time to demonstrate consequences. However, focusing only on those who are at imminent risk of removal may be too narrow, and overreliance on evidence-based interventions could contribute to racial disparities in outcomes (Testa & Kelly, 2020). Additionally, there may be an incentive for child welfare agencies to neglect broader community preventive interventions and instead focus on mental health and substance use interventions supported by federal funding; restricting funds to a small range of preventive interventions takes away resources from broader interventions to prevent child abuse and family disruption (Testa & Kelly, 2020). Though the legislation addresses primary prevention by normalizing help-seeking and providing services to any who seek them, Testa and Kelly (2020) suggest that primary prevention should have a broader application than this legislation requires. They also wonder if most funding will be spent on interventions that occur too late in the process to make a meaningful difference for children and their families.

Effects on Communities of Color

As social workers, we know that issues such as child abuse are complex and have multiple contributing factors on many different levels. Contextual variables such as safe housing, adequate income to meet the demands of raising children, and availability of quality childcare all play a part in the well-being of children and families. While recognizing the importance of keeping families intact, this legislation limits support to primarily clinical services. This may not be sufficient to meet the needs of families and more effectively prevent child abuse and neglect. Milner and Kelly (2021) recommend doing more to prevent trauma and abuse from occurring in the first place. They further assert that if we fail to do all that we can do to support families before an imminent risk of removal, we are allowing inequity and disparity to continue. In addition, with limited evidence on the effectiveness of certain interventions with communities of color, we could inadvertently be contributing to ongoing racial disparity in child welfare (Testa & Kelly, 2020).

The question under the original ADC (changed to AFDC in 1962, eliminated and replaced with TANF in 1996) was whether income supports alone would be sufficient to keep children in their homes or if they needed social services support to address family challenges. The FFPSA reverses that question and seems to ask whether social services are adequate without income supports to keep families intact (Testa & Kelly, 2020).

Reflection Box 4.1

Many voices from many sectors have identified challenges with the child welfare system, including disproportionate effects on families of color, overzealous separation of children from their families, services that are not culturally responsive, continued abuse and neglect, and even child death. Due to these and other concerns, there have been many recommendations for extensive reform or even overhaul of the child welfare system. The FFPSA seeks to provide reforms by providing services to families at risk of child welfare involvement to reduce the number of out-of-home placements.

1. What are your thoughts about providing services to families, such as mental health counseling, substance use counseling, and teaching parenting skills?
2. Do you think such services can prevent out-of-home placement?
3. What are some of the pitfalls or weaknesses in the current child welfare system?
4. Where would you begin if you were to reform the existing child welfare system? What changes would you implement?
5. Is the FFPSA a step in the right direction? What is your assessment of this legislation?
6. What are some common public perceptions about the child welfare system? How would you create broader community support for child welfare and child well-being?

Safe Haven Laws: State Level

Safe haven laws are enacted at the state level to allow parents to leave their babies in a safe location if they cannot care for them. A mother in crisis may leave her infant in a designated location, such as a fire station or hospital, without charges or penalties for child neglect or abandonment. In some states, police departments or churches, if someone is present, can be sites to leave, rather than abandon, infants. The child is received into care, given medical attention as needed, and the local child welfare department is notified. They subsequently take custody and pursue termination of parental rights. Some states allow for procedures for parents to reassert custody of the infant within a specified time period, whereas in other states, parents relinquish their rights and cannot regain custody.

Context

Because of concerns about infant abandonment, including reports of babies left in such places as garbage bins or public restrooms, the issue of infant death or abandonment came to the attention of state legislatures. In the United States, homicide is the 13th leading cause of death of children under 1 year of age but is most likely to occur on the first day of life (Wilson et al., 2020). States began enacting safe haven legislation in 1999, with Texas being the first state to pass such laws, but now all 50 states, the District of Columbia, Puerto Rico, and Guam, have such laws in place (Child Welfare Information Gateway, 2022a). States vary in the time limits within which a mother must leave her baby, ranging from 72 hours to 30 days and beyond.

Effectiveness

In the first 20 years since the first safe haven law was enacted, an estimated 4,100 infants have been received into care (Wilson et al., 2020). Wilson and colleagues (2020) note that the homicide rate on the first day of life has decreased significantly when comparing the period from 1989 to 1998 (prior to any safe haven laws) to the period from 2008 to 2017, but that it remains high. Hammond et al. (2010) describe safe haven laws as *crime control theater*, laws that receive broad public support and were designed to address a specific social problem but have not demonstrated effectiveness. Safe haven laws may create the impression that the social problem of infant abandonment and homicide is being addressed, thereby stifling public discourse about the actual causes of the problem or ways to address it (Hammond et al., 2010; Krauss et al., 2021). Since homicide rates on the first day of life occur most frequently among younger mothers with lower educational attainment, perhaps with a concealed pregnancy, and nonhospital birth, Wilson and colleagues (2020) recommend strengthening financial support, improving access to affordable childcare, and providing training for young parents. Hammond and colleagues

(2010) recommend implementing programs and services that address the *causes* of infant abandonment and death. They further recommend additional research into the effects and consequences of such legislation, both intended and unintended. Finally, comprehensive sexual health education and access to services can reduce unwanted pregnancies.

POLICIES THAT AFFECT CHILDREN AND FAMILIES DIRECTLY AND INDIRECTLY

Many policies are not specific to child abuse and neglect, but still significantly impact the well-being of children, youth, and families. These include, but are not limited to, drug policies, immigration policies, and housing policies, and they will be briefly touched upon here.

The *"War on Drugs"* was first coined as a term during the Nixon administration, though recreational drug use has been part of the history of the United States since before its founding. Rosino and Hughey (2018) describe the War on Drugs as a method of social control of low-income Black and Latinx populations due to the ways it has been implemented, including disparate sentencing policies and increased surveillance of low-income communities. In many ways, these policies target families of color, breaking up families rather than addressing substance use. Media coverage in the 1980s and 1990s of "crack babies" and predictions of negative outcomes that were vastly exaggerated created negative stereotypes. In 1986, Congress passed the Anti-Drug Abuse Act, establishing the 100 to 1 punishment disparity between crack and powder cocaine. This led to the explosion of the U.S. prison population, a growth largely due to the incarceration of Black and Latinx populations (Elliott, 2021) and accompanied by the separation of children from their parents. It wasn't until 2010 that the Fair Sentencing Act was passed, essentially reducing the sentencing disparities between crack and powder cocaine from 100:1 to 18:1. In more recent years, we have seen the different treatment of crack versus opioid use, where crack is criminalized and opioid addiction is viewed more sympathetically, with referral to social services (Harp & Bunting, 2020).

Stable housing is essential for family life; unstable and unsafe housing creates stress. Unsafe communities limit the opportunity for children to play outside or for families to be engaged in their community or to access resources. The shortage of affordable housing for families, rising housing costs, and the widening wealth and wage gap are continuing concerns. Significant numbers of children are being raised in shelters, cars, as well as public housing developments that may be unhealthy and unsafe. This can make children feel insecure, self-conscious, and embarrassed to have their peers discover their living circumstances (Elliott, 2021). Inadequate housing may not provide places for restful sleep, quiet homework completion, or access to such things as computers and internet connections, increasingly viewed as necessities. Also, homeless families often come to the attention of child welfare authorities (Dettlaff et al., 2020), increasing the risk of the removal of children.

Some families may face delays in having their children return from foster care simply because they don't have stable housing (Dettlaff et al., 2020). A better solution is to ensure stable, safe, affordable housing for every family.

Immigration practices create challenges for child well-being. Children in mixed-status families, where some members are citizens or have documentation and others do not, may live with the fear of deportation of a family member. If a parent is deported, they face the heartbreaking decision of leaving their children in the United States and being separated from them or taking their children with them into an uncertain future. Some of these children who remain in the United States are placed into foster care. Unaccompanied minors face challenges and exploitation after arriving and are at increased risk of physical and sexual abuse and trafficking. They need support to protect them, to provide for basic needs, and to facilitate this difficult transition to a new culture. A well-documented challenge is the now obsolete policy of separation at the border, where even very young children were separated from their parents and kept in different facilities. Even with later attempts to reunify families, those children experienced trauma and sometimes had difficulty reconnecting with their parents. Not all families were reunited; some parents were deported while children remained in the United States. Finally, youth who were brought to the United States when they were young, in some cases so young that they may not realize that they are not citizens, may be unable to access the same services as their peers. These youth have been called *dreamers*; President Obama established, through executive action, the Deferred Action for Childhood Arrivals (DACA) program in 2012 so that these youth would not need to live under fear of deportation and could access benefits, such as the ability to attend college. Through different administrations and court decisions, the future of the program and participants' futures remain tenuous. There is still no legislation to protect these youth permanently, and many are now young adults raising their own families.

EFFECTS OF RACISM AND COLONIALISM ON CHILD WELFARE PRACTICE AND POLICY: TYING IT ALL TOGETHER

Historically, children of color were ignored by the child welfare system, and families and communities were left to care for dependent children or they were placed in segregated orphanages (Mallon, 2020). Mallon (2020) notes that children of color began entering the child welfare system in the 1950s, and their numbers grew exponentially. At the same time, the system became more punitive (Milner & Kelly, 2021). Funding for out-of-home care was greater than in-home services, leading to increased numbers of children removed from their families.

Native American children were separated from their families at alarming rates, sent to boarding schools away from their communities, and forced to adopt Western/European practices. They were forbidden from speaking their language. As an extreme example of colonialist attitudes, their families and communities were viewed as inferior and countless children were removed from their homes and adopted by White families. Though ICWA was established to address this systematic destruction of family and culture, Native American children are still heavily involved in the child welfare system.

Because children of color, particularly African American and Native American children, are disproportionately overrepresented in the child welfare system, they and their families and communities experience to a greater degree the negative, life-altering effects of being in the system. Once in the system, they are less likely to find permanency and more likely to age out with the increased risk of negative outcomes, including lower educational attainment, fewer and poorer employment opportunities, earlier and more pregnancies, increased likelihood of involvement with the criminal justice system, increased stress, poorer health outcomes, and increased prescriptions of psychotropic drugs. Additionally, Black males are more likely to be in congregate settings such as group homes rather than family settings (Martin & Connelly, 2015).

For lower-income families, the child welfare system represents one more means of surveillance (Elliott, 2021). Milner and Kelly (2021) note the punitive approaches to child welfare intervention, the criminal justice types of procedures, and the value judgments about those parents and families whose children are in the system. Harp and Bunting (2020) argue that child welfare policies may represent one more way of regulating Black bodies, particularly those of women, as Black women are disproportionately affected by the child welfare system. They are more likely to be drug tested during pregnancy; they are disproportionately reported for abuse and neglect, accompanied by the removal of their children.

While the focus appears to be moving toward the prevention of child removal, much can be done to promote family and child well-being more broadly, including addressing the root causes of poverty and systemic racism. Harden and colleagues (2020) note that child maltreatment is complex and likely results from an interaction of multiple variables. They summarize research findings that increased income through Earned Income Tax Credits (EITC), expansion of Medicaid, and supportive housing services is associated with reductions in family involvement with the child protective services system, suggesting that expansion of these programs and services may decrease rates of abuse and neglect.

The connection between poverty and involvement with the child welfare system is complex, though we do know that as financial hardship increases, the likelihood of being involved with the system under neglect charges increases (Feely et al., 2020). Though child abuse has decreased, rates of child neglect remain high, in part because we have not acknowledged the relationship between neglect and income hardship and continue to think of neglect as an individual rather than a systemic problem (Feely et al., 2020). Though abuse and neglect may occur together, they are different with different causes (Feely et al., 2020), suggesting that different interventions may be required.

Neglect is less clearly defined than abuse, leading to more subjectivity; therefore, the potential for more explicit and implicit bias in assessment. It, by far, represents the largest number of founded cases. Historically, there was the sense that children in poverty suffered, but rather than providing families with an adequate income, the thought was to put children in other homes. As an example, after the Indian boarding schools began closing, people were concerned that children would be returning to impoverished families and communities. The Bureau of Indian Affairs hired social workers to find alternative placements for these children (Williams et al., 2015).

CHAPTER SUMMARY

As we have seen, certain themes emerge in the history of child welfare policy. The earlier attempts to provide assistance to children through widow pensions have been replaced by a more punitive stance. Also, racism has played a role in establishing and implementing certain policies. The system, as it currently exists, does not meet family needs broadly. In some ways, it has moved to criminalizing child abuse rather than treating families with the goal of strengthening them. Judgments are made about families, which affect services. Though poverty and neglect are not the same concept, they sometimes are seen and treated as the same, especially by a privileged public. We also have seen how policies may be created to address a specific issue but often create new problems.

DISCUSSION QUESTIONS

As social workers, we say that policy informs practice.

1. What should your role be in advocating for policy change to make policies more equitable?
2. What relationship, if any, do you see between neglect and poverty? Describe the distinctions between neglect and poverty.
3. If we addressed poverty adequately, what might happen to rates of neglect referrals?
4. How could addressing poverty reduce child abuse and neglect rates?
5. We know that neglect represents *omission*, and abuse represents the *commission* of an act. Are interventions different for neglect versus abuse? In what ways should they differ?

RESOURCES

Prevent Child Abuse America:
https://preventchildabuse.org

"Imagine a New Child Welfare System"—Milner, Children's Bureau:
https://vimeo.com/276889408

A robust set of instructor resources designed to supplement this text is located at **http://connect.springerpub.com/content/book/978-0-8261-5285-5.** Qualifying instructors may request access by emailing **textbook@springerpub.com.**

REFERENCES

Adoption Assistance and Child Welfare Reform Act of 1980. P.L. 96–272. 42 U.S. C. 1305 (1980). https://www.congress.gov/96/statute/STATUTE-94/STATUTE-94-Pg500.pdf

Association on American Indian Affairs. (2022, February 28). *Press Release: US Supreme Court will hear challenge to ICWA.* https://www.indian-affairs.org/uploads/8/7/3/8/87380358/2022-02-28 _pr_re_sct_cert_statement.pdf

Berger, L. M., & Slack, K. S. (2020). The contemporary U.S. child welfare system(s): Overview and key challenges. *Annals of the American Academy of Political and Social Science, 692,* 7–25. https://doi .org/10.1177/0002716220969362

Child Abuse Prevention and Treatment Act P. L. 93–247. U.S.C. 42 § 5101 (1974). https://www .govinfo.gov/content/pkg/STATUTE-88/pdf/STATUTE-88-Pg4.pdf

Child Welfare Information Gateway. (n.d.). *Group and residential care.* https://www.childwelfare. gov/topics/outofhome/group-residential-care/

Child Welfare Information Gateway. (2017). *Extension of foster care beyond age 18.* U.S. Department of Health and Human Services, Administration on Children, Youth and Families, Children's Bureau. https://www.childwelfare.gov/pubPDFs/extensionfc.pdf

Child Welfare Information Gateway. (2019a). *About CAPTA: A legislative history.* U.S. Department of Health and Human Services, Administration on Children, Youth and Families, Children's Bureau. https://www.childwelfare.gov/pubPDFs/about.pdf.

Child Welfare Information Gateway. (2019b). *Major federal legislation concerned with child protection, child welfare, and adoption.* U.S. Department of Health and Human Services, Administration on Child Youth and Families, Children's Bureau. https://www.childwelfare.gov/pubPDFs/majorfedlegis .pdf

Child Welfare Information Gateway. (2019c). *Mandatory reporters of child abuse and neglect.* U.S. Department of Health and Human Services, Administration for Children and Families, Children's Bureau. https://www.childwelfare.gov/topics/systemwide/laws-policies/statutes/manda/

Child Welfare Information Gateway. (2021). *The Indian Child Welfare Act: A primer for child welfare professionals.* U.S. Department of Health and Human Services, Administration for Children, Youth, and Families, Children's Bureau. https://www.childwelfare.gov/pubPDFs/icwa.pdf

Child Welfare Information Gateway. (2022a). *Infant safe haven laws.* U.S. Department of Health and Human Services, Administration for Children, Youth, and Families, Children's Bureau. https:// www.childwelfare.gov/pubPDFs/safehaven.pdf

Child Welfare Information Gateway. (2022b). *Extension of foster care beyond age 18.* U.S. Department of Health and Human Services, Administration for Children and Families, Children's Bureau. https://www.childwelfare.gov/topics/systemwide/laws-policies/statutes/extensionfc/

Children's Bureau. 42 U.S.C. 42 Ch. 6, §191 & 192 (1912). https://uscode.house.gov/view .xhtml?path=/prelim@title42/chapter6&edition=prelim

Children's Bureau. (2023). *The Child Abuse Prevention and Treatment Act.* U.S. Department of Health and Human Services, Administration for Children and Families, Administration for Children, Youth, and Families. https://www.acf.hhs.gov/sites/default/files/documents/cb/capta.pdf

Children's Bureau. (2020). *Title IV-E implementation program updates.* U.S. Department of Health and Human Services, Administration for Children, Youth, and Families. https://www.acf.hhs.gov /sites/default/files/documents/cb/iv_e_ppp_webinar_march9.pdf

Congressional Research Service. (2022). *The Temporary Assistance for Needy Families (TANF) block grant: A legislative history.* https://crsreports.congress.gov/product/pdf/R/R44668

Daily, E. F. (1941). Maternal and child health programs under the Social Security Act. *American Journal of Public Health, 31*(2), 117–120. https://www.ncbi.nlm.nih.gov/pmc/articles/PMC1531281/pdf /amjphnation00717-0009.pdf

Dettlaff, A. J., Boyd, R., Merritt, D., Plummer, J. A., & Simon, J. D. (2021). Racial bias, poverty, and the notion of evidence. *Child Welfare, 99*(3), 61–89.

Dettlaff, A., Weber, K., Pendleton, M., Reiko Boyda, R., Bettencourt, B., & Burton, L. (2020). It is not a broken system, it is a system that needs to be broken: The upEND movement to abolish the child welfare system. *Journal of Public Child Welfare, 14*(5), 500–517. https://doi.org/10.1080/15 548732.2020.1814542

Elliott, A. (2021). *Invisible child: Poverty, survival & hope in an American city.* Random House.

Family First Preventive Services Act. (2018). https://www.childrensdefense.org/wp-content /uploads/2018/08/ffpsa-pages-from-law-language.pdf

Feely, M., Raissian, K. M., Schneider, W., & Bullinger, L. R. (2020). The social welfare policy landscape and child protective services: Opportunities for and barriers to creating systems synergy. *Annals of the American Academy of Political and Social Science, 692,* 140–161. https://doi .org/10.1177/0002716220973566

Feely, M., Raissian, K. M., Schneider, W., & Bullinger, L. R. (2021). Creating systems synergy across the social welfare policy landscape. *Focus on Poverty, 37*(2), 21–28. https://www.irp.wisc.edu /wp/wp-content/uploads/2021/09/Focus-on-Poverty-37-2d.pdf

Fletcher, M. L. M. (2009). The origins of the Indian Child Welfare Act: A survey of the legislative history. *Indigenous Law & Policy Center Occasional Paper Series 2009–04.* http://www.law.msu.edu /indigenous/papers/2009-04.pdf

Goetz, S. L. (2020). From removal to incarceration: How the modern child welfare system and its unintended consequences catalyzed the foster care-to-prison pipeline. *University of Maryland Law Journal of Race, Religion, Gender & Class, 20*(2), 289–305. https://digitalcommons.law .umaryland.edu/rrgc/vol20/iss2/6/

Gordon, L., & Batlan, F. (2011). *The legal history of the Aid to Dependent Children Program.* Social Welfare History Project. https://socialwelfare.library.vcu.edu/public-welfare/aid-to-dependent -children-the-legal-history/

Hammond, M., Miller, M. K., & Griffin, T. (2010). Safe haven laws as crime control theater. *Child Abuse & Neglect, 34*(7), 545–552. https://doi.org/10.1016/j.chiabu.2009.11.006

Harden, B. J., Simons, C., Johnson-Motoyama, M., & Barth, R. (2020). The child maltreatment prevention landscape: Where are we now, and where should we go? *Annals of the American Academy of Political and Social Science, 692,* 97–118. https://doi.org/10.1177/0002716220978361

Harp, K. L., & Bunting, A. M. (2020). The racialized nature of child welfare policies and the social control of Black bodies. *Social Politics: International Studies in Gender, State and Society, 27*(2), 258–281. https://doi.org/10.1093/sp/jxz039

Haskins, R. (2020). Child welfare financing: What do we fund, how, and what could be improved? *Annals of the American Academy of Political and Social Science, 692,* 50–67. https://doi.org/10.1177 /0002716220970909

Indian Child Welfare Act P.L. 95–608. 25 U.S.C. § 1901 (1978). https://www.govinfo.gov/content /pkg/STATUTE-92/pdf/STATUTE-92-Pg3069.pdf

Krauss, D. A., Cook, G. I., Song, E., & Umanath, S. (2021). The public's perception of crime control theater laws: It's complicated. *Psychology, Public Policy, and Law, 27*(3), 316–327. https://doi .org/10.1037/law0000302

Lawrence-Webb, C. (1997). African American children in the modern child welfare system: A legacy of the Flemming Rule. *Child Welfare, 76*(1), 9–30. http://www.jstor.org/stable/45399315

Lieberman, A., & Nelson, K. (2013). *Women & children first: The contribution of the Children's Bureau to social work education.* CSWE Press.

Mallon, G. P. (2020). Black and brown children's and families' lives matter: Addressing racial bias and oppressive policies and practices in the U.S. child welfare system. *Child Welfare, 98*(3), v–ix.

Martin, M., & Connelly, D. D. (2015). *Achieving racial equity: Child welfare policy strategies to improve outcomes for children of color.* Center for the Study of Social Policy. PolicyforResults.org. https:// files.eric.ed.gov/fulltext/ED582913.pdf

McRoy, R. G. (2013). The Indian Child Welfare Act and Multi-Ethnic Placement Act: Implications for vulnerable populations. In A. Lieberman & K. Nelson (Eds.), *Women & children first: The contribution of the Children's Bureau to social work education* (pp. 71–87). Council on Social Work Education.

McRoy, R., & Griffin, A. (2012). Transracial adoption policies and practices: The US experience. *Adoption & Fostering, 36*(3–4), 38–49. https://doi.org/10.1177/030857591203600305

Milner, J., & Kelly, D. (2021). The need for justice in child welfare. *Child Welfare, 99*(3), 1–29.

National Archives. (n.d.). *Social Security Act of 1935.* https://www.archives.gov/milestone-documents/social-security-act

National Association of Black Social Workers. (1972, September). *Position statement on trans-racial adoptions.* https://cdn.ymaws.com/www.nabsw.org/resource/resmgr/position_statements_papers/nabsw_trans-racial_adoption_.pdf

National Association of Black Social Workers. (2003, January 10). *Preserving families of African ancestry.* https://cdn.ymaws.com/www.nabsw.org/resource/resmgr/position_statements_papers/preserving_families_of_afric.pdf

Nelson, L. R. (2020). Discourses and themes in adoption and child welfare policies and practices in the U.S. throughout the 19th and 20th centuries. *Adoption Quarterly, 23*(4), 312–330. https://doi.org/10.1080/10926755.2020.1790450

Renick, C. (2018). The nation's first family separation policy. *The Imprint: Youth and Family News.* https://imprintnews.org/child-welfare-2/nations-first-family-separation-policy-indian-child-welfare-act/32431

Rosino, M. L., & Hughey, M. W. (2018). The war on drugs, racial meanings, and structural racism: A holistic and reproductive approach. *American Journal of Economics and Sociology, 77*(3–4), 849–892. https://doi.org/10.1111/ajes.12228

Schreiber, J. C. (2011). Parenting, policies, and practice: Christian influence on child welfare in America. *Social Work & Christianity, 38*(3), 293–314.

Social Security Administration. (1999, November 24). *The Foster Care Independence Act of 1999.* https://www.ssa.gov/legislation/legis_bulletin_112499.html

Temporary Assistance to Needy Families. 42 U.S.C. 601 (n.d.).

Testa, M. F., & Kelly, D. (2020). Child welfare policy through the Family First Prevention Services Act of 2018: Opportunities, barriers, and unintended consequences. *Annals of the American Academy of Political and Social Science, 692,* 68–96. https://doi.org/10.1177/0002716220976528

U.S. Department of Health and Human Services. (2019). *About TANF.* Administration for Children and Families, Office of Family Assistance. https://www.acf.hhs.gov/ofa/programs/tanf/about

U.S. Department of Health and Human Services. (2020). *The multiethnic placement act 25 years later.* Office of the Assistant Secretary for Planning and Evaluation, ASPE Research Summary. https://aspe.hhs.gov/sites/default/files/private/pdf/264526/MEPA-Research-summary.pdf

U.S. Government Accountability Office. (2019). *Foster care: States with approval to extend care provide independent living options for youth up to age 21.* https://www.gao.gov/products/gao-19-411

Williams, J. R., Maher, E. J., Tompkins, J., Killos, L. F., Amell, J. W., Rosen, J. E., Mueller, C., Summers, A., Cain, S. M., Moon, M., McCauley, G., & Harris, L. (2015). *A research and practice brief: Measuring compliance with the Indian Child Welfare Act.* Casey Family Programs. https://www.casey.org/media/measuring-compliance-icwa.pdf

Williams-Butler, A., Golden, K. E., Mendez, A., & Stevens, B. (2020). Intersectionality and child welfare policy. *Child Welfare, 98*(4), 75–96. https://www.jstor.org/stable/10.2307/48623697

Wilson, R. F., Klevens, J., Williams, D, & Xu, L. (2020). Infant homicides within the context of safe haven laws—United States, 2008–2017. U.S. Department of Health and Human Services. *Morbidity & Mortality Weekly Report, 69,* 1385–1390. http://dx.doi.org/10.15585/mmwr.mm6939a1

Child Welfare Practice

5

Decolonizing Child Welfare: Social, Economic, Environmental, and Racial Justice

We pay homage to decolonizing theorists and recognize the importance of their work. Paying homage is a decolonizing practice that recognizes and honors the contributions of Indigenous scholars and scholars of color in writing their own histories, truths, theories, and concepts. It balances the scholarly knowledge base and adds value to the practice of any profession. Finn (2020) credits Yellow Bird and Gray for their focus on a decolonizing approach to collaborating with Indigenous people, the purpose of which was to re-examine the Eurocentric nature of social work practice. The authors believe the same focus is needed as we write about the child welfare system (as it pertains to the United States and how it affects Indigenous people and people of color). Child welfare practice, like social work practice, is rooted in colonial knowledge and colonial structures, which are included in professional standards, practices, nomenclature/language, professional values and ethics, and basic epistemological assumptions made within the profession (Finn, 2020). This chapter seeks to make space for decolonizing thought and decolonizing possibilities in the profession of child welfare to acknowledge the need for social, economic, environmental, algorithmic, and racial justice.

LEARNING OBJECTIVES

By the end of the chapter, you will be able to:

- Identify key concepts related to decolonizing child welfare.
- Consider the effects of social, economic, environmental, and racial injustice on child welfare practices.
- Reflect on the plight of children and families of color related to service provision.

- Discuss the unintended effects of biased investigations.
- Describe ways to develop more effective and equitable practices in child welfare.

INTRODUCTION

Decolonization appears in the literature to mainly address Indigenous populations. However, Coates (2016) notes that "decolonization involves the recognition of colonization and the efforts of Indigenous Peoples and other marginalized groups to break free—to decolonize—from the hegemony of modernist Western thinking that has supported political, economic, [and] cultural ideological imperialism" (p. 63). Decolonizing practice must consider the humanization of services and conduct child welfare practice from an unbiased lens. Unbiased practices can help professionals avoid judging people based merely on differences. This type of practice seeks to protect children from existential threats of harm based on the biased assumptions professionals may hold regarding clients of low-income status, lower educational attainment, and varying ethnic/cultural backgrounds. When child welfare workers are able to see the humanity of the families and children they serve, it can help avoid bias. Professional self-reflection on attitudes, biases, and proper protocol is a disciplined habit that aids in decolonizing one's practice.

Decolonization is about divesting cultural power that reigns over those with little power; it is a divestment that eschews the assertion of political, social, and economic control and authority over others. People of color, Indigenous and non-Indigenous marginalized groups, must assert their own knowledge, experience, and scholarship to challenge the vestiges of colonialism. "It is important that social workers become better able to identify and critique the colonizing values and 'regimes of truth' so as not to inadvertently continue to oppress through ill-informed efforts under the guise of 'good intentions'" (Coates, 2016, p. 64). Decolonizing practice includes challenging oppressive and unjust practices that impact our clients. Child welfare workers and social workers specializing in child welfare practice must protect children and advocate for just, fair, and unbiased treatment of under resourced families.

In the United States, the current thought by some conservative groups is to downplay the country's history of slavery and racism. But critical thinking must embrace counterviews and allow for the "refutation of dominant racial ideology" (Holton, 2007, p. 236) in a discursive space separate from the national narrative. "History must restore what slavery took away" (Schomburg, 1925, p. 237). The legacy of hatred, discrimination, and oppression aimed at people of color has had profound effects on every social institution in society. So, professionals cannot ignore the historical truths of the Western world and the persistence of oppression and injustice in society. We must acknowledge, publish, create policies, and embrace practices that challenge the status quo! Acknowledging the full history of the United States is by no means an affront to patriotism.

In fact, the high proportion of African American children in child welfare demonstrates the perpetual need to address the overrepresentation of minoritized communities of color. Black children and youth make up 40% to 50% of children involved in the child welfare system, while African Americans only account for 13% of the total U.S. population. Belanger (2018) acknowledges the relationship between poverty and race, as low-income status is a high indicator of child removal. The disproportionate representation of African Americans in the child welfare system is correctable with the proper checks and balances in place. The child welfare system must continue to intensify and stress cultural training and work on safeguarding against cultural and racial biases in determining risk.

Decolonizing practices aim to mitigate harm to vulnerable people within these institutions. It is the ethical, social, political, and professional responsibility of child welfare workers and social workers to challenge systems that treat people unfairly. The goal of protecting children is about shielding them from harm and not creating more harm in the process. This implies a great responsibility for conducting child welfare practices in ways that do not penalize people who are already marginalized and oppressed. In this chapter, the authors present discourse on decolonizing child welfare; consider examples of social, economic, environmental, algorithmic, and racial injustice; and make recommendations for change. It is critical to begin brainstorming to create pathways to fairness and just practices.

DECOLONIZING CHILD WELFARE

Concerns for Social Justice

Martin and Connelly (2015) write about equity and racial justice in child welfare; they assert that families of color are generally overrepresented in child welfare across the nation. In addition, Martin and Connelly report that families of color are more likely to have worse outcomes, to have children removed from their homes, to be engaged in foster care longer, and to receive fewer opportunities for family preservation services than White families. The literature shows how disproportionately families of color are affected within the child welfare system. "Disproportionality refers to the differences in the percentage of children of a certain racial or ethnic group in the country as compared with the percentage of children in the same group in the child welfare system" (Hill, 2007, as quoted in Martin & Connelly, 2015, p. 5). They further explain that disparity means unequal treatment when comparing a racial or ethnic minority with a nonminority (Hill, 2007, as quoted in Martin & Connelly, 2015, p. 5). According to Martin and Connelly (2015), there are many consequences for families of color (see Figure 5.1).

Figure 5.1 Child Welfare and Social Justice: Consequences for Families of Color

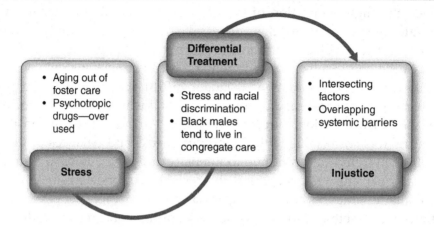

Source: Based on Martin, M., & Connelly, D. D. (2015). *Achieving racial equity: Child welfare policy strategies to improve outcomes for children of color.* Center for the Study of Social Policy. https://files.eric.ed.gov/fulltext/ED582913.pdf

1. *Aging out of the system*—This is associated with negative consequences. Historically, over half of the children who age out of the system are youth of color.

2. *Psychotropic drugs*—These are often overused and unequally applied to the youth of color who are in foster care (e.g., historically, it has been nearly five times more than their peers who are not in foster care). dosReis and colleagues (2011) report that youth of color who are in care are prescribed psychotropic medications more than White youth in care.

3. *Stress and racial discrimination*—These affect physical health and can have a lasting negative effect on youth of color.

4. *Black males are more likely to live in congregate care*—Placed in group homes or other institutional settings, Black males also experience more moves than other youth. Youth in congregate care tend to have worse outcomes than similar children placed in family foster care settings.

5. *Intersecting factors*—These have a strong impact on children and youth of color. Intersectionality calls for an examination of one's experience through multiple intersecting experiences (race, ethnicity, class, sexual orientation, gender, gender expression, identity, ability, immigration status, and many more dimensions). More importantly, to understand children's experiences in the child welfare system, it is crucial to consider the ways systems "create overlapping and interdependent systems of discrimination or disadvantage" (Martin & Connelly, 2015, p. 6). Overlapping factors can have an impact on children and youth of color in the child welfare system.

6. *Overlapping systemic barriers are faced by families*—These occur especially when parents of color experience discrimination "in many basic aspects of daily life, including housing and employment" (Martin & Connelly, 2015, p. 6). These challenges create additional barriers for those who are mired in the depths of poverty and disadvantage.

Children and youth of color face additional challenges in the child welfare system that can potentially do more harm than good. Child welfare workers and system administrators must go the extra mile to advocate for better services and lower caseloads. There also needs to be a focus on improving the quality of placement for children and youth of color who deserve safe and stable housing. Many child welfare systems have struggled with the provision of stable, caring foster homes for children and youth of color and must continue the struggle to attract the best environments for them. It is a professional standard and a social justice ethic to ameliorate the adverse effects of bias and discrimination that plague our country—especially for professionals entrusted to care for our most vulnerable citizens.

Dorothy Roberts, a legal scholar, has written extensively about the social injustices Black and other people of color face in the United States. In her latest book, *Torn Apart* (2022), Roberts documents how the child welfare system destroys Black families. "Every year government agents invade the homes of hundreds of thousands of families in poor and low-income communities, without a warrant or any other kind of judicial authorization" (p. 21). In 2018, 3.5 million children were involved in child protective services (Roberts, 2022). Some scholars use the numbers to point to the need for child welfare services, while Roberts, on the other hand, highlights the disproportionate representation of Black families. Black families are subjected to state intrusion, and more often than not, if they experience a lack of food, insecure housing, inadequate medical care, and other problems associated with poverty, they are viewed as unfit parental units. She also asserts that child welfare is a system of policing families, metaphorically likening the termination of parental rights to capital punishment. "Termination of parental rights [. . .] is the death penalty of the family-policing system—the ultimate punishment the family court can impose. The United States extinguishes the legal rights of more parents than any other nation on Earth" (Roberts, 2022, p. 23).

Roberts argues for the abolishment of the child welfare system. She states that poor parents have herculean tasks to complete to regain custody of their children, noting that to succeed in completing the mandated tasks for family reunification requires parents to navigate transportation, employment, and treatment terrain that remain overwhelming for parents trapped in poverty (Roberts, 2022). Roberts also describes the power of the child welfare system as abusive. She asserts that child welfare workers have a singular authority to destroy families. "Such a *powerful mechanism* for reinforcing racial capitalism—the [U.S.] system of wealth accumulation grounded in racist hierarchy and ideology—parallels the function of police and prisons" (Roberts, 2022, p. 23). Roberts's critique of the system is a stark reminder of the powerful function of such a system: " Child welfare agencies hold the power to break families, especially vulnerable and underresourced families, and if it happens in error, what recourse do these families have? If child welfare workers who care about social justice view the profession critically, they can make a difference by challenging the status quo."

Economic Justice

Despite child welfare agencies striving to preserve families and not remove children from their homes due to poverty (Eamon & Kopels, 2004), many families experience separation for reasons of poverty (Pelton, 1989, 1994). Many of the reasons for such high representation of poor families include factors like "biased community reporting, increased exposure [of] poor families to public scrutiny, and parietal problems such as mental illness or substance abuse" (Eamon & Kopels, 2004, p. 822). Eamon and Kopels write about the role of poverty when children have been relegated to out-of-home placements and highlight the low percentage of them who achieve family reunification. Eamon and Kopels remind readers of the toll economic hardships tend to have on families:

1. Experiencing economic hardship impedes access to safe and adequate housing, adequate food and clothing, medical treatment, food, and other basic human needs.

2. Poverty can lead to myriad psychological and social problems like financial stress, depression, family conflict, low levels of social support (a known buffer for mitigating stress), and disadvantages of being situated in blighted communities—with dismal opportunities for social or financial growth.

3. These impediments can hinder parental success in mitigating the issues that brought them to the attention of the child welfare system in the first place.

Child protective services (CPS) must provide adequate resources to strengthen familial caregiving, especially once the family has to complete mandated services if they are to be reunited.

One way of explaining poverty and child welfare involvement is the *family stress model of economic hardship* (Maguire-Jack & Font, 2017), which proposes that severe problems can overwhelm the family system, evoking depression (as aforementioned) and leading to complications of stress and low support. The fallout for families can be devastating. Not only do children experience the effects of impoverishment, but then they are traumatized by the process of family separation. Child abuse and neglect, and even family violence, whether "through witnessing or directly experiencing it, may trigger a cycle of adversities, including re-victimi[z]ation, mental problems and other life difficulties" (Jirapramukpitak et al., 2011, p. 829). Rossman (2001) coined the term "adversity package" to describe the multiple stressors in the lives of young people. Children and youth experience all types of hardship before entering the child welfare system. Often, this includes financial hardship and lack of resources. Additionally, they are at a higher risk of other adverse effects beyond the initial trauma they experience. "Multiple studies document that children who are removed from their homes are at risk for a host of negative outcomes including *low educational attainment, homelessness, unemployment,* [and] *economic hardship*" (Dettlaff & Boyd, 2020, p. 255).

Dettlaff and Boyd (2020) provide a historical review of racism that has led to poverty, oppression, and institutionalized marginalization of Black people in the United States: "The history of enslavement and dehumanization of Black people, forced family separation, and policies to maintain White supremacy . . ." (Dettlaff & Boyd, 2020, p. 259) are contextual factors that must be understood. This history is what reinforces an inequitable foundation that has a lasting impact on the "social, legal, and political factors that shape [the] experiences of Black children and families" (Dettlaff & Boyd, 2020, p. 259). Child welfare professionals must appreciate how and why disparities exist to fully apprehend this historical context and how it affects families today (Dettlaff & Boyd, 2020). Dettlaff and Boyd (2020) make current and historical connections relating to the impact of socioeconomic status and lack of resources on Black families. "Current and historic racism continues to negatively impact the economic status of Black families and is a root cause of racial disparities in poverty" (Dettlaff & Boyd, 2020, p. 260). Dettlaff and Boyd assert that the enduring legacy of racism has impacted residential segregation, labor markets, job opportunities, and unequal access to quality education for Blacks in the United States. These scholars also acknowledge the role of bias (whether implicit or explicit) in maintaining a system that disproportionately affects Black families. Although the link between child maltreatment and poverty is uncontested, the link between poverty and racism is rarely acknowledged, according to Dettlaff and Boyd (2020). The CPS must recognize these connections in order to adequately address racial disparities in the system. "Applying a historical view that properly accounts for racism is key to accurate contextualization . . . of these disparities. It provides a basis for understanding that racial disparities attributed to disproportionate need are also fundamentally attributable to racism and its enduring effects" (Dettlaff & Boyd, 2020, p. 260).

An ounce of prevention is worth a pound of cure could be applied here. If the child welfare system engaged in advocacy work to address the known factors that lead to child maltreatment, that would be a pound of cure. What if the system engaged in meaningful collaborations with scholars/academicians, clinicians, other agency administrators, and key department heads/agencies like the Department of Health and Human Services, Head Start Programs, legal scholars/legal advocates, and families who have navigated the child welfare system to create comprehensive solutions? Poor families are dependent on various systems that bring great exposure and subsequent surveillance regarding private family matters. The more families are surveilled, the more distrust they have for systems. The stress placed on families who do not have adequate resources is profound. A transformative systemic approach would be to provide intensive support for vulnerable children and families.

Environmental Justice

The literature has established that racism/ethnicity and class have cumulative effects on vulnerable populations (McKane et al., 2018). Transportation, environmental hazards, and other stressful environmental conditions place low-income people in untenable positions, and spatial segregation is known to amplify the concentration of environmental hazards that contribute to poor outcomes for people living in affected areas. Because of the harsh realities of environmental injustice in certain communities, anti-oppressive practices are necessary to support families in need.

Dominelli (2014), the social work scholar who ushered the concept of *anti-oppressive social work* into the profession, writes about environmental justice. She notes that Robert Bullard (2008) was the sociologist who highlighted the unequal impact of environmental conditions on the poor. Industries that dump waste in poor communities promote environmental injustice. Dominelli (2014) notes that Bullard "coined the term *environmental racism* to expose the disproportionate burden borne by African American communities and the price they paid for a degraded environment that jeopardized their health and well-being while locking them in low paid jobs associated with industrialization processes" (Dominelli, 2014, p. 339). Dominelli further credits Ungar (2002) for introducing the concept of *environmental justice* into the social work profession since protecting the environment protects the health of children adversely affected by environmental racism. Social work and child welfare practitioners have a significant role to play in bringing attention to environmental justice.

In addition, many low-income communities face disproportionate consequences related to health and other environmental threats. Poor communities lack green spaces and tend to be food deserts void of adequate proximity to affordable fresh food sources of nutritional value. The Annie E. Casey Foundation (2021) indicates that food deserts exist due to transportation challenges, convenience food stores in low-income areas, divestment (added investment risks of being in low-resourced areas), and income inequality Solutions may include incentivizing businesses to invest in low-income areas, expanding pilot projects to benefit local grocers, creating community partnerships, and funding city-wide programs to encourage the promotion of healthy living. Further, food and nutrition education can help support families with young children.

Environmental justice affects children living in poverty and the resources available to them. Social capital may be lacking in the areas of support, social networks, peer relations, adequate and affordable housing, and conditions in the neighborhood. Parental units, single parents, and other family members raising children need support because they often work jobs where they may have little flexibility in scheduling and providing childcare and supervision for their children.

Racial Justice

BLACK FAMILIES

Dettlaff and Boyd (2020) provide an overview of the disproportionate reality youth of color experience in the child welfare system. "Research has observed the overrepresentation of children of color in the child welfare system for 50 years" (Dettlaff & Boyd, 2020, p. 253). Dettlaff and Boyd also highlight that Black children make up 23% of children in foster care while only being about 14% of the general U.S. population.

Dettlaff and Boyd (2020) also provide key terms and definitions in their discussion of the inequities that exist within the system. "While racial disproportionality refers to one group's representation in the child welfare system being out of proportion with their representation in the population, racial disparity refers to inequality in group representation in the child welfare system" (Dettlaff & Boyd, 2020, p. 254). Racial disparity describes the inequitable outcomes that one group experiences compared to another (Dettlaff & Boyd, 2020). They further illustrate how pervasive racial disparities are within the system and at each step (see Figure 5.2). Dettlaff and Boyd highlight the points of contact at which Black youth are more likely to experience racial disparities within the child welfare system:

Figure 5.2 Disparities Points in the Child Welfare System

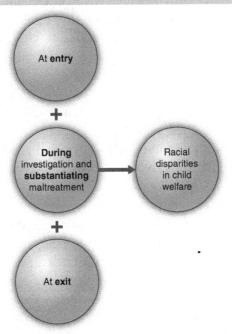

Source: Adapted from Dettlaff, A. J., & Boyd, R. (2020). Racial disproportionality and disparities in the child welfare system: Why do they exist, and what can be done to address them? *The ANNALS of the American Academy of Political and Social Science, 692*(1), 253–274. https://doi.org/10.1177/0002716220980329

1. Regarding *entry into the system*, Black parents or families are more likely to be reported for suspected child maltreatment than other ethnic groups and more likely to have their cases proceed to investigations.

2. *During the investigation* period, Black parents or families are more likely to be *substantiated* for having committed child maltreatment.

3. *Exiting the system* takes longer for Black children once they are placed into foster care. Once in care, Black children do not experience reunification with their families as frequently as White children in care; consequently, they spend more time in the system (Dettlaff & Boyd, 2020, p. 254).

In summary, the child welfare system investigates Black families more, finds cases or substantiates child maltreatment more frequently than with White families, and maintains them in the system longer (Dettlaff & Boyd, 2020). Dettlaff and Boyd also found in their critical review that an overwhelming amount of literature focused on racial disproportionality, while fewer studies report that race is not a factor. Nonetheless, long stays in foster care tend to show negative outcomes for youth of color placed in care, especially when compounding disadvantages are taken into consideration. "For Black youth in care, we contend that these risks are heightened, resulting in a condition of compound disadvantage for youth who are already at increased vulnerability for negative outcomes" (Dettlaff & Boyd, 2020, p. 255).

Dettlaff and Boyd (2020) provide clarity for understanding key concepts like the adverse outcomes, structural and institutional racism, and underreporting of other children and key definitions related to the racial injustice children of color experience like racial disproportionality and racial disparities (see Table 5.1). "Although the risk of these adverse outcomes exists for all children who enter foster care, Black children are at greater risk of experiencing these outcomes due to the added impact of the ongoing legacy of structural and institutional racism in America" (Dettlaff & Boyd, 2020, p. 500).

Dettlaff and colleagues, in another article, argue that Black children have been oversurveilled and overpoliced by the child welfare system. The harm caused by the child welfare system leaves irreparable damage (Dettlaff et al., 2020). "Thus, when Black children and families are systematically oversurveilled and subsequently forced to participate in an intervention known to cause harm, the child welfare system itself becomes a source of their ongoing and continued oppression" (Dettlaff et al., 2020, p. 500). Dettlaff and colleagues (2020) call for a new form of intervention rather than the forced separation of Black families that perpetuates inequality. These critiques are not meant to discourage professionals from working in child welfare but rather to offer a realistic view of such a powerful system's inner workings and consequences. It is good to know both the strengths and challenges of the child welfare system. Also, understanding child welfare from a critical stance positions child welfare workers to become change agents to consider how child welfare might be transformed into a system that supports families while protecting children. Imagining what can be done to improve the lives of disadvantaged families is only a start.

TABLE 5.1 KEY TERMS AND KEY FACTORS OF DISPROPORTIONALITY IN CHILD WELFARE

DISPROPORTIONALITY/CHILD WELFARE	KEY TERMS	KEY FACTORS
1. Higher percentage of Black parents/families referred for and investigated for maltreatment. 2. Higher percentage of substantiated findings for child maltreatment for Black parents/families. 3. Higher percentage of Black youth who end up in foster care and stay in foster care longer than their White peers. 4. If there is a high concentration of poverty it decreases the chance of placement for Black youth. Points 1 to 4 apply here as well. Also consider the disproportionate numbers of people of color who are low income and involved in the child welfare system.	**Compound Disadvantage (CD):** *CD related to child welfare describes the multiple and compounding effects of disadvantage due to preexisting adverse experiences like trauma, family separation, and other ecological adverse conditions. CD increases vulnerability for negative outcomes.* **Racial Disproportionality:** *The Children's Bureau defines [racial] disproportionality as the overrepresentation or underrepresentation of a racial or ethnic group compared with its percentage in the total population.*	**Adverse Outcomes (AO):** *AO related to child welfare describes the negative consequences of child welfare involvement for youth.* Adverse risks: • Dual system involvement increases adverse outcomes (e.g., CPS and Juvenile Justice system). • Economic hardship, poor health, low educational attainment, emotional distress, and suicidal ideation(s) (Dettlaff & Boyd, 2020). **Structural/Institutional Racism:** This occurs when laws, rules, practices, and sanctioned behaviors are enacted in ways that cause disadvantages and harm to specific groups of people over other groups. These systems of rules underlie racial hierarchy in the United States (Bailey et al., 2021). Bailey et al. provide the following examples of structural/institutional racism: • Slavery and Jim Crow • Redlining and housing inequality • Racialized segregation

(continued)

TABLE 5.1 KEY TERMS AND KEY FACTORS OF DISPROPORTIONALITY IN CHILD WELFARE *(continued)*

DISPROPORTIONALITY/CHILD WELFARE	KEY TERMS	KEY FACTORS
Points 1 to 4 apply here as well. Also consider overrepresentation of certain groups over others.	**Racial Disparity:** *According to Dettlaff and Boyd (2020), this "is used to describe inequitable outcomes experienced by one racial group when compared to another racial group" (p. 254).* Disparities can affect each disposition of the case throughout their time in the system.	**Structural/Intuitional/Individual Racism:** Children who spend time in foster care exhibit adverse outcomes behaviorally, economically, and through their life-course. They may also have health-related consequences. Due to societal inequality (structural/institutional and individual), Black youth reap lifelong consequences which further disadvantage them in life (i.e., compound disadvantage).

Source: Adapted from Dettlaff, A. J., & Boyd, R. (2020). Racial disproportionality and disparities in the child welfare system: Why do they exist, and what can be done to address them? *The ANNALS of the American Academy of Political and Social Science, 692*(1), 253–274. https://doi .org/10.1177/0002716220980329

Other scholars challenge the harsh reality of anti-Black sentiment in the child welfare system. "Black parents know the pain of legally sanctioned and socially accepted separation from their children in a profound way" (Stephens, 2022, p. 3). Stephens makes a poignant argument for contextualizing the country's treatment of and blatant disregard for the Black family. Based on malignant notions of humanness, Whites have used racialized frames (or stereotypes) as fact, despite being shrouded in half-truths and devoid of the larger picture or context of people's lived experiences.

To understand the rationale for this argument, Stephens (2022) presents the historical context of slavery to help readers grasp the legacy of oppression in relation to current practices. White racist beliefs about people of color became institutionalized and used as a standard of practice for one of the greatest abuses committed against humanity; that is, the institution of slavery. "For centuries, their bodies were viewed as profit machines, units of labor and reproduction, [with] their parental rights stripped to sustain America's institution of chattel slavery" (Stephens, 2022, p. 3). Further, she writes that utilizing research that focuses only on the failings of people of color allows people in power to remain blind to "investigating and recording any White racist role in the poor social and health outcomes that are a consequence of being targeted" (Stephens, 2022, p. 1). It is the equivalent of blaming the victim after creating the conditions that victimize them in the first place. Stephens further calls for a focus on social justice, especially for the profession of social work in relation to the child welfare system.

Stephens asserts that it is the responsibility of social workers to seek out and advocate for transformative solutions that mitigate or root out the disadvantage Black families face in the child welfare system. The system itself has incentivized out-of-home placements that have adversely impacted Black families. In addition, Stephens warns, the child welfare system spends less money on in-home support, a budgeting priority that must be contested as it only supports the perpetuation of family disruption.

LATINX FAMILIES

Recent studies show mixed reporting nationwide regarding the representation of Latinx families in the child welfare system (Maguire-Jack et al., 2015). Based on regional or state differences, Latinx families are either overrepresented or underrepresented in child welfare (Hines et al., 2004; Lanesskog et al., 2020; Maguire-Jack et al., 2015). Lanesskog and colleagues (2020) discuss the low representation of Latinx families in child welfare. However, they further assert that once involved, Latinx families "are more likely than their English-speaking peers to encounter barriers to the human services needed to keep their families together" (Lanesskog et al., 2020, p. 435). Among the barriers faced by Latinx families are:

1. *Language*—Services are often not provided in Spanish.

2. *Noncitizen*—Parents who are not U.S. citizens are not eligible for services.

3. *Immigration Status*—This creates fear of deportation among undocumented families.

Lanesskog and colleagues acknowledge the struggles of the most dedicated bilingual human service workers to work across languages and cultures within a system that does not provide enough support to its workers.

In their study, Lanesskog and colleagues report that workers lamented that clients were not communicated with in Spanish on documents. One worker who participated in their study explained, "Our court reports are never . . . never provided to families in Spanish" (Lanesskog et al., 2020, p. 444). The participant further explained their view of this as an unfair practice that violates Latinx families' rights.

Other problems related to citizenship status for impoverished families include, but are not limited to, ineligibility for public benefits. Undocumented parents/caregivers are not eligible to apply for welfare, housing, emergency assistance, and health insurance (Lanesskog et al., 2020), which places them at a disadvantage and makes them vulnerable to child protection. Children of undocumented parents/caregivers may remain undetected if they are able to avoid being in spaces where mandated reporters work. The exception would be school systems, of course. Nonetheless, the tradition, cultural value, or practice of *"familismo"* may serve as protection for people with undocumented status. Familismo represents the importance of family relationships, loyalty, and closeness among the family of origin, extended family, and kinship networks. Familismo as a protective factor may help to provide the support needed when other resources are not readily available due to being undocumented.

ASIAN FAMILIES

Xu and colleagues (2018) indicate that the United States receives immigrants from all over the world each year, and most immigrants are currently from Asia. Low-income immigrant parents face additional stress when parenting since material hardship impacts family resources to provide for the family's basic needs. They may also encounter emotional stress and depressive symptoms that perhaps are derived from the isolation and discrimination they experience (Xu et al., 2018). Overall, these scholars note immigrant families face greater stressors, have less social support, and experience the pains of integrating into a new culture that is discriminatory. Xu and colleagues (2018) note that many of the factors related to the immigrant experience can elevate immigrant parenting stress. "Thus, it is important to examine factors associated with maternal parenting stress among non-U.S. born mothers and provide implications to promote healthy family functioning and child development among immigrant populations" (Xu et al., 2018, p. 62). Interventions that are culturally responsive and help immigrant families by providing needed resources can help tremendously to support children growing up in safe environments free from abuse and neglect.

In general, the literature and child welfare system reports show a smaller percentage of Asian and Pacific Islander families' involvement in child welfare in relation to other ethnicities. Nonetheless, as Asian immigration grows, so will the need to support these communities. Some researchers report spatial or regional variations in reporting, which at times yield mixed results. Edwards, for instance, states that "race plays a powerful role in explaining the geography of family surveillance" (Edwards, 2019, p. 63).

INDIGENOUS FAMILIES

Native populations in the United States frequently live in desolate areas with high unemployment, environmental stress, and entrenched forms of social injustice and governmentally enforced marginalization. Some researchers report that "race plays a powerful role in explaining the geography of family surveillance" (Edwards, 2019, p. 63). Youth living on tribal lands have a high rate of substantiated child maltreatment (14.2 per 1000). Forty-two percent of the Native population is below the age of 24, and they are 3.3 times more likely to be in the child welfare system than their White peers (Child Welfare Information Gateway, 2017; Kids Count Data Center, 2016). Additionally, although not related to child welfare, Native youth have the highest suicide rates of any other ethnic group in the United States.

The historical context of Native Americans is critically important to consider, especially in light of historical trauma. "Historical trauma is multigenerational trauma experienced by specific groups of people and refers to cumulative and psychological wounding over the lifespan and across generations, emanating from massive group trauma" (Brave Heart et al., 2011, p. 283). Understanding historical trauma provides a rationale for seeking to decolonize practices in child welfare, governmental assistance, and tribal relations in general.

> Decolonizing or anti-colonial work seeks to actively de-center and dismantle colonial institutions, modalities, systems, structures, and ways of knowing and being that continue to dispossess Indigenous peoples of their lands, families, homes, languages, and rights. In this article, we are invested in anti-colonial work that seeks to decolonize the current state of child welfare. We suggest that applying ideas of cultural safety to child-welfare practices might enable this. (de Leeuw & Greenwood, 2017, p. 144)

de Leeuw and Greenwood also point out that "colonial benevolence" (2017, p. 145) claims an intention to better the lives of those living outside the mainstream dominant culture. The reality is that this inimical act caused more harm than good to Indigenous people. Ecumenical entities have a history of benevolence for the good of those they colonize (de Leeuw & Greenwood, 2017). The historical atrocities of the residential boarding schools illustrate this misguided sense of helping that besmirched the developmental trajectories and well-being of many Native children.

Such devastating trauma and oppression create generational problems like poverty, substance use, and domestic violence experienced by many child welfare-involved families (Haight et al., 2018). These effects may be more intensely experienced by Indigenous families and contribute to disparities in child welfare, especially in instances of neglect (Brave Heart et al., 2011; Bunting et al., 2018; Haight et al., 2018). Haight and colleagues (2018) indicate that the historical past and all its trauma have led to current-day conditions that place Indigenous people at risk in North America (e.g., many forms of oppression, violence, structural racism, and child welfare involvement). Brave Heart passionately calls for Indigenous nations to reclaim their way of life and embrace the *Seven Generations Philosophy*, which considers how each decision made today will affect the next seven subsequent generations (Haight et al., 2018). Haight and colleagues (2018) warn that this is a "long emergency" (p. 398) that warrants great concern. "Indigenous people in the United States and Canada also have endured a long emergency from systemic actions to destroy their families, cultures, lands, and spiritual belief systems beginning" (Haight et al., 2018, p. 398), which began more than 500 years ago through the colonization of North America. Through the early 1800s into the 20th century, "Indigenous families and children were victims of U.S. and Canadian government's efforts to forcefully and brutally assimilate Indigenous people" (Haight et al., 2018, p. 398). This process included ethnocide and was enacted through the child welfare system.

The unjust practice of ethnocide ripped Indigenous children away from their families and placed them in off-reservation boarding schools where many children were deprived of their birth families' love, care, and nurturance (Haight et al., 2018). Children were taken from all they knew and removed from the community that played a strong role in their lives. In addition, Indigenous children were subjected to institutional maltreatment that took the forms of physical, sexual, emotional, and psychological torture, leaving behind a legacy of harm that plagues Indigenous communities today.

LGBTQ+ YOUTH

LGBTQ+ youth are placed in congregate care more often than their peers and stay for longer periods of time (Mountz & Capous-Desyllas, 2020). In addition, LGBTQ+ youth experience a high percentage of residential change while in foster care and the emotional fallout from it. LGBTQ+ youth report feelings of being mistreated while in care, chronic physical and verbal aggression, and enacted stigma (daily microaggressions and other devaluing sentiments expressed toward them). Mountz and Capous-Desyllas also indicate that LGBTQ+ youth in foster care experience foster parent rejection and hostility related to their identity or sexual expression. LGBTQ+ youth in care are not accepted for who they are at a critical time in their development. This rejection may, in fact, compound the trauma and mistreatment they have already experienced prior to entering the system. LGBTQ+ youth of color experience compounded disadvantages related to their identity and more disparities within the child welfare system (i.e., overrepresentation, longer stays, and multiple forms of maltreatment).

In 2018, the Family First Prevention Services Act (FFPSA) was signed into law, focusing on prevention, early intervention, and evidence-based interventions and practice within child welfare. The purpose is to bolster the support and services youth receive in foster care in four main ways: (a) by allowing Title IV-E dollars to be used to fund up to 1 year of evidence-based prevention services for children and families who are at imminent risk of child welfare involvement (as candidates for foster care), (b) by regulating financial support for youth in congregate care to minimize long residential stays, (c) by providing residential treatment options for youth in care with clinical needs, and (d) by establishing criteria for qualified residential treatment programs (QRTPs).

Specifically, the FFPSA calls for reform in child welfare related to foster care placements and policies to provide enhanced support to children and families and prevent foster care placements, and, if removal is needed, it urges that children be placed in loving foster homes rather than congregate care where LGBTQ+ youth are overrepresented. The legislation recognizes the poor outcomes for LGBTQ+ youth compared to their cisgender and heterosexual peers. The FFPSA also calls for the recruitment, retention, and support of homes that are affirming of all youth in care despite sexual orientation. Mountz and Capous-Desyllas (2020) recommend the child welfare system utilize "culturally affirming mental health and substance abuse prevention and treatment programs, practices, and counselors within and external to child welfare agencies" (Mountz & Capous-Desyllas, 2020, p. 10). Engaging the needs of all children in an equitable manner implies that the system should seek to understand the developmental needs of children in care in a culturally responsive and trauma-informed way. This includes understanding the importance of cultivating an affirming, respectful, and accepting practice with LGBTQ+ youth in care and finding ways to enhance their identity development. Social and racial justice must be afforded to all children/youth in care.

Case Scenario: Supporting LGBTQ+ Youth

John is a 15-year-old White male. He has recently been placed in out-of-home foster care with a nonrelative family. John recently came out to his biological parents. His mother was supportive, but his father was not. A call was made to the hotline because his dad punished him severely. Although his father was contrite, due to the severity of the beating the court determined that John would go to foster care until the father completed parenting classes, anger management, and general counseling. John has been placed with a family that has successfully provided youth foster care previously. This family, however, is very conservative, although this has never been an issue in the past. They are not accepting of John's sexual identity and expression. John recently has been asking to be identified as "they/them." The school personnel have been very supportive and accepting of his identified pronouns. His foster parents,

(continued)

Case Scenario: Supporting LGBTQ+ Youth *(continued)*

however, have been challenged by this new request. They think this is a phase John is going through and refuse to refer to John using nonbinary terms.

DISCUSSION QUESTIONS

1. How do the foster parents' values clash with more current views of sexual expression?
2. What interventions should the child welfare professional take with the foster family to support John?
3. How can the child welfare professional support John so they can feel safe in this environment?
4. To encourage family reunification, what interventions would help the family to be more accepting and unified to support John?

Algorithmic Justice

In this section, we consider algorithmic justice, a more current concept. Today's society depends on big data and artificial intelligence to inform social platforms and shape how decisions are made in the banking, insurance, and financial industries. Algorithms can be useful tools when used properly and in unbiased ways. However, when algorithms are used in the political arena, they have produced a political contagion during elections, similar to the emotional contagion which occurs on social platforms (Završnik, 2021). Despite the need to mitigate built-in bias in algorithmic programming, the child welfare system uses algorithms to make critical decisions about the safety and welfare of children.

Keddell (2019) writes about the use of algorithms in the field of child protection and its rapid acceptance. Keddell considers algorithmic programs a challenge when trying to achieve social justice, noting that "fairness expects an algorithm not to reproduce or exacerbate social inequalities relating to group rights, such as those related to race, class or gender" (Keddell, 2019, p. 5). Edwards and colleagues (2015) describe the problem with norming parental expectations and acknowledge that services are shaped by these expectations. Sadly, most Anglophone countries "operate as a key site of the reproduction of social inequalities, have both care and control functions and, while offering protection, can also promote normative parenting ideals mired in cultural and class specificities" (Keddell, 2019, p. 5).

Decisions made by child welfare caseworkers had more to do with "individual practitioner values, location, decision-making variability, and service supply and demand factors" (Keddell, 2019, p. 9) rather than fairness and equity. It is important to understand human rights, ensure reasonable inferences are made from computer-generated software/algorithms when making assessments that will affect people's lives, and assess them in a relational way. Algorithms categorize people using available data and group them according to statistical similarities across a population. However, this data may be distal and incomplete, which can cause network or algorithmic bias. "This can also exacerbate raciali[z]ed bias, as people's personal networks are likely to reflect histories of racialized disadvantage and poverty, leading to networked bias, where parents may be considered high risk due to family members, neighbours, or community location" (Keddell, 2019, p. 15). Others assert that "big data" (Hannah-Moffat, 2019) is not always used accurately to depict reality in social phenomena. Hannah-Moffat writes, "Still, we have little understanding of where 'big data' actually comes from, how it is used or how it lends authority and justifies decisions" (Hannah-Moffat, 2019, p. 455). Child welfare professionals must consider the possibility of human and technological errors (e.g., large data errors). All decisions should consider the humanity of each child, parent, and family to provide an unbiased view in case workers' assessments to "first do no harm" similar to the oath physicians take.

FOCUSING ON SOCIAL JUSTICE: FEEDFORWARD

The authors believe that focusing extensively on the past without any remedy for the future is futile. Toward that end, Hirsch (2017) provides ways to avoid staying focused on the past. Hirsch posits five ways that traditional feedback (looking back) in the field of business needs fixing and gives examples from the business sector. These lessons are appropriate for any system requiring critical thought about its operations or procedures. Hirsch (2017) suggests:

- First, looking back consumes too much time and productivity. Looking back at child welfare practices consumes time and effort, diminishing the energy to create solutions.

- Second, focusing on the past does not help, as it cannot be changed, and "we resist the change we cannot control" (Hirsch, 2017, p. 18). Child welfare is a complex system with complex problems and requires the synergy of multiple systems for creating real change.

- Third, looking back and giving critique come across as judgmental. We believe in the concept of accountability and not blame. Society and the child welfare system tend to engage in a cycle of blame that sometimes cascades from one system to another. Parents blame workers, the system, and the child; the system blames the parents and the community when they lack resources; and sometimes the government and politicians blame system administrators, who in turn blame the workers.

- Fourth, looking back perpetuates negative behaviors and beliefs, which may also lead to feelings of helplessness as systems struggle to grapple with their flaws. If workers feel helpless in the bureaucratic cog of child welfare, it may create negative behaviors leading to burnout.

- Fifth, looking back diminishes the prospect of growth. "The self-defeating tone of traditional feedback pins people to an unchanging narrative about their own intelligence and abilities" Hirsch, 2017, p. 28). This is particularly true in the child welfare system, as it expects people with few resources and material support to navigate the system. How might we avoid the blame game and build on the strengths of parents and families?

Moreover, Hirsch provides recommendations for looking forward as a way of demonstrating value for every individual and promoting clarity over intuition. Accordingly, Hirsch outlines the steps for feedforward. Feedforward is a concept of providing valuable input without being mired in the past. Professionals can learn from taking stock of what needs to be done. For Hirsch, this is the concept of repair (i.e., REPAIR, which is explained in the following):

1. *Regenerates*—Instead of affirming what the worker already knows (i.e., what is observable), regeneration considers how the worker may move forward to use their skills and talents.

2. *Expands*—Instead of pointing out the problem and focusing on what is believed to not work, this concept reveals possibilities and expands options.

3. *Particular*—Instead of overwhelming the system with data, the focus should be on just a few particular things (so they may be targeted and embedded in instruction). Too much feedback, Hirsch warns, can lead to information overload and poor decision-making.

4. *Authentic*—Instead of sugar-coating things to manipulate others, the concept of authenticity describes the problem and its impact, then elicits input to develop solutions.

5. *Impact*—Instead of focusing strictly on measurement, the concept of impact considers the creation of a specific plan with steps for improvement (in manageable steps to guide the process).

6. *Refines*—Instead of delegating from a top-down hierarchical approach, the concept of refinement considers ways to gain input from a diverse group of people with different viewpoints and skills.

Applying the concept of feedforward creates greater opportunities for enacting socially just practices. One benefit of feedforward is that it regenerates the talent it attracts and retains top prospects, especially when organizations/systems can view them as an investment and not an expense. Child welfare systems are better situated to create change when they engage other stakeholders. For instance, child welfare systems may invite the innovative ideas of grassroots advocates and other crucial input from leaders who have relational ties with and respect from the families the system serves. They also look for improvement through organizations like Chapin Hall and the Annie E. Casey Foundation, which conduct critical research related to child welfare and child well-being.

CULTURALLY RESPONSIVE INTERVENTIONS IN CHILD WELFARE

General Recommendations

Culturally responsive interventions in child welfare must become standard with a commitment to anti-racist practice. Dettlaff and colleagues (2020) indicate that anti-racist work involves the continuous and rigorous interrogation of institutional motives and a commitment to opposing policies that produce and maintain racial inequity. "Applying an anti-racist framework to child welfare begins by acknowledging that racial disproportionality and disparities are produced and maintained through the policies and practices of the system in which they exist" (Dettlaff et al., 2020, p. 508). Dettlaff and colleagues further state that efforts to remedy child welfare disparities include examining the policies that create the disparities.

Complex problems require complex solutions. Recommendations should be created with the end-user in mind and with their input from the beginning. It should be truly a collaborative effort.

- First, child welfare practitioners and social workers must think critically about whom to involve in examining the problems and exploring solutions to create a decolonized system in child welfare.
- Second, child welfare practitioners and social workers must commit to creating multiple solutions in manageable parts:
  - Immediate solutions,
  - Upstream strategies for change,
  - Workforce changes,
  - Professional development changes, and
  - Increased family support to avoid the system.
- Third, child welfare practitioners and social workers must evaluate our efforts and include all partners (parents, children/youth, child welfare professionals, legislators/policymakers, and scholars).
- Fourth, child welfare practitioners and social workers must continue to do this work irrespective of media coverage about what is needed. In other words, crises and public media should not lead the focus. We must consider how to address those things that impact public perception while continuing to work on long-term strategies for decolonizing child welfare practices.
- Fifth, child welfare practitioners and social workers must consider the role of trauma, even in the lives of parents/family members, who may be helped through therapeutic interventions versus child removal (when deemed safe and appropriate). In some systems, intact family services operate in this way but perhaps should advocate for parental support and education prior to families being involved in the child welfare system. This is a big request and

requires a proactive stance versus being reactive. In other words, what can child welfare systems do to drive prevention?

- Sixth, child welfare practitioners and social workers must respect and embrace the cultural uniqueness of vulnerable and marginalized groups and provide cultural safety in our interface with culturally diverse families and children.

Other considerations include creating a stepwise plan for addressing child welfare's structural and functional inequalities. In order to set the tone for doing this work, the authors recommend *addressing the issue directly, acknowledging structural racism,* and *creating new policies.* First, *addressing the issue* head-on means acknowledging the role of racism in the United States and how it is perpetuated through institutional practices, laws, standards of care, and policies. Second, *acknowledging structural racism* and following up by planning a course of action to rectify these disparities within the system, remove barriers for people of color, and enact anti-racist practices in child welfare services. This means providing greater accountability (not blame), providing intensive supervision, and requiring the professional habit of self-reflection to enhance cross-cultural decision-making to create more culturally responsive systems. Third, *creating newer policies* and allocating funds to serve families can mitigate problems before forcibly separating families.

Additional considerations in becoming more child inclusive include:

1. Reflecting on how the child welfare system unintentionally affects the child,

2. Finding ways to amplify children's voices in the development of services, and

3. Ensuring child safety (postremoval) to prevent retraumatization and enhance family reunification processes.

The child welfare system must also consider ways of incorporating Indigenous knowledge and cultural customs, values, and traditions for family life in ongoing professional development. The system must hire more people from diverse backgrounds, including Indigenous people and other people of color, within the child welfare system.

Another thought is how child welfare systems and the social work profession might engage in think tanks to tackle complex systemic problems. There is a great benefit to conducting group-think activities that are unencumbered by thoughts of defeat. The best brainstorming activities are those in which participants are *uncensored* and engaged to think about solutions *as if money were no object.* We often engage students and workshop participants in these types of activities. But to tackle the larger, more pressing issues, this is only a start and must be followed by prioritizing the ideas that are generated, considering realistic assessments about managing barriers, engaging larger systems in change, and making sure the right people are at the helm to work collaboratively toward real change.

Moreover, in a *Stanford Social Innovation Review* article, Wilkerson (2022) made three suggestions for increasing greater social connection to enhance well-being through belonging:

1. Adopt a *social in all policies mindset* to guide the efforts of key stakeholders like policymakers, social change organizations, funders, and other important professionals who engage in this type of work. Social connection must become threaded throughout policymaking and must be a collaborative effort between other large entities that directly or indirectly impact the social problem that needs to be addressed (urban planners, social services, transportation, and the like). In child welfare, the agencies could include health and behavioral health, educational, and transportation systems, childcare, and other services for children and families.

An example of this in child welfare would be examining policies about mandated services and compliance issues. How can parents make it to mandated services when their job hours conflict with the times services are offered? Effective case management must be flexible and understanding of the parental/familial context (i.e., the need to work). In addition, transportation, childcare, and the location of services compound the barriers parents face. This example demonstrates the need for child welfare policies, social service providers, and transportation services to be coordinated to maximize possible parental cooperation. How can the child welfare system truly support families by incorporating what they need versus only providing what is convenient?

This example of a *social in all policies* perspective demonstrates a commitment toward equity and inclusion, which can lead to fair practices for families with limited work flexibility. In turn, this has the potential to enhance compliance because families' needs are being considered.

2. *Increase investments in social infrastructure* to address the physical elements of communities. As a prevention strategy, child welfare systems should advocate for underresourced communities by providing the types of services and interventions that enhance social connection for families who live in those communities. Taking steps to lower the impact of environmental stress in low-income areas can go a long way in supporting family life.

Social infrastructure includes everything that connects people with each other such as parks and recreation, libraries, public transportation, and commercial shopping centers. "Such investments should be made while working across sectors and with communities to create places and programs that better connect people with each other" (Wilkerson, 2022, p. 60). Social support is a known buffer for stress, and it decreases the isolation some families may feel in communities that are grossly disconnected from mainstream living. Broadening the support systems for children and families involved in the child welfare system is critical for low-resourced families.

3. *Embrace social connectedness as a norm.* According to Wilkerson (2022), "changing policies and practices can influence social norms, but hosting inclusive conversations where people can collectively create norms that support social connections tends to be more effective at eliminating harmful,

isolating practices and policies and supporting new, inclusive ones" (p. 60). Wilkerson gives the example of how "some cities have declared themselves compassionate or welcoming communities, resilient communities, or stigma-free zones" (Wilkerson, 2022, p. 60). This is a practice that can be used in foster care communities and communities in general to produce environments that embrace the humanity of all their citizens.

Other recommendations from the literature should also be considered. Stephens (2022) suggests that social work educational institutions create *"mandated supporter training"* (Stephens, 2022, p. 3), a term, she writes, that was coined by parent advocates in the New York City grass-roots advocacy movement. The purpose is to prepare new social workers to assess the impact of racism on families as they navigate their involvement in the child welfare system. This training would include a line of inquiry asking about the barriers that ensnare families in the system:

1. What challenges do parents face in securing adequate/sustainable housing?
2. What challenges do parents face in securing sustainable employment?
3. What other foundational supports are needed for families to have security?
4. A mandated supporter would explore what a parent needs and connect them to resources before a report is made.

Stephens concludes by asserting that all social work institutions should strongly consider the potential racial bias practitioners may have as they perform their duties as mandated reporters. How might institutions of higher education serve as ethical gatekeepers in the fight against racial bias and unjust practices? More importantly, she poses a question about how we may track these injustices and bar those whose biased practices unnecessarily and disproportionately disrupt Black family life. The system must train workers to avoid race-based judgments that create an extra layer of disadvantage for families of color. Further, all mandated reporters would benefit from this type of training.

In addition to these recommendations, consider:

1. What supports are needed for families to provide guidance, supervision, and monitoring for their children when they must work?
2. What can agencies do to assist in providing viable solutions for childcare and after-school programming?
3. How might the child welfare system advocate for services to accommodate parents with nontraditional needs (transportation, evening hours, childcare)?
4. How can child welfare expand the implementation of "system navigators" to help parents understand the system and access needed services? Many systems provide liaisons or parent advocates who address issues and help problem-solve for parents.

Reflection Box 5.1

Use the following steps to conduct a classroom debate about a topic in child welfare. The example provided is related to algorithmic justice and the documentary Coded Bias).

PREPARATION

1. *Make sure students read the article by Keddell.*

   Keddell, E. (2019). Algorithmic justice in child protection: Statistical fairness, social justice and the implications for practice. *Social Sciences, 8*(10), 281. https://doi.org/10.3390/socsci8100281

2. *Have your students determine ground rules for the debate to increase civility and decorum.*

AFTER VIEWING THE DOCUMENTARY *CODED BIAS* IN CLASS

1. Assign students to debate teams. Configure the debate teams based on the pros and cons of algorithms used to make determinations of abuse and neglect in child welfare.

2. Students may select roles within their group. Speakers may focus on the opening/closing responses or rebuttal. Students may also select tasks such as researcher or organizer.

3. Provide direction about the types of "credible" sources you want them to use; for example, newspaper articles, government sites, the film itself.

4. During the debate, the instructor may select one student who will be the moderator.

5. Before the debate, provide students with the proposition statement that shapes the arguments (i.e., *algorithmic tools are fair and just tools to use regarding child welfare workers' decisions about removing children from their homes/parents*).

6. Designate how much time each team will have:

   a. Pro—10 minutes

   b. Rebuttal—5 minutes

   c. Con—10 minutes

   d. Rebuttal—5 minutes

   e. Team conferral—5 minutes

   f. Closing statements—5 minutes for each team to make their closing arguments

(continued)

Reflection Box 5.1 *(continued)*

7. After the debate, take time for debriefing as a large group activity (see Figure 5.3). Consider the following:

   a. How did it feel to present a position that you may not have agreed with?

   b. In what way does this defense of an opposite view help you understand the issue in a more critical way?

   c. Were there any surprises, or were you left with any questions?

   d. What is your biggest takeaway from this activity?

   e. Discuss which side (pro or con) presented the most compelling argument and why.

Figure 5.3 Debate Prompts

Useful Debate Prompts

Students may benefit from the list of quick phrases to utilize as they form their responses:

- For instance
- To put it another way
- In opposition
- Indeed, certainly
- Nevertheless
- However
- More importantly
- Ultimately
- In summary

When introducing their side, students may use the following phrases:

- In society, there are many instances of _____. We are here to discuss what this means if we agree (or if we disagree) with _____.
- My opponents may tell you _____; however, evidence shows _____.
- In conclusion, my opponents have argued for _____, but the issue is about social justice and _____.

CHAPTER SUMMARY

This chapter discussed decolonizing child welfare and its rationale and considered steps for engaging in decolonizing practices that are culturally responsive and fair. The authors provided a review of social, economic, environmental, racial, and algorithmic justice related to the child welfare system. Additionally, the chapter ended with thoughts about how to take the necessary steps to challenge the typical manner of conducting this work.

DISCUSSION QUESTIONS

1. Discuss ways that algorithmic methods can aid in child welfare decisions.
2. Discuss ways that algorithmic methods create coded bias.
3. Discuss ways of contesting practices ingrained within the child welfare system that no longer support families.
4. Discuss ways to support LGBTQ+ youth in foster care settings.
5. Discuss a plan to be more inclusive of children's/youths' voices in the services they receive.

RESOURCES

Native Child and Family Services of Toronto /
https://nativechild.org/child-welfare/decolonizing-child-welfare-learning-series/

Decolonizing Child Welfare Webinar Learning Series #1 / [1 hour 28 minutes]
https://www.youtube.com/watch?v=GAixoLSpaAU&t=1s

Decolonizing Child Welfare Webinar Learning Series #2 /[1 hour 33 minutes]
https://www.youtube.com/watch?v=fgFUgGQF13M&t=2s

Decolonizing Child Welfare Webinar Learning Series #3 / [1 hour 27 minutes]
https://www.youtube.com/watch?v=G_SwB9wgbc4&t=2s

Decolonizing Child Welfare Webinar Learning Series #4 / [1 hour 28 minutes]
https://www.youtube.com/watch?v=W0wMszz6g9Q&t=487s

Decolonizing Child Welfare Panel https://nativechild.org/child-welfare/decolonizing-child-welfare-learning-series/

Youth Villages (Non-Profit Organization) /[5 minutes 12 seconds]
Testimonial of Youth Voice - LifeSet Maria's Story
https://www.youtube.com/watch?v=o7weq5yFa1Y

A robust set of instructor resources designed to supplement this text is located at **http://connect.springerpub.com/content/book/978-0-8261-5285-5**. Qualifying instructors may request access by emailing **textbook@springerpub.com**.

REFERENCES

Annie E. Casey Foundation. (2021). *Food deserts in the United States*. https://www.aecf.org/blog/exploring-americas-food-deserts

Bailey, Z. D., Feldman, J. M., & Bassett, M. T. (2021). How structural racism works—Racist policies as a root cause of US racial health inequities. *New England Journal of Medicine, 384*(8), 768–773. https://doi.org/10.1056/NEJMms2025396

Belanger, K. (2018). Examination of racial imbalance for children in foster care: Implications for training. In K. Briar-Lawson & J. L. Zlotnik (Eds.), *Evaluation research in child welfare: Improving outcomes through university-public agency partnerships* (pp. 162–176). Routledge.

Brave Heart, M. Y. H., Chase, J., Elkins, J., & Altschul, D. B. (2011). Historical trauma among indigenous peoples of the Americas: Concepts, research, and clinical considerations. *Journal of Psychoactive Drugs, 43*(4), 282–290. https://doi.org/10.1080/02791072.2011.628913

Bullard, R. D. (2008). *Dumping in Dixie: Race, class, and environmental quality*. Avalon Publishing.

Bunting, L., Davidson, G., McCartan, C., Hanratty, J., Bywaters, P., Mason, W., & Steils, N. (2018). The association between child maltreatment and adult poverty—A systematic review of longitudinal research. *Child Abuse & Neglect, 77*, 121–133. https://doi.org/10.1016/j.chiabu.2017.12.022

Child Welfare Information Gateway. (2017). *Foster care statistics 2016*. U.S. Department of Health and Human Services, Children's Bureau. https://www.acf.hhs.gov/cb

Coates, J. (2016). Ecospiritual approaches: A path to decolonizing social work. In M. Gray, J. Coates, M. Yellow Bird, & T. Hetherington (Eds.), *Decolonizing Social Work* (pp. 63–86). Routledge.

de Leeuw, S., & Greenwood, M. (2017). Turning a new page: Cultural safety, critical creative literary interventions, truth and reconciliation, and the crisis of child welfare. *AlterNative: An International Journal of Indigenous Peoples, 13*(3), 142–151. https://doi.org/10.1177/1177180117714155

Dettlaff, A. J., & Boyd, R. (2020). Racial disproportionality and disparities in the child welfare system: Why do they exist, and what can be done to address them? *The ANNALS of the American Academy of Political and Social Science, 692*(1), 253–274. https://doi.org/10.1177/0002716220980329

Dettlaff, A. J., Weber, K., Pendleton, M., Boyd, R., Bettencourt, B., & Burton, L. (2020). It is not a broken system, it is a system that needs to be broken: The upEND movement to abolish the child welfare system. *Journal of Public Child Welfare, 14*(5), 500–517. https://doi.org/10.1080/15548732.2020.1814542

Dominelli, L. (2014). Promoting environmental justice through green social work practice: A key challenge for practitioners and educators. *International Social Work, 57*(4), 338–345. https://doi.org/10.1177%2F0020872814524968

dosReis, S., Yoon, D. M., Riddle, M. A., Noll, E., & Rothbard, A. (2011). Antipsychotic treatment among youth in foster care. *Pediatrics, 128*, 1459–1466. https://doi.org/10.1542/peds.2010-2970

Eamon, M. K., & Kopels, S. (2004). 'For reasons of poverty': Court challenges to child welfare practices and mandated programs. *Children and Youth Services Review, 26*(9), 821–836. https://doi.org/10.1016/j.childyouth.2004.02.023

Edwards, F. (2019). Family surveillance: Police and the reporting of child abuse and neglect. *RSF: The Russell Sage Foundation Journal of the Social Sciences, 5*(1), 50–70. https://doi.org/10.7758/RSF.2019.5.1.03

Edwards, R., Gillies, V., & Horsley, N. (2015). Brain science and early years policy: Hopeful ethos or 'cruel optimism'? *Critical Social Policy, 35*(2), 167–187. https://doi.org/10.1177/0261018315574020

Finn, J. L. (2020). *Just practice: A social justice approach to social work* (4th ed.). Oxford University Press.

Haight, W., Waubanascum, C., Glesener, D., & Marsalis, S. (2018). A scoping study of Indigenous child welfare: The long emergency and preparations for the next seven generations. *Children & Youth Services Review, 93*, 397–410. https://doi.org/10.1016/j.childyouth.2018.08.016

Hannah-Moffat, K. (2019). Algorithmic risk governance: Big data analytics, race and information activism in criminal justice debates. *Theoretical Criminology, 23*(4), 453–470. https://doi.org/10.1177/1362480618763582

Hill, R. B. (2007). *An analysis of racial/ethnic disproportionality and disparity at the national, state, and county Levels*. Casey Family Programs and the Center for the Study of Social Policy. https://www.aecf.org/resources/an-analysis-of-racial-ethnic-disproportionality-and-disparity-at-the-nation

Hines, A. M., Lemon, K., Wyatt, P., & Merdinger, J. (2004). Factors related to the disproportionate involvement of children of color in the child welfare system: A review and emerging themes. *Children and Youth Services Review, 26,* 507–527. https://doi.org/10.1016/j.childyouth.2004.01.007

Hirsch, J. (2017). *The feedback fix: Dump the past, embrace the future, and lead the way to change.* Rowman & Littlefield.

Holton, A. (2007). Decolonizing history: Arthur Schomburg's afrodiasporic archive. *The Journal of African American History, 92*(2), 218–238. https://doi.org/10.1086/JAAHV92N2P218

Jirapramukpitak, T., Harpham, T., & Prince, M. (2011). Family violence and its 'adversity package': A community survey of family violence and adverse mental outcomes among young people. *Social Psychiatry and Psychiatric Epidemiology, 46*(9), 825–831. https://doi.org/10.1007/s00127-010-0252-9

Keddell, E. (2019). Algorithmic justice in child protection: Statistical fairness, social justice and the implications for practice. *Social Sciences, 8*(10), 281. https://doi.org/10.3390/socsci8100281

Kids Count Data Center. (2016). *Child population by race.* A Project of the Annie E. Casey Foundation. https://www.aecf.org/resources/2016-kids-count-data-book

Lanesskog, D., Muñoz, J., & Castillo, K. (2020). Language is not enough: Institutional supports for Spanish speaking client-worker engagement in child welfare. *Journal of Public Child Welfare, 14*(4), 435–457. https://doi.org/10.1080/15548732.2019.1621235

Maguire-Jack, K., & Font, S. (2017). Intersections of individual and neighborhood disadvantage: Implications for child maltreatment. *Children and Youth Services Review, 72,* 44–51. http://doi.org/10.1016/j.childyouth.2016.10.015

Maguire-Jack, K., Lanier, P., Johnson-Motoyama, M., Welch, H., & Dineen, M. (2015). Geographic variation in racial disparities in child maltreatment: The influence of county poverty and population density. *Child Abuse & Neglect, 47,* 1–13. https://doi.org/10.1016/J.chiabu.2015.05.020

Martin, M., & Connelly, D. D. (2015). *Achieving racial equity: Child welfare policy strategies to improve outcomes for children of color.* Center for the Study of Social Policy. https://files.eric.ed.gov/fulltext/ED582913.pdf

McKane, R. G., Satcher, L. A., Houston, S. L., & Hess, D. J. (2018). Race, class, and space: An intersectional approach to environmental justice in New York City. *Environmental Sociology, 4*(1), 79–92. https://doi.org/10.1080/23251042.2018.1429177

Mountz, S., & Capous-Desyllas, M. (2020). Exploring the families of origin of LGBTQ former foster youth and their trajectories throughout care. *Children and Youth Services Review, 109,* 104622. https://doi.org/10.1016/j.childyouth.2019.104622

Pelton, L. H. (1989). *For reasons of poverty: A critical analysis of the public child welfare system in the United States.* Praeger Publishers.

Pelton, L. H. (1994). The role of material factors in child abuse and neglect. In G. B. Melton, & F. D. Barry (Eds.), *Protecting children from abuse and neglect: Foundations for a new national strategy* (pp. 131–181). Guilford Press.

Roberts, D. (2022). *Torn apart: How the child welfare system destroys Black families--and how abolition can build a safer world.* Basic Books.

Rossman, B. R. (2001). Time heals all: How much and for whom? *Journal of Emotional Abuse, 2*(1), 31–50. https://doi.org/10.1300/J135v02n01_04

Schomburg, A. A. (1925). "The Negro digs up his past". In A. Locke (Ed.), *The new Negro.* The Schomburg Papers, Schomburg Center for Research in Black Culture. https://www.sobtell.com/images/questions/1496201498-arthur-schomburg-the-negro-digs-up-his-past_1.pdf

Stephens, T. (2022). Black parents love their children too: Addressing anti-Black racism in the American child welfare system. *Social Work, 67*(2), 191–195. https://doi.org/10.1093/sw/swac013

Ungar, M. (2002). A deeper, more social ecological social work practice. *Social Service Review, 76*(3), 480–497. https://doi.org/10.1086/341185

Wilkerson, R. (2022). A sense of belonging. *Stanford Social Innovation Review, 20*(3), 59–60. https://doi.org/10.48558/1HR2-CF58

Xu, Y., Wang, X., Ahn, H., & Harrington, D. (2018). Predictors of non-US born mothers' parenting stress across early childhood in fragile families: A longitudinal analysis. *Children and Youth Services Review, 89,* 62–70. https://doi.org/10.1016/j.childyouth.2018.04.012

Završnik, A. (2021). Algorithmic justice: Algorithms and big data in criminal justice settings. *European Journal of Criminology, 18*(5), 623–642. https://doi.org/10.1177/1477370819876762

6 Engagement and Assessment

LEARNING OBJECTIVES

By the end of the chapter, you will be able to:

- Consider the various aspects of the assessment process in child welfare.
- Understand multiple ways of assessing families.
- Consider the use of professional development to enhance engagement.
- Understand the use of genograms, ecomaps, and culturagrams.
- Review effective strategies for interviewing parents and children.
- Consider the importance of a strengths-based perspective even in child welfare.

INTRODUCTION

The field of child welfare recognizes the importance of engaging families in assessment processes but has mixed reviews about how that is accomplished (Toros et al., 2018). Effective engagement is a critical component of interacting with family systems to ensure child safety. Toros and colleagues highlight the glaring gaps in how assessments are conducted. First, the process has typically been imposed on families and children, as their input in social work evaluations has been excluded, rather than demonstrating true collaboration with them (Toros et al., 2018)—a critique that applies broadly across other helping professions and fields of practice. Assessment of parents/families in child welfare should also be collaborative. In the field of child welfare, collaboration occurs in a very dynamic manner and is dependent on the family's willingness to engage in a process that requires/mandates their participation. Second, the roles of child welfare professionals and parents/families occur within a highly complex context. Third, public scrutiny of the child welfare system overshadows some work. Child welfare professionals often find themselves in untenable binary positions; they get blamed for leaving children in unsafe environments and for breaking up families. The image the public sees paints a picture that often vilifies child welfare professionals. Fourth, the parents/families are often riddled with ambivalent feelings related to the adversarial nature of the role of the child welfare professional. Fifth, the child welfare professional must contend with the dual nature of the client–worker relationship. As Toros and colleagues (2018) aptly note, "It is challenging for families and practitioners to deal with the duality of the relationship given expectations that workers engage in conflicting roles of supporting families on the one hand and ensuring children's safety on the other" (p. 599). This type of power dynamic and use of authority can cause parents to distrust the system, a reaction that permeates subsequent interactions between the child welfare worker and parents.

There are myriad perceptions about the barriers to engagement from all sides (parents, children, child welfare professionals, administrators, and even the public). Moreover, Toros and colleagues (2018) highlight the factors that promote engagement from a comprehensive literature analysis. Trust and open communication provide pathways for parents/families to engage in the process positively. A wide array of support facilitates greater engagement. Parents/families often require material support to provide for their children's basic needs. Emotional support enables parents/families to engage in a long and challenging process toward reunification. Therapists can help in this regard if the child welfare protection worker is unable to do so in light of their dual relationship. Therapists often describe providing a holding environment for parents/families entangled in the child welfare system. In this chapter, the authors provide detailed information about the importance of and skills needed for the effective engagement of parents/families involved in the child welfare system.

ENGAGEMENT

Engagement is defined in multiple ways; however, scholars generally agree that engagement is essential, especially in child welfare, since it expedites family reunification and decreases recidivism (Rawlings & Blackmer, 2019). Effective outcomes depend on quality engagement. There is an adage in the helping profession that change happens within the context of the therapeutic relationship. Not all engagement is therapeutic, but one may contend that in child welfare, change happens due to respectful and effective engagement with clients, parents, families, and children. Each interface within family systems is critical to positive outcomes. Respectful engagement is vital in assessing families, especially when services are perceived as intrusive. Respectful engagement implies meeting parents/families where they are despite the worker's own stressors and time constraints. Although it may be difficult to do when the child welfare worker has so many competing demands, it is critical to establish a beginning level of trust as a precursor to engagement. Engagement is critical in cases where parents or families are resistant, and, perhaps more importantly, successful engagement is key to understanding the familial context. Rawlings and Blackmer (2019) draw attention to the need for effective engagement and note that "it has been long recognized as a critical component of the helping process" (p. 441). What is the child welfare worker's role in engaging understandably reticent families?

Rawlings and Blackmer (2019) assert that "child protection workers must skillfully balance both the development of [the] relationship and the use of mandated authority. Yet child welfare workers are often unprepared in how to effectively engage a client presenting as resistant" (p. 441) as they execute their mandated duties. The responsibility of child welfare professionals is to balance establishing a relational interface with clients while also using their mandated authority. This balance presents a significant level of complexity to the engagement process. The ability to remain flexible can be challenging when dealing with complex issues like abuse and neglect. The balancing act does not always come naturally. This skill is not inculcated enough through training and professional development opportunities (Rawlings & Blackmer, 2019). Nevertheless, supervision and opportunities for peer mentoring/support, modeling/video simulations, and other empathy-building exercises enhance professional child welfare professionals' abilities to engage with families more effectively (see Table 6.1).

Engagement requires acceptance of services, participation in services, and acceptance that change is inevitable (Ingram et al., 2015). Engagement occurs in varying degrees. It may be either hampered or enhanced depending on a multitude of factors that affect the engagement process (e.g., context, values, flexibility, rigidity, ability to convey empathy, transference, and countertransference issues). Any of these factors hindering engagement may amplify parent/family noncooperation. Even with the best levels of engagement, there will be instances where parents/families will not cooperate. Parents/families, for a number of reasons, may not choose to engage, may not understand the demands of the system, may become aggressive or violent, may not understand cultural and linguistic nuances, and may experience mental health challenges that prevent them from cooperating (see the Case Scenario: Family Reunification Counseling and the Angry Client).

TABLE 6.1 PROFESSIONAL DEVELOPMENT TO ENHANCE ENGAGEMENT SKILLS

WHERE PROFESSIONAL DEVELOPMENT HAPPENS	PROFESSIONAL DEVELOPMENT	IMPORTANCE OF PROFESSIONAL DEVELOPMENT IN CHILD WELFARE
Supervision *(Individual or Group)*	Weekly supervision can go a long way in child welfare. Ensuring that proper procedures are followed and engaging in reflective practice with expert feedback are critical to quality work. Individual and group supervision is critical to professional growth. Group supervision can provide critical peer feedback.	Preparing for supervision is key to professional growth. It is the responsibility of both parties to organize an agenda, add to it, and stick with it. The idea of mutual agenda setting sets the tone for the professional responsibility one should take in executing their clinical duties. Supervision may be a great place to do the anticipatory work needed when meeting a parent/family for the first time.
Peer Mentoring/ Support	Peers or more experienced workers can be responsible for mentoring newer workers. Mentors provide guidance about agency policies and procedures and model the way for others. Mentors provide key professional support, encouragement, knowledge, and skills transfer.	Peer support can be crucial in understanding the parent/family perspective and may provide insights into depersonalizing negative interactions. Mentors can help new workers understand typical reactions parents may have to child welfare involvement.
Modeling/ Video Simulations	Rawlings and Blackmer (2019) point to the importance of using *simulation* in order to prepare and train new workers for critical elements of practice, including micro skills focused on how to enter a home, interviewing, and risk assessment.	Modeling and video simulations are important tools for training new workers and helping them understand what to anticipate while trying to engage parents/families.

(continued)

TABLE 6.1 PROFESSIONAL DEVELOPMENT TO ENHANCE ENGAGEMENT SKILLS
(continued)

WHERE PROFESSIONAL DEVELOPMENT HAPPENS	PROFESSIONAL DEVELOPMENT	IMPORTANCE OF PROFESSIONAL DEVELOPMENT IN CHILD WELFARE
Cultural Empathy Building	Empathy is a cornerstone of the helping profession and plays a critical role in understanding, assessing, and engaging others. Empathy and cultural empathy help professionals understand the intersectional realities of people's life experiences. In child welfare, it is important to recognize when cultural differences may be strained due to previous experiences. For instance, in cases where there has been little cross-cultural contact and past experiences have been negative, the worker's ability to understand and empathize with the parent/family may be key to effective engagement.	The best way of cultivating empathy among child welfare professionals is to accept differences, look for strengths, see the humanity of the parent/family, embrace the dignity and worth of every human being, and conduct a fair and unbiased assessment. If the worker is able to engage the parent/family in an unbiased manner it can lead to greater participation in services.
Continuing Professional Development and Training	Professional development training provides opportunities to remain current on the latest evidence-based interventions and practices, increases the professional's knowledge and skill repertoire, and expands networking opportunities outside of one's organization.	Continuing educational and professional development are ways of engaging in lifelong learning. Child welfare professionals have an ethical responsibility to maintain their skills.

Case Scenario: Family Reunification Counseling and the Angry Client

Ms. Hicks, who grew up in poverty, had her two children removed from her home. The child welfare system removed her children despite her protests that she was innocent and did not break her toddler's arm. Ms. Hicks blamed it on her ex-boyfriend and his girlfriend. However, she had little proof that this was the case. Ms. Hicks was extremely angry about losing custody of her children and being accused of harming her baby. During a meeting with the child welfare investigator (prior to the system taking custody), she cursed the worker out, became very defensive, and spat in the worker's face, causing an abrupt end to their interview. She refused any attempts to engage in the system and became closed almost immediately. Several months after the removal of her children, Ms. Hicks engaged the system to begin working on reunification. She was referred to a social work therapist who worked well with angry clients. The therapist also participated in clinical supervision to assist in her ability to engage and work with the client, who, at this point, had also been diagnosed with borderline personality disorder. The therapist understood at intake that the parent had been resistant to engagement and had, in fact, by this point, spat on a couple of different caseworkers. The therapist began working with Ms. Hicks and allowed her to vent during the first sessions providing an opportunity for the client to be heard and establish trust. The point was that Ms. Hicks was angry and needed time to express her frustrations about how she felt she had been treated throughout the process. After allowing for this expression, explaining how counseling works, and explaining what the system requested of her, the therapist established a beginning level of rapport with Ms. Hicks, who felt heard and could move to the next level of treatment. According to the therapist, Ms. Hicks did not understand the system or the requirements she was facing to achieve family reunification. However, in addressing many cognitive distortions and assessing her desire to regain custody of her children, Ms. Hicks was better able to comply with mandated services.

Before answering the discussion questions below, review the problem again from the parent's perspective. Problem: Ms. Hicks complained of having multiple workers she could never connect with or see as a source of support. In addition, she had multiple public defenders who represented her with little time to prepare for court or get to know her case.

Ms. Hicks also had a difficult time expressing her emotions and did not speak standard English—which she felt disadvantaged her in many ways. Ms. Hicks stated that the lawyers assigned to her case and the family court judge did not listen to her and acted as if they did not understand her. In fact, she expressed feeling dismissed and invisible to them, as if she was not important. It appeared that these professionals did not extend much patience to her, which hampered her from feeling understood and engaging with the system.

(continued)

Case Scenario: Family Reunification Counseling and the Angry Client *(continued)*

Ms. Hicks felt dismissed throughout her initial contact with child welfare professionals, public defenders, and the family court judge. When she felt dismissed, she lashed out angrily and acted out the frustrations she could not adequately express.

DISCUSSION QUESTIONS

1. What type of micro-skills would have been helpful to the investigator as they attempted to engage Ms. Hicks (i.e., do you believe they did everything right or not)?

2. Why is it important to understand Ms. Hicks's diagnosis of borderline personality disorder?

3. Was the client resistant, or did the investigator fail to engage Ms. Hicks?

4. What could the other caseworkers have done differently to engage Ms. Hicks more successfully?

5. What other concerns or questions do you have about this scenario?

Barriers to Positive Engagement in Child Welfare

Barriers to positive engagement include (a) the expectation that parents/families will be willing and happy to participate in a process/system that is blaming them for harming their children; (b) the allegation of child abuse or neglect places parents/families in a defensive frame of mind; (c) the feeling of parents/families that an assumption of guilt is cast upon their entire experience; (d) is the innate and legal inability of the child welfare worker/social worker to afford the client the same level of confidentiality that other settings provide (Rawlings & Blackmer, 2019); (e) the entire process is usually overshadowed by the involuntary nature of the child welfare system itself; (f) parents/families face other societal stressors like unemployment/underemployment, low-income status, housing, and food insecurity (Rawlings & Blackmer, 2019); (g) mandated services are often shrouded with multiple demands that do not accommodate parents/family members who work lower-wage jobs, have little flexibility in their work schedule, have few social supports, lack childcare services/assistance, transportation, and other accommodations that make it possible to comply with mandated services. The parent/family may focus on systemic factors contributing to their circumstances, versus the child welfare worker, who focuses on the parent's role in the problem (Rawlings & Blackmer, 2019), which tends to place blame on them; and (h) the process of blame cascades throughout the child welfare system (e.g., the worker blames the parent, the parent blames the worker, the system blames the worker when something goes wrong, and the cycle of blame continues). Blame may impede engagement and the true process of accountability.

One way to mitigate these barriers is to contextualize them. It is important to understand reactance versus resistance in considering the context. When professional workers view resistance as reactance, they may understand it as a common and normal response (Rawlings & Blackmer, 2019). Blaming the victim can be avoided by providing a positive reframe regarding reactance and viewing it as a motivational desire to regain control (Rawlings & Blackmer, 2019). This conceptualization does not excuse parental harm or neglect of their child(ren). However, it does provide a much more cogent frame of reference when attempting to engage parents/families, especially in the initial phases of their child welfare involvement.

Furthermore, the sobering reality is that "child safety trumps other demands that may include time spent developing trust and a positive working relationship" (Rawlings & Blackmer, 2019, p. 444). With this in mind, it is critical to understand that while safety is first and foremost, engaging families is still essential at every junction in their involvement in the system. As the case example shows, while parents may be very resistant at one point in the process, they may become less resistant at other stages of their involvement in the system. Child welfare professionals must not grow weary of their attempts to engage parents/families. Successful engagement does not imply that child welfare professionals should dismiss the need to protect their safety. Nonetheless, believing in the human capacity for change may serve as a reminder of the importance of the work they do to protect children from harm.

Reflection Box 6.1

BARRIERS TO ENGAGEMENT IN THE CHILD WELFARE SYSTEM

1. Can you think of additional barriers to engaging families in child welfare?
2. Can you identify effective ways to address each of these barriers?
3. What other barriers can you identify related to systemic racism that impedes positive engagement?
4. What can child welfare professionals do to avoid the negative impact of racism on the children/families they serve?

Addressing Barriers Through Culturally Responsive Practices

Culturally responsive practices include *not* buying into the "melting pot" theory and *not* treating people as if their cultural context is unimportant. It is also essential to avoid using archetypal default positions to understand family systems and parenting practices. Other helpful tips include the following:

- Understand that all words do not mean the same thing to all people. In communication, there is a sender and a receiver who both have their own subjective interpretations of word usage and meanings.

- Avoid the assumption that everyone thinks and processes information in the same ways. Meanings of messages are influenced by more than spoken language; words and messages are often subject to individual experiences.

- Realize that parents/children may feel suspicious of a child welfare professional. Parents/families often feel threatened by the child welfare system itself. Any entity that has the power to remove children controls a family's ability to remain together.

- Avoid the pretense that one is color-blind (it ignores who people are and the racism that is endemic within our world).

- Ensure that child welfare professionals have a wide array of evidence-based interventions (EBI) available. Selecting the best EBI depends on the professional's knowledge of the gaps in service and the needs or contexts of the family/parent.

It is also essential to engage parents/children utilizing strengths-based values to promote success:

- Seek to understand how the parent/child understands their problem(s).
- Learn what the parent/child needs to maintain the child safely at home.
- Consider environmental and community strengths that may be untapped.
- Assess the family in multidimensional ways.
- Assess the family for uniqueness and potential for collaboration in goal setting.
- Avoid blame (or cause-and-effect thinking). Stress personal accountability versus blame.

It is crucial to have a genuine dialogue with parents/families/children and establish positive expectations when able, identify natural resources from their environment, and learn what they need from each other. As child welfare professionals engage parents, families, and children, it is important to identify their strengths. Discovering their strengths involves inquiring about what they know of themselves; their personal qualities, traits, and virtues (but also realistically viewing it against their actual practices); and attempting to understand the client system through the stories they tell about their culture and community.

The strengths-based perspective values the positive attributes of client systems and recognizes they are more than simple pathological organisms, even in child welfare practice. How one understands people derives from how one sees or defines problems (see Figure 6.1). Professionals may lean toward pathology-laden views rather than seeing strengths in the client system. Conversely, when

Figure 6.1 Pathology vs. Strengths

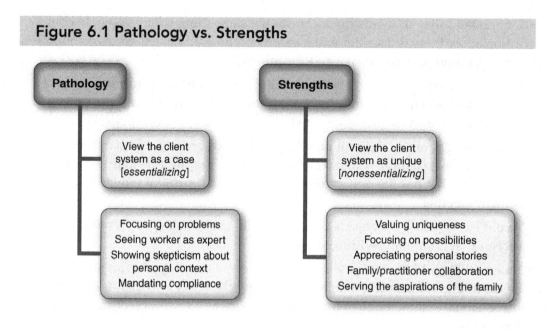

professionals view only strengths and do not assess the challenges in the client system, this can constitute a positive bias. Positive bias may favor the client system but should not ignore the need to protect the child(ren). Perhaps more fitting in the field of child welfare is to understand how to balance both challenges and strengths within client systems and always conduct self-reflection to understand how our biases prejudice our decisions in the field.

Empowering Families

Essentializing people based on an all-negative portrayal is not a realistic picture of who they are, nor is it helpful. People are more than just their labels. From a pathology-laden perspective, child welfare professionals are viewed as consummate experts and ascribe little value to the family's contribution or strengths. On the other hand, the worker utilizing the strengths perspective, despite the problem(s), still looks for uniqueness, considers possibilities in light of their strengths, and honors the family's aspirations from a collaborative vantage point.

The child welfare system operates naturally from the pathology perspective since problems are what usher families into the system. Child welfare professionals may draw on family strengths once they engage families in the assessment and service identification process. A child and family team meeting provides an opportunity to identify strengths within the family system. It also allows families to recognize and tap into their resources as another source of support.

Every child, parent, and family has strengths and challenges. The ability to engage families as partners in developing and implementing a service plan is one way to utilize their strengths and gain more cooperation. It is important for child welfare professionals to view parents/families with an understanding that "each of us is more than the worst thing we've ever done" (Stevenson, 2019, p. 17). When this concept is a part of the professional's clinical ethos, they can appreciate the humanity in every client and avoid essentializing them, which in turn unwittingly dehumanizes them. Essentializing people reduces them to prescribed categories instead of recognizing people's intersectional and unique identities.

Increasing family efficacy, empowering families, and increasing their social support networks are critical for keeping families together. Equally important is the task of child welfare professionals to realize critical components of client engagement. Workers learn to assess situations quickly but must also consider how to contextualize them as they work with parents/families. They must also utilize skills of engagement and empathy as they balance those skills with their authority. During the worker's interface with the client system, they should provide transparency by helping the parent/family understand what the system expects of them. Offering the support and resources needed to all clients is critical to successfully reaching their goals. Clients may need help acclimating to the expectations of such a large and powerful system (such as the state's child protection system) and may require a good orientation to the process. Workers should also continue to *make every* attempt to gain cooperation from the parent/family to help them achieve their goals for reunification (see Figure 6.2).

Additional strategies for engagement are:

1. *Preparation and preparatory empathy*—Review all the available information first and notice contextual cues that should not be overlooked for safety reasons. Preparatory empathy involves putting oneself in the position of a parent who will encounter the professional as an outsider intruding in their lives. It is also critical to consider how to balance agency-given authority with the need to be engaging and relational with parents/families. It is equally important to avoid

Figure 6.2 Child Welfare Worker Engagement

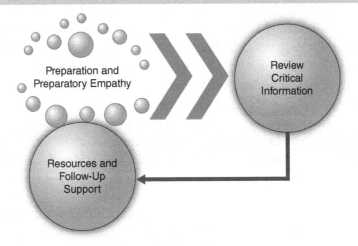

over-identifying with the parent/family; child welfare professionals must maintain professional boundaries to be effective and address biases.

2. *Critical information*—This will promote better engagement and provide critical information through honest, ethical, and transparent communication. Parents/ families need to know what is expected of them, what the next steps involve, their rights, and how their progress will be monitored. It is essential for child welfare professionals to check for clarity with the parents/families to ensure they have a mutual understanding. The child welfare professional should orient clients about their role, the processes toward reunification, the exact steps parents/families are required to take, what it means to appear before the judge in family court, and what to expect about intervention and closure.

3. *Resources and follow-up support*—Offer resources to parents/families whenever indicated and safe to do so. Parents/families should not be punished for being impoverished. The system should offer and collaborate with other systems to provide resources to help families meet their children's basic needs (e.g., housing and food assistance before removing children from their homes). In addition, child welfare professionals make continuous attempts to engage parents/families and should closely monitor cases and follow up for the best outcomes.

These strategies are critical to enhancing engagement, trust, and strengthening the parent and worker alliance. Preparing for cases and using preparatory empathy allows the worker to see the parent(s)'s humanity and anticipate their needs. Transparency demonstrates trustworthiness, a step that should not be undervalued. Providing concrete resources and follow-up support demonstrates care, builds trust, and facilitates future efficacy.

UNDERREPRESENTED FAMILIES: RACE, SOCIAL CLASS, AND ENGAGEMENT

Pellecchia and colleagues (2018) conducted a comprehensive literature review to identify the most effective strategies for supporting and engaging underrepresented families who receive child welfare services for their children. Underrepresented families include clients from minority ethnic groups or low-income households and are overrepresented within the child welfare system. Their findings suggest that "researchers and practitioners require guidance in selecting engagement strategies to reduce attrition of underrepresented families in treatment" (Pellecchia et al., 2018, p. 3141). Pellecchia and colleagues identify promising strategies for engaging families, such as:

- Collaboration with parents and foster parents on problem-solving and goal setting;

- Promotion of accessibility (to ensure parents and foster parents can access services);
- Therapist reunification counseling and monitoring (to increase internal motivation and participation, with the goal of completing services);
- Cultural respect and acknowledgment and the use of culturally informed practices (e.g., Burgos v. The State of Illinois; the Multi-ethnic Placement Act);
- Peer-pairing (pairing seasoned and new workers for field visits to model the expected professional behavior and procedural processes);
- Engagement, relationship, and rapport building;
- Role-play and rehearsal in preparation for cases (e.g., consultation and supervision).

The most successful strategies are peer support, culturally informed practices, collaboration, shared goal setting, and incentives for participation. Combining strategies of cultural acknowledgment, accessibility, and collaboration around goal setting and assessment can achieve greater engagement (see Figure 6.3).

Parent engagement has been operationalized as attitudinal engagement, referring to the beliefs parents hold about the need for treatment and its effectiveness, and behavioral engagement, which translates to their physical participation (attendance, completing homework, retention, and completing treatment; Pellecchia et al., 2018). From a cognitive behavioral lens, it is easy to see how one's belief system influences one's actions (i.e., the behavior that follows).

Figure 6.3 Commonly Combined Engagement Strategies

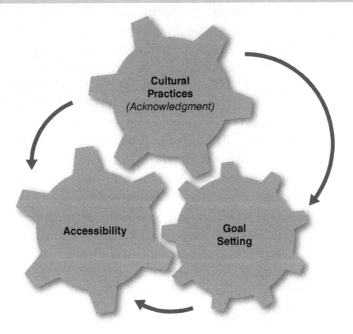

Engagement may also be affected by power differentials. Child welfare professionals must reflect on the underlying power dynamics organic to the child welfare system. Parents/families are at the mercy of child welfare professionals, lawyers, guardians ad litem, and judges. Parents/families may mistrust systems and feel powerless as they face them.

Power Differentials

The power differential of language, who decides what terms will be used for oppressed groups, is important to note. How society views people can be discerned through language. The language used to describe families living in poverty vastly differs across ethnically categorized people. For instance, in 2005, the natural disaster of Hurricane Katrina portrayed Black people in the media as looters when they took merchandise from stores to survive, while White people who did the same thing were described as people seeking sustenance for survival (Sommers et al., 2006). Is not food the sustenance necessary for all humans' survival? While recognizing that some people of all races engaged in looting, the point is that how one is portrayed in the media depends on those in power.

Power differentials exist when there is a difference in power between people in positions of authority and those in subordinated positions. Child welfare professionals operating from a position of cultural humility recognize power differentials and seek to understand a family's cultural expressions while learning from clients (Harp & Bunting, 2020). Practicing cultural humility also requires an appreciation for context and intersectional differences.

Understanding intersectionality along with interlocking social oppressions is critical. Child welfare professionals must empathize with clients to see them as fully human despite their transgressions. Empathy is needed when they are in their most vulnerable state. When clients are not respected or viewed through an empathetic lens, the interaction professionals have with them can be disempowering and even dehumanizing, depending on how much bias enters the client-worker interface. Seeing everyone's humanity is critical to enacting social justice.

Kikulwe and colleagues (2021) highlight practices in Canada's child welfare system that contribute to perceived discriminatory practices undermining social justice. Phillips and Pon (2018) describe bio-power (management/control) that is "implicated in the fear of Blackness [and] demonstrated in instances when child welfare professionals solicit the accompaniment of police officers on home visits to Black families" in a targeted way (p. 95). In the United States, on the other hand, having a police presence at home visits is a welcomed practice when done so to protect child welfare professionals and when Black communities are not singled out. Nonetheless, the disempowerment, over surveillance, and use of power over Black families are oppressive and demonstrative of the power differential exercised without restraint or caution. Kikulwe and colleagues assert the importance of Foucault's ideas of governmentality and how child welfare systems oversurveil or criminalize communities of color.

To correct for governmentality, Kikulwe and colleagues suggest that professionals do the work of self-reflection, challenge biased and damaging views that promote anti-Blackness, and reshape systems that perpetuate power differentials. Child welfare professionals can use cultural humility, "which calls for an ongoing process of stepping back to understand one's own assumptions, biases, and values during interactions with individuals with different identities" (Kikulwe et al., 2021, p. 19). These scholars also highlight the importance of life-long learning and organizational responsibilities for inculcating more culturally responsive practices. Organizations and child welfare professionals must do more than merely attend training to reshape systems and change practices that adversely affect disenfranchised populations. It is the integration of unbiased practices and the development of self-critique that will aid in addressing power imbalances. Kikulwe and colleagues argue for a change in practices that affect immigrants/newcomers (specifically) to help them realize environmental changes/nuances and how they affect family relations, family dynamics, and parenting rules. Child welfare professionals may forge relationships with other service organizations that serve immigrant populations (Kikulwe et al., 2021).

Child welfare professionals must be able to perform a self-critique and consider their own biases and must do this as a professional habit. We next turn our attention to assessment. It is important to recognize that we all have biases and that it is critical to recognize them to mitigate them effectively.

Reflection Box 6.2

ASSESSING YOUR OWN BIASES
Assessing one's own biases requires an examination of one's own thoughts about oneself in relation to others. Begin by asking yourself questions like:

1. What do you believe about human suffering? Understanding what you believe about why people have problems is key here.

2. How do you react to people who are different from you? Do you become nervous, anxious, fearful, or judgmental, or do you embrace differences?

3. What stereotypes or assumptions do you believe about others (race, ethnicity, gender, religion, sexuality, socioeconomic status, educational level, ability/disability, immigration status, and other differences)?

4. Do your words and actions reflect how you really feel? Do you tend to stereotype when you are under pressure or overwhelmed with work demands?

5. How do you get to know people who do not live near you or frequent the same places as you?

(continued)

6. Have you ever used your privilege (if you have it) to help someone else?

7. Do you put yourself in the shoes of other parents and families and empathize with their situation when you meet them for the first time?

To learn more about yourself and your biases, go to the Implicit Project: Implicit Project Tests. There you will learn what biases you may hold about many types of differences. The tests are free, easy to take, and provide more insight into your own unencumbered thought processes.

Engaging and Empowering Families

Indeed, successful engagement requires the suspension of the view that neglect is intentional. Understanding neglect as unintentional allows the practitioner to minimize bias and to connect with parents. Optimally effective engagement contains multiple components (see Figure 6.4). In essence, respecting the dignity and worth of all individuals and utilizing a human-centered perspective positions the child welfare professional to operate from a culturally humble lens that recognizes context and systemic issues that contribute to abuse and neglect. From this perspective, the worker can empower and collaborate with parents, which encourages their participation at every level. Successful engagement may also include trauma-informed and strengths-based approaches.

The most effective way to engage families is to remember their humanity. Social work values espouse a belief in the dignity and worth of all human beings. Child welfare is a field of practice within the profession of social work (Rycus & Hughes, 1998), although pathways to child welfare include more than social work education. Nevertheless, embracing respect for differences and unique cultural values within diverse family systems is crucial for maintaining the dignity of parents/families.

Understanding how oppression and marginalization affect families' pathways into the child welfare system is important. As Harp and Bunting (2020) note, "concomitant prejudices about the moral character of those living in poverty" have a bearing on the stereotypes ascribed to such individuals in ways that "make them appear less redeemable" (p. 271). Although the authors do not specifically address child welfare in their example, economic disadvantage is a factor for the majority of parents/families involved in the system.

Empowering parents/families to participate fully in all aspects of planned interventions and inviting parental voices in decisions may enhance the process of engagement. Effective engagement also includes supporting a parent-driven process to encourage parental and familial support throughout their involvement with the child welfare system. "Consultation with and inclusion of clients is one

Figure 6.4 Effective Engagement

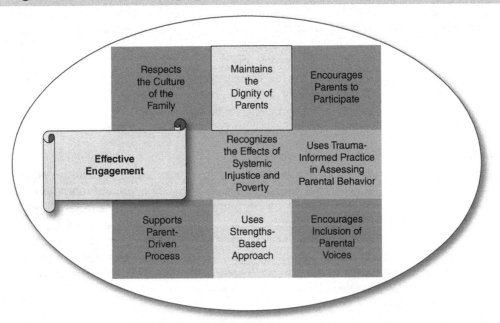

of the central tenets of quality casework. But in child welfare, birth parents have never enjoyed the position of prominence that is now standard in many agencies" (Berrick et al., 2011, p. 179). The goal is to create a helping alliance with parents that can be implemented seamlessly throughout their involvement in the system. In addition, understanding and applying a trauma-informed perspective is necessary when assessing parental behavior and decision-making. Understanding the context of an individual's behavior is key to intervening in ways that resonate with their experience and needs. The strengths perspective helps professionals understand the sobering reality that although parents/families fail to keep children safe, there are still strengths inherent within all people. The real challenge is balancing the mandate to keep children safe and bolster existing parent/family strengths.

Other fundamental principles for successful engagement include our own preparatory work. Child welfare professionals should get into the habit of preparing themselves for the meeting depending on the time allotted and the urgency of the situation (see Table 6.2).

ASSESSMENT

Interviewing the Parents/Family

Consider the parent(s)' or family's point of view at the first contact with child protective services. It starts with a knock at the door or the ring of the doorbell. All of a sudden, one of your worst nightmares has come true. A person at your door is

TABLE 6.2 PRINCIPLES FOR SUCCESSFUL ENGAGEMENT

PROCESS	SELF-REFLECTION	ACTION
Prepare for the First Visit	Consider any possible biases you may hold and why. Consider how your pre-judgments may affect your ability to conduct a fair assessment. Consider how family members may feel (fearful of the process, thinking they may be judged)	Make a plan to review all files prior to meeting the family/parent(s). Do so in a way that considers child safety and parental need.
Set the Right Tone	Consider the importance of acceptance and how you are able to convey it in an authentic manner. This means being genuine and connecting genuinely to moments that may at first appear to be disruptive but are issues that concern the parent. Reaffirm the process; convey that you are working as a team.	Plan how you will convey to the group that everyone has a voice. Plan how you will encourage families to include their own support system. Make a plan to use supervision for mitigating any possible concerns you may have.
Amplify Your Listening	Listen more rather than ask questions—sometimes listening with the *third ear* (a clinical concept) can provide keys to what questions need to be asked. Listen to the parent/family intently. Look for the unspoken parts of communication (body language, vocal tone).	Make a plan to respect all people because of a deeper belief system you have. Consider how you might intentionally build trust. Consider how you may modify your own communication based on the client's ability to understand and process information.
Strengths Based	Recognize the strengths that are present within the existing family structure. Respecting their culture and seeing how it is demonstrated is important. (This may include becoming familiar with the family's traditions, food, and activities.)	Plan how you will be collaborative with parents/families throughout the process. Identify existing supports and work on building a support network that benefits the family.

explaining that they are from the local child welfare authority and there has been a report of potential abuse or neglect involving your children. A multitude of emotions may overwhelm you. You feel frightened, confused, and angry, all at the same time. Your mind becomes perplexed by a flurry of questions. What should you do? How do you react? Do you let the person in your house? Should you call a lawyer? Do you even know a lawyer to call? Will they believe anything you say? Are they going to take your children away? All these thoughts and feelings could be accurate depending on what you have heard or what you may have previously experienced. The question remains for parents: What happens when they open the door?

Child welfare professionals have the arduous task of forging a relationship with the parent/family after their first point of contact with investigators. The task, depending on the goal (e.g., family reunification, intact family services, child removal), becomes one requiring ongoing services, case management, monitoring, or referral and support services. No matter the length of the interactions between the child welfare professional and the parent/family, a relational approach is essential. Building effective relationships with families of color can be more challenging due to distrust of the system, systemic racism, family surveillance, and overzealous community policing. Establishing trust is the first level of building a successful collaborative relationship where parents feel empowered enough to share their needs and develop plans for meeting them.

Interviewing the Child

Newlin (2015) and colleagues provide guidelines for child forensic interviewing. Several things should be considered:

1. No two children relate their experiences the same way, so the level of detail and clarity may differ. How the child recounts the story of their abuse may depend on the interviewers' behavior and ability to engage the child, the familial context and relational ties, and the child's sense of agency.
2. The literature on child interviewing shows that repeated questioning and duplicating interviews are not necessarily helpful (Brubacher et al., 2019; Child Welfare Information Gateway, 2017; Swerdlow-Freed, 2017).
3. Generally, interviewers should learn to sit with silence, avoid prompting too soon, use open-ended questions, and establish rapport with the child.
4. Interviewers should elicit detailed responses from children early in the interview because it enhances their responses later. This may encourage more detailed responses and increase their comfort with the interviewer.

It is also suggested that those newer to the field of child welfare conduct child interviews under the supervision of more skilled workers. It is also essential to understand metacognition, development, children with disabilities, and the type of abuse and duration.

Metacognition and Child Interviews

Metacognition (i.e., thinking about thinking) in child interviewing is important. Metacognition involves the practitioner's ability to perceive whether or not the child understands the interview question(s). An older child may have a greater fund of knowledge and recall, enabling them to answer more questions (Newlin et al., 2015).

Development may impact a child's ability to engage in forensic interviewing. Depending on a child's chronological age, they may not understand concepts that frame time (e.g., tomorrow, for a long time, how long). Culture also shapes development. "A child's family, social network, socioeconomic environment, and culture influence his or her development, linguistic style, perception of experiences, and ability to focus attention" (Newlin et al., 2015, p. 4).

CHILDREN WITH DISABILITIES

Children with disabilities are at a high risk of maltreatment. Interviewing such child victims of abuse can be challenging as there may be limits to their ability to communicate effectively (Wyman et al., 2019). Wyman and colleagues note that while deficits in intellectual functioning impact a child's "ability to use age-appropriate communication, abstract thinking, reasoning, and judgment in everyday situations . . . deficits in learned adaptive behaviors . . . can limit a child's ability to meet community standards of personal independence and social responsibility" (p. 170). They also note that these "cognitive and adaptive deficits cannot be attributed to linguistic diversity and cultural differences" (Wyman et al., 2019, p. 170). A child with an intellectual disability can have trouble with recall, affecting their overall ability to be descriptive about their abuser. Besides intellect, the emotional needs of the youth with intellectual disabilities must be addressed during the interview. Depending on the perpetrator's actions, the child may also have difficulty discerning when a personal boundary has been crossed. Because of these and many other issues related to the developing needs of intellectually disabled children, Newlin and colleagues (2015) suggest that interviewers utilize the services and expertise of local disability specialists. Local area experts who already work with children with disabilities and their parents can suggest specific accommodations necessary to place the child at ease. It is important to note that while it is generally recommended to limit the number of interviews, conducting more than one interview may be necessary to gain the child's trust and adapt to the child's specific needs for communication and time usage. However, practitioners are cautioned not to interview the child too often, as this can contribute to the child's confusion.

Sumampouw and colleagues (2020) recommend that adults who conduct interviews use open-ended questions and standard protocols to elicit the strongest testimonials from children. They suggest the following protocols that may be used:

- The Cognitive Interview (Fisher & Geiselman, 1992)
- The Memorandum of Good Practice (Davies & Westcott, 1999)
- The Step-Wise Interview (Yuille et al., 1993)
- The Ten Step Investigative Interview (Lyon, 2005)
- The National Institute of Child Health and Development (NICHD) Interview Protocol (Lamb et al., 2018)

These interview protocols have the potential to maximize the child's narrative while minimizing the contamination of that information (Sumampouw et al., 2020). It is critical to provide a safe and child-friendly environment regardless of the protocol. These protocols are intended to be victim-sensitive to preserve the child's well-being and avoid contaminating the information gathered. These interview guidelines also promote a certain level of fidelity.

Assessment Tools

Use of Ecomaps

In 1975, the ecomap was introduced as an assessment tool for child welfare (Hartman, 1978). Hartman developed the ecomap as a part of the Child Welfare Learning Laboratory at the University of Michigan's Social Work Program for continuing education in human services. Since then, ecomaps have become standard practice in child welfare by some practitioners. It is essential to know how a child and family are situated within their immediate environment. Hence, family systems are assessed by using ecomaps to determine an individual's connections within their social and community settings (Libbon et al., 2019). It is important to note the number of connections one has in a community and the quality of those connections. In essence, the ecomap can help detect where boundaries are open or closed and how the individual perceives the self in relation to others (e.g., their social acceptance). "These systems can include immediate family, extended family, or community groups such as church[es], school[s], peer groups of friends, or other social groups" (Libbon et al., 2019, p. 437).

The ecomap may be drawn by starting with the client as the center of the graphic, then creating circles representing relational and community ties. Next, the practitioner draws lines to depict the quality of the relationships in the ecomap to determine where relationships with family, friends, and community supports may be weak, broken, strained, closed, strong, independent, or dependent. Additionally, a practitioner may assess how an individual engages with other systems to ascertain how they either impede or enhance family or individual functioning. Community systems may include schools, service agencies, churches/synagogues/mosques/temples/halls, police systems, courts, city government, federal support, and mental and physical healthcare.

It is also critical to pay attention to power relations and how immigrant or undocumented parents engage when using ecomaps. For example, if a family is undocumented, they may hide information about extended family or connection to community resources for fear of deportation. In addition, in some communities, people may not venture out of their immediate community for fear of racist treatment and oppression. In antiracist sentiment, this is referred to as the *foot of oppression*. The foot of oppression highlights historical and current relationships where those in power enact policies and practices that limit access for vulnerable communities (e.g., immigrant, Black, poor, and other communities of color). As

Figure 6.5 Ecomap

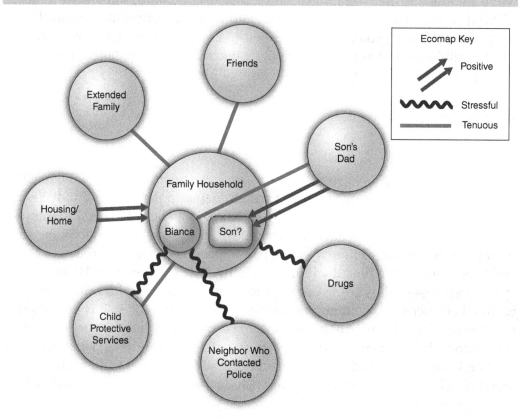

a result, vulnerable communities continue to be leery of outsider input and may view these systems as a threat to their family's stability. Therefore, when an ecomap is devoid of vital connections to support services in the community, it is crucial to understand the context of immigrant families. The ecomap may also include involuntary connections to authoritarian entities (e.g., court, police, child welfare, or mandated substance use services), which should be denoted by lines indicating stress (see Figure 6.5).

Use of Genograms

Genograms have been used for over 50 years and may be as in-depth or brief as needed. Genograms visually depict a family's composition, structure, and relationships across multiple generations. Genograms can be helpful to child welfare professionals and clients; some practitioners believe it helps them recall families for years after their cases have been closed. It is the visual picture that may reveal family secrets or shed light on certain elements of the family an individual has just discovered. Genograms may reveal family patterns, connections, disconnections, and secrets or even bring a sense of honor, guilt, survival, or pride.

Genograms are widely used to help detect the family's ways of functioning, contexts, relationships, and sources of strength over several generations. It is generally recommended to include a minimum of three generations. Genograms tell a story that illustrates the complexities of the family system.

The practitioner uses standard symbols to convey the details about a family, who is connected to whom and how, living and deceased relatives, relational ties (strengths and weaknesses), work and school information, and other contextual patterns (e.g., sobriety, substance use, births, miscarriages, marriages, divorces, trauma, well-being, education, medical and mental health histories). Generally, double lines identify the person for whom the genogram is made; circles represent females, squares represent males, circles with triangles inserted inside represent homosexual females, squares with triangles inserted inside represent homosexual males, and dotted broken triangles inside either box represent bisexual males or females (squares or circles). To depict a transgender male transitioning to a female, use a circle surrounded by a square; a transgender female to male is represented by a square surrounded by a circle (Barsky, 2022). There are numerous symbols that each practitioner decides how and when to use to identify gender fluidity, gender unknown, pregnancies, and other life occurrences. See Figure 6.6.

Figure 6.6 Genogram Symbols for Gender Inclusivity, Expression, and Identity

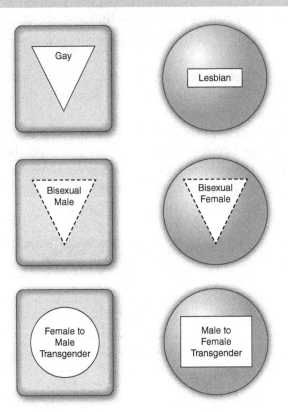

Some questions are helpful when meeting with a client to make a genogram during the assessment process. As the practitioner gains experience in co-creating genograms with clients, they may add additional questions to the list. A beginning list of prompts and questions follows:

Prompts/questions to use when creating a genogram:

- Tell me about your parents. Are they still together?
- What values were stressed in your family when you were growing up?
- What kind of relationship did your parents have?
- How was affection demonstrated (between parents and children)?
- How were you disciplined as a child?
- How did your family handle conflict? How was it addressed?
- What role did spirituality or religion play in your upbringing?
- Is there a history of substance abuse, mental health, or health concerns?
- Describe your parents' educational level and history.
- Describe your parents' current occupation(s) and employment history.
- Describe family relationships. Were you close to your parents? Were you close to your siblings?
- How did your family interact with one another (e.g., boundaries)?
- Who held family knowledge and who did not (e.g., were there family secrets)?

These prompts may be used across generations. The purpose of the genogram is to assess relationships among family members. Start with the individual's parents, then grandparents, and themselves.

Figure 6.7 is a basic genogram that shows multiple parental units, ethnicities, and current relationships between a client named Sam and the men in his family. Generally, genograms cover at least three generations; however, there may be some instances where aspects of family history are unknown. Gaps in information may also be informative of family relationships and patterns.

Reflection Box 6. 3

Applying Knowledge

1. Create a narrative explaining Sam's relational patterns in the genogram depicted in Figure 6.7. Talk about this in class as a beginning discussion about the use of genograms with clients.

2. Develop a genogram of your own (e.g., your own family, a client's family using pseudonyms, or someone you interview on campus). Depict three generations. Bring the genogram to class to discuss.

Questions for discussing the genograms:

a. Were there any surprises in completing the genogram?

b. How comfortable did you feel in completing the genogram?

c. Talk about any unconventional symbols you may have used.

d. What patterns did you notice?

e. Were there generational family secrets?

f. What did you notice about strengths and challenges?

Figure 6.7 Basic Genogram Depicting Multiple Fathers

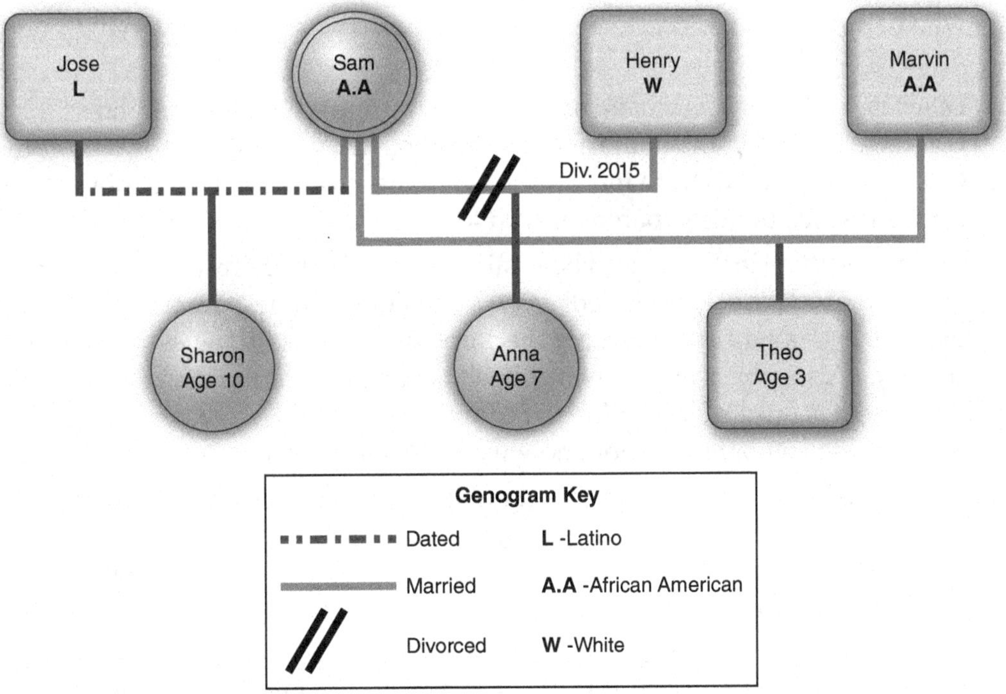

Use of Culturagrams

Culturagrams were developed by Elaine Congress, a social worker, in 1994. Her research agenda focused on cultural diversity, social work education, and social work values and ethics. Congress has continued to refine the culturagram over time; it now includes 10 categories and yields narrative information about the family's cultural background and experiences. It helps the practitioner to comprehend an immigrant family's context from a broader perspective. Yeshiva University (2021) provides a useful overview of the culturagram:

1. *Reason for relocation*—People immigrate for many reasons: to escape poverty, violence, and oppression or to join family in the United States. Many factors may influence trends in immigration.

2. *Legal status*—Family members may have mixed legal statuses (i.e., documented, undocumented, refugee, or other). When one family member is vulnerable, it can also place the entire family system at risk.

3. *Time in country/community*—It is good to understand the arrival circumstances of families and their current residence within their community. The length of time a family member has been in the country will influence their overall adjustment. The psychology of a newcomer versus someone who has already adjusted to life in a new country can produce varying points of view, familial strain, and generational differences.

4. *Language spoken at home/community*—It is important to understand how language is used in the home and community and who interprets for whom. Often children are used to interpret for parents, creating possible role confusion (i.e., between parent and child).

5. *Health benefits*—Healthcare can be vastly different in the family's country of origin and well-care expectations may differ. For example, parents may not seek well-baby care or preventive checkups since it is not done in their home country. "Also, physical and mental health are more interwoven in the United States, so it is uncomfortable for some immigrants to share personal issues with a doctor who they do not know well" (Yeshiva University, 2021, para. 11).

6. *Impact of trauma and crisis events*—Many immigrants have endured some type of premigration trauma (e.g., war, rape, violence, torture, murder of relatives, or other). These traumatic events may lead to unresolved trauma and developmental crises for children unless addressed.

7. *Contact with cultural and religious institutions, holidays, food, and clothing*—Immigrants may need help understanding holiday traditions in the new country and may continue with their own traditions. In addition, they may require a great deal of assistance in securing their basic needs (such as food and clothing).

8. *Oppression, discrimination, bias, and racism*—Immigrants have bias, prejudice, and conflicts that shape how they see things. There may be people from the same area who view the world differently. "Also, many immigrants have left a

country where they are the majority and now find themselves as the minority facing prejudice in their new home" (Yeshiva University, 2021, para. 14).

9. *Values about education and work*—Many immigrants revere authority figures and value education. "They come from backgrounds where parents would bring a child to school, and the teachers would take over. This practice is quite different from the American educational system in which parents and teachers form a partnership" (Yeshiva University, 2021, para. 15).

10. *Values about family: Structure, power, myths, and rules*—"Many immigrant families come from traditional, patriarchal backgrounds in which the father is the head of the house. Meanwhile, other cultures consider family needs to trump that of the individual" (Yeshiva University, 2021, para. 16). Child welfare professionals should seek to understand the context of the family structure and how power is arranged and how rules are carried out.

Congress warns professionals about the danger of essentializing others: "Considering a family only in terms of a generic cultural identity, however, may lead to over generalization and stereotyping" (2004, p. 251). Understanding the full context of all family members' cultural experiences, traditions, journeys, and beliefs is essential. It is also important to listen and to gain an understanding of each client's uniqueness. When it comes to culture and values, the family is the expert of their own experience, and the child welfare professional should not make assumptions about people based solely on their cultural background. Cultural background is only one piece of the picture and may not be understood as a monolithic experience. We cannot place people in neat little boxes devoid of personalized meanings (see Figure 6.8).

Figure 6.8 Culturagram

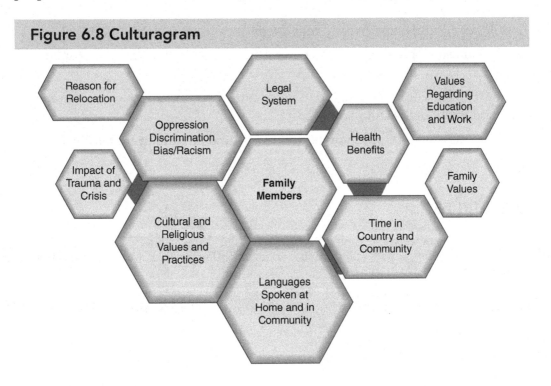

Each state will have its own assessment tools. The professional must effectively assess the adequacy of the tool as an unbiased instrument. Child welfare professionals should learn what is expected of them based on where they work and honor the humanity of the families they serve. The point is to use the tools and relational connections when assessing people.

CHAPTER SUMMARY

This chapter focused on effective ways of engaging families and children in child welfare. The authors conducted a robust discussion of the barriers to engagement and the elements of successful engagement. A review of several protocols for forensic interviews was provided. Additionally, an explanation and examples of assessment tools such as the ecomap, genogram, and culturagram have been included. It is important in child welfare to understand the family within its full context. The ecomap shows the person's connections to others; the genogram is helpful in understanding family patterns, and the culturagram is useful in contextualizing a family's cultural strains and cultural interpretations of traumatic events. Being sensitive to cultural belief systems can also be viewed as a way of respecting differences. Child welfare professionals need to engage in preparatory work, cultural empathy, and supervision/mentoring for guidance in the field.

DISCUSSION QUESTIONS

1. What is cultural empathy, and how might it be used in child welfare?
2. What are some possible reasons parents or families may disengage from the system? (Answer this from a cultural viewpoint.)
3. How can an ecomap be used to identify existing or missing resources in the environment of the child and family?
4. What assessments would you use to understand an immigrant family and why?

RESOURCES

Annie E. Casey Foundation
https://www.aecf.org/topics/child-protection?gclid=EAIaIQobChMIr6XXmYDP-wIVFcmUC
    R3s4g89EAAYAiAAEgIAqvD_BwE

Child Welfare Information Gateway
https://www.childwelfare.gov/topics/systemwide/assessment/family-assess/sources/

Harvard Project Implicit
https://implicit.harvard.edu/implicit/

Family Assessment in Child Welfare: The Illinois DCFS Integrated Assessment Program in Policy and Practice / Chapin Hall at the University of Chicago
https://eric.ed.gov/?id=ED507227

NASW - Child Welfare
https://www.socialworkers.org/Practice/Child-Welfare

 SPRINGER PUBLISHING **CONNECT™** | A robust set of instructor resources designed to supplement this text is located at **http://connect.springerpub.com/content/book/978-0-8261-5285-5.** Qualifying instructors may request access by emailing **textbook@springerpub.com.**

REFERENCES

Barsky, A. E. (2022). Sexuality- and gender-inclusive genograms: Avoiding heteronormativity and cisnormativity. *Journal of Social Work Education, 58*(2), 379–389. https://doi.org/10.1080/10437797.2020.1852637

Berrick, J. D., Young, E. W., Cohen, E., & Anthony, E. (2011). 'I am the face of success': Peer mentors in child welfare. *Child & Family Social Work, 16*(2), 179–191. https://escholarship.org/uc/item/0nc6p0dj

Brubacher, S. P., Poole, D. A., Dickinson, J. J., LaRooy D., Szojka, Z. A., & Powell, M. B. (2019). Effects of interviewer familiarity and supportiveness on children's recall across repeated interviews. *Law and Human Behavior, 43*(6), 507–516. https://doi.org/10.1037/lhb0000346

Child Welfare Information Gateway. (2017). *Forensic interviewing: A primer for child welfare professionals.* U.S. Department of Health & Human Services, Children's Bureau. https://www.childwelfare.gov/pubs/factsheets/forensicinterviewing

Congress, E. P. (1994). The use of culturagrams to assess and empower culturally diverse families. *Families in Society: The Journal of Contemporary Human Services, 75*(9), 531–540. https://doi.org/10.1177/104438949407500901

Congress, E. P. (2004). Cultural and ethical issues in working with culturally diverse patients and their families: The use of the culturagram to promote cultural competent practice in health care settings. *Social Work in Health Care, 39*(3–4), 249–262. https://doi.org/10.1300/j010v39n03_03

Davies, G. M., & Westcott, H. L. (1999). Interviewing child witnesses under the memorandum of good practice: A Research Review (No. 115). Home Office, Policing and Reducing Crime Unit, Research, *Development and Statistics Directorate.* ISBN 1-84082-328-3

Fisher, R. P., & Geiselman, R. E. (1992). *Memory-enhancing techniques for investigative interviewing: The cognitive interview.* Charles C. Thomas Publisher. ISBN 0-398-06121-1

Harp, K. L., & Bunting, A. M. (2020). The racialized nature of child welfare policies and the social control of Black bodies. *Social Politics: International Studies in Gender, State & Society, 27*(2), 258–281. https://doi.org/10.1093/sp/jxz039

Hartman, A. (1978). Diagrammatic assessment of family relationships. *Social Casework, 59*(8), 465–476. https://doi.org/10.1177/104438947805900803

Ingram, S. D., Cash, S. J., Oats, R. G., Simpson, A., & Thompson, R. W. (2015). Development of an evidence-informed in-home family services model for families and children at risk of abuse and neglect. *Child & Family Social Work, 20,* 139–148. https://doi.org/10.1111/cfs.12061

Kikulwe, D., Falihi, A., & Watkinson, A. M. (2021). Newcomer parents with child welfare histories: Dilemmas of caring and control. *Journal of Public Child Welfare, 17*(1), 1–23. https://doi.org/10.1080/15548732.2021.1965941

Lamb, M. E., Brown, D. A., Hershkowitz, I., Orbach, Y., & Esplin, P. W. (2018). *Tell me what happened: Questioning children about abuse* (2nd ed.). John Wiley & Sons. ISBN 9781118881675.

Libbon, R., Triana, J., Heru, A., & Berman, E. (2019). Family skills for the resident toolbox: The 10-min genogram, ecomap, and prescribing homework. *Academic Psychiatry, 43*(4), 435–439. https://doi.org/10.1007/s40596-019-01054-6

Lyon, T. D. (2005). *Ten step investigative interview*. http://works.bepress.com/thomaslyon/5

Newlin, C., Cordisco Steele, L., Chamberlin, A., Anderson, J., Kenniston, J., Russell, A., Stewart, H., & Vaughan-Eden, V. (2015). *Child forensic interviewing: Best practices*. Office of Juvenile Justice & Delinquency Prevention. Bulletin. https://ojjdp.ojp.gov/sites/g/files/xyckuh176/files/pubs/248749.pdf

Pellecchia, M., Nuske, H. J., Straiton, D., McGhee Hassrick, E., Gulsrud, A., Iadarola, S., Vejnoska, S. F., Bullen, B., Haine-Schlagel, R., Kasari, C., Mandell, D. S., Smith, T., & Stahmer, A. C. (2018). Strategies to engage underrepresented parents in child intervention services: A review of effectiveness and co-occurring use. *Journal of Child and Family Studies, 27*(10), 3141–3154. https://doi.org/10.1007/s10826-018-1144-y

Phillips, D., & Pon, G. (2018). Anti-Black racism, bio-power, and governmentality: Deconstructing the suffering of Black families involved in child welfare. *Journal of Law and Social Policy, 28*, 81–100.

Rawlings, M. A., & Blackmer, E. R. (2019). Assessing engagement skills in public child welfare using OSCE: A pilot study. *Journal of Public Child Welfare, 13*(4), 441–461. https://doi.org/10.1080/15548732.2018.1509760

Rycus, J. S., & Hughes, R. C. (1998). *Field guide to child welfare: Foundations of child protective services* (Vol. 1). CWLA Press (Child Welfare League of America).

Sommers, S. R., Apfelbaum, E. P., Dukes, K. N., Toosi, N., & Wang, E. J. (2006). Race and media coverage of Hurricane Katrina: Analysis, implications, and future research questions. *Analyses of Social Issues and Public Policy, 6*(1), 39–55. https://doi.org/10.1111/j.1530-2415.2006.00103.x

Stevenson, B. (2019). *Just mercy: A story of justice and redemption*. One World.

Sumampouw, N. E., Otgaar, H., La Rooy, D., & De Ruiter, C. (2020). The quality of forensic child interviewing in child sexual abuse cases in Indonesia. *Journal of Police and Criminal Psychology, 35*(2), 170–181. https://doi.org/10.1007/s11896-019-09342-5

Swerdlow-Freed, D. (2017). The nuts and bolts of a child forensic interview. Forensic Interviewing of Children, Forensic Services. *Swerdlow-Freed Psychology*. https://www.drswerdlow-freed.com/nuts-bolts-child-forensic-interview/#:~:text=A%20properly%20conducted%20forensic%20interview,cognitive%20abilities%20and%20verbal%20skills

Toros, K., DiNitto, D. M., & Tiko, A. (2018). Family engagement in the child welfare system: A scoping review. *Children and Youth Services Review, 88*, 598–607. https://doi.org/10.1016/j.childyouth.2018.03.011

Wyman, J. D., Lavoie, J., & Talwar, V. (2019). Best practices for interviewing children with intellectual disabilities in maltreatment cases. *Exceptionality, 27*(3), 167–184. https://doi.org/10.1080/09362835.2018.1425623

Yeshiva University. (2021). *Practical applications of the culturagram in social work*. https://online.yu.edu/wurzweiler/blog/practical-applications-culturagram-social-work

Yuille, J. C., Hunter, R., Joffe, R., & Zaparniuk, J. (1993). Interviewing children in sexual abuse cases. In G. S. Goodman & B. L. Bottoms (Eds.), *Child victims, child witnesses: Understanding and improving testimony* (pp. 95–115). Guilford Press.

7

Placement Disruption and Family Reunification

LEARNING OBJECTIVES

By the end of the chapter, you will be able to:

- Understand attachment in the context of the child welfare system.
- Demonstrate the ability to assess the needs of children and families.
- Review the various ways the child welfare system impacts children.
- Understand the different types of placements available to children in the child welfare system.
- Discuss the importance of family connections and lifelong implications.

INTRODUCTION

It is important to discuss the impact that entering the child welfare system has on children and families. Disruptions in the family system and children being separated from their families can be highly traumatic, particularly when children are placed outside the family into nonrelative foster care. Depending on the stage of development of the child during the family disruption, children can be impacted in various ways. Trauma often manifests in children differently, and their behavior can vary depending on their age, personality, and family circumstances. Additionally, the duration and intensity of disrupted attachment can also impact the severity and subsequent level of trauma. Attachment disruption affects the child's ability to connect with others, regulate emotions, and achieve academic success. The decision to remove children from families should be made with great care, considering the impact of this action on families, and finding ways to involve extended family members when possible. Extended family members provide the children with a sense of support and security because of preexisting familiarity and possible connections. Being placed with family decreases the level of trauma that the separation causes. Extended family and fictive kin also hold some level of comfort and familiarity with children in care. Families, even distant ones, have similar connections, values, cultures, or routines, which may bring comfort and belonging to the child. Whether a child is placed with a relative or in a traditional foster home, foster care providers must work toward providing stable and nurturing environments for the child and minimize placement disruptions whenever possible. Providing professional support, such as therapy, is critical to address the emotional and psychological impact of being placed in foster care.

Additionally, many children in foster care experience disruptions in their foster care homes. The best outcomes require stability for the children and youth who have already been separated from their families. Changing foster placements can add to the trauma these children experience.

Family reunification services, which include assessments, child and family team meetings, service planning, parent/child visitation, and referrals, are critical in planning for children to return to their families. Engaging parents and working closely with families can create an environment of trust and commitment and potentially increase the success of reunification. Risk and safety assessments and aftercare services are paramount in families' continued success after reunification.

This chapter addresses the trauma of family disruption, attachment theory, challenges of foster placement disruption, and the journey to reunification. It also explores the intersection of media and political influence on child welfare and how they shape the public's opinion of the work being done in this field. Media and political influence also impact child welfare professionals' self-efficacy. In the aftermath of tragedy, public, legal, and political opinions shape child welfare policies and procedures.

ENTRY INTO THE SYSTEM

Entry into the child welfare system can happen in many different ways. Through a hotline call, an assessment is made to determine if child protection should intervene. If an investigation is warranted, once the investigation is completed, a determination is made regarding the disposition of the case. There are several directions that investigations can go. If an investigation is unfounded, the case can be closed, or if there is reason to believe that the family can benefit from supportive services, the case could be opened as an intact family case where the children are left in the parents' home. A child welfare professional is assigned to work with the family in the home, visiting the family consistently, assessing for safety continuously, and recommending any service referrals the family needs.

Reviewing how different ethnicities are represented is vital when discussing entry into the child welfare system. According to the Child Welfare Information Gateway (2021), American Indian and Alaska Native children comprised 1% of the U.S. child population and 2% of the foster care population. In 2019, African American children were 14% of the U.S. child population and made up 23% of the children in foster care. In 2018, Latinx children, while underrepresented in the national picture, were overrepresented in 20 states (Child Welfare Information Gateway, 2021). Racial disproportionality in child welfare exists when one's ethnic group is a lower percentage in the population compared to the high percentage in the child welfare system. "Racial disparities occur at nearly every major decision-making point along the child welfare continuum" (Child Welfare Information Gateway, 2021, p. 2). African Americans and other ethnic groups are adversely affected by this occurrence which happens all too frequently.

Many scholars note that African American, American Indian, and Alaska Native families experience more reports of maltreatment that are substantiated, longer involvement in the system, more out-of-home placements, longer reunification timeframes, and increased likelihood of having their parental rights terminated than their White counterparts (Garcia et al., 2016; Maguire-Jack et al., 2020; Wildeman et al., 2020; Yi et al., 2020).

If safety conditions do not allow the youth to remain in the home with their parents, the youth is taken into custody and placed in an alternative placement. There are various types of placement options for youth who come into care. The least restrictive setting for any youth is to be placed with relatives to preserve family connections and reduce the trauma caused when youth are removed from their parents and everyday family lives. If there are no relatives available, foster home placement is the next level of placement for the youth.

Being away from the familiarity of the family can cause significant trauma for youth in the care of child welfare agencies and, at times, lead to significant social and emotional concerns. There are also times that youth come into the care of child welfare agencies with preexisting social, emotional, or medical concerns due to being in an abusive or neglectful environment. These youth need a higher level of care, which requires a specialized/treatment foster home, group home, or residential facility. Specialized treatment means that professionals who work in group homes and residential facilities have specific training related to structure, behavior modification, and clinical treatment. Foster parents operate specialized foster homes with specific training to manage behavioral and medical needs.

In some instances, children come to the attention of child welfare agencies due to habitual delinquency. These youth have a history of uncontrollable behavior or behaviors that parents are unable to manage. Youth with these extreme behaviors will likely be placed in secured (i.e., locked) residential treatment programs. The goal is to provide structure and clinical support to alleviate or decrease unmanageable symptoms. The overall aim is to stabilize the behavior and provide a safe and successful transition back into the community.

No matter how children enter the system, the objectives are to address the child's clinical needs, treat the dysregulation of behavior (i.e., rehabilitation), and launch the child successfully into the next phase of their journey. Some youth return home, some move into a less restrictive setting, and some move into independence (as young adults).

Children who enter the child welfare system have different levels of attachment, which can affect the stability of their placements. Child welfare professionals must understand the child's connection to their families regardless of their experiences.

ATTACHMENT THEORY

The question of how human beings form close connections with caregivers is important for understanding what happens in child welfare when children are separated from their parents. Attachment theory was developed by British psychologist John Bowlby (1907–1991) more than 70 years ago and was further studied by Mary Salter Ainsworth (1913–1999; Bretherton, 1992). Attachment begins in infancy and continues throughout one's life span. "The primary caregiver is usually the mother, and strong bonds are formed within minutes of giving birth" (Lee, 2003, para. 4). The premise is that babies need basic care and a reliable caregiver to take care of them.

Bowlby spent more than 2 years in a medical facility where he observed children separated from their parents due to hospitalization. Bowlby recognized children's dependence on their parents to meet their basic needs and their mothers' dependence on the larger society to meet their economic needs. To grow up mentally healthy, Bowlby (1952) asserted that "the infant and young child should experience a warm, intimate, and continuous relationship with his mother (or permanent mother substitute) in which both find satisfaction and enjoyment" (p. 11). Bowlby viewed attachment and the need to connect to caregivers as a natural occurrence. According to Bowlby, attachment happens in four stages (see Figure 7.1). These stages are not fixed or rigid categories.

Ainsworth expounded on Bowlby's attachment theory and viewed mother–child attachments in three basic stages (see Figure 7.2). One major premise is the importance of a child's secure attachments before expanding to other attachment figures.

A secure attachment occurs when children demonstrate a sense of security. Children can rely on their parents/primary caregivers to meet their basic needs and provide support and comfort when securely attached. Children know they can depend on caregivers' support and know their needs will be met. Children with secure attachments may adjust to their out-of-home placements with fewer behavioral concerns than children with less secure attachments.

An insecure attachment results when children experience uncertainty and become upset when their parent/caregiver leaves (Keller & Grumbach, 2022). When children's parental attachments have been insecure due to abuse/neglect, it is further exacerbated when children are placed in foster care in unfamiliar environments.

Figure 7.1 Bowlby's Four Stages of Attachment

Pre-Attachment	Indiscriminate Attachment	Specific Attachment	Multiple Attachments
(Birth–6 weeks) Infants are seen as asocial and may respond to many types of stimuli.	**(6 weeks–7 months)** Infants can now enjoy the company of their caregiver and are responsive to them.	**(7–9 months)** Baby looks to specific caregivers to meet their needs. Child needs a secure foundation and nurturing environment. During this time, babies show a fear of strangers and separation anxiety.	**(10 months and older)** Baby is more independent and has begun to form many attachments. The parents are usually the main attachment but extended family, friends, and alternate caregivers also serve as attachment figures.

Figure 7.2 Ainsworth's Three Stages of Attachment

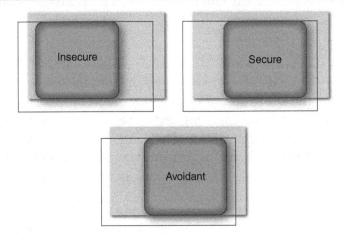

Avoidant attachment—Children who have experienced abuse or neglect may sometimes appear indifferent to their caregivers. They have learned that although they seek attachment, the parent/caregiver does not always meet their needs (Van Rosmalen, 2015).

An understanding of attachment theory is necessary for child welfare professionals. It will provide them with a better understanding of the child's experiences. A child may react differently when separated from their parents/caregivers, despite their harmful or abusive relationship, depending on their level of prior attachment. Interpreting children's behavior in new situations, including post-separation adjustment, is crucial to addressing the child's holistic needs. Children who have experienced an attachment disruption early in their development may struggle to establish and maintain new relationships. The child welfare professional should use this knowledge to appropriately anticipate the child's emotional, social, educational, and developmental needs. Understanding how the child is impacted in these areas will allow the child welfare professional to support foster parents as they work to stabilize the child in their placement. This understanding can also aid foster parents in anticipating the needs of the child whose life has just been upended.

After a thorough investigation, if a determination is made that a child has been abused or neglected, the child is either left in the home of the parent and referred to intact family services or family preservation services, or the child is removed from the home and placed either with a relative or in foster care. If a child is placed in care, the assigned caseworker ensures that parent–child visitation is arranged within 5 days (this may vary from state to state), and the caseworker begins the initial assessment. Once the assessment is completed, a child and family team meeting is arranged to discuss the assessment and service referrals. During this meeting, the client service plan is developed with the family. Collaborating with parents/families can bolster trust and help with buy-in and cooperation.

The Developing Child

When a child is removed from their family and placed in foster care, they are impacted emotionally. Being placed in foster care is a complex issue and can give rise to various developmental concerns and behavioral problems that need to be clinically addressed. Although foster care is a protective measure to provide a safe environment for youth, being removed from family and a familiar environment can lead to anxiety and depression, manifesting in many ways.

- *Trauma*—This can result from both the cause and remedy of the situation; that is, the abuse or neglect a child experiences and the subsequent separation from their parents and family. Children who experience trauma may demonstrate behavioral dysregulation, anger, and social and academic failure.

- *Emotional toll*—Being separated from one's family has an increased emotional impact on a child. As children experience multiple disappointments and failed promises, they may feel abandoned. Children's confidence, feelings of safety, and sense of self-worth may be undermined.

- *Disrupts family routine*—The family/parental routine is disrupted, the parents' responsibilities are unsettled, and they may even lose financial resources (e.g., housing vouchers when children are no longer in the home, leading to a loss of housing, which also interrupts their work schedules). Parents may lose benefits, including *Section 8* since they are no longer eligible for the program when they lose custody of their children. Parents may go back on a waitlist, delaying reinstatement for several months or years.

- *Loss of the breadwinner*—This affects the economic stability of the family. Even when the partner has been abusive, if they are the breadwinner, there may be an emotional, financial, and relational backlash that the family experiences.

- *Changes in family dynamics*—Family disruptions may usher in a new set of household rules, disciplinary consequences, and overall structural changes, making it difficult for children to adjust. Disruptions may include placement in foster care and an abusive parent being mandated to leave the home.

- *Self-image/cultural identity*—Children's cultural grounding can be compromised, which creates issues with low self-esteem and lower self-confidence. Children who are placed across cultures can lose their sense of self and cultural connections. For instance, Spanish-speaking children placed in non-Spanish-speaking homes can potentially lose their ability to speak their native language, impacting their ability to communicate with their birth families.

The child welfare professional must be aware of how involvement in the system affects the developing child. Although the child is brought to safety, they still love their parents/families and have strong connections that impact their emotional, social, and cognitive functioning.

Family Disruptions and Attachment

Robertson and Bowlby (1952) identified several phases of separation: protest, despair, and detachment. As children were separated from their parent(s), these scholars found the following patterns of behavior (phases). *Protest* was viewed as separation anxiety. *Despair* manifested as grief and mourning. *Detachment* was viewed as a defense mechanism, along with denial and repression. As research further developed in the field, it affirmed earlier theories. Bretherton (1992) wrote, ". . . Bowlby maintained that infants and children experience separation anxiety when a situation activates both escape and attachment behavior" (p. 763). In essence, children who are separated from their parents experience these emotions in distinct ways based on their stage of development, maturity, life experiences, and family/cultural context.

Case Scenario: Supporting the Mendez Family

The Mendez family came to the attention of the Department of Children and Family Services because of domestic violence in the home as well as abuse against older children. Neither parent spoke English, although the eight children involved were bilingual. In addition, the parents were undocumented.

(continued)

Case Scenario: Supporting the Mendez Family (*continued*)

The father, the breadwinner in the family, was removed from the home and arrested. The children, ranging from age 2 to 18 years, were placed in various foster homes. Unfortunately, the case manager was not able to identify Spanish-speaking homes. The mother could not identify any available family members to foster the children. The mother indicated early on that she had family who would help but later denied having family members who could care for her children. The caseworker thought the mother was concerned about the legal status of relatives and refused to identify any.

CHALLENGES

1. Lack of financial resources/lack of employment.
2. Eviction from her apartment.
3. Language barrier: The judge ordered that the children be placed in Spanish-speaking homes, but the case manager could not identify any available Spanish-speaking homes.

SOLUTIONS

1. Mom was able to secure a job at McDonald's.
2. The child welfare agency assisted the mom in finding a new apartment.
3. The child welfare agency finally located three licensed foster parents that spoke Spanish.
4. The child welfare agency found a translator (for court) and Spanish-speaking community providers.

The 2-year-old in the family was entirely dependent on her older siblings, who managed her care on a daily basis (as parentified children). Parentification is assuming or being assigned total and excessive adult/parental duties. The parentified child takes on the responsibilities of caregiving and providing emotional support for their younger siblings, soothing family members, and even caring for the adult in the family (as needed). The parentified child and parent(s) engage in a role reversal (Masiran et al., 2022), and parents may seek them out for advice on important family matters.

DISCUSSION QUESTIONS

1. What are some of the possible reasons (not specifically mentioned) the children were removed from the home?

(continued)

Case Scenario: Supporting the Mendez Family (*continued*)

2. How might this attachment disruption affect each of the children's developmental progress? Think specifically of the 2-year-old as well as the other siblings who are parentified.

3. What should the case manager do to consider the cultural needs of the children as they enter foster care?

4. What more can the case manager do to support the mother in her goal for family reunification? (Consider what other resources and concrete supports would the mother need to support and nurture her children.)

Attachment and Neurodevelopment

Dr. Bruce Perry is a psychiatrist with extensive clinical research on children's mental health, trauma, and neurodevelopment. Perry's (2021) research has focused on understanding the long-term effects of trauma on children, adolescents, and adults, with the belief that childhood traumatic events change the brain's biology. In response to his research on trauma, Perry developed a model called the Neurosequential Model of Therapeutics (NMT), which is based on the idea that the impact of trauma on a child's brain can be measured and addressed through a comprehensive assessment and treatment plan. NMT considers the child's developmental history, trauma exposure, and current functioning and uses this information to guide individualized treatment intervention.

The brain grows amazingly fast during the first years of a child's life. By the time a child is 3 years old, their brain is developed at 90% of an adult brain. The first few years of a child's life are critical because of what they experience. All parts of the brain (e.g., brainstem, midbrain, limbic, cortex) may be affected by trauma. The brainstem controls blood pressure, heart rate, and body temperature. It essentially regulates the automatic functions of our bodies connected to the spinal cord, making it a part of the central nervous system. The midbrain is related to vision, hearing, arousal, sleeping/waking, and motor skills. The brain's limbic area controls our behavioral and emotional responses. As children face traumatic circumstances, it is important for child welfare professionals to understand the impact of trauma on the developing brain. The limbic area is most impacted because this is part of the brain that drives behavioral responses when survival is crucial. The cortex is at the top of the brain and processes memory, thinking, learning, problem-solving, and functions related to the five senses. Because of trauma, parts of the brain become overstimulated while other parts are not. This type of interruption to brain development has serious and lasting consequences.

Placements are often disrupted when youth in care display extreme behavioral symptoms that cannot be managed. These disruptive behaviors are due to prior trauma, separation from family, and multiple placements, which may require hospitalization. Youth in care may experience a myriad of acting out behaviors:

- Poor impulse control;
- Emotional dysregulation;
- Depression and anxiety;
- Attention deficit hyperactivity disorder; and
- Misdirected anger.

Ensuring placement stability is one way to mitigate some of the trauma the child has experienced; it helps to prevent retraumatization. Children may demonstrate internalizing or externalizing behaviors interrupting their development and household relationships. Foster parents may struggle to manage the foster child's behavior and connect with them relationally. An experience with multiple placements is known to exacerbate childhood trauma further. Disruptions can frequently occur within the child welfare system and adversely affect the child's present and long-term well-being (Vreeland et al., (2020). The more placements a child experiences, the more likely the child is to display internalizing and externalizing behaviors. Children who encounter multiple placements "may experience an increased sense of rejection and impermanence as well as difficulty forming attachments or trusting" others (Vreeland et al., 2020, p. 2).

Chambers and colleagues (2020) identify the negative impact of multiple placements for youth, including loss of relationships, low self-esteem, difficulty trusting others, exclusion from placement decisions, difficulty graduating high school, feeling unwanted by caregivers, and other long-term negative consequences. The lasting effects create long-term instability and emotionally distant relationships into adulthood.

Psychiatric, Emotional, and Behavioral Challenges

The negative impact of multiple placements for youth and all that comes with them gives rise to psychiatric, emotional, and behavioral challenges that often lead to placement disruption. The cascade of disruptions can ultimately lead to an alternative structured placement, such as a group home or residential placement. If behaviors are severe enough, they can lead a youth to become psychiatrically hospitalized due to safety concerns for the youth and those around them.

The problem with multiple placements is that, over time, youth become accustomed to having to leave their placement when foster parents are unable to manage their behaviors or they feel rejected and unable to connect or form an attachment with any foster family. Youth in foster care tend to develop their own coping strategies due to a lack of trust, lack/loss of connection, separation from their biological families, and a history of past trauma. When youth have unresolved trauma, they may sabotage placements for fear of rejection and to avoid the emotional pain of being removed from foster homes.

Engler and colleagues (2022) note that many studies show the connection of a lifetime of mental health concerns for foster children (approximately 60%). Youth in foster care with unresolved trauma may develop reactive attachment disorder (RAD). Understanding the foster child's trauma exposure is key to understanding why the behaviors exist and what interventions may be appropriate. "The number of maltreatment types experienced by a child was found to be the strongest predictor of a mental health disorder" (Engler et al., 2022, p. 260). Adverse childhood experiences (ACEs) refer to experiences that could potentially be traumatic during childhood. Children who experience traumatic events will react differently depending on the trauma's nature, severity, and frequency. In efforts to circumvent subsequent pain and stress, it will be necessary for the child to have the support of community providers, extended family, and child welfare professionals.

Broad screenings for ACEs are often recommended. The screening poses several questions about childhood experiences from a predictive framework. Critics suggest that predictions based on ACE screenings do not take resiliency into consideration and do not consider a broad enough spectrum of adversities that could impact biopsychosocial development (Engler et al., 2022; McLennan et al., 2020; Cooke et al., 2019). Defenders of ACE screenings assert that early trauma disrupts neurodevelopment; causes social, emotional, and cognitive impairment; influences health risk behaviors; impacts overall life potential; is likely to increase disease, disability, and social problems; and can lead to an early death (Centers for Disease Control and Prevention [CDC] 2019; see Figure 7.3). These experiences have long-lasting effects on a child's emotional and psychological development.

The fears of attachment, loss, and disappointment are often linked to the child's history. For instance, a child who is promised that they will be returned home when their parents meet their goals for reunification can be seriously disappointed if the parents fail to meet those goals. That disappointment may lead the

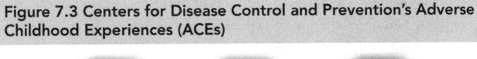

Figure 7.3 Centers for Disease Control and Prevention's Adverse Childhood Experiences (ACEs)

child to protect themselves from vulnerability in the future. Avoiding vulnerability may interfere with developing a positive connection with foster parents. Trust becomes impossible for many foster youth who have had to experience multiple disappointments. However, there is hope for children/youth with even just one caring adult in their lives. A nurturing, safe, and stable environment where the youth can establish a healthy relationship with a caring adult may prevent the ill effects of their trauma (CDC, 2019).

To mitigate the child's disillusionment, helping them understand a realistic picture of the reunification process is helpful. Child welfare professionals must determine when to include the child in reunification planning. In some states, the child may be involved in family planning meetings only after age 12 or when mature enough to understand the process. Removing the veil of ambiguity can ease the child/youth's level of anxiety and provide some form of clarity and comfort. It also provides the youth an opportunity to voice their concerns over their future.

FOSTER CARE PLACEMENT DISRUPTION

Generally, the purpose of foster care is to provide a safe and secure environment for children who have encountered abuse and neglect. The official purpose of foster care in the United States is to provide "safe and stable out-of-home care" (Children's Bureau, 2020, para. 1) for children who cannot safely live with their original caregivers. In an effort to create a safe environment for children/youth, foster parents receive comprehensive training to prepare for their role.

Foster parents are trained during their licensure process on what to expect and how to manage the dynamics of foster care. The foster parent must learn how to navigate the process:

- Introduce the child to the home.
- Ensure the home is a warm and safe environment for the child.
- Work alongside the case manager by:
  o complying with the mental and physical healthcare needs of the child,
  o complying with the child/youth's educational plan, and
  o ensuring availability with caseworker/child visits.

In addition, foster parents must understand the age-appropriate developmental needs of children. The most successful foster parents understand context, have empathy, support the child and family's permanency goals, and can manage predictive and challenging behaviors. Successful foster parents are able to depersonalize the child's behaviors and are able to view the child with unconditional positive regard.

However, fostering is not for the faint of heart. Some foster parents may begin with the best intentions but do not fully understand what it means to foster because of the sacrifices that must be made. Placement disruptions can also occur when foster parents can no longer manage the child in their home due to their own life circumstances or when the child requires a higher level of care than the foster parents can provide.

The foster child's behavior may play a considerable role in the placement disruption (consciously or unconsciously). When a child/youth seeks protection from emotional harm and disappointment, they may act out behaviorally, project their fears of abandonment, and display a number of defenses. They may react by refusing to accept loving kindness and the support of a new caregiver. If the foster child/youth is old enough to articulate their needs, they may voice a desire to live in a more independent environment to determine their own connections and life choices. Foster youth may go to transitional living or independent living programs. The overall goal is to reduce multiple placements, which retraumatizes the youth and exacerbates the dysregulation of behaviors.

One service that helps remediate trauma and addresses the stress of trauma that children experience as they transition to foster homes is specialized treatment programs. For instance, Yale University School of Medicine has implemented an evidence-based, early treatment model called the *Child and Family Traumatic Stress Intervention* (CFTSI). The CFTSI is a new brief treatment model designed for children and youth ages 7 to 18 and their parents or other caregivers (foster parents). The program focuses on increasing family support, improving communication about the child's symptoms and reactions to their trauma, and helping the caregivers learn to manage the child's dysregulated behavior. The goal of CFTSI is to begin treatment immediately after a traumatic event.

The CFTSI trains agencies on this new intervention, studies its efficacy, and collects data to inform the project. Agencies benefit from real-time scoring of assessments, ongoing analysis of client outcomes, support for intervention fidelity, and access to data for reporting and accountability. Agencies may learn more about this treatment model by visiting the Yale University School of Medicine's website.

Reflection Box 7.1

WHEN FOSTER CARE BECOMES A SAFE HAVEN FOR YOUTH

When children realize that the foster home is working in their best interest, they may decide it is not beneficial for them to return home. Although this is a rare occurrence, it happens. Despite valuing their biological family and loving their parents, their time away from family has allowed them

(continued)

Reflection Box 7.1 (*continued*)

to experience different ways of life. It has provided them with a level of stability they were not accustomed to, and they realize how being in a stable home will affect their future. When foster youth experience the development of a more favorable opportunity structure, they may excel. These youth begin to self-actualize, which may cause a disconnection from their biological families. For instance, when the foster youth applies for college, the biological family may not value those experiences, and the relationship becomes strained. At this time, the tables may turn, and communication may deteriorate.

THINK, PAIR, SHARE ACTIVITY

1. As a case manager, how would you engage the family to enhance the parent–child relationship while supporting the youth's decision to remain in the foster home?

2. Can you think of ways to involve foster and biological parents to help the child/youth manage ambivalence and identify their goals?

3. Does the child welfare system have an obligation to support the youth's decision when they choose not to return home?

4. How might you help the biological parent understand the youth's decision?

5. How does the child/youth's desire to remain with the foster family interfere with family reunification?

6. How might you support the youth's desires while respecting the initial plan for family reunification?

FAMILY REUNIFICATION SERVICES

In child welfare, family reunification is required of children placed in out-of-home care. Toombs and colleagues (2018) assert that family reunification is the most common goal for families. In the United States, when a child is removed from their biological family, child welfare services typically work toward the goal of family reunification, except in particularly egregious cases. Family reunification is a process that requires continuous assessment, and parents must progress through stages. In the beginning, the case manager completes an assessment to identify the needs and strengths of the family. Once the needs have been assessed, a child and family team meeting is held to discuss recommendations for services, referrals, and planning. The service plan is further developed with the case manager and family outlining the service, education, and visitation needs/plan. Every 6 months, the plan is reviewed with the family to determine progress toward the goal of reunification. As parents progress toward the goal of returning the child to the home, the visitation plan is expanded from supervised to unsupervised. As progress continues, ultimately the family is reunified and monitored for a period of time, leading to case closure (this may vary from state to state).

Family reunification is about family preservation. When children are not removed from their parent's custody, intact family services can provide much-needed interventions to preserve the family unit.

FAMILY PRESERVATION: INTACT FAMILY SERVICES

Generally, when an investigation occurs, and it is determined that the risk to a child is low and the child does not need to be removed from the home, an intact family case is opened. It is a voluntary service in which families are assigned a case manager who visits the home three to four times per month and provides services to support the family and the conditions which caused the family to be investigated. The case manager provides weekly visitation to the home to ensure the child's continued safety and to offer additional service referrals as needed. Families are provided service for 6 months and assessed for closure. After 6 months, there are two options for the supervisor and case manager: (a) either the services are complete, the family is stable, and the case can close, or (b) the family is still in need of services, and the case will be extended.

At any time during the life of the case, the risk level can rise, and the children may no longer be safe in the home. The child welfare professional is responsible for screening the case with the office of the state's attorney to assess whether or not custody needs to be taken of the children. If custody is taken, the parents are asked about possible relatives or fictive kin that may be available to care for the children. If there are no viable family members, a non relative foster home within the child welfare system is found.

Additional services to preserve stability in the home may also be used to support the family. The types of services offered may vary according to the family's needs. The following is a list of possible services:

• Family counseling;

• Substance use treatment;

• Parenting classes/coaching;

• Assistance with household expenses (utilities/rent/furniture);

• Domestic violence resources;

• Case management visits; and

• Referral services.

This list is not exhaustive and may vary from state to state and case to case. The services may be specifically tailored to meet the individual needs of families.

EFFECTIVENESS OF ENGAGING FAMILIES AND DEVELOPING PLANS

Child and Family Team Meetings

Child and family team meetings provide an opportunity for case managers, parents, court personnel, and service providers to collaborate and discuss the family case. The parents can also invite their formal and informal support systems to participate. Parents and guests must adhere to ground rules, and parents must understand the parameters of confidentiality.

During this meeting, the parents can also exercise their voices and communicate their concerns that are ultimately integrated into the plan. This method allows for a mutually agreed upon plan to be developed. Completing these meetings and ensuring participation allows the family to buy into the plan and take ownership because they were involved in helping to develop it. When this happens, parents are more likely to be successful in completing services. When families invite their support system, they are empowered to take ownership and promote successful outcomes (Martínez-Rico et al., 2022). It is important to note that informal support systems should not be discounted, as families value informal support networks. These informal supports include church members, pastors, close relatives, and neighbors who are trusted resources in their communities.

Positive outcomes are more likely with an effective team comprised of the family, their support system, and providers. Child and family team meetings allow participants to discuss, review, and renew the plan each quarter. The meetings are collaborative and encourage everyone to have an investment in the plan and hold one another accountable. For example, the pastor may offer pastoral counseling to support the family, or a neighbor may agree to pick a child up from school, helping to support the family plan. These meetings are most effective when they are held consistently with participants who are invested in the process throughout the life of a case.

Newer Approaches for Child and Family Team Meetings

Historically, child and family team meetings were led by child welfare professionals. Meetings were held with little input from the parents who were informed during these meetings about what services had been identified for them. Child welfare professionals acted as experts, and parents had little to no voice. Child welfare administrators and other professionals began acknowledging that parents had no voice in the process, and changes began to happen over time. Research, policies, and parental advocacy are among the efforts that helped to change the system. Approaches have been enhanced over time to improve child and family team meetings. Evidence-based practices have shown that improving communication, creating a sense of teamwork, and developing goals together improve the overall outcome for children and families.

The Annie E. Casey Foundation (2013) suggests four approaches to involving families in child welfare decisions:

- The first is *family team conferencing*, establishing a flexible support network to sustain the family after the agency involvement ends.
- The second is *family group decision-making*, which allows time for the family to make plans. These meetings may be used as a breakout session from a larger child and family meeting or as a stand-alone meeting so families can determine what they need.
- The third is *permanency teaming*, which uses a mixture of individual, joint, and large team meetings to determine a child's needs. Permanency teaming is the equivalent of coordinating all efforts and determining the areas of deficit.
- The fourth is *a team decision-making meeting* that focuses on special needs as they arise. This meeting may provide a time to resolve conflict, determine a child's placement, and make as-needed decisions about the case.

Engagement

Engagement is a significant part of working with families. The child welfare system can be very intimidating, particularly because it can involve removing children from their families during vulnerable times. Case managers are meeting families in crisis, which can result in emotions running high. When emotions run high, the child welfare professional may be called upon to respond in a neutral, non defensive way, refusing to take it personally. The key is to remain calm while reassuring the parents that the child welfare professional's role is to ensure the child's safety. The child welfare professional may ask themselves how the parents might be feeling to try and empathize with them. The goal in every area of child welfare is safety first.

Case Scenario: Managing Hostitlity: Safety Tips

Josie is a new case manager who just received the Jones case. The children were recently removed from the home by the investigator due to allegations of inadequate supervision. This call was not the first; similar allegations were made earlier that year. Josie contacted the mother, Helen Jones, to introduce herself and set up the first home visit. Mrs. Jones immediately began to curse and berate Josie—indiscriminately blaming her for removing her children. Her voice escalated as Josie remained silent. Mrs. Jones eventually hung up on Josie. When Josie's supervisor returned to the office, she immediately consulted her supervisor regarding the best approach to work with this family. Josie explained

(continued)

Case Scenario: Managing Hostitlity: Safety Tips (continued)

the experience she had with Mrs. Jones the day before. Her supervisor commended her for not reacting, educated her on possible responses, and suggested that she schedule a meeting to take place in the office.

Josie also learned the following general safety tips during her first case experience:

1. Refrain from entering into a hostile dialogue with the irate parent(s).
2. Always assess the safety level when engaging with upset or agitated parents.
3. Pay attention to nonverbal/verbal cues (e.g., balled-up fists, taking off earrings, clenching jaws, elevated voice, pressured speech).
4. Pay attention to who may be in the home (e.g., how many shoes are at the door/number of coats).
5. Always know where the exits are and position yourself by the door for a quick exit if needed.
6. Retreat if you see signs of aggression.
7. If you know this is an aggressive family, go with a colleague or ask for police accompaniment.

This scenario can very well play out in the field of child welfare. The child welfare professional must be committed to serving and protecting children. Violent encounters are unpleasant and should be avoided at all costs.

DISCUSSION QUESTIONS

1. How do these tips help when facing hostile reactions from parents?
2. How should you prepare for visits in anticipation of aggressive encounters with parents (verbal or physical)?
3. Why is it important not to engage in hostile dialogue?
4. How do you manage your own emotions and not take it personally when attacked verbally?

The child welfare professional should work hard to engage families to build a trusting relationship. Trust is built when child welfare professionals are responsive, follow through by honoring their word, consider the family as critical decisions are made, and keep families well informed. Trust develops when a child welfare professional demonstrates credibility, integrity, and fairness.

Understanding the context of families involved in the child welfare system is important. Families are often at a crisis point, and their children are at risk and are no longer safe in their homes. There could be many reasons for the lack of safety. However, some leading causes of child maltreatment are parental substance abuse, mental illness, physical abuse, sexual abuse, and inadequate supervision. In extreme circumstances, child welfare cases may involve abandonment and serious harm (which may include homicide). Regardless of the reasons for being involved in the child welfare system, as a child welfare professional, it is important to be empathic toward the family, understanding that they are dealing with significant issues and are in need of support. It can be difficult to show empathy when a child has been harmed. Parents and youth can become highly emotional and make inappropriate and negative comments toward the child welfare professional due to feelings of anger, resentment, and mental health challenges. It is so important for the child welfare professional to remain empathic during this time, considering the parents' circumstances and the source of their sadness and anger. The role of the child welfare professional is not one of moral judgment but one of assessing the family's need for services to strengthen their ability to provide a safe environment for their children. Comprehensive service planning facilitates this complex process.

Service Planning

Berliner and colleagues (2015) note that many state and federal laws have determined the child welfare system's policies: ". . . The child welfare mission has historically been characterized by two key goals—safety and permanence—operationalized as efforts to keep children safe and settled within a permanent family home, preferably with their own family when safely possible" (p. 7). The service plan is a dynamic document that can change over time and outlines mandated and recommended services.

The information derived from the child and family team meeting is used to develop the client *service plan*. This plan is a written contract that identifies services to the parents and children. These services may include therapy, parenting classes, substance use treatment programs, educational resources, and visitation plans for the parent and children. Depending on the child's needs, additional tasks may need to be completed by the foster parent. For example, a child with special needs or who is medically complex will need additional support, and it is up to the foster parent to ensure the child is receiving the identified services. Every 6 months, the plan is evaluated and reviewed for progress. The goal for returning home depends on the parents' progress within the service plan. As they make progress, they move closer to reunification.

When parents do not make satisfactory progress, the child welfare professional should plan concurrently for a different permanency outcome for the child. An alternative option includes asking the foster parents to consider guardianship or adoption so the child can have some sense of permanency. Parents are allowed a reasonable time frame for reunification before they lose total custody.

Good case management involves tailoring the recommended services to fit the specific and unique needs of the family. A one-size-fits-all generic approach is not effective.

Follow-Up to Ensure Continued Success

When families are reunified after being separated from one another for any length of time, it is always an adjustment. Learning new household rules and boundaries can be difficult for children and the parent. The child welfare professional needs to remain engaged with the family for at least 6 months after the case is closed. This follow-up contact supports the family as they adjust to their new and healthier family environment. Providing support may mean that the child welfare professional (a) visits the home at least monthly, (b) provides needed community services, and (c) supports the family as they readjust to their new family life.

MEDIA INFLUENCE

Child welfare is a highly challenging area of social work, primarily due to the unpredictable nature of working with people during life-altering times as families. With child welfare involvement, families face a looming threat of being dismantled. Nonetheless, children are abused or neglected, and child welfare professionals cannot always prevent tragedies from happening (Levin Keini et al., 2022). When grievous incidents of child maltreatment occur within the system, the media tends to shine more of a light on negative outcomes than on positive ones. Society may, at times, vilify the child welfare system as a result of the negative publicity it receives. The media's information influences public opinion regarding child welfare organizations and the public's misperceptions of dereliction of duty. Media portrayal of child welfare gives rise to a lack of respect for child welfare professionals and thoughts that perhaps not enough is being done to keep children safe. Levin Keini and colleagues (2022) assert that media and public sentiment can directly impact child welfare professionals' self-esteem. Ultimately, the onus falls on the professional, although they cannot always predict the occurrence of child maltreatment.

Developing a realistic picture of child welfare is needed. It is important to note that many good stories exist in child welfare that are rarely, if ever, publicized. If the media publicized some successes, it would show communities a more balanced view of the system. Successes could include a spotlight on:

- Successful family reunifications;
- Someone-you-should-know stories about youth in care, foster parents, and families that succeed and improve in vast ways because of services offered by the system;
- Family restoration due to the system's intervention and services;

- Youth transitioning to state colleges with state-funded scholarships; and
- Youth who excel by using what the system offers and enter into successful career paths (e.g., becoming physicians, attorneys, establishing their own law firms, and much more).

These stories, if elevated, could help other families in the community understand how the system can work with families to enhance functioning and protect the child while serving the entire family. Success stories could give other families hope for positive outcomes and a sense of what to expect.

POLITICAL INFLUENCE

Pine (1986) aptly writes about how politics influence the child welfare system. She asserts that federal policy-making is expressed through federal statute as a dynamic and complex process involving "many participants, numerous events, and a number of confluent forces" (p. 340). Kingdon (2014) writes about policy windows as a confluence of opportunities political actors take advantage of to seize moments to push political agendas. When the media portrays the child welfare system's flaws, it indirectly influences policy agendas. For instance, when the system was reviewed, and it was discovered that children were spending too much time in the system, child welfare critics demanded greater accountability. The message was that children were languishing in the child welfare system, and the system was not meeting its permanency goals. In 1997, First Lady Hillary Clinton helped to usher in the Adoption and Safe Families Act during the Clinton administration. This process was fueled by public sentiment, media influence, political agenda-making, and a demand for reform. Lawmaking also influences public funding that agencies receive to provide resources for these families. More recently, public opinion and research have broadened the discussion of trauma experienced by children and youth entering the foster care system. Public opinion influenced the passage of the Family First Prevention Services Act of 2018, which received bipartisan (political) support. This act was intended to decrease the number of children entering foster care by increasing services for vulnerable families to stay together.

CHAPTER SUMMARY

This chapter focused on mitigating some of the disparities in the child welfare system, understanding what it is like to have a child removed from the home, and contextualizing the experience to understand the family's plight, needs for support, and reaction to child welfare involvement. In addition, it is important to understand child attachment and trauma reaction to a child's separation from family to best intervene on behalf of the child and family. The types of placements and placement processes are discussed in detail to help new child welfare professionals understand the system. When placement disruptions occur, it is critical to understand what factors help to prevent and mitigate them. Children and youth are served more effectively when they receive treatment for the trauma caused by abuse/neglect and the system's involvement. Despite children/youth being saved from harm, they still love and may be deeply connected to their families. Understanding the complex emotional reactions of children can better situate worker expectations and planning for families and youth in care.

DISCUSSION QUESTIONS

1. Is it the child welfare system's responsibility to protect the agency's image?
2. What could the system do to market a better image?
3. How can supervisors enhance the professional esteem of child welfare workers after a tragedy occurs, especially when the worker did all they could to protect the child?
4. In what ways might fear and blame play a role in how child welfare professionals are viewed?
5. What are some strategies to reduce trauma when children enter the child welfare system?
6. How can foster parent training be enhanced to make foster placements more stable?
7. How might a child welfare professional de-escalate a tense situation with an angry parent?
8. What supervisory activities are essential when supporting new child welfare professionals?
9. What are the benefits of engagement when conducting child and family team meetings?
10. What are some strategies for joining/partnering with families to be successful in permanency planning for youth and children?

RESOURCES

Nadine Burke Harris TED Talk "How Childhood Trauma Affects Health Across a Lifetime" www .ted.com/talks/nadine_burke_harris_how_childhood_trauma_affects_health_across_a_lifetime

James Redford film: "Resilience: The Biology of Stress; The Science of Hope"

A robust set of instructor resources designed to supplement this text is located at **http://connect.springerpub.com/content/book/978-0-8261-5285-5**. Qualifying instructors may request access by emailing **textbook@springerpub.com**.

REFERENCES

Annie E. Casey Foundation. (2013, January 1). *Strategies in child welfare: Four approaches to family team meetings.* https://www.aecf.org/resources/four-approaches-to-family-team-meetings

Berliner, L., Fitzgerald, M. M., Dorsey, S., Chaffin, M., Ondersma, S. J., & Wilson, C. (2015). Report of the APSAC task force on evidence-based service planning guidelines for child welfare. *Child Maltreatment, 20*(1), 6–16. https://doi.org/10.1177/1077559514562066

Bowlby, J. (1952). *Maternal care and mental health.* World Health Organization. https://pages.uoregon.edu/eherman/teaching/texts/Bowlby%20Maternal%20Care%20and%20Mental%20Health.pdf

Bretherton, I. (1992). The origins of attachment theory: John Bowlby and Mary Ainsworth. *Developmental Psychology, 28*(5), 759. https://web.s.ebscohost.com/ehost/pdfviewer/pdfviewer?vid=0&sid=ddf9845f-f03f-43f3-920e-c672564c98a4%40redis

Centers for Disease Control. (2019). *Preventing adverse childhood experiences: Leveraging the best available evidence.* National Center for Injury Prevention and Control, Centers for Disease Control and Prevention. https://www.cdc.gov/violenceprevention/aces/about.html#:~:text=The%20ACE%20Pyramid%20represents%20the,being%20throughout%20the%20life%20course

Chambers, R. M., Crutchfield, R. M., Willis, T. Y., Cuza, H. A., Otero, A., Goddu Harper, S. G., & Carmichael, H. (2020). "Be supportive and understanding of the stress that youth are going through": Foster care alumni recommendations for youth, caregivers and caseworkers on placement transitions. *Children and Youth Services Review, 108*, 104644. https://doi.org/10.1016/j.childyouth.2019.104644

Child Welfare Information Gateway. (2021). *Child welfare practice to address racial disproportionality and disparity.* U.S. Department of Health and Human Services, Administration for Children and Families, Children's Bureau. https://www.childwelfare.gov/pubPDFs/racial_disproportionality.pdf

Children's Bureau. (2020, June 25). *Title IV-E foster care.* U.S. Department of Health and Human Services, Administration for Children and Families. https://www.acf.hhs.gov/cb/grant-funding/title-iv-e-foster-care

Cooke, J. E., Racine, N., Plamondon, A., Tough, S., & Madigan, S. (2019). Maternal adverse childhood experiences, attachment style, and mental health: pathways of transmission to child behavior problems. *Child Abuse & Neglect, 93*, 27-37. https://doi.org/10.1016/j.chiabu.2019.04.011

Engler, A. D., Sarpong, K. O., Van Horne, B. S., Greeley, C. S., & Keefe, R. J. (2022). A systematic review of mental health disorders of children in foster care. *Trauma, Violence, & Abuse, 23*(1), 255–264. https://www.doi.org/10.1177/1524838020941197

Garcia, A. R., Kim, M., & DeNard, C. (2016). Context matters: The state of racial disparities in mental health services among youth reported to child welfare in 1999 and 2009. *Children and Youth Services Review, 66*, 101–108. https://www.doi.org/10.1016/j.childyouth.2016.05.005

Keller, J., & Grumbach, G. (2022). *School social work: A skills-based competency approach.* Springer Publishing Company.

Kingdon, J. W. (2014). *Agendas alternatives and public policies.* Pearson Education Limited. http://www.dawsonera.com/depp/reader/protected/external/AbstractView/S9781292053875

Lee, E. J. (2003). *The attachment system throughout the life course: Review and criticisms of attachment theory.* Rochester Institute of Technology. http://www.personalityresearch.org/papers/lee.html

Levin Keini, N., Ben Shlomo, S., Shoval, R., & Ramon, D. (2022). Media coverage of child welfare social workers and its effect on professional self-esteem: The moderating role of family and social support. *The British Journal of Social Work, 53*(5), 2539–2559. https://doi.org/10.1093/bjsw/bcac222

Maguire-Jack, K., Font, S. A., & Dillard, R. (2020). Child protective services decision-making: The role of children's race and county factors. *American Journal of Orthopsychiatry, 90,* 48–62. https://doi.org/10.1037/ort0000388

Martínez-Rico, G., Simón, C., Cañadas, M., & Mcwilliam, R. (2022). Support networks and family empowerment in early intervention. *International Journal of Environmental Research and Public Health, 19*(4), 2001. https://doi.org/10.3390/ijerph19042001

Masiran, R., Ibrahim, N., Awang, H., & Ying, L. P. (2022). The positive and negative aspects of parentification: An integrated review. *Children and Youth Services Review, 144,* 106709. https://doi.org/10.1016/j.childyouth.2022.106709

McLennan, J. D., MacMillan, H. L., & Afifi, T. O. (2020). Questioning the use of adverse childhood experiences (ACEs) questionnaires. *Child Abuse & Neglect, 101,* 104331. https://doi.org/10.1016/j.chiabu.2019.104331

Perry, B., D., & Winfrey, O. (2021). *What happened to you: Conversations on trauma, resilience, and healing.* Flatiron Books. ISBN: 9781250223180.

Pine, B. A. (1986). Child welfare reform and the political process. *Social Service Review, 60*(3), 339–359. https://www.jstor.org/stable/30011846

Robertson, J., & Bowlby, J. (1952). Responses of young children to separation from their mothers. *Courrier du Centre International de l'Enfance, 2,* 131–142.

Toombs, E., Drawson, A. S., Bobinski, T., Dixon, J., & Mushquash, C. J. (2018). First Nations parenting and child reunification: Identifying strengths, barriers, and community needs within the child welfare system. *Child & Family Social Work, 23*(3), 408–416. https://doi.org/10.1111/cfs.12430

Van Rosmalen, L. (2015). From secure dependency to attachment: Mary Ainsworth's integration of Blatz's security theory into Bowlby's attachment theory. *History of Psychology, 19*(1), 22. http://hdl.handle.net/1887/33739

Vreeland, A., Ebert, J. S., Kuhn, T. M., Gracey, K. A., Shaffer, A. M., Watson, K. H., Gruhn, M. A., Henry, L., Dickey, L., Siciliano, R. E., Anderson, A., & Compas, B. E. (2020). Predictors of placement disruptions in foster care. *Child Abuse & Neglect, 99,* 104283. https://doi.org/10.1016/j.chiabu.2019.104283

Wildeman, C., Edwards, F. R., & Wakefield, S. (2020). The cumulative prevalence of termination of parental rights for U.S. children, 2000–2016. *Child Maltreatment, 25,* 32–42. https://www.doi.org/10.1177/1077559519848499

Yi, Y., Edwards, F. R., & Wildeman, C. (2020). Cumulative prevalence of confirmed maltreatment and foster care placements for US children by race/ethnicity, 2011–2016. *American Journal of Public Health, 110,* 704–709. https://www.doi.org/10.2105/AJPH.2019.305554

8   Foster Care and Adoption in Child Welfare Practice

INTRODUCTION

National data from the Adoption and Foster Care Analysis Reporting System (AFCARS, 2022) show the numbers reported by the foster care system. In 2021, 207,000 children entered the child welfare system; 54,200 children were adopted; 114,000 were awaiting adoption; 65,000 had parental rights terminated; and 215,000 children exited the system. The number of children under age 18 in foster care has been declining since 2017 (Annie E. Casey Foundation, 2023). The pandemic may have affected the number of allegations and families referred to the child welfare system. Since schools were delayed in opening, there was a decrease in the number of children who came to the attention of mandated reporters (AFCARS, 2022).

Since 2019, the number of children in the system has fallen by 2.5%. This downward trend continued into 2021 with a 3.9% decrease (AFCARS, 2021). According to AFCARS (2022), there were 391,000 children in care in fiscal year 2021, representing a decrease of 10.5% from fiscal year 2017, when numbers were at a high of 437,000 children in care. In addition, with the increased awareness of the trauma experienced by children who are separated from their parents, more emphasis is placed on keeping children with their families when it is safe to do so.

Most recently, it has been noted that slightly less than 50% of children who exit foster care return home to their parents or previous caregiver. From 2018 through 2021, 25% of children exiting foster care were adopted, and one in six exited the system to live with a relative or guardian (Annie E. Casey Foundation, 2022). Roughly 5% of youth age out of foster care each year (AFCARS, 2022). These percentages reflect the latest statistics on children in the child welfare system nationwide. While the primary function of the child welfare system is to ensure the safety of children, and by default, the focus of the foster care system is to ensure the safety of children in out-of-home care, federal policies and practices in recent years have also focused on legal permanency for children and youth in care (Rolock & White, 2016).

FOSTER CARE

The primary purpose of foster care is to provide a safe and stable environment for children who cannot be with their parents. It is necessary to provide a safe placement for children who have been living in unsafe home situations. Foster care is meant to be a temporary arrangement that should protect the child until it is deemed safe to return the child to the family or until parental rights are terminated, and the child can find permanency through adoption or subsidized guardianship. "Foster care provides round-the-clock substitute care for nearly 700,000 U.S. children who are temporarily or permanently separated from their family of origin each year. Each state manages its own foster care system according to federal regulations" (Font & Gershoff, 2020, p. 1). With federal oversight, foster care is enacted at the state level; therefore, regulations may have nuanced differences depending on state needs, challenges, and focus. Once an allegation of abuse or neglect is made, the allegation is investigated, and a determination of the case is made to substantiate or rule that the allegations are founded, or the allegations are not. Child welfare agencies have the legal authority to remove children from their biological homes when they are in imminent danger of harm under the authority of their parents (Font & Gershoff, 2020). In most states, a child may be removed, and court approval obtained within 24 to 72 hours.

Foster placement can take many different forms; foster care can be classified as a relative home, a nonrelative foster home, or a group/treatment facility. Many factors go into determining the most appropriate placement for a child in out-of-home care. These factors include but are not limited to, first, safety and stability, but also considering placement with relatives, placement with siblings, remaining in the same school, and overall well-being of the child, while also taking into account the availability of foster homes, the time involved in searching for family, and weighing other placement options. Font (2015) asserts that meeting all of the above factors may be impossible. The child welfare professional must treat each child individually as they prioritize the child's unique needs.

Relative Placement

Within child welfare, efforts have increased to place children and youth with relatives (Font, 2015). Logically, relative placement, also known as kinship foster care, may have many benefits. For example, children and youth may already have a connection with or attachment to a relative. Relatives may be more familiar with cultural and family customs, foods, traditions, and values. The relative caregiver may be more committed to working to make the placement successful and less traumatic for the child. There may be other benefits, as well. In a review of research on children's mental health, Xu and Bright (2018) found that children in kinship care had better mental health outcomes than children in nonrelative care when considering internalizing behaviors, externalizing behaviors, total behavioral problems, and socio emotional problems. They do caution, though, that there are gaps in the research, inconsistent findings across studies, and other variables such as the child's mental health status prior to placement, the type(s) of abuse or neglect experienced by the child, the foster family makeup, and the community context. However, they note that children's mental health status changes, with improvement for those in kinship care and increased challenges over time for those in non-kinship placements (Xu & Bright, 2018).

Relative foster placement is not without its challenges, however. Families are complex systems; sometimes, family dynamics and geographic location can create complicating factors. Sometimes it takes time to find relatives willing to take a child. Consider the following case scenario.

Case Scenario: Supporting Families, Culture, and Religion

A child welfare professional, David has been working with a family for about 2 months. The child, Amirah, is 21 months old. She was born in Cleveland but currently lives in Nevada. Her mother, Sarah, is White; her father is Arabic and a recent immigrant to the United States. The father's relationship with Sarah ended abruptly shortly after Amirah's birth. Amirah was placed in

(continued)

Case Scenario: Supporting Families, Culture, and Religion (*continued*)

foster care for 8 months following her birth due to Sarah's drug use. She was returned to Sarah, and Sarah relocated to Nevada, where she said she would be living with her mother in a stable home environment. However, she was found living on the streets with her daughter and received assistance getting into a shelter. A short time later, she and Amirah were asked to leave the shelter due to the destruction of property. Sarah continues to struggle with substance use. Amirah is Sarah's fifth child. She relinquished custody of her first child, who was subsequently adopted. Sarah's parental rights to the other three children were terminated in Cleveland, Ohio, due to neglect and exposure to domestic violence.

David, the child welfare professional, has been working with Sarah and Amirah, who has been in care for six months. The initial plan was to return Amirah to Sarah, who was mandated to complete random urine analyses, have a psychological evaluation, maintain stable housing, attend counseling with medication management, and be present for visitation with Amirah twice a week for 2 hours each visit. The court found Sarah to only comply with some of the objectives after 6 months. She also is living with a new partner, where she has reported being involved in mutual domestic violence. Considering that Sarah has been making some progress but is not yet ready to parent, David is looking for a more permanent placement for Amirah. Sarah's mother is not able or willing to assume care. Amirah's father, Eli, has been contacted and is willing to take Amirah. In order to do so, Eli must complete a paternity test to verify he is Amirah's father, begin virtual visits with her, and visit her in Nevada. In addition, both Eli and Sarah are practicing Muslims. Currently, Amirah is in a non-Muslim foster home. Sarah wants her daughter to be exposed to the Muslim religion.

The case scenario illustrates some challenges that can arise in relative placement. Sarah would still like to have contact with Amirah and have her returned to her at some point. Maintaining visits if Amirah is out of state will be complicated. Eli has yet to have consistent contact with his daughter. However, he is interested in providing stability and becoming more involved with Amirah. He also hopes that Sarah will make progress in drug treatment and be able to assume custody. Finally, he is committed to raising Amirah in the Muslim faith.

DISCUSSION QUESTIONS

1. From this scenario, what is the most important consideration for placing Amirah?

Case Scenario: Supporting Families, Culture, and Religion (*continued*)

2. Considering Sarah's unstable and volatile relationship and continuing drug use, what support can be provided to help her maintain sobriety and focus her attention on stabilizing her home environment for possible reunification?
3. How would temporary custody affect Eli's chances of gaining full custody later?
4. What should the child welfare system do to properly vet Eli for custody?

Nonrelative Foster Placement

Many foster parents are not related to the child and do not know the child prior to placement. They have decided to open their homes to children needing care. Both couples and single persons can be licensed to be foster parents. Each state has its own guidelines regarding minimum age, training, background checks, home study, and other requirements for licensure. Foster parents receive payment for assuming care. Some foster placements are considered receiving homes or emergency foster care and provide short-term support (which may vary across states). Ideally, short-term care does not exceed 30 days and serves as an emergency placement. Most foster parents provide long-term care. Foster parents are expected to support the permanency plan for the child. If the plan is for the child to return home, the foster parents partner with the biological parents to support this goal. Some foster homes are considered foster-adopt placements, where the families foster children whose parental rights have been or likely will be terminated. After a period of time, they can move toward adoption.

Challenges of Foster Care

Children and youth in foster care face many challenges. Many have unmet mental health needs. Due to the complex trauma that many children and youth in foster care experience, both from abuse and neglect before entering care and from separation from their home and families, adults who have been in the foster care system experience posttraumatic stress disorder nearly five times as much as the adult population in general (Child Welfare Information Gateway, 2023). McGuire et al. (2018) found that the severity of abuse and the number of placement changes were independently positively correlated with both externalizing and internalizing mental health behaviors. Thus, both contribute to behavioral health challenges for youth in foster care.

Additionally, behavioral health symptoms increased for those in care who experienced multiple placement changes, while they decreased for those who experienced stability in their foster placement (McGuire et al., 2018). In other words, mental and behavioral health problems may contribute to placement instability, but placement instability can also contribute to mental and behavioral health problems (McGuire et al., 2018). Chambers et al. (2020) asked foster care alums who had experienced three or more placements what advice they would give to foster youth, foster care providers, and caseworkers to assist youth better. Advice to youth included just dealing with the placements, knowing it is part of the process, and expressing how they feel. They also recommended maintaining relationships as much as they could. For caregivers, including foster parents and group home staff, they recommended focusing on the youth, understanding what they are going through, and considering the true purpose of foster care before committing. They also recommended welcoming youth but giving them time and space to adjust as well as safe spaces to express their feelings. The foster care alums recommended that caseworkers do better jobs of investigating foster families, try to understand what the youth are going through, and be transparent about the placement process (Chambers et al., 2020). Knowing that children and youth in foster care have experienced countless challenges, the role of the child welfare professional in supporting children becomes critical.

Despite the vast criticisms, what is the alternative to foster care? Without foster care, vulnerable children will be abused, neglected, and traumatized. Child maltreatment-related deaths may be rare, but recurrent victimization is not. By age 12, one in seven American children is reported to Child Protective Services (Font & Gershoff, 2020). The child welfare system is not perfect; it has continuous improvements to make, but the overarching goal is to protect children from abuse/neglect. "Foster care is never an ideal situation for a child, but it may be the least worst alternative for children whose parents intentionally, recklessly, or negligently harm them" (Font & Gershoff, 2020, p. 4).

Case Scenario: Finding Strengths to Make Authentic Connections

Morgan has worked at Washington State's Department of Children, Youth, and Families (DCYF) for approximately 1 year. Part of Morgan's role is to provide supervised visits for parents on her caseload for whom allegations of abuse or neglect have been *founded*, resulting in the removal of the children from their care. Depending on the case, visitations can occur in the community, home, or child welfare office.

Today Morgan is supervising a visit with a mom who was *founded* for neglecting her 6-year-old daughter, Jasmine, due to the mother's drug

(continued)

Case Scenario: Finding Strengths to Make Authentic Connections (*continued*)

addiction. Mother and child both are identified as Hispanic. Morgan is meeting the mother at the child welfare office that provides rooms with cameras, so Morgan can watch the visit from another room and intervene if necessary. Morgan checked out a state car for the day and picked up Jasmine from her foster home. Jasmine had no trouble going with Morgan despite not knowing Morgan, and she hopped right in her car and into her car seat. Morgan knows that Jasmine has had many social workers transport her over the last year since entering the foster care system. Jasmine is primarily quiet except when Morgan is communicating with her, asking her questions about her favorite things.

Morgan can also hear Jasmine singing most of the songs on the radio. The mother was already there when Morgan and Jasmine arrived at the office. The mother's presence was a happy sight due to previous reports of the mother being a frequent no-show to visitation. Jasmine ran to her mother in excitement. The mom was standoffish and initially did not want to look at Morgan. Morgan introduced herself to her biological mother and said she would watch the video from the other room since this was a supervised visit. The visit went well, and Morgan informed the mother that they could set up another time that would work within her schedule. Jasmine began to get visibly upset that she was going to leave her mom and began crying, clinging to her mom. The parent started crying and began to provide her with comforting words. Morgan asked the mom if she would like to walk out to the car with them and put her daughter into the car seat. The mom smiled and very much wanted to be part of the process. Morgan could hear the parent singing to her daughter as they walked to the car. Morgan inquired if they enjoyed music. The parent stated that she would sing all the time with her daughter, and their family loved music. Mom put Jasmine into the car seat and thanked Morgan for letting her help. Morgan got curious and asked the parent about the type of music they would listen to and things her daughter liked.

The mom's face lit up in response to the question; she discussed things they would do and the music they enjoyed the most. As they said goodbye to the parent, Jasmine was still crying. Morgan checked in with the child on how she was feeling. Morgan put on some music that the mom recommended, and Jasmine slowly began to sing. Morgan began to sing and move along with the music, also. Morgan and Jasmine had fun singing all the way to her foster home. When they pulled up to her foster home, Morgan let Jasmine out of the car and walked her to the door. Jasmine said goodbye to Morgan as she ran into the foster home. Even though her mom continued to struggle with addiction, Morgan was happy to connect with the parent by demonstrating an interest in how music was important in her and her daughter's lives. She began to be more curious about identifying the mother's other strengths.

(continued)

Case Scenario: Finding Strengths to Make Authentic Connections (*continued*)

In this case scenario, one can identify three parties: the child welfare professional, the mother, and the child. Each has their own perspective and their part to play in the process. The child welfare professional may feel overworked and frustrated with a mother who has not always shown up at supervised visits. It would be easy to fall into the trap of negativity and judgment. However, Morgan could see the mother through a different lens, could identify strengths, and was interested in looking for more strengths. Morgan also identified a way to connect more completely with Jasmine and recognize some of Jasmine's strengths, including her love and loyalty to her mother, her musical talents, and her adaptability.

Jasmine is still clearly attached to her mother. She has experienced several disappointments in her 6 years. She was only 5 when she was taken from her mother and placed with her foster family. Before this, neighbors had reported that she was often left unattended while her mother was out. Sometimes, when her mother was home but passed out or high, Jasmine would tend to her mother, even at age 4 and 5, bringing her food, water, and other things. Jasmine did not fully understand why she had to leave her mother since she thought she and her mother were doing fine. Jasmine was very sad when she was removed and withdrew for a while. She is adaptable and has adjusted to her new home and school. However, the visits are sometimes painful as her mother does not show up occasionally, and when she does, the separation brings back those feelings she had when she was first taken from her mother. Listening to music and singing with Morgan helped Jasmine feel better, and she looks forward to the next visit.

The mother has struggled with addiction for several years, getting herself clean, then relapsing. She truly loves Jasmine and wants to do the best for her, but her addiction sometimes gets in the way. After Jasmine was removed, she first felt extraordinarily depressed and immobilized. More recently, though, she is motivated to do all she can to get Jasmine returned. Sometimes the mom has felt that the odds are stacked against her, and she fears she may never get Jasmine returned. In the past, she has felt that the child welfare workers are not really on her side, only see her in a negative light, and are not working with her to move toward reunification. However, Morgan seemed different. She picked up on the mom's and Jasmine's interest in music. Morgan gave her something happy to talk about and seemed genuinely interested in what she had to say. Morgan also complimented the mother on how well the visit went. This way of connecting helped the mother feel hopeful and promised she would arrive promptly at the next visit with a positive attitude.

(*continued*)

Case Scenario: Finding Strengths to Make Authentic Connections (*continued*)

DISCUSSION QUESTIONS

Divide the class into small groups and discuss each party's perspective and needs.

1. How does understanding each person's context help you enhance the relationship?
2. During parent–child visits, how would you utilize the strengths of the parent to increase communication?
3. How can the mother and foster parent work together to increase the mom's involvement in her child's educational programming?

Foster care protects many children, and the requirements of foster care and adoption may vary nationwide. As foster care is intended to be temporary, though it often extends longer than intended, it is crucial to determine what factors may contribute to greater stability in foster care placements. Chateauneuf et al. (2022) compared children and youth in kinship care, foster-to-adopt families (FAF), and nonrelative foster care (NRFC). They found that children placed in NRFC were more likely than either kinship care and FAF to experience more changes in placements, suggesting that the move toward increasing kinship care benefits children and youth as it promotes placement stability. It is important, though, to recognize each situation's uniqueness and consider the characteristics of the child, the intended foster/adopt/return trajectory, and the type of home placement (Chateauneuf et al., 2022). To support children and youth in care, knowing that increased changes in placements increase the likelihood of mental and behavioral health problems, giving children and youth support and preparation for transitions helps. Training foster parents on how to support youth facing transitions can be a proactive way of mitigating some of the additional challenges youth face in care (McGuire et al., 2018). In addition to foster care, permanency planning, subsidized adoption and guardianship, long-term care, and issues related to supporting families and youth/children who enter into foster care and guardianship arrangements are all part of the picture of child protection.

THE FAMILY FIRST PREVENTION SERVICES ACT (FFPSA)

The Family First Prevention Services Act (FFPSA) was signed into law in 2018 with much bipartisan support. According to Font and Gershoff (2020), this legislation provided the most significant overhaul of the child welfare system in

40 years. The Act now allows for funding under the Social Security Act, "which previously could only be used to pay for foster care services, adoption services, and assistance to kin guardians, to be used to prevent children from entering foster care" (Font & Gershoff, 2020, p. 6). Funding can be used for interventions that also benefit the biological parents' needs for substance use, mental health treatment, and in-home parenting services to bolster parenting skills. The goal is to support families to remain intact and support reunification goals for families where children have been removed. The caveat for this funding is that the money has to be used for evidence-based treatment services. Funds are partially reimbursed to states, and Title IV-E funds are the payer of last resort (Font & Gershoff, 2020).

In addition, when children are already in the system, Title IV-E provides limited reimbursement to states for Qualified Residential Treatment Programs (QRTP), meaning QRTPs must be licensed, have qualified professionals, use evidence-based interventions, and adhere to federal guidelines about time in care. Children/youth should not be placed in residential treatment for more than 18 months. Residential treatment is used when children/youth have psychological, behavioral, or mental health challenges that require more intensive treatment.

To ensure quality foster care placements, the FFPSA sets guidelines for licensure and provides funding to recruit qualified foster homes. To avoid foster care placement disruptions, children languishing in the system, or foster care drift, permanency planning must be integrated into the child/family's service plan.

PERMANENCY PLANNING

Once a child is in foster care, they are entitled to permanency. *Permanency planning* is a continuous process that happens over the course of a case. It seeks to remove barriers that caused the family's involvement in the child welfare system. Interventions, services, and referrals are provided to the family based on their needs. The child welfare professional, supervisor, and the family work collaboratively to monitor progress and reassess service needs.

Permanency planning ensures that children in foster care can have permanent homes that are safe and nurturing. Child welfare professionals work with families to make vital corrections in the home environment and provide interventions when needed so that children can return to a safe home with their parents. Whenever possible, the goal is initially set for reunification. Adoption and guardianship should be considered if reunification cannot be achieved with the birth parents. There are other permanency goals, such as subsidized guardianship and adoption, which we review next. It is always essential to have a concurrent plan to ensure a path for children to achieve a permanent and stable home.

SUBSIDIZED GUARDIANSHIP AND ADOPTION

Subsidized guardianship and adoption are permanency options for youth in care when the goal of returning home to their parents is no longer an option. Since the 1970s, there has been a movement toward permanency for youth in care through *subsidized guardianship and adoption*. The hope that all children in the foster care system can achieve permanency is a national goal. These outcomes are monitored each year with the expectation that children move quickly through the child welfare system to some form of permanency. The difference between guardianship and adoption is that guardianship can be temporary as the parents maintain their parental rights from a legal standpoint. Many relative caretakers choose guardianship because they do not want to sever the relationship between the children and their parents. *Adoption* is a more permanent option in which parental rights are terminated or surrendered voluntarily. Subsidies are offered in many states that chose these options to ensure children have permanent homes.

HOME STUDIES

In preparation for permanency for youth in care, *home studies* are required. It is an essential part of the process when moving toward guardianship or adoption. It provides the opportunity for child welfare professionals to learn more about the potential adoptive, foster parents, or guardians, but it also provides education to the foster parents about the process and what to expect as the process moves forward. The home study is a great tool to determine the compatibility of the foster parent with the youth in care as it relates to a permanent lifelong relationship. The home study covers all areas of life, which include family history, health, employment, home life, and the relationship between the foster parent and the child. The final part of the home study provides recommendations for proceeding with the adoption or guardianship process.

LONG-TERM FOSTER CARE

When planned permanent living arrangements do not work, other planned permanent living arrangements (OPPLA) are an option. Long-term foster care may be explored if family reunification, adoption, relative placement, or legal guardianship does not work (Child Welfare Information Gateway, 2018).

Long-term foster care is not the ideal goal for youth in care. In some situations, a child may stay in a stable foster home environment for many years until they age out of the foster care system and maintain a valuable connection with their foster family. In other cases, a child may have significant behavioral or medical concerns that make it difficult for some foster parents to commit to subsidized guardianship or adoption for fear of not having the same support they would have if the youth remained in foster care. However, some youth in care are older and able to make their own decisions about where they want to live and prefer not to go under the guardianship or adoption of a foster parent but maintain their placement until they age out of the system or go off to college, taking advantage of some of the educational supports that they may receive from state agencies. The truth of the matter is that every child deserves a home that is safe, secure, supportive, and loving. This is the ultimate goal for all children in the foster care system. If their biological families cannot provide permanency, it is important as child welfare professionals to work toward permanency for every child.

MAINTAINING CULTURAL IDENTITY

Race significantly affects a foster child's life trajectory and well-being (Annie E. Casey Foundation, 2014). The United States has a complex system of racial bias and inequities. Our country's history has indelibly impacted our institutions and culture. According to the Annie E. Casey Foundation (2014), systemic racism "routinely confers advantage and disadvantage based on skin color and other characteristics" (p. 2) and further asserts that this must be "clearly understood, directly challenged and fundamentally transformed. If our nation is to live up to its democratic ideals [. . .] then racial equity and inclusion must be at the forefront of how we shape our institutions, policies and culture" (p. 2). Understanding racial bias and inequities is vital for social workers and child welfare professionals when providing services to families in various communities. The disproportionate placement of children in the foster care system has been a standing issue for many years. All families deserve to be seen and assessed within their cultural context, which means that child welfare professionals must be culturally humble and astute.

Some suggested ways to help a child maintain their cultural identity are to:

- Match foster parents and foster children/youth with similar cultures/ backgrounds.
- Honor the cultural traditions of foster children/youth (holidays, foods, traditions).
- Demonstrate respect for children/youth's culture and values.
- Learn about cultural differences in hair care and grooming for foster children/ youth.
- Learn about cultural foods that are staples for foster children/youth.
- Socialize foster children/youth with experiences from their culture and background.
- Socialize foster children/youth with experiences they are accustomed to and enjoy.

- Recognize other cultures' strengths and nurture positive cultural identity development.
- Carefully screen foster homes for evidence of culturally diverse openness and respect for others.

In a qualitative study, Waniganayake et al. (2019) found that both caseworkers and foster parents believed that cultural matching between children and foster families represented the ideal way of providing the best and most stable placement for a child. Study participants identified various aspects of matching, including foods, religious practices and adherence, language, access to cultural texts, personal care and grooming, and social networks. Realizing the complexity of matching on all dimensions, they noted the difficulty of achieving the "ideal" match (Waniganayake et al., 2019). Brown et al. (2009) interviewed predominantly female foster parents who identified several benefits of cultural matching. These included stronger connections with the child and birth family so that both are more comfortable with the placement, provide a more immediate sense of safety and comfort for the child, and create less stress for foster parents and the child.

The first concern is for the child's safety and to place them in a timely manner. The most desirable outcome is to perform cultural place matching to the greatest extent possible while still protecting the child.

Reflection Box 8.1

In small groups, discuss two of the questions that follow. Choose a reporter and note-taker, and spend 15 minutes in dialogue. Each group should provide evidence for their position (using resources/references/experience). After the small group discussion, debrief in the larger classroom session.

1. How might you work with foster parents who may not be familiar with the culture of the child that is placed in their home?
2. How would you assess the foster parents' commitment and openness to diversity?
3. How does cultural identity affect a child's development?
4. How can you support the child's continued needs once placed in a culturally different foster home?
5. What ideas do you have about expanding culturally diverse foster homes?
6. Is cultural matching important? Why or why not?

ADOPTION AND SUBSIDIZED GUARDIANSHIP

Children and youth deserve a permanent home with a nurturing family. Adoption legally establishes a person(s) as the child's parent(s). Adoption gives that person(s) all the rights and responsibilities as if the child were born to them (Department of Children and Family Services [DCFS], 2022) and is only "possible when the birth parent/s have voluntarily relinquished their parental rights, are deceased or if the court has taken parental rights away from them" (DCFS, 2022, p. 3). When adoption is not an option, legal guardianship may be considered to provide a permanent family. Guardianship does not require relinquishing or terminating parental rights but names the permanent resource as the guardian. Guardianship happens when it is thought to be in the child's best interest for myriad reasons. If the potential guardian is a relative, they may not want to see the parents' rights terminated. At the foster youth's request, the guardian ad litem may advocate on their behalf not to have their parent's rights terminated.

According to DCFS (2022), legal guardianship gives the child a sense of permanence, curtails fear of living disruptions and uncertainty of their living situation, and provides a sense of security. Raising children comes with legal responsibilities for children/youth's medical, educational, and other decisions. Therefore, it must be a legal process as potential guardians make the decision to care for a child into adulthood. An example provided by DCFS states, "If the child welfare system continues to maintain legal responsibility for the child instead of you, . . . the child's caseworker must continue to monitor the care of the child and the court will continue to assess and review your case" (DCFS, 2022, p. 4). Without legal status, your control over a child's life is limited. Once legal permanency is established, the child welfare system can close the child's case, allowing the guardian to make independent decisions on the child's behalf without input from the state (DCFS, 2022). With legal status, the guardian can raise the child as if the child were their own. However, the court retains jurisdiction until the child/youth reaches 18 years of age. The DCFS writes, "Adoption and guardianship are strong commitments to children. Although guardianship legally ends when the child reaches adulthood, most legal guardians have family ties" (p. 15) and a lifelong commitment to the child.

Subsidized guardianship and adoption provide financial assistance, health insurance, and other services from the child welfare department. Subsidies may include:

1. Payment for expenses that are unrepeatable for reasonable and necessary costs and legal fees related to subsidy review and the court hearing.
2. The monthly amount for support of the child may vary from state to state and is based on the needs of the child.

3. The child welfare system provides health insurance.

4. The department must approve costs before they are incurred.

5. Employment-related day care payments may be made for children under the age of 3 years if the guardian is employed or is in a training program that will lead to employment. This rule applies to Illinois and may vary depending on the state's guidelines.

6. Therapeutic day care may be available for children with special needs.

Subsidized guardianship and adoption are crucial for some families, and resource development must be made in the child's best interest. As the child matures, the child welfare worker and the prospective guardian must anticipate what special services or interventions are needed (if any). Knowing the child's medical, social, emotional, and educational needs is the best way to determine what may be needed for the future.

There are slight differences between adoption and guardianship (Figure 8.1), and prospective parents must weigh the benefits of whether they are adopting or consenting to legal guardianship. The main distinctions between adoption and guardianship are:

1. *Legal status and autonomy from the child welfare system differ for cases of adoption versus guardianship.* Guardianship has consistent child welfare involvement whereas adoption ends the intrusion of the child welfare system into their lives.

Figure 8.1 Adoption or Guardianship

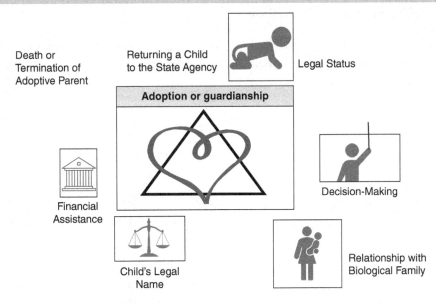

2. *Legal status of the child differs between adoption and guardianship.* In cases of adoption, it becomes a permanent status, and the adoptive parent has all rights and responsibilities of the child as if the child were their own.

3. *Legal name of the child differs in cases of adoption.* The child may take the adoptive family's name, whereas guardianship makes no provision for this type of change.

4. *Child's relationship with the birth family may remain intact through guardianship.* It is up to the discretion of the adoptive parent whether or not contact continues.

5. *Decisions made on the child's behalf can be done without any hesitation or consultation with the system in the case of adoption or guardianship.*

6. *Autonomy and independence are granted to adoptive parents.* Guardians, *in some states*, remain involved with the child welfare system and do not have executive authority over the child. Some states grant total independence and discontinue further system involvement.

7. *When an adoptive parent dies, or their rights are terminated, the child may be up for adoption again or reenter guardianship status.*

Each family must consider their options and how much interaction and support they need from the child welfare system. Additionally, guardians need to have a backup plan to make contingencies if they can no longer care for the child. These and other considerations are important in deciding whether to adopt a child or enter a subsidized guardianship arrangement with continued system involvement. For specific details, consult the state's guidelines on adoption and guardianship.

Adoptive Parents and Guardians

Adults seeking adoption or guardianship have the right to ask for certain information to properly care for and support the child/youth. They are entitled to know about the birth parents'

- age
- race
- religion
- ethnic background
- mental or physical conditions
- education
- occupation
- existing siblings
- birth grandparents
- country of origin
- reasons for immigrating to the United States (if applicable)
- relationship between birth parents, and
- detailed medical and mental health histories of the child, birth parents, and immediate kin

Per the DCFS, "none of this information will include the names or the last known address of the birth parent/s, grandparent/s, the siblings of the birth parent/s or any other relative of the adopted child" (DCFS, 2022, p. 17). This information is essential for continuity of care, understanding the child's development, and the family's medical and mental health history.

Beyond what the adoptive parent needs to know, they should remember the importance of sibling relationships and decide how to maintain those connections. According to child welfare systems, any involvement with the birth parent(s) is at the discretion of the adoptive parent. "However, adoptive parents should realize that connections to siblings and other birth relatives can be very important to adopted children" (DCFS, 2022, p. 17). These recommendations come with a caveat: Connections must be healthy and benefit the child; otherwise, chaotic connections can be harmful.

Postpermanency Discontinuity

"Permanency policy and child welfare practice have prioritized the safe movement of children out of state custody, yet little is known about the lasting and binding nature of families formed through adoption or guardianship" (Rolock et al., 2018, p. 11). The goal is to provide a safe and nurturing environment for children/youth to have life-long relationships and a sense of belonging with a family (Rolock et al., 2018). Although this is the goal, relationships and legal arrangements do not always endure. Studies have shown that 10% to 15% of children who achieve permanent placement through adoption or guardianship may experience postpermanency discontinuity (Rolock & White, 2016; Rolock et al., 2018). Postpermanency discontinuity happens for many reasons.

Postpermanency discontinuity refers to children and youth who achieve legal permanency through adoption or guardianship and later reenter the child welfare system, emancipate from the system, or choose an alternative placement. Postpermanency discontinuity can happen formally or informally. If an adoptive parent can no longer care for the child they have a legal relationship with, they can *formally* request a change in custody with the state child protective agency. When adoptive parents make a plea to discontinue caring for the child, it can go two ways: (a) The child protective services attorney may *"motion the case up"* in court to consider bringing the child back into the foster care system due to failure of adoption, or (b) adoptive parents may refuse to abide by their legal agreement and could be charged with neglect (this may vary from state to state). In the case of a guardian who wants to relinquish the child, they can make a plea to give the child/youth back to the foster care system. Depending on their mental health needs, children/youth may also go into mental health facilities or long-term facilities. These placements happen formally, but if an adoptive parent refuses to take the youth back into their home, this could be considered to be a *"lock-out."* It is important to know all the facts because any caregiver—foster or adoptive parent or guardian—may have extenuating circumstances or safety concerns about the youth. Each state has its own guidelines for managing these circumstances.

Informal permanency discontinuity occurs when the youth finds an alternative place to live (without the consent or knowledge of the adoptive parent/guardian). The alternative placement could be with a friend, relative, or biological parents. Alternative placements may be due to instability, broken relationships in the adoptive home, or the youth's desire to return home.

Suggestions to Strengthen Postadoption/Guardianship Permanency

Although most children and families report stability after adoption or guardianship, it does not ensure the continued well-being of adoptive relationships (Rolock et al., 2018). Postadoption support and services are gravely needed to ensure that postpermanency stability occurs. Continued support can help buffer against life challenges and typical transitions such as divorce, loss of a spouse through death, retirement, the birth of children, natural disasters, and more. The ebbs and flows of life cannot be predicted, and a once stable environment can be destabilized as families navigate through life. For example, adopting an infant brings such joy to families that consideration may not be given to the complete medical history and future consequences of the adoptive child having biological parents who suffer from mental health issues that the child may be genetically predisposed to later in life. Consequently, this family may need support postadoption many years later.

The authors make a few suggestions to strengthen postpermanency supports:

1. Survey postpermanent homes every 5 years to inquire about family/child well-being.
2. Ensure smaller postadoption worker caseloads to enhance case management.
3. Implement a tracking and reporting system to examine a child's well-being after adoption.
4. Create a postpermanency task force (i.e., postadoptive parents, foster children, case managers, supervisors, policy specialists) to discuss innovative ways to support youth and families.

In addition, it is helpful to understand what variables are associated with an increased likelihood of placement disruption. Prepermanency characteristics that are related to postpermanency discontinuity include (a) a higher number of foster placements—those with more placements were *more likely* to experience discontinuity; (b) placement with siblings—those placed with at least one sibling were *less likely* to experience discontinuity; (c) length of time in care—those who spent 3 or more years in foster placement were, perhaps surprisingly, *less likely* to experience discontinuity, which may reflect increased services from the child welfare system and better preparation for adoption or guardianship; and (d) age of the child—the younger the child, the *less likely* they are to experience placement discontinuity (Rolock & White, 2016). Knowing what factors are associated with a greater or lesser likelihood of placement disruption can suggest where preventive efforts can be directed, ideally before a family is in crisis (Rolock & White, 2016).

Reflection Box 8.2

Consider the child welfare system and, in small groups, discuss your suggestions for strengthening families postpermanency. Choose a reporter who will review your suggestions with the larger group. Slides or white boards may be used to display the answers. While other groups present their solutions, consider any patterns or surprises encountered.

1. What can be done to strengthen the adoptive parent–child relationship over time?
2. What specific information should be provided to prospective adoptive parents before the finalization of adoption?
3. What specific information should be reviewed periodically with the adoptive parent?
4. What types of resources should be available in the life of an adoptive family?
5. What other enhancements may be made to assist these families?

YOUTH: AGING OUT OF FOSTER CARE

Spinelli et al. (2021) report that transition-age youth (TAY) are a large subpopulation of youth in child welfare. Nationwide, TAY typically are emerging into adulthood (ages 14 to 26), and the start of transition planning may vary from state to state. Transition planning is vitally important to the success of youths as they enter adulthood. Foster youth can get lost in the system if they display troubling behavior, truancy from school, and an unwillingness to follow the goals in their service plan. "Studies of youth that have exited foster care show that TAY have high rates of homelessness, decreased employment rates, low rates of high school graduation, and high rates of arrests when compared to same-aged peers" (Spinelli et al., 2021, p. 2). Approximately 20,000 foster youth age out of the system per year; however, without needed support, they may not be able to thrive as they should if they were adequately prepared for adulthood (Annie E. Casey Foundation, 2022).

Trauma affects foster youth in ways that impede their ability to plan for the future. Some foster youth suffer from arrested development impacted by childhood trauma. Unaddressed trauma can lead to runaway behavior, homelessness, depression, risky sexual behavior, sexual exploitation, substance use, gang membership, and other detrimental pathways (Rebbe et al., 2017). In addition, foster youth may struggle with adult transitions for many reasons.

Still, as youth transition from the foster care system into adulthood, they may experience the additional challenge of not having the necessary support systems to guide them through the decision-making process (see Figure 8.2). There are many pathways for youth transitioning out of the child welfare system. A youth who chooses an alternative path with negative consequences could end up in mental health environments or the criminal justice system. Not all youth take full advantage of programming and opportunities for growth. Unfortunately, youth may experience serious challenges into adulthood. Foster youth with little exposure to the workforce and no educational or vocational guidance opportunities may have unrealistic expectations about self-sufficiency. Transition planning should be viewed as a process that considers the youth's long-term plans and breaks them down into smaller, manageable short-term goals.

The SMART goals are specific, measurable, attainable, realistic, and time-bound (see Table 8.1). Foster youth could benefit from extended foster care services if they remain in the system. Some, however, leave the system before they are fully ready for self-sufficiency. A sober look at their life skills readiness is recommended starting at age 14. Youth must engage in a variety of advanced skills for adult living, such as: (a) navigating the child welfare system, (b) managing transportation, (c) practicing daily living and self-care skills, (d) budgeting, (e) accessing community resources, (f) becoming civically engaged, (g) becoming

Figure 8.2 Youth Transitioning Out of the Child Welfare System

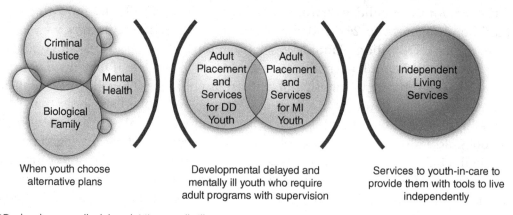

DD, developmentally delayed; MI, mentally ill.

TABLE 8.1 SMART GOAL

A SMART GOAL EXAMPLE FOR TRANSITION AGE YOUTH		
Specific	A *short-term* goal is to research apartments to check costs (immediate action).	A *long-term* goal is to have an apartment by the age of 18.
Measurable	Check-in with the case manager or residential counselor and maintain a log of activities.	Obtain a list of affordable apartments in 2 weeks. Obtain a job to maintain housing within 6 months.
Attainable	Understand: The goal is attainable by breaking the task into smaller, more manageable chunks.	Have regular check-ins to monitor progress toward their goal. Achieve step by step progress.
Realistic	Understand: This goal must also align with what the youth can afford.	Check-in with the youth as a relational practice to monitor progress and ensure adequate fit is made.
Time-bound	Understand: The goal is time limited and is expected to be met within 1 year.	Have regular check-ins to monitor progress toward their goal.

computer literate and practicing online safety, and (h) maintaining healthy relationships. However, some youth in care are resilient despite the trauma they have endured. These young people are able to create plans and imagine possibilities for a better life for themselves.

For example, a long-term goal could be having an apartment by age 18, and an accompanying short-term goal could be looking up the average cost of rent in the area and identifying two potential apartments by a specific time (Child Welfare Information Gateway, 2018).

Transition planning is an essential part of youth exiting the child welfare system because it is important for youth in care to understand how to set achievable goals that will sustain them as they take steps toward independence. Keeping in mind the trauma and adversities that youth in the foster care system have to overcome, it may be difficult for them to visualize a realistic picture of their future. Child welfare professionals should be prepared to work with youth to create a transition plan. This plan can involve career/education/vocational exploration and planning, financial literacy, and even researching the price of housing and the cost of living on their own.

Federal legislation called the Fostering Connection Act of 2008 has implications for working with youth and planning for their discharge from the foster care system well before they reach the age of 18 or 21. Transition planning depends on the state, as rules may vary. Foster youth who remain in the system and work or take vocational training will receive extra funds for completing certain tasks. They undergo financial literacy training and other life skills training (daily living, self-care, work, and study habits, using community resources, and more). This Act extends time in care for foster youth to support them as they transition into adulthood. Some youth in this age group remain in foster care due to developmental delays or mental health challenges that impede their ability to care for themselves. It will be important to begin working with this population early in their teens to obtain the proper assessments to identify a clear diagnosis and recommendations for adult transition services and living arrangements beyond foster care. In these circumstances, placements like adult Community Integrated Living Arrangement (CILA) housing and adult group home settings with supervised independent living programs are generally explored. In some cases, adult guardianship may be needed depending on the level of disability.

Case Scenario: Rosario: A Case for Resiliency

Rosario came into the child welfare system as a result of neglect. Her mother abused drugs and often left her home alone. After her mother left her home for a week, Rosario, who was 11 years old, began to ask her neighbors for food. One of the neighbors called the hotline, a report was substantiated, and Rosario was brought into care. She was initially placed with her maternal grandmother. Rosario lived with her grandmother until she was 13 years old when her grandmother suddenly passed away. She was then moved to live with her maternal aunt. Despite the moves, she maintained good grades and was a good student. The boyfriend of Rosario's aunt began to make inappropriate sexual remarks toward her and touched her inappropriately. Rosario told her aunt, who in turn blamed Rosario, causing a rift between Rosario and her aunt. The aunt began calling her names and locking her out of the house. Things got so heated one night that Rosario's aunt began hitting her with a stick. Rosario grabbed everything she could and ran out of the home, vowing never to return. She was allowed to stay with one of her classmates and informed her teacher about what happened the next day. Rosario's case worker came to the school and took her to the child welfare office to discuss placement. Rosario stated that she did not want to go back to another foster home; she would rather go to a group home where she could be around other girls her age. By the time Rosario was 15, she had learned about all the resources the state child welfare agency had offered youth in care. She spoke with her guardian ad litem, who encouraged her to take

(continued)

Case Scenario: Rosario: A Case for Resiliency (*continued*)

advantage of those resources. Rosario contacted her case worker to ask for help making a transition plan.

Discuss this scenario in groups of four. In class, report back to the larger group and answer the following questions.

DISCUSSION QUESTIONS

1. What is Rosario's support system?
2. How might the case worker begin helping Rosario create an adult transition plan?
3. How might the case worker outline the steps and identify the resources needed?
4. How can the case worker support Rosario in reaching her goals?
5. What resources do you anticipate Rosario may need?

Although names have been changed, this scenario is based on a real-life case. Rosario became independent and worked hard in school. She worked while in college, saved her money, and proclaimed she wanted everything she was entitled to get. Rosario used the resources to further her education and support herself through the process. Her guardian ad litem so inspired Rosario that she decided to go to law school and became a lawyer to advocate for youth in the child welfare system.

CHAPTER SUMMARY

This chapter focuses on the importance of permanency for children and youth in the foster care system. In this chapter, the authors focus on family preservation, foster care, and permanency for youth in care. Child welfare professionals need to understand that time in care for a child seems much longer than it really is, particularly when they are separated from their families. It can cause anxiety and frustration that can manifest in behavioral and emotional dysregulation. It is important to work diligently on the front end when youth enter the child welfare system to return them to their parents when possible. Engagement, assessment, planning, consistent communication, and visitation are critical throughout the life of a case. When returning home to parents is not an option, other permanency options should be considered, such as subsidized guardianship and adoption. These options provide youth with a safe and nurturing environment to support them as they grow into adulthood. This chapter explored the differences between subsidized guardianship and adoption and what type of permanent relationship these options may offer the youth.

It should be noted that both are excellent options and provide permanency for youth. However, there are variances in the decision about which option to choose. The age of the youth and connections with biological families, guardians, and adoptive parents can play a role in making decisions about the type of permanency goal they choose. Once permanency has been established, it is vital to honor the youth's identity and wishes as they relate to faith, sexuality, and culture, while finding ways in the community to affirm and support them so that they can thrive and become secure and healthy adults.

Trauma affects youth in so many different ways. Sometimes it affects the youth's mental health, impacting their behavior and decision-making. Depression, anxiety, and mental health–related behavior can affect foster care placements when those behaviors become disruptive to the home leading to multiple placements. Some youth may be unable to thrive in traditional foster home placements. These youth tend not to reach permanency through adoption or guardianship and remain in the foster care system as they transition to adulthood. Adult transition services offer a variety of ways that youth can become independent and care for themselves. Youth can benefit from vocational and educational services and live in transitional and independent environments where they learn financial literacy, budgeting, and daily living skills to prepare them for life on their own. Youth transitioning to adulthood can also take advantage of state-funded educational opportunities to attend college or vocational school to prepare them further to be self-sufficient. Although resources are available, some youth make alternative decisions that render them homeless and unable to care for themselves. Youth may become involved in alternative systems such as various mental health facilities or the criminal justice system. There are also youth who make the decision to return to their biological families.

DISCUSSION QUESTIONS

1. What are the differences among foster care, adoption, and subsidized guardianship?
2. What role would you most prefer to work in: postadoption permanency or the foster care system?
3. What factors lead to greater resiliency in foster care youth?
4. What are the benefits of adoption for foster care youth?
5. What are the most significant concerns for youth aging out of the system?
6. What is postpermanency discontinuity?
7. How does postpermanency discontinuity affect youth in the child welfare system?

RESOURCES

Department of Children and Family Services
http://www2.illinois.gov/DCFS

Annie E. Casey Foundation/Casey Life Skills Toolkit / Casey Family Program
https://www.casey.org/casey-life-skills/

The Child Welfare Gateway
www.childwelfare.gov/pubs/transitional-plan/

Kids Count Data Center
https://datacenter.aecf.org/data#USA/2/35/36,38,40/char/0

National Youth in Transition Database (NYTD)/Children's Bureau
https://www.acf.hhs.gov/cb/fact-sheet/about-nytd

 A robust set of instructor resources designed to supplement this text is located at **http://connect.springerpub.com/content/book/978-0-8261-5285-5.** Qualifying instructors may request access by emailing **textbook@springerpub.com.**

REFERENCES

Adoption and Foster Care Analysis Reporting System. (2021). *Trends in foster care and adoption: FY 2012–2021.* AFCARS data, U.S. Children's Bureau, Administration for Children, Youth and Families. https://www.acf.hhs.gov/sites/default/files/documents/cb/trends-foster-care-adoption-2012-2021.pdf

Adoption and Foster Care Analysis Reporting System. (2022). *The AFCARS report.* U.S. Department of Health and Human Services, Administration for Children and Families, Administration on Children, Youth and Families, Children's Bureau. https://www.acf.hhs.gov/sites/default/files/documents/cb/afcars-report-29.pdf

Annie E. Casey Foundation. (2014). *Race equity and inclusion action guide: Seven steps to advance and embed race equity and inclusion within your organization.* https://www.aecf.org/resources/race-equity-and-inclusion-action-guide

Annie E. Casey Foundation. (2022). *Foster care explained: What it is, how it works and how it can be improved.* https://www.aecf.org/blog/what-is-foster-care

Annie E. Casey Foundation. (2023). *Kids count data center.* https://datacenter.aecf.org/data/line/6242-children-ages-birth-to-17-in-foster-care?loc=1&loct=1#1/any/false/2048,574,1729,37,871,870,573,869,36,868/asc/any/12985

Brown, J. D., George, N., Sintzel, J., & St. Arnault, D. (2009). Benefits of cultural matching in foster care. *Children and Youth Services Review, 31,* 1019–1024. https://doi.org/10.1016/j.childyouth.2009.05.001

Chambers, R. M., Crutchfield, R. M., Willis, T. Y., Cuza, H. A., Oteroe, A., Goddu Harper, S. G., & Carmichael, H. (2020). "Be supportive and understanding of the stress that youth are going through:" Foster care alumni recommendations for youth, caregivers and caseworkers on placement transitions. *Children and Youth Services Review, 108,* 1–9. https://doi.org/10.1016/j.childyouth.2019.104644

Chateauneuf, D., Poitras, K., Simard, M-C., & Buisson, C. (2022). Placement stability: What role do the different types of family foster care play? *Child Abuse and Neglect, 130,* 1–10. https://doi.org/10.1016/j.chiabu.2021.105359

Child Welfare Information Gateway. (2018). *Working with youth to develop a transition plan.* U.S. Department of Health and Human Services, Children's Bureau. www.childwelfare.gov/pubs/transitional-plan/

Child Welfare Information Gateway. (2023). *National foster care month.* U.S. Department of Health and Human Services, Children's Bureau. https://www.childwelfare.gov/fostercaremonth/awareness/facts/

Department of Children and Family Services. (2022, November). *Making the adoption guardianship decision.* Illinois Department of Children and Family Services. http://www2.illinois.gov/DCFS

Font, S. A. (2015). Is higher placement stability in kinship foster care by virtue or design? *Child Abuse & Neglect, 42,* 99–111. https://doi.org/10.1016/j.chiabu.2015.01.003

Font, S. A., & Gershoff, E. T. (2020). Foster care: How we can, and should, do more for maltreated children. *Social Policy Report, 33*(3), 1–40. https://doi.org/10.1002/sop2.10

McGuire, A., Cho, B., Huffhines, L., Gusler, S., Brown, S., & Jackson, Y. (2018). The relation between dimensions of maltreatment, placement instability, and mental health among youth in foster care. *Child Abuse & Neglect, 86,* 10–21. https://doi.org/10.1016/j.chiabu.2018.08.012

Rebbe, R., Nurius, P. S., Ahrens, K. R., & Courtney, M. E. (2017). Adverse childhood experiences among youth aging out of foster care: A latent class analysis. *Children and Youth Services Review, 74,* 108–116. https://doi.org/10.1016/j.childyouth.2017.02.004

Rolock, N., Pérez, A. G., White, K. R., & Fong, R. (2018). From foster care to adoption and guardianship: A twenty-first century challenge. *Child and Adolescent Social Work Journal, 35*(1), 11–20. https://doi.org/10.1007/s10560-017-0499-z

Rolock, N., & White, K. R. (2016). Post-permanency discontinuity: A longitudinal examination of outcomes for foster youth after adoption or guardianship. *Children and Youth Services Review, 70,* 419–427. https://doi.org/10.1016/j.childyouth.2016.10.025

Spinelli, T. R., Bruckner, E., & Kisiel, C. L. (2021). Understanding trauma experiences and needs through a comprehensive assessment of transition age youth in child welfare. *Child Abuse and Neglect, 122,* 105367. https://doi.org/10.1016/j.chiabu.2021.105367

Waniganayake, M., Hadley, F., Johnson, M., Mortimer, P., McMahon, T., & Karatasas, K. (2019). Maintaining culture and supporting cultural identity in foster care placements. *Australasian Journal of Early Childhood, 44*(4), 365–377. https://doi.org/10.1177/1836939119870908

Xu, Y., & Bright, C. L. (2018). Children's mental health and its predictors in kinship and non-kinship foster care: A systematic review. *Children and Youth Services Review, 89,* 243–262. https://doi.org/10.1016/j.childyouth.2018.05.001

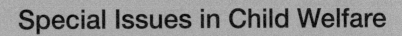

III   Special Issues in Child Welfare

9 Addressing the Needs of Foster Children in School Settings

CASSANDRA MCKAY-JACKSON, SARA CASTILLO, ARELY CERDA, AND ERIC VELASCO

LEARNING OBJECTIVES

By the end of the chapter, you will be able to:

- Understand the challenges children and youth face in foster care as they navigate the educational system.
- Understand principles of trauma-informed care in the schools and their relevance to children in care.
- Apply Positive Youth Development (PYD) competencies to treatment planning and collaboration with foster care youth.
- Discuss the importance of advocacy and strategizing to reduce inequities in school settings faced by children and youth in foster care through the engagement of youth voice.
- Discuss the importance of developmentally and culturally appropriate social and emotional support that can be provided collaboratively between the child welfare and educational systems for children and youth in foster care.

INTRODUCTION

Beyond the family, the school system is one of the most significant influences in a child's or youth's life. Children and youth spend countless hours in this system, where they ideally are supported in their intellectual, social, emotional, and physical development through interactions with adults and peers. In the best circumstances, parents/caregivers and school personnel are engaged in *collaborative efforts* to enhance healthy development and acquisition of skills to help youth transition into adult roles.

Compulsory schooling in the United States parallels two stages of psychosocial development, based on Erik Erikson's model: In the school-age phase (industry vs. inferiority, ages 6–12), the child must master new skills or feel a sense of defeat and failure. Ideally, in the school setting, children have opportunities and support to learn new skills and develop a sense of mastery. The opportunities may occur within or outside school settings. For instance, a child who engages in organized sports can master specific skills that enhance confidence. Students who experience unremediated failure in the school setting or do not have other opportunities for success may fail to develop a sense of mastery/industry. This phase is significant for all children to build confidence by mastering skills and being recognized for that mastery. It may be even more critical for children in out-of-home care, as they often face obstacles in their development.

During adolescence (identity vs. role confusion, 12–18 years of age), the youth must discover a sense of self through social relationships, experimentation with different roles, and how they relate to the culture and larger community (Knight, 2017). Youth who experience a disruption in their home placement have often had less opportunity to form and maintain healthy social relationships and may not have had the support for healthy experimentation with different roles, so crucial in identity development and in their sense of how they fit into their community and culture.

For children and youth experiencing a disruption in their home placement, their mastery of tasks in each stage of development may suffer. In many cases, they have yet to receive support and encouragement from parents/caregivers or other learning and mastery opportunities, such as sports or artistic endeavors. They may not develop the skills they need for mastery at one stage, preparing them to move on to the next successfully. They may need more social support to accomplish the tasks at these stages of development. Child welfare professionals can partner with schools and foster parents in these cases to provide a supportive space to restore and enhance growth.

This chapter highlights the (a) challenges experienced by children and youth in foster care in the context of the school; (b) manifestation of traumatized behavior in school-based settings; (c) role of child welfare professionals in working collaboratively with school social workers and other personnel to advocate for appropriate accommodations and interventions, including trauma-informed approaches such as restorative practices; and (d) constructs from the Positive Youth Development (PYD) approach that can be applied to work with youth in foster care.

CHILD WELFARE, TRAUMATIZED BEHAVIOR, AND THE SCHOOL SETTING

Within the United States, there continue to be significant differences in rates of child maltreatment by type. In 2021, neglect accounted for 76% of cases, physical abuse represented 16%, and sexual abuse accounted for 10% (U.S. Department of

Health and Human Services [DHHS], 2023). Neglect and abuse can lead to childhood trauma and have lifelong consequences.

Children/youth in the foster care system who already may have experienced trauma from the abuse or neglect they have sustained may experience additional trauma through the separation from their families. Further, youth in these circumstances may also be more likely to have experienced exposure to their parent's/caregiver's intimate partner violence (IPV), subsequently contributing to behavioral, social, and cognitive challenges because of their caregiver's inability to attend to the youth's needs fully (Bernstein et al., 2019). Witnessing IPV leads to trauma and possible symptoms of post traumatic stress. These traumatic experiences have grave consequences for the child's intellectual, social, emotional, and physical development. Exposure to trauma affects brain development. Developing children and youth experience periods of significant brain growth at various times in their young lives. Specific regions of the brain are particularly sensitive at certain stages of children's development. The brain is also very adaptable to positive or negative environmental circumstances (Child Welfare Information Gateway, 2023). As a result, children and youth may develop responses to a negative environment that help them survive but may not be adaptive in other situations. They may suffer from compromised brain development manifesting in poor academic performance, absenteeism, disruptions to attachment, and other significant problems in schools. These issues are further compounded when children fall behind their peers academically and have difficulty making and maintaining social connections (Child Welfare Information Gateway, 2017). Understanding the relationship between trauma and school performance prepares school and child welfare professionals to collaborate more effectively to support the student involved in the child welfare system.

Relationship Between Foster Care Placement and School Performance

The U.S. Department of Education (DOE) and DHHS assert that "Children and youth in foster care represent one of the most vulnerable student subgroups in this country" (DOE & DHHS, 2016, p. 3). Children and youth in foster care are more likely than their peers to have lower academic achievement and fall behind in school (Somers et al., 2020). They receive special education services at higher rates than their peers, have more school absences (Palmieri & LaSalle, 2017), are more likely to be retained for at least 1 year (Jaramillo & Kothari, 2022), and are less likely to graduate from high school (DOE & DHHS, 2016). Some of these poorer outcomes are associated with increased mobility and instability at home and school, as significant numbers of foster youth make unplanned school changes during the school year compared to their peers (DOE & DHHS, 2016) and likely attend more schools throughout their academic careers.

Youth in foster care also tend to have more disciplinary referrals than their peers not involved in the child welfare system (Somers et al., 2020). Children who are removed from their families by the child welfare system may be preoccupied with thoughts of returning home and may be worried about their parents or siblings. This preoccupation with the family of origin may divide their attention throughout the school day. In addition, transferring from school to school can negatively impact their school performance and subsequent connection to a new academic environment. School disciplinary referrals can also impede academic achievement, as they may involve removal from instruction and encourage a lack of connection or even alienation from the school environment.

Intervention Strategies to Support System-Involved Children and Youth

It is essential to recognize that each student's experience is unique, each student's response is unique, and no single intervention or approach may work for all students (Palmieri & LaSalle, 2017). However, no matter what their previous experiences have been, students in foster care have experienced a remarkable separation from their parents/caregivers, school, friends, possibly siblings, pets, and community. In short, they have been separated from what was familiar to them. In addition, early relationships with parents/caregivers may have been marked by a lack of trust. These patterns can affect future relationships, even those with teachers (Palmieri & LaSalle, 2017) and other adults.

While all students require a nurturing and stable environment to succeed, the needs of students in foster care may differ significantly from their peers not in care. There are many approaches school personnel can take to address these needs. Students who feel more connected tend to perform better in school. In contrast, children and youth in foster placements tend to feel less connected (Somers et al., 2020) and are more likely to experience academic struggles. School settings can support children and youth in foster care in various ways. School social workers can assist by supporting child welfare–involved students using the following inclusive practices (see Figure 9.1):

1. Contributing to a welcoming environment (e.g., recognizing diverse family compositions, including foster families).
2. Encouraging cultural representation in school personnel, communications, events, and activities.
3. Facilitating safe spaces by promoting diversity, inclusion, access, and belonging.
4. Using a trauma-informed lens to support the foster student in acclimating to a new environment.

It is essential to anticipate the fears, doubts, and reservations of a child whose home life has been disrupted. A welcoming environment facilitates students'

Figure 9.1 Supporting Child Welfare Youth in Schools

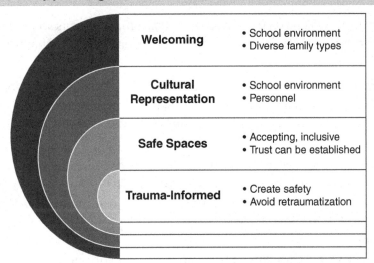

Welcoming	• School environment • Diverse family types
Cultural Representation	• School environment • Personnel
Safe Spaces	• Accepting, inclusive • Trust can be established
Trauma-Informed	• Create safety • Avoid retraumatization

connection to the school and may enhance student engagement with teachers and peers. In addition, cultural representation is vital for students in establishing a sense of belonging. Seeing people like you can be powerful and may affect students' aspirations and achievements. School personnel should ensure that child welfare–involved youth have safe spaces that are diverse, inclusive, and accessible. Safe spaces allow these youth to establish a sense of belonging and trust where they can share their experiences with someone who cares. Finally, a trauma-informed lens helps create safety for child welfare–involved students and families. It is crucial to avoid retraumatizing students who are already vulnerable.

In addition to steps to create a welcoming and nurturing school environment, there are other recommendations to support students who are child welfare involved. Children and youth in foster care are likely to change schools at the time of placement into a foster home, and many go through several school changes when they are in care. Schools may not have received updated information about foster students' backgrounds or former experiences (Palmieri & LaSalle, 2017).

The child welfare and educational systems must share information so that teachers, school social workers, and other school personnel will have the information they need to provide appropriate and timely services (Fouck & Esposito, 2016). Additionally, youth who experience multiple school transitions have a weaker future orientation, associated with lower academic success (Somers et al., 2020).

Palmieri and LaSalle (2017) recommend using:

1. *School-home partnerships* to include the school staff, child welfare worker(s), and foster parents. School workers and other key professionals involved in the student's life may be added.

2. *Structured and supportive environment* for all students in the school.

3. *Social skills support* to address any deficits that children and youth in care may have.

4. *A schoolwide framework such as Positive Behavior Interventions and Support (PBIS)* to meet the needs of students regarding social, emotional, behavioral, and [academic] concerns.

5. *Extracurricular activities* to further support students' connections to the school. Students who are child welfare involved may benefit from the extra incentive to participate and improve overall attendance.

Students will have an array of mental health needs. Interventions may include trauma-focused cognitive behavioral therapy (TF-CBT)—an evidence-based intervention. In addition, schools can implement a behavior management system that sets clear expectations for student behavior and provides positive support for reinforcement.

One of the most significant predictors of school completion is literacy, or the ability to read and write in English. Children and youth in foster care are more likely to have lower literacy levels than their peers, but most are not receiving early intervention services for reading (Fouck & Esposito, 2016). Thus, intensive services in reading help students with reading deficits perform better academically. School mobility may play a role in the need for more services. In schools with a multitiered system, all students should be screened as early as preschool to identify preliteracy skills, ensuring literacy instruction for children in foster care (Fouck & Esposito, 2016).

Child welfare professionals and school social workers should investigate evidence-based interventions, refer students for additional services when needed, and consider schoolwide approaches such as trauma-informed schools and restorative practices. Countless schools nationwide have moved toward a multitiered approach for academics and behavior (multitiered systems of support [MTSS]), beginning with schoolwide intervention, then moving into more focused and restrictive interventions. The MTSS model addresses the whole child and goes beyond basic academics and behavior; it is well-suited for implementing trauma-informed practices (Williams, 2023). Additionally, the emphasis on students' social, emotional, and behavioral functioning has been increased. School districts are following the lead of child welfare and mental health professionals in their promotion of trauma-informed practices (Eber et al., 2020), and there are ways of incorporating trauma-informed practices within a schoolwide multitiered model to enhance social, emotional, and behavioral development of children. These practices can be helpful to children and youth in out-of-home placements who have encountered trauma exposure in their lives.

It is important to recognize the strengths and resilience of children and youth in foster care (Jaramillo & Kothari, 2022). They have survived many challenges. Sometimes school staff make an assumption that students in foster care cannot achieve or will present behavior problems. These assumptions can limit how teachers and other school personnel view the child. These limitations also influence how teachers interact with child welfare–involved youth and the level of behavioral and academic expectations they set for them.

Trauma-Informed Schools

Many schools have been applying principles of trauma-informed care to become more responsive to student needs, reduce bullying and other forms of school violence, and develop more positive and less punitive approaches to discipline. Trauma-informed practices address both behavioral and academic challenges, encourage resilience, and emphasize social and emotional development and well-being (Williams, 2023). Integrating trauma-informed practices into a multitiered approach can provide a solid pathway to addressing the social, emotional, and behavioral aspects of development that have an impact on student learning (Eber et al., 2020), and this may be especially important for children and youth in foster care who have experienced multiple traumas. Recognizing that increasing numbers of children and youth have experienced some form of trauma and knowing that these traumatic events affect academic and behavioral performance compels more and more schools to implement trauma-informed practices (Williams, 2023). In fact, for many youth, schools are safe havens for both escape from and space to process traumatic experiences. Ethically, then, the school must implement ways of helping youth recover from trauma (Williams, 2023).

The Substance Abuse and Mental Health Services Administration (SAMHSA, 2014) has defined a trauma-informed approach, which can be applied to any system, including schools and child welfare:

> A program, organization, or system that is trauma-informed realizes the widespread impact of trauma and understands potential paths for recovery; recognizes the signs and symptoms of trauma in clients, families, staff, and others involved with the system; and responds by fully integrating knowledge about trauma into policies, procedures, and practices, and seeks to actively resist re-traumatization. (SAMHSA, 2014, p. 9)

Trauma-informed practices are strengths based and seek to avoid retraumatization of children and youth (Williams, 2023). One approach compatible with trauma-informed strategies is restorative practices. Because they consist of preventive measures and interventions, restorative practices can fit within a multitiered school-wide system (Gregory et al., 2016).

RESTORATIVE PRACTICES

Restorative practices in schools grow out of restorative justice in the judicial system. *Restorative practices* are a broader term encompassing restorative justice, healing and restoring relationships, and proactive, preventive steps to build community. The exact origins of restorative practices are unknown but include indigenous cultures and traditions, faith communities, and correctional system reform movements. Restorative practices intend to identify and focus on the harm that was caused and work to restore relationships. One strategy involves having the wronged party explain their perspective and the impact of the harm they experienced. The offending party has an opportunity to learn about the effects of their actions on both the victim and the community as a whole and find ways to make restitution (Vincent et al., 2021).

Though many schools have adopted multitiered intervention models, they still struggle with finding effective, equitable, and appropriate interventions for the setting (Zakszeski & Rutherford, 2021). Many schools are seeking alternatives to zero-tolerance practices and exclusionary discipline, such as suspension and expulsion, which are ineffective and harmful in many cases (Zakszeski & Rutherford, 2021). In addition, such practices are affected by both implicit and explicit bias, leading to disparate results with higher percentages of Black, Indigenous, and Other People of Color (BIPOC) students on the receiving end of these harmful practices. Youth in foster care also may face more disciplinary exclusion.

Restorative practices have been implemented in many schools as a way of addressing inequities and developing a school-wide approach to discipline that is focused on relationships, accountability, meeting needs, addressing imbalances in power, and utilizing conflicts as opportunities for learning. Though the approach appears promising, implementation has outpaced research on its effectiveness (Gregory et al., 2016; Zakszeski & Rutherford, 2021). Further, there may be differences in how schools identify and implement restorative practices. For example, Zakszeski and Rutherford completed a review of the literature on restorative practices. They found a need for more clarity regarding what was considered restorative practice. They noted that the most commonly mentioned approaches included reactive practices—restorative conferences, responsive circles—and proactive practices—community-building circles, peer mediation, and impromptu restorative meetings. However, some of the articles reviewed described less frequently mentioned activities, including peace education, circles for re-entry, dialogue about equity and social justice issues, and peer juries.

School settings that do not support restorative justice practices may inadvertently promote marginalizing social spaces. Youth experiencing a restrictive environment may cope through escapism, manifesting as (a) retaliation—in this response, the youth may rebel against what feels like a caged social experience; or (b) withdrawal and emotional and physical disengagement from the school setting; this may take the form of absenteeism, lack of interaction with teachers or peers, avoidance of social or other activities. For youth who wage war in the school setting, punishment and exclusion are often used to manage their behavior.

For adults working with rebellious youth, "punitive 'get tough' or avoidant 'kick out' strategies are feel-good responses. [. . .] they lessen immediate adult stress or settle the school environment. However, adults who become counter aggressive or rejecting further rupture a youth's social bond and thus reinforce antisocial behavior" (Brendtro et al., 2005, p. 10).

Such punitive responses dismiss the traumatic experiences of children served within the child welfare system. Disruptive students and zero-tolerant environments do not mix. Broad-stroke push-out policies (i.e., suspensions or expulsions) are not the answer to *convert* these youth into becoming compliant students. Such policies threaten the development of many youth and create barriers to them feeling connected to the school, attaining academic and social-emotional competence, and having a positive identity, as the "preoccupation with punishment and pathology only fuels defiance and discouragement" (Brendtro et al., 2005, p. 69).

Operating as a social contract, schools promise to provide opportunities and benefits through the educational process and a developmental community for belonging (i.e., an age-appropriate communal space for growing and learning). Yet students who experience a restrictive environment, such as zero-tolerance policies, view schools as places of empty promises. Their retaliatory responses suggest that they are fighting against the school's social norms and practices, which confine them, and the youth are demanding retribution for the broken social contract (Noguera, 2003).

Foster children may be prone to missing a lot of classroom instruction time and may have been transferred from school to school or experienced frequent absences. Youth who are behind academically often engage in disruptive behavior either out of frustration, boredom, or embarrassment. Fixated on silencing, containment, or punishment, some schools will reprimand youth for their responses while contributing factors to these responses go unnoticed and unaddressed. Punitive responses point to the psychopolitical nature of oppression often manifested within harsh and indiscriminate zero-tolerance practices. This vicious cycle is so ingrained within the school setting that "the tendency to punish the neediest children, especially those who are Black and Latino, occurs without conscious planning and deliberate orchestration" (Noguera, 2003, p. 349). Vulnerable students in the child welfare system must be given preventive attention if expected to adhere to strict policies. School practices of containment can foster oppression through inequitable tolerance and restrictive participation of marginalized students, promoting a passive citizenry by implementing zero-tolerance policies. It is no wonder that when asked, "What is the problem with schooling? [a] student replied, this place hurts my spirit" (Bane, 1992, p. 11). Children who are child welfare–involved often fall subject to these zero-tolerance policies without considering the full context of their life circumstances and experiences.

Case Scenario: Rebekah Moves to a New School

Rebekah is 6 years old and lived with her mother, father, and two younger siblings until recently. For the first 4 years of her life, Rebekah's father was employed out of the home, working the second shift at his job, and her mother stayed home with the children. The parents had both struggled with alcohol use before having children. Rebekah's mother has been in recovery for 7 years, but Rebekah's father continues to struggle off and on. His struggle with alcohol has been a source of tension in the home, such that Rebekah's mother began planning a way to live independently with the children, if necessary. That meant securing employment, which she did 2 years ago. Rebekah's dad would stay home with the children while their mother was at work. This arrangement worked well until he began staying out with his friends, drinking after work. He would then fall asleep on the couch and would not be tending to the children's needs.

Over approximately 18 months, there were multiple reports to child protective services (CPS), where neighbors and school personnel would express concerns over these unattended or neglected children. Each time there would be a visit to the family. Rebekah's mother consistently demonstrated apparent concern and affection for the children, and Rebekah's father always vowed to maintain sobriety, which he did for a few months before relapsing. The 2½- and 4-year-olds were sometimes out in the front yard unsupervised. Rebekah had to get herself to school and sometimes appeared disheveled and unfed. She also would arrive late, as she was helping to get her younger siblings dressed and fed. She sometimes tried to wake her dad by splashing cold water on his face. After repeated calls to CPS and repeated visits to the home, the court determined that the situation was not improving and the children were at risk. The mother is working hard at taking parenting classes, exploring other resources for childcare, and counseling. The plan is to reunite the family. However, the children are in a nonrelative foster care placement until the parents demonstrate consistent, safe, and nurturing care. The closest available foster placement is approximately an hour away from the family. Thus, the decision was made to change schools. Rebekah had started first grade at her home school, but she was moved a month into the new school year. Rebekah is a quiet but competent student who likes school. However, in her new school, she sometimes has bouts of crying and seems withdrawn.

DISCUSSION QUESTIONS

1. How can the child welfare professional and school social worker work together to support Rebekah in transitioning to a new, unfamiliar school environment?

(continued)

Case Scenario: Rebekah Moves to a New School (*continued*)

2. Consider the many losses and changes that Rebekah has experienced in a short time. Identify as many losses as possible and note how each may affect a developing child.

3. More recently, school and child welfare teams make *best interest* decisions about school placement for children in foster care. What factors do you think went into this decision for Rebekah?

4. What factors would you have considered in determining the best educational placement for Rebekah?

5. There is increasing recognition of the challenges children and youth in care face regarding their educational experiences, often affecting their achievement and later opportunities. What are some of these challenges, and how can they be mitigated?

6. How should the child welfare professional determine the effectiveness of their decisions regarding children's foster placement and education?

THE IMPACT OF RACIAL DISPARITIES IN CHILD WELFARE AND SCHOOLING

Many schools fail to adopt a developmental model when working with youth. A developmental model assumes that students go through similar growth patterns (emotional, social, and intellectual), although depending on life circumstances, the rate at which these growth areas are reached varies. The variability of development is especially important in understanding vulnerable (foster care youth, minority, and low-income) students' social and emotional needs within the educational environment. The racial demographics of children involved in the child welfare system further expound on the inequitable manner by which children are removed from their home environments (Child Welfare Information Gateway, 2021). In 2021, while American Indian and Alaska Native children only made up 1% of the U.S. population, they accounted for 2% of children in foster care, and African American children made up 22% of the foster care population, while only accounting for 14% of the U.S. population (Annie E. Casey Foundation, 2022).

In contrast, White children make up 43% of the foster care population while accounting for 50% of the child population in the United States (Annie E. Casey Foundation, 2022; Puzzanchera & Taylor, 2022). Recognizing these disparities, child welfare professionals must be vigilant in advocating for school policies that reduce inequities and provide culturally affirming and developmentally appropriate social-emotional support.

Restorative justice practices were implemented in schools to counter the ineffective zero-tolerant practices of the 1990s and 2000s (Hoffman, 2014; Wadhwa, 2016). In contrast, restorative justice promotes rebuilding the community and repairing harm. This approach is critical for youth who have experienced family disruption and are now involved in the child welfare system. A framework affiliated with restorative justice and complementary to its principles is PYD.

Positive Youth Development

PYD was established to counter a pathological view of youth and young adulthood. PYD strategies offer a paradigm shift from correcting deficits in individual youth to enhancing their potential for healthy development (Barton et al., 1997).

Based on the research of Bowers et al. (2010) and Lerner et al. (2005), PYD comprises five components (see Figure 9.2):

1. *Competence*: Lerner et al. (2005) describe this component as the cognitive, social, academic, and vocational competencies. These competency components denote problem solving, logical thinking, and decision-making in the cognitive component. Academic competence can be observed through a student's performance in school (grades, attendance, test scores). Social competence relates to how the student/youth interacts with their environment (get along with others and how they manage conflict). In contrast, vocational competence may be reflected in developing a work ethic and exploring career options.

Figure 9.2 Lerner's Five Cs for PYD Leading to Contribution

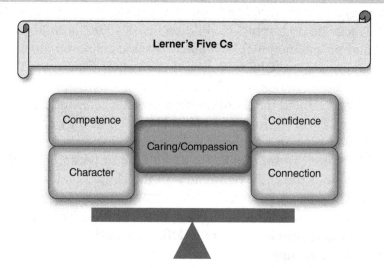

2. *Confidence*: May be explained as the student's/youth's global outlook and trust in their own capacities.

3. *Connection*: May be explained as the student's/youth's positive relationships and interconnection to others within their environment.

4. *Character*: May be explained as the student's/youth's values and standards that guide their behavior (Shek et al., 2019). It concerns the student/youth's morality, integrity, and respect for social expectations.

5. *Caring/Compassion*: The student's/youth's ability to have sympathy and empathy for others. It is essential to develop a sense of concern for others. These components, known as the five Cs, interact with a sixth component, contribution.

When student's/youth's development has been disrupted, it may also impact their ability to contribute or extract meaning from their environments. The disruptions of traumatic child maltreatment must be understood for what they are and how they affect students/foster youth. However, through a series of coordinated activities and experiences, researchers hypothesize that participation in youth development programming may foster the increase of these components, lessen risk behaviors, and heighten contribution (Catalano et al., 2004). The PYD approach "aims at understanding, educating, and engaging children in productive activities rather than [. . .] correcting, curing, or treating them for maladaptive tendencies or so-called disabilities" (Damon, 2004, p. 15).

According to Erikson, industry versus inferiority and identity versus role confusion are foundational challenges in school-age through adolescent development. When youth develop a sense of mastery in school settings, they develop feelings of competence, confidence, and connection. Students with consistently high attachment to school showed less violent behavior and aggressive beliefs, perceived the school climate more positively, and displayed greater academic motivation (Darling-Hammond & Cook-Harvey, 2018). Moreover, boys with consistent high school attachment during their transition from middle to high school had reduced levels of violent behavior. Both boys and girls in the group with high levels of school attachment had lower levels of aggressive beliefs and higher levels of perceived academic motivation, and more positive perceptions of school climate than students who had consistently low school attachment over time (Griner Hill & Werner, 2006).

Positive bonding promotes a youth's trust in self and others, whereas inadequate bonding establishes patterns of insecurity and self-doubt. Extremely poor bonding with an adult fosters a fundamental sense of mistrust in self and others. Further, disruptive students are often isolated from the larger student body because of their behavior. Instead, schools must create ways to engage this population, supporting their sense of belonging and restoration to the larger student population. Restorative practice in schools is about building, maintaining, and repairing relationships. The approach recognizes that relationships among the school community (i.e., between teachers and students, among the youth themselves, colleagues, staff, and caregivers) are critical to learning (Hendry, 2009).

Positive Youth Development: Applications for Children and Youth in Foster Care

Strategies to rebuild or sustain positive bonding with adults include creatively engaging families and marginalized youth. While youth learn skills, caregivers should be informed of these strategies and progress in acquiring them. Child welfare professionals facilitate this by exchanging letters and cards or conducting home visits to celebrate successes, not just problems. These activities support youth–family bonding, family and school community connections, and parents' engagement in collaborative interventions. Additionally, through group work, youth who are often marginalized due to their behavior and rarely receive public affirmation of their skills can strategize how to give back to the school community in meaningful prosocial ways and then receive public affirmation (e.g., a letter from the principal or small assembly acknowledging their efforts).

Although trust is an early benchmark in development, mistrust creates an emotional emptiness that youth may try to fill later in development through drugs, impulsive acts, or antisocial peer relations (Catalano et al., 2004). In contrast, research shows that school environments that promote healthy school boundaries (Gomez & Ang, 2007), elevated expectations for academic achievement and social skill competencies (Bryk & Driscoll, 1988) and school attachment (Frey et al., 2006) are negatively correlated with problematic behaviors. Students who are child welfare–involved must receive multiple opportunities to learn how to work through conflicts and practice this skill within the school setting. Mistakes are part of the learning experience and critical to developing active and productive citizens. Nevertheless, schools that advocate for immediate harsh and punitive measures during this developmental stage will only further ostracize youth, propelling them into self-destructive and externally harmful acts (Noam et al., 2001). Allowing students to learn from their mistakes by participating in a type of discourse to learn within schools requires schools to create a climate that is knowledgeable of, understands, and respects the culture of the students and their families.

As mentioned, a service-learning supplement can foster the contribution of a sixth C of PYD. Service learning, partly through its effects on students' sense of community and positive school climate, may especially help increase marginalized students' engagement and motivation (Golombeck, 2006). Service learning emphasizes youths becoming empowered to see themselves as partners to others in order to bring about change in their environments (Muscott, 2000), fostering a positive identity. Service-learning projects may reduce alienation and isolation by encouraging individual and collective efficacy through meaningful participation in the critical analysis of structural forces and power.

According to Mitra (2004), student voice initiatives support PYD outcomes in the areas of increased agency, belonging, and competence and in fostering feelings of industry. Students who have been abused or neglected and are involved in the child welfare system may believe they have less agency as they often feel powerless and unheard. Service learning, partly through its effects on students' sense of community and positive school climate, may especially help to increase the engagement and motivation of marginalized and traumatized students (Golombeck, 2006). Moreover, *critical service learning* (CSL) builds on these areas of engagement, expands social justice principles, and raises questions about the roots of social inequality (Johnson et al., 2018).

Effective critical service learning projects are not adult-dominated activities that suppress or direct marginalized youth. Instead, they act as a youth–adult partnership, countering a pathological perspective devoid of observing young people's strengths and social consciousness (see McKay, 2010, for further details).

THE CHILD WELFARE PROFESSIONAL AND THE SCHOOL

Child welfare professionals must partner with school social workers who act as a bridge between the school community and youth. They must also view the educational setting as a community where students are empowered, resources are created to support their development, and youth are seen as participating citizens learning to navigate social communities.

With social community, youth may find it easier to engage in a positive way with the environment. Youth who rebel or withdraw in school settings are often referred to the school social worker for remediation. However, the school social worker must be conscious to avoid becoming complicit in oppressive practices by ignoring them. Recognizing students' context and the environmental circumstances that impact them is crucial. Enacting fair practices involves a refusal to blame and punish the victim. In collaboration with the child welfare professional, the school social worker can advocate for specific policies to mitigate harm and provide trauma-informed practices necessary for child welfare involved youth. That said, social work practice must traverse multiple practice levels within school settings to be effective. School social workers are often confined to micro-level practice providing counseling and case management services to youth and their families to curtail disruptive behaviors.

When necessary, child welfare professionals must seek accommodations and modifications for youth to ensure their educational success. Children impacted by the child welfare system may have experienced a breach in their development. However, with the aid of adult allies (e.g., child welfare professionals, school social workers, other school personnel), self-efficacy can be fostered through the process of skill development and mastery. As youth successfully navigate typical crises or challenges at each stage of development, a clear and positive identity emerges.

Further, youth establishment of belief in the future predicts better social and emotional adjustment in school and a more robust internal locus of control. This belief also acts as a protective factor in reducing the adverse effects of high stress on self-rated competence (Wyman et al., 1993). Opportunities for skill development encourage youth to learn, master, and apply cognitive and prosocial competencies (intrapersonal, relational, communicative, decision-making, and action-taking skills) in rehearsed and real-life settings, followed by positive and constructive feedback.

POLICY LEVEL CHANGES

Policymakers have been aware of the educational disparities experienced by youth in foster care. Following the signing into law of the Every Student Succeeds Act (ESSA), a reauthorization of the Elementary and Secondary Education Act, the U.S. Departments of Education (DOE) and DHHS issued nonregulatory guidance for school districts, specifically to address concerns for children and youth in foster care (2016). In addition to the above recommendations (see Figure 9.3) for child welfare agencies and local education agencies (LEAs) to work collaboratively to maintain school stability as much as possible, the DOE and DHHS jointly encourage child welfare agencies and LEAs to facilitate positive outcomes for youth who transition out of care. These recommendations include supporting youth in college and career preparation so that they can successfully move into adult roles.

Figure 9.3 Elements of Interagency Collaboration

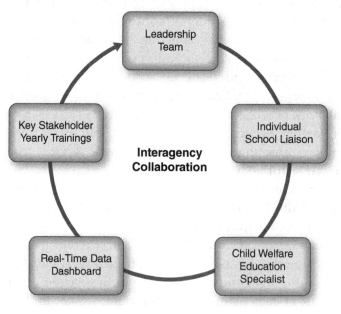

As a response, some school districts may hire staff to support children and youth in foster care to address the additional challenges they experience. Some districts require a *point-of-contact* in each building. In Washington State, for example, the law requires, under RCW 28A.320.148, *foster care liaisons*. The foster care liaison position often is described as one that increases equity by creating a safe, affirming, family-centered environment for families and students who have often felt marginalized and have faced barriers in the schools. Additionally, the foster care liaison facilitates *"best interest determination"* meetings whenever a student in foster care changes placement to match the student with the school that best meets their needs. This legislation was implemented to reduce the number of placement changes and address any gaps in attendance (school disruptions) that can occur when transitioning. Best practice would suggest that school and child welfare professionals make introductions to improve communication and give people someone to contact as needs arise. For examples of implementing best interest determination and other resources, visit the Office of the Superintendent of Public Instruction (OSPI) Foster Care Resources and Training website.

Reflection Box 9.1

Advocacy in the Schools—Practice, Pair, and Share:
Practice advocacy skills by *writing a letter* to a school principal or school social worker requesting specific support for a student who is involved in the child welfare system. Consider promoting a *critical service-learning project* (Johnson et al., 2018) and the use of student voice to encourage individual and collective efficacy through meaningful participation in the critical analysis of structural forces and power. Be specific about the age, grade, and developmental level of the student or group.

CONNECTION BETWEEN CHILD WELFARE AND THE PUBLIC SCHOOL SYSTEM

Education is one of the most essential systems in a child's life. While over 400,000 children and youth are in out-of-home placement at any given time, approximately two thirds are school-age (Farnsworth et al., 2022). Children in foster care face more negative school outcomes than their peers, consequences that include school instability, placement in more restrictive educational settings, suspension or other exclusion from school, and increased risk for disengagement from school (Farnsworth et al., 2022). At the same time, the school setting can become a safe and stable environment for children and youth in foster care (Farnsworth et al.,

2022). Children and youth in the child welfare system often have experienced multiple adverse childhood experiences (ACEs) and benefit from trauma-informed settings and practices.

School social workers, administrators, and teachers can support these children by having easy transitions across schools and strategies to increase school engagement and connection. School professionals need to understand laws that apply to youth in foster care. Those educational professionals who are aware of the legal rights of students in foster care are more likely to follow due process in special education, keep students as much as possible in the same school setting, implement research-based interventions, and ensure that student records are complete (Farnsworth et al., 2022).

Several laws are relevant to education and foster care, including the Individuals with Disabilities Education Act (IDEA), Family Educational Rights and Privacy Act (FERPA), and ESSA (reauthorization of the Elementary and Secondary Education Act). Under IDEA, educators must determine who can legally consent for services and make educational decisions. The parent may consent unless their rights have been limited or terminated by the court. Farnsworth et al. (2022) recommend that educators determine if the child has a court appointed special advocate (CASA) or guardian ad litem (GAL) and include that person in that process—they know the child, the child welfare system, and the legal system. They can help to represent the interests of the child. Farnsworth et al. (2022) further state that educators need to consider that youth in foster care are overrepresented in the emotional and behavioral disorders (EBD) category. Students must receive the services they need while being mindful of this overrepresentation. In addition, students identified as EBD may be placed in more restrictive settings, including out-of-school placements, more than their peers, partly because they may not have adults advocating for them.

Regarding FERPA, if parents have retained their rights, they are the ones who should consent for educational records to be shared with child welfare, foster parents, and outside agencies (Farnsworth et al., 2022). However, educational records must be shared when school placement changes to ensure a smooth transition. The Uninterrupted Scholars Act of 2013 (USA) was passed to reduce delays in sharing records. Under FERPA, records can now be shared with child welfare and tribal communities without parental consent (Farnsworth et al., 2022).

The DOE (2016) recommends increased collaboration and decision-making between child welfare and educational agencies. Limiting educational disruption also is crucial; hence, children and youth entering foster care are to remain in their current school unless it is determined to be in their best interest to change schools (DOE, 2016). There are many considerations when determining if it is in the child's best interest to remain in the same school or transition to a new one. These factors include the preference of the child, the preference of the parent(s) or educational decision-maker, the placement of the child's siblings, the child's connections to the school, possible effects of the length of the commute based on the child's age and developmental stage, considerations for children receiving special education services, considerations for children who are English learners (DOE &

DHHS, 2016). If a school transition is necessary, the child can enroll immediately without waiting for school records. Under ESSA and the Fostering Connections to Success and Increasing Adoptions Act of 2008, a child must be immediately enrolled in a new school if it is not in their best interest to remain in their school of origin. The receiving school should immediately obtain the child's educational record. Children in foster care should be enrolled without delay, even if required documentation is not readily available, to ensure there is no gap in support for the child or youth. ESSA also addresses school stability and puts shared responsibility with LEA, SEA, and child welfare agencies. "The educational stability of children in foster care is a joint responsibility of educational and child welfare agencies, and to successfully implement these provisions, these entities will need to collaborate continuously" (DOE & DHHS, 2016, p. 5).

If parental rights have been terminated, the foster parent often can consent to services. However, this varies from state to state, so the child welfare professional should be familiar with their state's policies. Ultimately, children and youth do better when there are strong connections with caring adults; schools can support these connections by involving them in the process and engaging families and the child welfare agency.

When appropriate, child welfare professionals and school social workers must participate in interorganizational (mezzo level) practice, working collaboratively with teachers within the classroom and larger school communities. In fact, researchers advocate "policies and practices designed to increase collaboration between school social workers, teachers" (Brewster & Bowen, 2004, p. 64). Child welfare professionals and other professionals can foster social support for youth and schools.

Interagency Collaborations

Children and youth are often involved in multiple systems aside from school and child welfare. These systems do not always communicate with each other to develop a coherent approach to supporting the well-being of the child. When these systems fail to collaborate in the assessment, planning, and intervention processes, it may lead to misaligned goals and an incomplete understanding of the child's ecosystem, undermining progress. The DOE and DHHS (2016) prepared a document to address this gap in serving children in the field. This document highlights one example of a community's approach to effective collaboration with multiple systems (see Figure 9.3).

In Figure 9.3, there are five components to this interagency collaboration:

1. *Leadership Team:* A core leadership team facilitated monthly meetings and effective communication among partners.
2. *Individual School Liaison:* The county, in the example, suggested that each school identify a liaison who will communicate regularly with the child welfare education specialist.

3. *Child Welfare Education Specialist:* "Two child welfare agency education specialists [should] liaison with the child welfare agency caseworker assigned to the child's case and assist in education-related issues" (DOE & DHHS, 2016, p. 27).

4. *Real Time Data Dashboard:* The child welfare agency used a real-time data dashboard to incorporate vital information from both collaborating systems—the child welfare agency and the school. Using a real-time data dashboard enhanced case management decisions using up-to-date educational information (DOE & DHHS, 2016), allowing them to better serve the child.

5. *Key Stakeholder Yearly Training:* The collaborative partnership included yearly training for professionals such as judges, supervisors, caseworkers, GAL, court-appointed special advocates, mentors, foster parents, school psychologists, principals, and school social workers.

Agency collaborations are crucial for upholding the best interest of child welfare involved students. Agency collaborations are essential for adequately coordinating services and planned interventions, taking a holistic approach, demonstrating respect for the student's station in life, and creating multiple opportunities to understand the student's mental and emotional health and educational and social needs.

Reflection Box 9.2

Describe how your current or future interactions with youth involved in the child welfare system promote the 5 Cs (i.e., Competence, Confidence, Connection, Character, and Caring/Compassion plus Contribution) of positive youth development.

1. How will you collaborate with the school social worker to help the youth develop a sense of *competence*?

2. What activities will help the child/youth develop their self-*confidence*?

3. What activities increase social *connection* in schools and foster care settings?

4. How might the school social worker enhance the youth's identity development while building *character* (similar to social emotional learning standards [SEL] in schools)?

5. How will you foster a student's sense of empathy, *caring, and compassion* for others?

6. How do all of these components of the 5 Cs assist youth in making a *contribution* to their school, family, and other communities? Are there specific concrete contributions they can make?

CHAPTER SUMMARY

School is one of the most critical systems for children and youth beyond the family. A positive school environment is essential for healthy development. Youth involved in the child welfare system experience tremendous trauma, yet many school settings struggle with supporting their unique emotional, behavioral, and educational needs. Child welfare professionals should advocate for specific educational practices that benefit youth in foster care. These can include school-wide positive behavioral supports, trauma-informed approaches, restorative practices, PYD, and other evidence-based interventions. In addition, they should collaborate with school personnel, become familiar with educational policies relevant to youth in care, and learn more about the process of determining the child's best interest in making school placement decisions.

DISCUSSION QUESTIONS

1. How can zero-tolerant school environments further exacerbate harm for traumatized youth?
2. How do youth–adult partnerships support PYD?
3. What practices can support positive connections between child welfare and public school systems?
4. How can school-wide restorative practices assist children and youth in foster care?
5. How important are trauma-informed approaches in child welfare and school settings?

RESOURCES

National Child Traumatic Stress Network. *Child Trauma Toolkit for Educators* is a resource that informs educators on the specific needs of traumatized children and how to help them overcome the effects of trauma at multiple developmental stages.
https://www.nctsn.org/resources/child-trauma-toolkit-educators
https://www.nctsn.org/sites/default/files/resources//child_trauma_toolkit_educators.pdf

Office of Superintendent of Public Instruction, Washington State.
Foster Care Resources and Training is a resource-rich site for supporting child welfare involved youth /children in school settings.
https://www.k12.wa.us/student-success/access-opportunity-education/foster-care/foster-care -resources-and-training

---

 SPRINGER PUBLISHING **CONNECT™** A robust set of instructor resources designed to supplement this text is located at **http://connect.springerpub.com/content/book/978-0-8261-5285-5**. Qualifying instructors may request access by emailing **textbook@springerpub.com**.

REFERENCES

Annie E. Casey Foundation. (2022, June). *KIDS COUNT data center. Children in foster care by race and hispanic origin in the United States.* https://datacenter.aecf.org/data/tables/6246-children-in-foster-care-by-race-and-hispanic-origin#detailed/1/any/false/2048/2638,2601,2600,2598,2603,2597,2602,1353/12992,12993

Bane, M. W. (Ed.). (1992). *Voices from the inside: A report on schooling from inside the classroom.* Claremont Graduate School, The Institute for Education in Transformation. https://searchworks.stanford.edu/view/4500707

Barton, W. H., Watkins, M., & Jarjoura, R. (1997). Youths and communities: Toward comprehensive strategies for youth development. *Social Work, 42*(5), 483–493. https://www.jstor.org/stable/23718335

Bernstein, R. E., Timmons, A. C., & Lieberman, A. F. (2019). Interpersonal violence, maternal perception of infant emotion, and child-parent psychotherapy. *Journal of Family Violence, 34*(4), 309–320. https://doi.org/10.1007/s10896-019-00041-7

Bowers, E. P., Li, Y., Kiely, M. K., Brittian, A., Lerner, J. V., & Lerner, R. M. (2010). The Five Cs Model of Positive Youth Development: A longitudinal analysis of confirmatory factor structure and measurement invariance. *Journal of Youth and Adolescence, 39*, 720–735. https://doi.org/10.1007/s10964-010-9530-9

Brendtro, L., Ness, A., & Mitchell, M. (2005). *No disposable kids.* National Educational Service. https://www.solutiontree.com/no-disposable-kids.html

Brewster, A. B., & Bowen, G. L. (2004, February). Teacher support and the school engagement of Latino middle and high school students at risk of school failure. *Child and Adolescent Social Work Journal, 21*(1), 47–67. https://link.springer.com/content/pdf/10.1023/B:CASW.0000012348.83939.6b.pdf

Bryk, A. S., & Driscoll, M. E. (1988). *The school as community: Theoretical foundations, contextual influences, and consequences for students and teachers.* National Center on Effective Secondary Schools. https://files.eric.ed.gov/fulltext/ED302539.pdf

Catalano, R. F., Berglund, M. L., Ryan, J. A. M., Lonczak, H. S., & Hawkins, J. D. (2004). Positive Youth Development in the United States: Research findings on evaluations of Positive Youth Development programs. *The Annals of the American Academy of Political and Social Science, 591*(1), 98–124. https://doi.org/10.1177/0002716203260102

Child Welfare Information Gateway. (2017). *Supporting brain development in traumatized children and youth.* U.S. Department of Health and Human Services, Children's Bureau. https://www.childwelfare.gov/pubPDFs/braindevtrauma.pdf

Child Welfare Information Gateway. (2021). *Child welfare practice to address racial disproportionality and disparity.* U.S. Department of Health and Human Services, Administration for Children and Families, Children's Bureau. https://www.childwelfare.gov/resources/child-welfare-practice-address-racial-disproportionality-and-disparity/

Child Welfare Information Gateway. (2023). *Child maltreatment and brain development: A primer for child welfare professionals.* U.S. Department of Health and Human Services, Administration for Children and Families, Children's Bureau. https://www.childwelfare.gov/pubs/issue-briefs/brain-development/

Eber, L., Barrett, S., Scheel, N., Flammini, A., & Pohlman, K. (2020). *Integrating a trauma-informed approach within a PBIS framework.* Technical Assistance Center on Positive Behavioral Interventions and Supports. http://idahotc.com/Portals/0/Resources/858/Integrating%20a%20Trauma-Informed%20Approach%20within%20a%20PBIS%20Framework.pdf

Damon, W. (2004). What is positive youth development. *The Annals of the American Academy of Political and Social Science, 591*(1), 13–24. https://www.jstor.org/stable/4127632

Darling-Hammond, L., & Cook-Harvey, C. M. (2018). *Educating the whole child: Improving school climate to support student success* (research brief). Learning Policy Institute.

Farnsworth, E. M., Cordle, M., Kromminga, K., Shayer, E. L., Szydlo, T., & Frederick, J. (2022). Protecting the educational rights of students in foster care: Legal considerations for educational professionals. *Children and Youth Services Review, 141*, 1–8. https://doi.org/10.1016/j.childyouth.2022.106585

Fouck, S. M., & Esposito, M. C. K. (2016). Ensuring educational equity for children and youth in foster care. *Leadership, 46*(1), 30–33.

Frey, L. L., Beesley, D., & Miller, M. R. (2006). Relational health, attachment, and psychological distress in college women and men. *Psychology of Women Quarterly, 30*, 303–311. https://doi.org/10.1111/j.1471-6402.2006.00298.x

Golombeck, S. B. (2006). Children as citizens. *Journal of Community Practice, 14*(1–2), 11–30. https://doi.org/10.1300/J125v14n01_02

Gomez, B. J., & Ang, P. M. M. (2007). Promoting positive youth development in schools. *Theory Into Practice, 46*(2), 97–104. http://www.jstor.org/stable/40071475

Gregory, A., Clawson, K., Davis, A., & Gerewitz, J. (2016). The promise of restorative practices to transform teacher-student relationships and achieve equity in school discipline. *Journal of Educational and Psychological Consultation, 26*(4), 325–353. https://doi.org/10.1080/10474412.2014.929950

Griner Hill, L., & Werner, N. (2006). Affiliative motivation, school attachment, and aggression in school. *Psychology in the Schools, 43*(2), 231–246. https://doi.org/10.1002/pits.20140

Hendry, R. (2009). *Building and restoring respectful relationships in schools: A guide to using restorative practice.* Routledge. https://www.routledge.com/Building-and-Restoring-Respectful-Relationships-in-Schools-A-Guide-to-Using/Hendry/p/book/9780415544276

Hoffman, S. (2014). Zero benefit: Estimating the effect of zero tolerance discipline policies on racial disparities in school discipline. *Educational Policy, 28*(1), 69–95. https://doi.org/10.1177/0895904812453999

Jaramillo, J., & Kothari, B. H. (2022). Supportive caseworkers, school engagement, & posttraumatic symptoms among youth in foster care. *Child and Adolescent Social Work Journal, 39*(4), 391–407. https://doi.org/10.1007/s10560-021-00749-w

Johnson, A., McKay-Jackson, C., & Grumbach, G. (2018). *Critical service learning toolkit: Social work strategies for promoting healthy youth development.* Oxford University Press.

Knight, Z. G. (2017). A proposed model of psychodynamic psychotherapy linked to Erik Erikson's eight stages of psychosocial development. *Clinical Psychology and Psychotherapy, 24*(5), 1047–1058. https://doi.org/10.1002/cpp.2066

Lerner, R. M., Lerner, J. V., Almerigi, J. B., Theokas, C., Phelps, E., Gestsdottir, S., Nausea, S., Jelicic, H., Alberts, A., Ma, L., Smith, L., Bobek, D., Richman-Raphael., D., Simpson, I., Christiansen, E. D., & von Eye, A. (2005). Positive youth development, participation in community youth development programs, and community contributions of fifth-grade adolescents: Findings from the first wave of the 4-H study of positive youth development. *The Journal of Early Adolescence, 25*(1), 17–71. https://doi.org/10.1177/0272431604272461

McKay, C. (2010). Critical service learning: A school social work intervention. *Children and Schools, 32*(1), 5–13. https://doi.org/10.1093/cs/32.1.5

Mitra, D. (2004). The significance of students: Can increasing student voice in schools lead to gains in youth development? *Teachers College Record, 106*(4), 651–688. http://curriculumstudies.pbworks.com/w/file/fetch/52018177/Mitra2004TheSignificanceofChildrensVoice_TCRecord.pdf

Muscott, H. (2000). A review and analysis of service-learning programs involving students with emotional/behavioral disorders. *Education and Treatment of Children, 23*(3), 346–368. https://www.jstor.org/stable/42899624

Noam, G., Warner, L., & Van Dyken, L. (2001). Beyond the rhetoric of zero tolerance: Long-term solutions for at-risk youth. *New Directions for Youth Development, 92*, 153–182. https://doi.org/10.1002/yd.23320019209

Noguera, P. (2003). Schools, prisons, and social implications of punishment: Rethinking disciplinary practices. *Theory into Practice, 42*(4), 341–350. https://www.jstor.org/stable/1477398

Palmieri, E., & LaSalle, T. P. (2017). Supporting students in foster care. *Psychology in the Schools, 54*(2), 117–126. https://doi.org/10.1002/pits.21990

Puzzanchera, C., & Taylor, M. (2022). *Disproportionality rates for children of color in foster care dashboard.* National Council of Juvenile and Family Court Judges. https://ncjj.org/AFCARS/Disproportionality_Dashboard.asp

Shek, D. T., Dou, D., Zhu, X., & Chai, W. (2019). Positive youth development: Current perspectives. *Adolescent Health, Medicine and Therapeutics, 10*, 131–141. https://doi.org/10.2147/AHMT.S179946

Somers, C. L., Goutman, R. L., Day, A., Enright, O., Crosby, S., & Taussig, H. (2020). Academic achievement among a sample of youth in foster care: The role of school connectedness. *Psychology in the Schools, 57*, 1845–1863. https://doi.org/10.1002/pits.22433

Substance Abuse and Mental Health Services Administration. (2014). *SAMHSA's concept of trauma and guidance for a trauma-informed approach* (HHS Publication No. 14-4884). https://store.samhsa.gov/system/files/sma14-4884.pdf

U.S. Department of Education & U.S. Department of Health and Human Services. (2016, November 29). *Non-regulatory guidance: Ensuring educational stability for children in foster care.* https://www2.ed.gov/policy/elsec/leg/essa/edhhsfostercarenonregulatorguide.pdf

U.S. Department of Health & Human Services, Administration for Children and Families, Administration on Children, Youth and Families, Children's Bureau. (2023). *Child maltreatment 2021.* https://www.acf.hhs.gov/cb/data-research/child-maltreatment

Vincent, C., Inglish, J., Girvan, E., Van Ryzin, M., Svanks, R., Springer, S., & Ivey, A. (2021). Introducing restorative practices into high schools' multi-tiered systems of support: Successes and challenges. *Contemporary Justice Review, 24*(4), 409–435. https://doi.org/10.1080/10282580.2021.1969522

Wadhwa, A. (2016). *Restorative justice in urban schools: Disrupting the school to prison pipeline.* Routledge.

Williams, T. (2023). Implementation of trauma-informed care in a urban school district. *Education and Urban Society, 55*(4), 418–432. https://doi.org/10.1177/00131245221076100

Wyman, P., Cowen, E., Work, W., & Kerley, J. (1993). The role of children's future expectations in self-system functioning and adjustment to life stress: A prospective study of urban at-risk children. *Development and Psychopathology, 5*(4), 649–661. https://doi.org/10.1017/S0954579400006210

Zakszeski, B., & Rutherford, L. (2021). Mind the gap: A systematic review of research on restorative practices in schools. *School Psychology Review, 50*(2–3), 371–387. https://doi.org/10.1080/2372966X.2020.1852056

10

Special Topics in Child Welfare Practice

LEARNING OBJECTIVES

By the end of the chapter, you will be able to:

- Demonstrate an understanding of the intersection of child welfare with a number of other systems.
- Discuss the importance of knowing how other systems operate when working with children and youth in care.
- Discuss the importance of understanding linkages between foster care and juvenile and adult corrections systems and ways to break this link.
- Demonstrate an understanding of the connections between child welfare and healthcare systems and identify ways to meet the health needs of children and youth more effectively.
- Identify some of the inequities and injustices within the child welfare system, particularly as it intersects with other systems.

INTRODUCTION

Child welfare is a complex field of practice. In addition to usual considerations surrounding the assessment of abuse and neglect, protecting children, respecting family integrity, and promoting the well-being of children, families, and communities, we have seen how contextual factors, such as poverty, affect our understanding of abuse and neglect and the appropriate interventions to prevent as well as remediate unsafe situations for children and youth. This chapter explores a range of special circumstances that are important in understanding abuse and neglect and providing the most effective interventions. Essentially, the chapter explores the layers of complexity at the intersection of child welfare with different systems, including health care, corrections, immigration, education, and the military. Youth in out-of-home care are often involved in multiple systems, including but not limited to special education, mental/behavioral health, and juvenile corrections. Abuse and neglect, as well as involvement in the child welfare system, occur in a context. This chapter further explores that context and the interrelationships among different systems. Not only do youth in care often find themselves involved with various systems, but the majority of screened-in referrals come from legal/law enforcement, education, medical, social services, and mental health professionals (U.S. Department of Health and Human Services [DHHS], 2023). Thus, the influence is bidirectional, with professionals in each setting influencing who is referred and identified as potential abuse and neglect victims.

CHILD WELFARE AND THE HEALTHCARE SYSTEM

The child welfare system intersects with the healthcare system in many ways. Child well-being is connected to access to quality healthcare, beginning before birth and lasting throughout childhood and beyond. Specific issues relate directly to healthcare, including adequate nutrition, teenage pregnancy, substance use by parents and youth, physically unhealthy environments, and other health-related concerns.

Teenage Parents

Adolescence can be a challenging time with increased risk-taking and experimentation with different roles, behaviors, and identities. These challenges and risks increase when a youth goes through adolescence without a strong familial or community support system in place. One of the challenges for youth, particularly those without adequate social support, is understanding the consequences of choices around sexual behavior and being able to make fully informed choices. Youth in out-of-home care face an increased risk of unintended pregnancy, HIV, and STIs (Finigan-Carr et al., 2018). Young women exiting foster care are more likely than their peers who have not been a part of the child welfare system to become pregnant, in some cases giving birth while they are still in the system. Approximately one third of teenage women leaving foster care have become pregnant by age 17, and nearly half of those women experience a second pregnancy by age 19 (Rouse et al., 2021).

Young women aging out of the system as parents may find themselves as single mothers with few role models or social support. Without a support system, this may lead to generational involvement with the child welfare system. Risks may be cumulative over time, potentially leading to social isolation, increased risk-taking, and diminished educational opportunities (Rouse et al., 2021). In fact, Rouse and colleagues (2021) found that these young mothers indicated that they wanted their birth mothers' emotional support and physical presence at the time of delivery but often did not receive this.

There are already many known risks to aging out of the foster care system, including abbreviated education, increased likelihood of poverty and homelessness, and increased chance of involvement with the juvenile or adult corrections system. Additional risks associated with becoming a parent before age 21 include an increased likelihood of substance use, poorer quality of interpersonal relationships, decreased economic stability, and poorer physical and mental health (Rouse et al., 2021). Exiting while pregnant or parenting can compound those risks, as early parenthood can be disruptive to educational and economic advancement; foster care–involved youth experience early parenthood more frequently than the general population (Font et al., 2019). However, Font and colleagues argue that other variables, including low-income status and experiencing neglect or abuse, are also related to an increased likelihood of early parenting. In other words, it is difficult to sort out the relative influence of the many variables that are part of the lives of these youth.

In a mixed methods study, Rouse and colleagues (2021) found that foster care youth may seek to become pregnant or not actively work to prevent pregnancy because having a child may be viewed as a relational connection or a way to work through one's own trauma and healing process. They also found that some young women view pregnancy and parenting as a way to demonstrate their maturity; that is, that they are no longer children. Additionally, many youth in foster care tend to have earlier sexual experiences and more sex partners than their peers who are not in care (Rouse et al., 2021).

Recommendations

Due to the many challenges faced by children and youth in foster care, the American Academy of Pediatrics (AAP, 2021b) has recommended an enhanced medical schedule of two visits per year at minimum for ages 24 months to 21 years, with more frequent visits for younger people. They further recommend a health screening within the first 72 hours of entering foster care and comprehensive medical, mental health, and dental examinations within 30 days of placement.

Because youth in foster care have less access to educational opportunities or supportive personal relationships than non foster care youth, Rouse and colleagues (2021) recommend increased educational and supportive programs focusing on such topics as reproductive health, pregnancy, and parenting, as well as providing opportunities to expand social support networks, which are so crucial for new parents. Additionally, they recommend sex education that goes beyond the biological aspects of reproduction and is broadened to include healthy relationships. Finigan-Carr and colleagues (2018) note that youth in foster care may receive inconsistent and confusing messages about their reproductive health and sexual behaviors and may have less access to contraceptive and reproductive health services than their peers. Finally, Finigan-Carr and colleagues (2018) note that in the system, children and youth should have an annual physical and providers need to ensure that they receive an exam and information relevant to reproductive health and screening for STIs.

Rouse and colleagues (2021) found that foster care youth reported that their sex education came primarily from the schools, not their foster parents, case workers, or anyone in the child welfare system. Thus, because of the increased risks to parenting at a young age or while in the foster care system, it seems essential to provide consistent, quality education to this population so they can make decisions from a position of strength. As youth in foster care may change schools more frequently than their peers, it is important to ensure that they have received adequate sex education. Additionally, potentially high-risk behaviors occur at younger ages when sex education is lacking than they do when sex education is presented. Thus, Finigan-Carr and colleagues (2018) recommend providing reproductive health information and resources at earlier ages for this population.

Social Determinants of Health and Foster Care

One way of thinking about the challenges youth in foster care face regarding reproductive health and other health concerns is to consider the social determinants of health (see Figure 10.1).

Essentially, social determinants of health are those social, environmental, and economic factors that affect a broad range of health outcomes. For youth, system involvement may be considered a social determinant of health (Finigan-Carr et al.,

Figure 10.1 Social Determinants of Health

Education Access and Quality

Healthcare Access and Quality

Economic Stability

Neighborhood and Built Environment

Social and Community Context

2018). Systems involved youth face increased challenges due to "inconsistent, disrupted relationships, multiple placements, trauma and other adverse childhood experiences (ACEs), chronic depression, exposure to domestic violence, engagement in high-risk behaviors, fractured or nonexistent support systems to help youth transitioning out of care, and barriers to pregnancy prevention" (Finigan-Carr et al., 2018, p. 312). All of these variables can affect their health choices and outcomes.

The Office of Disease Prevention and Health Promotion (Office of the Assistant Secretary for Health [OASH]) has identified five domains relevant to health, each broken down into subcategories. Some of those are directly relevant to health issues experienced by children and youth in the child welfare system. For example, *Health Care Access and Quality* is one of the domains, with one of the objectives being to increase the percentage of adolescents who speak privately with their providers during healthcare visits. This opportunity to speak privately to their provider is important in developing a sense of autonomy and responsibility for their healthcare, especially for youth in foster care. Approximately 50% of foster children and youth have chronic physical problems, such as asthma, visual or hearing loss, anemia, or neurological disorders, and approximately 10% are considered medically fragile or complex (AAP, 2021a). They also may have been exposed prenatally to substances as well as being born prematurely (AAP, 2021a).

Concerning *Education Access and Quality*, objectives include increasing the proportion of students who are proficient at reading and math for their grade level, increasing the proportion of children and youth who receive preventive mental health services in school, and ensuring that those with disabilities receive appropriate services while remaining in regular education programs as much as possible (DHHS, Office of Disease Prevention and Health Promotion, n.d.). Children and youth in foster care may be at increased risk for not achieving academic proficiency, being in more restrictive education placements, and not receiving consistent preventive mental health services due to less stability in educational settings. Additionally, youth in foster care are significantly more likely than their peers to face academic struggles and fall behind (U.S. Department of Education, 2016). One reason for this is academic instability and unexpected school changes; up to 75% of children and youth in foster care may make an unplanned school change in an academic year (U.S. Department of Education, 2016).

Another domain, *Social and Community Context*, acknowledges the critical role that social supports play in one's health and well-being. One of the objectives within this area is to increase the proportion of adolescents in foster care who show readiness to transition to adulthood. It is not uncommon for foster youth to wish to exit the system as soon as possible, not taking advantage of the extended foster care where they can continue receiving services to age 21. Therefore, they are not as adequately prepared for adult life, including employment, paying bills, and forming close relationships, as they might be with 3 more years of support and experience. These decisions affect their health and well-being. Transitioning to adulthood without social support can create additional challenges and barriers.

One of the objectives in the *Economic Stability* domain is to increase the proportion of children and youth in school or working. For children and youth in foster care, it is critically important that they remain in school as long as they can. As noted, youth in care are at increased risk of noncompletion of school, which affects long-term economic security and health and well-being. The transition to work is often difficult for youth exiting foster care because they may not have adequate preparation, training, or education for gainful employment, as well as the networks associated with securing employment.

Objectives under the *Neighborhood and Built Environment* domain that are relevant to foster care pertain to reducing the rate of crimes committed by youth and young adults, maintaining neighborhoods free of environmental toxins, and increasing the proportion of schools that have policies and practices to promote the health and safety of their students. All of these objectives are relevant to youth in or exiting foster care.

Substance Use and Its Effects on Children and Youth

Another issue related to the healthcare system is substance use. Depending upon the severity, substance use can interfere with providing quality and consistent parenting. While most parents love their children and want to provide the best care possible, addictions can disrupt the caregiver/child relationship and the ability to parent effectively, which may be a more widespread social issue than is widely known. Lipari and Van Horn (2017) have noted that approximately one in eight children and youth aged 17 or younger may live with at least one parent with a substance use disorder (SUD). According to the *Diagnostic and Statistical Manual of Mental Disorders, Fifth Edition-Revised (DSM-5-TR)* (American Psychiatric Association [APA], n.d.):

> SUD is defined as a complex diagnostic category in which there is an uncontrolled use of a substance despite harmful consequence[s]. People with SUD have an intense focus on using a certain substance(s), such as alcohol, tobacco, or illicit drugs, to the point where the person's ability to function in day-to-day life becomes impaired. People keep using the substance even when they know it is causing or will cause problems. The most severe SUDs are sometimes called addictions (para. 1).

Parents who have a problem with substance use may exhibit challenges at work or home and may have poor health outcomes (Lipari & Van Horn, 2017). People with SUD often vacillate between routine functioning and impaired functioning and can spend more time in the cycle of addictions (obtaining, using, and recovering from substance use). The APA (n.d.) describes further impairments, including:

- Distorted thinking and behaviors;
- Changes in brain functioning leading to intense cravings, personality changes, or atypical body movements;

- Changes in brain structure that can affect judgment, memory, learning, decision-making, impulse control, or other behaviors; and

- Long-lasting changes after repeated use that linger even when the substance has worn off.

Children raised by parents with SUD face an increased likelihood of academic difficulties, behavioral, emotional, or cognitive disabilities, and difficulties with social and family relationships (Lipari & Van Horn, 2017). Not all children living with a parent with SUD will experience abuse or neglect; however, children with parents who suffer from SUD are at increased risk for abuse or neglect, poorer health and developmental outcomes, and child welfare system involvement (Channell et al., 2023). Children in foster care with a parent with SUD have lower reunification rates, longer stays in foster care, and are more likely to re-enter the system following reunification than their peers whose parents do not struggle with SUD (Zhang et al., 2019). While treatment costs may be expensive, the long-term benefits for children suggest that treatment is essential and well worth the investment. Additionally, children who experience abuse and neglect are more likely to abuse substances as adults. It is vital to break the generational link between abuse and neglect, and misuse of substances (Channell et al., 2023). Approximately 33 states have included within their criminal code exposure of children to illegal drug activity, including manufacture, sales, being present where chemicals or equipment are stored, selling to children, or using in the presence of children if it impairs their ability to care for the child (Child Welfare Information Gateway, 2020b).

Family drug court is a common approach to intervening with families when a parent misuses substances. This approach began in the 1990s and has spread widely since then. Family drug court is characterized by frequent court hearings, provision of substance abuse treatment, and rewards and sanctions based on adherence to the program. A meta-analysis of family drug court effectiveness found promising but mixed outcomes (Zhang et al., 2019). More research needs to be conducted to determine what elements of family drug courts are most effective with which populations.

Pregnancy and Substance Use

One consideration related to substance use and parenting is the use of substances during pregnancy. Under the Child Abuse Prevention and Treatment Act (CAPTA), states are required to have policies and procedures in place for addressing the needs of infants who may be affected by prenatal drug exposure, including the requirement that healthcare providers notify the appropriate child welfare authorities (Child Welfare Information Gateway, 2020b). Additionally, states must have a safe care plan for the infant when leaving the care of health providers, which may include the treatment needs of other family members (Child Welfare Information Gateway, 2020b). In 26 states, statutes specifically require healthcare providers to report when treating infants who show evidence of prenatal drug exposure at birth (Child Welfare Information Gateway, 2020b). Twenty-three states include prenatal substance in their definitions of child abuse. A handful of states require reporting suspected substance abuse by pregnant persons to refer them for treatment.

While there are risks to both mother and baby with drug use during pregnancy, some interventions can promote positive outcomes. In several states, the reporting and interventions are intended to be supportive and include assessment of infant and family needs with appropriate referrals for treatment and other services (Child Welfare Information Gateway, 2020b). The effects of substance use during pregnancy depend on many variables, including timing during gestation, frequency, dose, and the source of the drug (Weber et al., 2021). Risks to the fetus include exposure during pregnancy and withdrawal symptoms following birth (Weber et al., 2021). Weber and colleagues (2021) also note the importance of language to describe parents and infants, including how terms like *addicts* or *addicted babies* can create stigma. Since most people who use substances seek to decrease or cease substance use when they learn they are pregnant, Weber and colleagues (2021) further recommend a trauma-informed treatment approach when working with expectant mothers due to the intense stigma that people who use substances experience. The stigma associated with substance use paints it as a moral failure demonstrating weakness and inability to exercise willpower (Weber et al., 2021). This stigma can lead individuals to isolate themselves and avoid prenatal care and substance abuse treatment, which can be detrimental to both the birthing parent and the baby. Weber and colleagues note that the intersection of being pregnant and using substances leads to more stigmatization, marginalization, and discrimination than experienced by pregnant people (not using substances) or other people who use substances but are not pregnant.

Reflection Box 10.1

Assume that you are a social worker in an agency that supports pregnant and parenting persons who may be considered *at risk* due to various factors, including age, substance use, homelessness, social isolation, mental illness, and other concerns. Understanding that the clients you encounter may mistrust systems and professionals within those systems, describe how you would work to engage your clients, including building trust, enhancing communication, providing concrete support, and reducing barriers.

Additionally, pregnant people of color using substances face even more discrimination. The criminalization of substance use contributes to injustices and is detrimental to patients (Kravitz et al., 2021). Policies tend to be punitive and create a false dichotomy between mother and baby. They are viewed as having competing needs, requiring choosing one over the other, when in reality, their health is intertwined (Harp & Bunting, 2020). Individual states, jurisdictions, and hospitals have different policies and criteria for interventions; therefore, healthcare providers have much latitude in the decisions that are made. Both implicit and explicit biases can lead to racial disparities in treatment.

The use of urinary drug screening must be viewed in the context of history and racism, seeing how it intersects with the war on drugs and mass incarceration of people of color (Kravitz et al., 2021). Other contextual dimensions include the criminalization of Black bodies, the stigma experienced by Black mothers, and injustices and discriminatory treatment at the hands of the healthcare system (Kravitz et al., 2021). A lot is riding on a positive drug test, depending on the state or locality, including criminal charges and separation of parent and baby. There are other implications of drug testing as well. For example, marijuana is legal in many states, but a positive toxicology result carries stigma and can trigger child welfare referrals. Alcohol use does not typically trigger a report to child protective services, although there is ample evidence of negative outcomes and no safe level of alcohol use during pregnancy (Perlman et al., 2021).

One concern related to equity in child welfare is drug testing at birth. The question becomes who gets tested more frequently and why. A large-scale study in an urban academic center found that neonates who were tested had younger mothers who self-reported as single, lived in lower-income zip codes, and were less likely to be White (Perlman et al., 2021). Another large-scale longitudinal study found that clinicians were significantly more likely to order drug testing of Black newborns (7.3%) compared with White newborns (1.9%) or other racial or ethnic groups (Schoneich et al., 2023). Furthermore, birthing parents who are Black or Latinx and those who are low-income are more likely to be drug tested than White parents. Perlman and colleagues (2022) found that verbal disclosure was the only valid indicator of substance use. However, in a retrospective cohort study of over 20,000 obstetrical patients, Black (4.76 times more likely) and Latinx (5.75 times more likely) birthing parents had an increased likelihood of having a toxicology screening without the presence of known substance abuse indicators (Perlman et al., 2022). There are no clear and systematic national standards for indicators of when drug testing is warranted, leaving open the possibility of discriminatory treatment of parents of color as well as low-income patients (Perlman et al., 2022). Toxicology testing risks false positives and does not distinguish between occasional and chronic use (Perlman et al., 2022). However, it can have serious ramifications. As noted, Black and Latinx birthing parents may undergo more toxicology screenings than their White peers without clear indicators. Without clear protocols for such screenings, there is much room for bias and discrimination.

Kravitz and colleagues (2021) note that the criminalization of substance use in pregnancy sets up a system in which parents are treated punitively by the criminal justice system rather than being treated therapeutically by the healthcare system.

The United States has the highest incarceration rate in the world, and the fastest-growing group is women, generally for drug or property crimes (Kravitz et al., 2021). Further, Black women are disproportionately overrepresented. Substance abuse can be grounds for removing children, as can incarceration. Both factors disproportionately affect Black mothers (Kravitz et al., 2021).

PLANS OF SAFE CARE

In order to receive CAPTA funds, states must have plans of safe care (POSC) for infants who are found to test positive for substances at birth or show signs of withdrawal or signs of fetal alcohol syndrome disorder (FASD; Child Welfare Information Gateway, 2020c). The POSC is intended to ensure that the infant is in a safe setting, getting their needs met, and may also include treatment for family members (Child Welfare Information Gateway, 2020c). States have a great deal of flexibility in designing POSC and, in some cases, may begin services pre-birth. In 42 states, reports to CPS are required when an infant has a positive toxicology report, shows signs of withdrawal, or demonstrates other physical or neurological signs of drug exposure, including FASD. However, 14 of these states specifically note that this notification does not constitute a report of child abuse unless there are other indications that the infant has been maltreated or is at risk of harm (Child Welfare Information Gateway, 2020c). Assessment of the infant and family should be ongoing to ensure that needs are met. A POSC should focus on strengthening the family unit and keeping the infant safe in the home environment.

New child welfare professionals should check their state's mandatory reporting laws and drug testing policies. Testing requirements vary from state to state and from hospital to hospital. Drug testing and reporting implications are significant, as they can lead to potentially negative consequences and increase stigma, separation from children, and even incarceration. These consequences contribute to continued racial disparities and disproportionality in the system. It is *privilege* that allows some parents and babies to avoid testing before and after birth and go undetected.

Perlman and colleagues (2022) suggest that, in light of the increased risk for adverse pregnancy outcomes for people of color, this bias toward toxicology screening of people of color may further incline clinicians to dismiss or not adequately explore other causes of pregnancy complications. Additionally, the stigma associated with substance use can become internalized, and the individual can give themselves the negative messages they assume others are sending, further destroying their self-esteem (Weber et al., 2021), which can impact their drive to complete services to reunite with their children.

RECOMMENDATIONS

Weber and colleagues (2021) recommend intentionally addressing stigma among pregnant persons by implementing a trauma-informed treatment approach. They further suggest using motivational interviewing and emphasize building relational trust. They also recommend helping the parent develop interpersonal skills, connecting with resources to support the parent and baby and their relationship, and building self-efficacy and empowerment.

For the social justice–minded child welfare professional who believes in the dignity and worth of all people, it is important to shift one's practice paradigm. Effective practices include engaging parents non judgmentally, convening child and family team meetings to enhance the relationship between the child welfare professional and the parent, and joining with the parents to collaboratively identify the best services to meet the child's and family's needs.

Case Scenario: Landy's Story: Positive Outcomes With Intact Family Services

Landy, age 19, identifies as biracial (Black/White) and has grown up in the foster care system since age 5 due to abuse by her mother and other family members. Landy's father has been in prison most of her life. Landy says she has bounced around to many foster homes throughout her life and couldn't make any connections. In addition, when she began to act out, foster families did not want to keep her: "I felt like a throw-away." Landy stated that this became her routine. "I didn't give a damn [sic]; nobody wanted me anyway. Why even try?" Landy recently gave birth to her first child. She is frightened that one day a social worker will take her baby away, and her baby will live the same kind of life she did. Landy is struggling with her mental health and has hesitated to seek help due to fear of being reported and having her baby taken away. Despite her fears, Landy was able to connect with a social worker at a community center for mental health support. With the social worker's help, Landy has connected with other services for support with the baby. Landy wants what is best for her baby. Despite all Landy's efforts, a child protective services (CPS) report was made on her for having a dirty house. Landy states that she was going to flip out and beat up the social worker if they tried to take her child. When Landy met the family volunteer services (FVS) social worker, she was surprised when the social worker stated that she did not want to take her baby but sought to help her keep her baby safe. The social worker showed Landy what she needed to keep clean and why it was important for the baby. She said the social worker told her she would be back in a few days to do a walk-through and promised that if Landy needed any support or resources, she would assist her. Landy was able to talk with the FVS worker to get resources and support. Landy felt empowered and stated she could get the things she needed and clean her home. Landy sometimes feels she is missing skills but is learning them. Landy's CPS case was closed, and Landy gained a new perspective. She even thinks about becoming a foster parent one day to help kids like her.

(continued)

Case Scenario: Landy's Story: Positive Outcomes With Intact Family Services (*continued*)

DISCUSSION QUESTIONS

1. Why do you think Landy was initially fearful of any involvement with the child welfare system?

2. How can child welfare professionals build trust with clients who are mistrustful of the system and people working in it?

3. Do you think Landy still has a difficult road ahead? If so, in what way(s)?

4. How can the child welfare professional assist Landy in navigating the challenges ahead of her?

Landy's scenario illustrates how various systems can interact—child welfare, corrections, health, mental/behavioral health, substance use, and household services (parenting/cleaning). Landy has faced health and mental health challenges. Her father was incarcerated. Her mother and other family members abused substances. Her life may not always go smoothly, but she has learned some skills and how to navigate and ask for resources to provide a more stable foundation for her family.

IMMIGRANT FAMILIES

Families that are at the intersection of child welfare and immigration face a unique set of circumstances and challenges not faced by other families. These families generally experience difficulties accessing services due to language barriers and fears of deportation, lack of knowledge about services, and perceived and actual legal barriers. Additionally, immigrant families may have already faced previous trauma through the immigration process, including leaving home and family behind; abuse, threats, and trials while immigrating; and their treatment after arriving. They also face the challenges of becoming part of another culture and needing to learn new customs and ways of living. Immigration is a contemporary critical issue to consider. The percentage of children with at least one immigrant parent has continued to grow, as fully one-quarter of children and youth currently are in this category, with half of these youth living in just four states: New York, Texas, Florida, and California (Carr, 2018; Finno-Velasquez & Dettlaff, 2018). Of the roughly 73 million children in the United States, approximately 5.5 million have at least one parent without legal status (Carr, 2018).

General Issues

There are many ways in which children and families face this intersection of systems. In 2016, the DHHS (2023) began requiring state child welfare agencies to collect data and report on their cases involving deportation and detention (Carr, 2018). Cabrera and colleagues (2018) found that many children and youth from immigrant families in the foster care system need therapeutic interventions, as they may suffer from depression, anxiety, and the fear that their families will never be safe. They may experience difficulty establishing relationships and may feel stuck between two cultures. Because of harmful policies that have reduced protections for children and families and such factors as Immigration and Customs Enforcement (ICE) raids and a generally hostile environment toward immigrants, they may be less inclined to access resources or services due to fear (Cabrera et al., 2018).

Additionally, rapidly changing and unclear immigration laws have destabilized immigrant communities, contributing to decreased participation in social programs, even if they are fully eligible. In turn, negative health and mental health outcomes may occur for children and families in these circumstances (Finno-Velasquez & Dettlaff, 2018). Additionally, biases and lack of knowledge about services in another country can make reunification more difficult. Families at the crossroads of immigration and child welfare may face many challenges, some of which are described in the following.

Children and Youth Separated at the Border

One category of families affected by immigration includes children and youth separated from their parents at the border. Cabrera and colleagues (2018) state that between October 2017 and April 2018, over 700 children were separated from their parents. Furthermore, in May 2018, people apprehended crossing the border were charged with a crime even if they presented themselves for asylum or were parents. At this point, over 2,300 children were separated from their parents, becoming unaccompanied minors and becoming part of the federal foster care system (Cabrera et al., 2018). Though an executive order effectively ended separation, these families were irreparably and unnecessarily harmed, and there was no clarity on how to reunite separated families; many parents may have been deported without their children (Cabrera et al., 2018).

Unaccompanied Minors

Another category of children entering the system includes unaccompanied minors; that is, youth under age 18 who arrive without a parent or guardian. Many of these youth are in long-term foster placements, placed under the auspices of the Office of Refugee Resettlement (ORR), pending immigration hearings (Crea et al., 2022).

These youth are in care because an appropriate caregiver cannot be found, unlike others in the child welfare system who are placed due to abuse or neglect. Most unaccompanied youth originate in Guatemala, Honduras, or El Salvador, countries with high homicide rates. Most unaccompanied children have been victimized while en route to the border. Youth presenting themselves at the border are initially taken into custody by Customs and Border Patrol, then transferred to ORR. They are typically placed in a shelter or transitional foster care program (Crea et al., 2022). There may not be enough shelter beds, so they may be placed in emergency shelters that are not child welfare placements and may not be able to adequately meet the needs of the youth (Crea et al., 2022). Further, the trauma they may have experienced en route and from being separated from their families may remain unaddressed and unresolved.

The Unaccompanied Refugee Minor (URM) foster care program for unaccompanied children and youth who are legally present in the country represents a partnership between ORR and the Department of State (DOS) and is administered through sectarian agencies, the Lutheran Immigration Refugee Service, and the U.S. Conference of Catholic Bishops (USCCB). There are at least 29 URM programs across the country, staffed by foster parents trained to work with children and youth born outside the country (Evans et al., 2018). Services include English language education, independent living skills, assistance with immigration status, and culturally relevant activities (Evans et al., 2018).

Immigrant minors face a number of challenges, not the least of which is understanding current laws. Immigrant youth under the age of 18, with no legal immigration status and with no parent or legal guardian in the United States, fall under the custody of the DHHS. The DHHS plays no role in the detention of minors, but if detained and under age 18, they are turned over to the custody of the DHHS. The ORR manages the unaccompanied children and URM programs to serve eligible children and youth. The ORR seeks vetted sponsors for the children, usually family members or close friends. Until placed, the ORR provides recreational, educational, and health-related services, and also provides wrap-around services while they seek a sponsor for the immigrant child/youth (DHHS, Office of Refugee Resettlement, 2023). The URM program requires an application to determine eligibility for participation. Eligible youth include refugees, asylees, victims of trafficking, and victims of abuse (DHHS, Office of Refugee Resettlement, 2022) and receive placement with a family or sponsor (i.e., resettlement in the United States).

The transition from adolescence to young adulthood is an important one for everyone. Adolescent tasks include developing a sense of identity with the capacity to form meaningful relationships. Identity development can be further complicated when youth must transition without the support of family or cultural ties (Citrin et al., 2018). Immigration status can further complicate this process as it affects youth's ability to access necessary resources and may increase their fear of deportation or detention. These youth may need help obtaining employment or advanced education, and their eligibility for certain services may change. For example, they previously did not qualify for financial support through the Foster Care Independence Program (Citrin et al., 2018). However, more recently, they have been eligible for the same support as other children in foster care. As immigrants and refugees, they are subject to federal law and are typically served through ORR rather than child welfare. It is essential to know the current laws and how to access services for eligible youth.

In addition, due to language barriers and lack of access to education, they may be behind in high school credits. They may run out of time to finish high school before reaching the upper age limit for foster care, essentially aging out before completion (Citrin et al., 2018). Compounding the challenges all youth who age out of foster care face, immigrant youth face racism and anti-immigration sentiment and must navigate a complex and ever-changing immigration and legal system. Essentially, upon reaching age 18, these youth fall under the custody of ICE. There are paths to legal status for them, but they need legal support and someone to inform them of their rights. It is important to remember that, despite their many obstacles, these youth are valued members of families and communities and have many strengths, not the least of which is resilience (Citrin et al., 2018). Consistent with good child welfare practice, it is essential to build on these strengths as this benefits the youth and the larger community.

Children in Mixed-Status Families: Deportation of Parent(s)

Another issue is related to the challenges faced by children in mixed-status families. Mixed-status families are those in which members do not have the same immigration status, where some members have documentation allowing them to remain in the country or are natural-born citizens, and other members do not have legal documentation. There are many risks faced by these children and families, including the trauma of separation, economic consequences related to limited access to employment or resources, the fear and trauma of ICE raids, and the increased likelihood of being placed in foster care (Cabrera et al., 2018; Carr, 2018). It is unclear how many children and youth become involved in the child welfare system due to immigration enforcement activities. However, many undocumented parents of U.S. citizen children have been deported (Finno-Velasquez & Dettlaff, 2018). Youth who come into the system not because of abuse but because they are separated from their parents may also experience the trauma of the system (Finno-Velasquez & Dettlaff, 2018).

Children who are U.S. citizens but have undocumented family members often have limited support. They are hoping that their parents will not be deported. They also may have a mistrust of systems. Despite regulations such as the Burgos Consent Decree in Illinois requiring bilingual caseworkers, interpreters, and foster families, there may be challenges in finding Spanish-speaking foster parents and case workers. Additionally, a background check may be required for foster parents, so many extended family members may not step forward for fear of deportation or drawing attention to other family members who may be undocumented.

Another challenge in mixed-status families exists when the breadwinner, often a male, is the perpetrator of abuse and is put out of the home. The family then faces challenges in surviving economically and socially. It could impact where they live, where the children attend school, and the overall community context, causing multiple transitions for the child.

Carr (2018) notes that detention and deportation do not legally alter one's right to parent or to participate in child welfare decisions. When detention and deportation occur, there may be a range of scenarios: (a) where no abuse is present, in which case the family should be able to place the child(ren) with other family members or friends; (b) where the child abuse/neglect investigation leads to finding out about a parent's undocumented status, resulting in deportation; and (c) where the nonabusive parent is the one without documentation, complicating the placement of child(ren) with them (Carr, 2018). The child welfare professional needs to be aware of these scenarios and the parents' rights. Ensuring that parents are aware of their rights contributes to the safety and well-being of the child. Honoring the parents' rights is important regardless of the political values the child welfare professional may hold.

Recommendations

Cabrera and colleagues (2018) make several recommendations to support children and families who are at the crossroads of these two systems of child welfare and immigration, including:

1. Therapeutic interventions for children and youth who may be dealing with depression, anxiety, anger, withdrawal, and insecurity.
2. Informing parents of their rights, as they may be unaware of the foster care processes, termination of parental rights, and adoption. When their children enter the child welfare system, parents may not be aware that they have rights, such as the right to consult with an attorney, the right to an interpreter, the right to communicate with their child(ren) and caseworkers, and the right to have and understand a reunification plan.
3. Increased training and knowledge related to the needs of immigrant families and increased cross-agency collaboration, including relationships with immigration agencies, consulates, government offices, and the ORR.
4. More Spanish-speaking caseworkers.
5. Relationships built on trust, transparency, and recognition of family strengths.

Additional recommendations include a pathway to permanent residency and citizenship, access to concrete supports, and assistance with developing relationships with caring adults. For example, Special Immigrant Juvenile Status (SIJS) requires a state court finding that the youth has been abused, abandoned, or neglected, and it is not in their best interest to return to their country of origin. Most youth would be unaware of these laws. Child welfare professionals need to be aware of this law and be able to connect the youth with immigration lawyers. Additionally, the youth may need assistance in securing employment authorization so that they have a chance to earn a living wage (Citrin et al., 2018).

Cabrera and colleagues (2018) further note the importance of "elevating youth and family voice, highlighting the value of cross-cultural humility and responsiveness, use of practice tools (e.g., genograms, eco-maps, family group conferences), forging new partnerships and becoming knowledgeable about a variety of legal procedures" (p.18). Additionally, it is crucial to recognize that this population may have many reasons not to trust the child welfare professional. As a result, engagement and the development of a positive working relationship may take longer and may be more complicated. Patience and good listening skills are required.

INTERSECTION OF CHILD WELFARE WITH THE CORRECTIONAL SYSTEM

The child welfare system intersects with the justice, correctional, and legal systems in many ways. The connection between foster care and juvenile and young adult incarceration is well known (Roberts, 2017; Summersett Williams et al., 2021), though the connection may be more complicated than it appears. There are other connections, including the effects on children whose parents have been incarcerated and the possible involvement of the child welfare system when a parent is detained. Children and youth who are runaways or trafficked represent another intersection of legal and child welfare systems. Additionally, domestic or intimate partner violence (IPV) can affect children and youth through exposure to violence and present other challenges in protecting children from abuse and neglect in homes where IPV is present.

Connection Between Child Welfare and Juvenile Justice Systems

The connection between child welfare and the correctional system is complex. Youth in foster care have already experienced a number of traumatic events that can place them at risk for criminal involvement (Font et al., 2021). They may have experienced abuse and neglect, lower academic achievement, and increased risk of poverty. They may have observed violence or illicit behaviors (Font et al., 2021). Youth in foster care are more likely than their peers to be arrested for a violent crime (Finigan-Carr et al., 2018). Trauma can increase the likelihood of juvenile justice involvement. As many as 30% of youth in the child welfare system are also involved in the correctional system; while they may be simultaneously under the supervision of both systems, the function of each system is different (Summersett Williams et al., 2021). Children and youth in the child welfare system have been exposed to trauma, abuse, or neglect, and these multiple stressors can lead to behavioral and mental health difficulties and substance use, increasing the likelihood of involvement with juvenile corrections. Moreover, youth involved in the child welfare system are at increased risk of becoming involved in the correctional system in adulthood.

Summersett Williams and colleagues (2021) studied a sample of child welfare involved youth to assess whether protective factors could mitigate the risk of juvenile corrections involvement. They explored data gathered at the beginning of system involvement and again at the exit from the system. They found that among youth not involved with the juvenile justice system, several protective factors were already present: spirituality/religion, optimism, and talents/interests. They further found that when certain protective factors—talents/interests, educational setting, spiritual/religious strengths, and community life—were increased during the time in care, the likelihood of justice system involvement decreased. In essence, protective factors before and during placement decrease the likelihood of correctional system involvement. Summersett Williams and colleagues (2021) suggest that for those youth who become involved with the juvenile justice system, professionals in that system should recognize and support growth in strengths rather than assuming the youth only carry deficits. Furthermore, all systems working with youth should build protective factors and identify youth strengths which are vital and may prevent correctional involvement later. A caring adult who can help the youth to identify and build on strengths can decrease the likelihood of later incarceration.

Children of Incarcerated Parents

The United States has the highest incarceration rate in the world. We have seen a dramatic increase in the number of people in prison since 1980 due to the war on drugs and other criminal justice policies (Phillips & Bloom, 1998). President Reagan signed the Anti-Drug Abuse Act of 1986, which focused on punishment over treatment, included mandatory minimum sentence requirements, and dramatically increased the incarcerated population. It targeted crack cocaine use over powder cocaine, giving much harsher sentences to those using crack cocaine, primarily impacting African Americans. It was not until the Fair Sentencing Act of 2010 that the disparity between crack and powder cocaine was addressed, though inequities still exist. Judges used to have discretion in sentencing mothers of young children and considered their need to be caregivers. Drug sentencing policies changed that, resulting in more mothers in prison (Phillips & Bloom, 1998).

Large numbers (over 2.6 million) of children have a parent incarcerated in prison or jail. This population tends to be concentrated among low-income and racial-ethnic minorities. Children who experience parental incarceration face more significant challenges in many areas that grow out of this trauma (Turney & Haskins, 2019). These children often have experienced multiple ACEs, potentially including separation from a parent, growing up with a parent with a mental illness, or growing up with a parent with SUD. Borja and colleagues (2015) note the cumulative effects of ACEs on health and their role in the intergenerational transmission of traumas and negative outcomes. Stress and adverse experiences can affect health; prisoners have more chronic health problems than the population at large, and these effects are also found in family members, including children (Borja et al., 2015). More specifically, they examine the risks and challenges with incarcerated parents and the accumulation of risk and adversity exposure over the lifespan. In addition to these challenges children face, when there is an incarcerated parent, the family is more likely to be impoverished and have lower educational levels. If the father is incarcerated, the family income is likely to decrease. The family also may reside in impoverished communities with fewer community resources. The incarceration of mothers is far more disruptive to children (Phillips & Bloom, 1998). Incarceration disrupts family relationships, exacerbated when parents are incarcerated far from the family. If no suitable caregivers are available, there may be an increased likelihood of involvement with the child welfare system. More attention should be paid to the children of incarcerated parents, their unique challenges, and the support they need to succeed.

Exploited or Trafficked Children (Missing Children)

There are different types of trafficking of minors, including for labor, sex, or adoption, but sex trafficking is one of the most prevalent forms. Trafficking for sexual exploitation includes commercial sexual activity, prostitution, or participation in pornography (Child Welfare Information Gateway, 2020a). It involves recruitment, deception, coercion, and abuse of power. Trafficking can occur within and across national borders. It is a global phenomenon, though this chapter will primarily address the trafficking of children and youth under the age of 18 in the United States. Most are recruited between the ages of 12 and 14 (Baird et al., 2020). All youth are at risk for sex trafficking simply because of their age, but youth involved in the child welfare system are at increased risk and are vastly overrepresented in the trafficked population (Baird et al., 2020). Youths' developmental stage makes them more vulnerable to trafficking, as adolescence is a time of exploring identities, risk-taking, and seeking connection with others.

Risk factors for Commercial Sexual Exploitation (CSE) include childhood neglect, sexual or physical abuse; family dysfunction; mental health needs; poverty; parental or youth drug abuse and addiction; parental involvement in the sex trade; and identifying as a member of a sexually (e.g., lesbian, gay, bisexual), gender (e.g., transgender, nonbinary), or racially marginalized community. Also, running away and homelessness can be predictive (Barnert et al., 2016). Youth who run away often have encounters with law enforcement because of engagement in activities to secure money, including shoplifting, sex for money, selling drugs, and fighting (Barnert et al., 2016).

Traffickers often target the youth's unmet needs for positive adult attachment, so those with difficult childhoods and fractured family relationships are more vulnerable than their peers. Children and youth in the foster care system are vulnerable to the enticement of traffickers simply by virtue of not having a strong connection with a protective parental figure. Youth who are trafficked are more likely than the population as a whole to have been abused, to have used alcohol and illicit drugs, and to have lived in a group home (Baird et al., 2020). Recruiters go to places where youth congregate and are largely unmonitored (malls, parks, bars, bus stations, courthouses, schools). Increased social media use creates another space for recruitment (Baird et al., 2020). Traffickers often use a *grooming process*, providing gifts, food, drugs, and connection, as well as aversive strategies where drugs, food, or shelter become a debt the youth must work to pay off (Baird et al., 2020). Perpetrators are more likely to be someone unknown to the youth or someone other than a parent, such as a stepparent or relative. Commercially sexually exploited youth face significant lifelong risks, including violence-related injuries, pregnancy, STIs, untreated chronic medical issues, and mental health issues such as depression, anxiety, and PTSD (Barnert et al., 2016).

Addressing Trafficking

The Victims of Trafficking and Violence Protection Act (VTVPA) of 2000 designated children/youth as victims rather than criminals and began the shift in thinking about sex crimes and minors as well as rethinking the needs of this population. The Stop Exploitation through Trafficking Act of 2015 furthered this process. Under the provisions of the VTVPA, the state may identify anyone up to age 24 as a child.

The U.S. Preventing Sex Trafficking and Strengthening Families Act of 2014 requires child welfare agencies to identify and document children involved in the child welfare system. Many states have included trafficking as a form of child abuse, regardless of whether the trafficker is the parent or not, which allows child protective agencies to provide services to the victims of trafficking.

In 2015 the federal definition of child abuse was expanded to include trafficking, requiring the state to provide services for youth in state care who may be at risk for CSE. Along with safe harbor laws, this legislation represents a significant change in how commercially sexually exploited children are treated, as they used to be treated as criminals.

Many states have enacted safe harbor laws to protect the needs of trafficked youth by redirecting them from the criminal justice system to the child welfare system. Safe harbor laws consist of various provisions, including training professionals providing intervention, trauma-focused care, and trafficking prevention programs. Some states enacted decriminalization but still have juvenile prostitution as a crime on the books, so they still have the option of prosecution (Barnert et al., 2016). Though safe harbor laws are a step in the right direction, challenges remain. In some states, there is no place for these youth to go, so police may lock them up simply to get them away from their pimp, suggesting the need for training for police and prosecutors (Barnert et al., 2016). Controversy exists regarding what to do when sheltering exploited youth. A locked facility can seem like jail, but these youth are at high risk of running (Barnert et al., 2016). As with other legislation, funding may be inadequate to provide services to meet the needs of the youth.

Global Trafficking

Global trafficking of children and youth, mainly for commercial sex, also occurs. The intersection of culture and trafficking is important to understand. For example, in Asian cultures, there is the concept of filial piety and helping one's family. Thus, girls may have mixed feelings about sex work seeing it as shameful but also as a way of earning money to help their family. However, if returned to their families and communities, these girls may experience rejection because of what they have done (Chung, 2009). Traffickers take advantage of the culture, including filial piety, shame, and the risk factors associated with poverty, to coerce and entice young females (Chung, 2009). The Western perception of Asian women as subservient also contributes to this injustice (Chung, 2009).

Prevention strategies include recognizing risk factors and identifying youth at heightened risk. Programs and interventions can be developed to mitigate those risks. Interventions should also focus on resiliency and aim to meet connection, love, and belonging needs. These interventions should be trauma and gender-focused, as most trafficking victims are female.

As a child welfare professional, it is essential to understand both domestic and global trafficking of youth. Child welfare professionals may encounter children and youth who have been sexually exploited or trafficked and must know to intervene and what resources are available. In these cases, knowledge of laws and resources specific to trafficked children is vital (such as T visa for children under 18) and trauma-informed services.

RUNAWAY CHILDREN/YOUTH ("RUN UNIT"): RISKS AND INTERVENTIONS

Runaway youth often have a child welfare connection and are at increased risk for trafficking (Baird et al., 2020). One study of youth in Washington State found that the mean age of the first runaway incident was 14.2 years. Youth in this study had an average of 27 placement disruptions, including running and detention, and moved or were placed an average of every 71 days (Pullmann et al., 2020). Children who run often are returned to a different foster home because foster homes with the capacity to care for more challenging youth are filled so quickly, leading to even more anxiety and subsequent runaway incidents (Pullmann et al., 2020). Some youth in foster care run back to their families or extended families.

A point-in-time study found that four to five thousand youth were on runaway status from foster care (Child Welfare Information Gateway, 2020d). Most youth who run from foster care are gone for only about a week or so before they are found and returned. However, many are missing for a month or more (Child Welfare Information Gateway, 2020d). Runaway or homeless youth are at increased risk for several challenges, including substance abuse, teenage pregnancy, involvement with juvenile corrections, dropping out of school, and mental illness (youth.gov, n.d.). Thus, it is vital to address the needs of this population.

Interventions

There are evidence-based interventions available that increase placement stability for adolescents in foster care who are prone to run away (Turner & Macdonald, 2011), such as Multidimensional Treatment Foster Care (Fisher & Chamberlain, 2000) and its related parent training intervention, Keeping Foster and Kin Parents Trained and Supported (KEEP) (Price et al., 2008). Child welfare professionals should diligently search for the latest evidence-based practices. Child welfare systems also play a role in the professional development of their staff to provide the best services to youth.

Intimate Partner Violence and Child Welfare

While there are clear connections between IPV and the child welfare system, the relationship is multitiered and complex. Children who witness IPV are at increased risk for physical and behavioral health challenges that may be long lasting (DHHS, Office of Women's Health, 2021). The National Child Traumatic Stress Network (NCTSN, 2014) notes that children may be exposed to domestic violence in various ways, including witnessing violence that causes physical harm to a parent, hearing a parent threaten the other, seeing an angry parent destroy property, seeing a parent who is extremely frightened, or even becoming a victim of violence themselves. Perpetrators of IPV have an increased likelihood of abusing children as well.

Children who are exposed to IPV may have a range of reactions, including fear, guilt, reverting to earlier behaviors (in the case of preschoolers, such things as bedwetting or thumb-sucking), sleep difficulties, separation anxiety, lower self-esteem, disengagement from peers or school, and, among adolescents, more acting out and risk-taking behaviors (DHHS, Office of Women's Health, 2021). The parent who is abused, most often the mother, may face isolation, increasing parenting challenges. They may have difficulty protecting their children from abuse or neglect and feel guilty and inadequate as a parent. Without a support system or access to resources, they may have a more challenging time getting out of the cycle of abuse.

Recommendations

Since many of the indicators of abuse and neglect are similar to indicators for exposure to IPV, the child welfare professional should tune in to the possibility that IPV is present. Support for the victimized parent is critical, including providing education about the effects of witnessing IPV, validating the concerns and experiences of the parent, and letting them know the importance of a stable, nurturing parent in the life of a child (NCTSN, 2014). Children need to feel safe, and while they may not forget the violence they have witnessed, children can learn healthy ways to express their emotions as they get older (DHHS, Office of Women's Health, 2021). Children and youth may need behavioral health intervention, as there are risks for their later life; for example, girls who witness domestic violence are six times more likely to experience sexual abuse than their peers from nonabusive homes, and boys who witness their fathers abuse their mothers are 10 times more likely to abuse female partners in adulthood (DHHS, Office of Women's Health, 2021). The child welfare professional must be aware that the abused parent's authority has been undermined, and it may take time and support for a healthy parent–child relationship to be developed or reestablished.

INTERSECTION OF CHILD WELFARE AND MILITARY FAMILIES

Families in the military experience several circumstances not routinely faced by civilian families. Multiple and prolonged deployments can strain families and disrupt family life (dePedro, 2015; Porter, 2013). With the closing of military bases and downsizing the military, deployments have tended to be longer (Porter, 2013), affecting family dynamics and relationships. Families may experience financial challenges; children and youth may be exposed to the trauma their parents may have experienced. Challenges can occur both pre- and post deployment (Porter, 2013). Families make adjustments in roles when members join or leave the family unit. With military families, children and youth may need to readjust their roles each time a parent is deployed or rejoins the family. It may be difficult for children and youth to take on or give up roles. Changing roles may be more stressful when a parent returns from deployment with physical or psychological trauma or injury (Porter, 2013).

Additionally, the stress the parents experience can lead to higher rates of abuse and neglect, contributing to the increase in child abuse during and post deployment (Porter, 2013). Typically, it is the non deployed parent who is the perpetrator (Porter, 2013), as they are the ones who are with the children and who feel increased stress to maintain home and family. Children and youth may also experience higher rates of depression and decreased sense of well-being (dePedro, 2015) due to deployment.

Children and youth who experience stress may act out in school (Porter, 2013). The majority of military youth are concentrated in 200 public school districts known as military-connected school districts. Districts meet this designation if at least 400 students, or 3% of the school population, have a caregiver in the military (dePedro, 2015). Staff within these school districts may be especially tuned in to some of these challenges and may implement programming to support this unique population. Staff outside military school districts may need more specialized training or information about the unique needs of children/youth from military families.

Travis and colleagues (2015) identify the military service core values, including honor, integrity, and self-discipline. They assert that these values can lead society to have higher expectations for this population. However, military families face high stress for many reasons and are not immune to problems and risk factors. While rates of child maltreatment are lower in the military than in the general population, the severity is worse (Porter, 2013). Additionally, there may be barriers to addressing or preventing child abuse. Soldiers may avoid seeking treatment for mental health problems because of stigma. Substance use may be an issue as well, one that may lead to a range of other challenges, including legal issues, domestic violence, and child maltreatment, as well as dishonorable discharge, which can ultimately lead to the loss of veterans' benefits (Porter, 2013). Thus, it becomes essential to focus on prevention as well as intervention.

Responses to Abuse and Neglect

The Department of Defense has established a range of resources for military families, including the Family Advocacy Program (FAP; Travis et al., 2015). All five military branches have FAPs focusing on prevention, identification, investigation, evaluation, treatment, rehabilitation, and follow up. Additionally, each military branch has a central registry to record cases of child maltreatment and must cooperate with civilian authorities (Travis et al., 2015).

As one example, the Air Force FAP provides training and outreach with mandated reporters and leadership, including commanding officers. They educate about risk factors, universal prevention, and selective prevention for those most at risk, including parents of young or teenage children (Travis et al., 2015). Workers in the FAP assess family well-being at the point of entry using the Family Needs Screener, a 58-item instrument that has been validated with mothers' responses (Travis et al., 2015). Similarly, the Navy has a prevention program called FOCUS (Families Overcoming Under Stress) through which they work on communication, dealing with war trauma, parenting, stress management, and emotional regulation (Porter, 2013).

The military seeks to both protect victims and hold offenders accountable. An intake interview is scheduled if a report of abuse is founded or indicated. The service member is mandated to participate, and relevant others are encouraged to attend the intake. Following the investigation, recommendations are made to the unit commander to initiate a safety plan. Collaboration between military and civilian agencies is required. In addition to engagement with the military, the family may be involved with a state child protection worker. Installation commanders ensure that appropriate services are provided and that the service member complies.

It is essential to recognize that military families are also resilient and resourceful. They may be able to rely on extended family members and community support groups. The family unit may be strengthened through dealing with stress, and parents may develop strong coping skills (Porter, 2013).

LGBTQ+ POPULATIONS: FAMILIES AND YOUTH

Sexual minorities face many challenges in the child welfare system. Issues are wide ranging and include placing children with gay parents for foster care or adoption, placing youth who identify as LGBTQ+ into foster care, and laws in some states charging parents with child abuse if they support their transgender children. In addition, some states have passed *don't say gay* legislation, which, though not directly a part of the child welfare system, can affect youth in foster care who identify as LGBTQ+ due to the hostile climate it creates. Foster youth who are sexual minorities have more negative health and social outcomes, including over-representation and longer time in the system, increased likelihood of abuse, and increased health and behavioral health challenges such as depression, suicide risk, unprotected sex, and substance abuse (Lorthridge et al., 2018). Once they are in foster care, it is not necessarily the safe place it should be, resulting from anti-gay biases and limited knowledge about the best ways to support LGBTQ+ youth (Lorthridge et al., 2018).

Further, LGBTQ+ youth in care are more likely than heterosexual and cisgender youth to remain longer, experience physical and verbal harassment, and face placement instability (Lorthridge et al., 2018). Lorthridge and colleagues (2018) found that interventions can help youth who are gender nonconforming or LGBTQ to make more and stronger connections with supportive adults, the LGBTQ+ community, and their families, facilitating a better understanding of their identity. Further, they are more comfortable disclosing their identity and experience less rejection from others.

CHAPTER SUMMARY

This chapter has considered the many systems that children and youth in the foster care system may encounter, as well as some of the risks and challenges inherent in those encounters. While all individual development and social interactions occur within an environmental context, with both positive and negative effects, involvement in the child welfare system can create additional challenges. Ideally, involvement within the system also can create opportunities to help those children and youth overcome some barriers. However, the child welfare system that exists in a society marked by racism, classism, and sexism, perpetuates discriminatory practices that further place marginalized populations at risk. The burden of *societal isms* plays out in all systems, including healthcare, education, immigration, and corrections.

DISCUSSION QUESTIONS

1. Considering the question of drug testing at birth, what are the ethical, moral, and social justice implications of this question?
2. What are some of the outcomes of drug testing, both intended and unintended?
3. What do you recommend regarding drug testing at birth?
4. Many have said that the immigration system within the United States is broken. What would you do to improve this system, particularly considering the needs of the children and youth in this system?
5. What efforts should child welfare professionals make to ensure the emotional safety of LGBTQ+ youth in foster care?

RESOURCES

Annie E. Casey Foundation. (July, 2023). Changing Course In Youth Detention: Reversing Widening Gaps By Race And Place. https://assets.aecf.org/m/resourcedoc/aecf-changingcourse-2023.pdf
Child Welfare Information Gateway Podcast Series. Episode 57: Connecting Cross-Border Families. https://www.childwelfare.gov/more-tools-resources/podcast/episode-57/
Child Welfare Information Gateway. (2023). Human trafficking and child welfare: A guide for caseworkers. U.S. Department of Health and Human Services, Administration for Children and Families, Children's Bureau. https://www.childwelfare.gov/pubs/trafficking-caseworkers/

 A robust set of instructor resources designed to supplement this text is located at http://connect.springerpub.com/content/book/978-0-8261-5285-5. Qualifying instructors may request access by emailing textbook@springerpub.com.

REFERENCES

American Psychiatric Association. (n.d.). *Addiction and substance use disorders*. https://www.psychiatry.org/patients-families/addiction-substance-use-disorders
American Academy of Pediatrics. (2021a, July 21). *Physical health needs of children in foster care*. https://www.aap.org/en/patient-care/foster-care/physical-health-needs-of-children-in-foster-care
American Academy of Pediatrics. (2021b, August 24). *Foster care: Health care standards*. https://www.aap.org/en/patient-care/foster-care/health-care-standards/
Baird, K., McDonald, K. P., & Connolly, J. (2020). Sex trafficking of women and girls in a Southern Ontario region: Police file review exploring victim characteristics, trafficking experiences, and the intersection with child welfare. *Canadian Journal of Behavioural Science, 52*(1), 8–17. https://doi.org/10.1037/cbs0000151

Barnert, E. S, Abrams, S., Azzi, V. F., Ryan, G., Brook, R., & Chung, P. J. (2016). Identifying best practices for "Safe Harbor" legislation to protect child sex trafficking victims: Decriminalization alone is not sufficient. *Child Abuse & Neglect, 51,* 249–262. https://doi.org/10.1016/j.chiabu .2015.10.002

Borja, S., Nurius, P., & Eddy, J. M. (2015). Adversity across the life course of incarcerated parents: Gender differences. *Journal of Forensic Social Work, 5,* 1670185. https://doi.org/10.1080/19369 28X.2015.1093992

Cabrera, J., Roberts, Y. H., Lopez, A., Lopez, L., Zepeda, A., Sanchez, R., Punske, C., Gonzalez, G., Nuño, M., Garay-Castro, L., Iris Lopez, Aguilera-Flemming, T., Pelczarski, Y. (2018). Working across borders: Effective permanency practices at the intersection of child welfare and immigration. *Child Welfare, 96*(6), 1–24.

Carr, P. B. (2018). Parental detention and deportation in child welfare cases. *Child Welfare, 96*(5), 81–101.

Channell, D. A., Jasczynski, M., Phillips, D. R., Robinson, J. L., Aden, F., Huq, M., Lee, K., Jones, G., Bernardi, C., & Aparicio, E. M. (2023). Experiences of child welfare social workers in addressing substance use among maltreated young mothers to prevent child maltreatment. *Child & Family Social Work, 28*(3), 846–857. https://doi.org/10.1111/cfs.13009

Child Welfare Information Gateway. (2020a). *Definitions of human trafficking.* U.S. Department of Health and Human Services, Administration for Children and Families, Children's Bureau. https://www.childwelfare.gov/topics/systemwide/laws-policies/statutes/definitions -trafficking/

Child Welfare Information Gateway. (2020b). *Parental substance use as child abuse.* U.S. Department of Health and Human Services, Administration for Children and Families, Children's Bureau. https:// www.childwelfare.gov/topics/systemwide/laws-policies/statutes/parentalsubstanceuse

Child Welfare Information Gateway. (2020c). *Plans of safe care for infants with prenatal substance exposure and their families.* U.S. Department of Health and Human Services, Administration for Children and Families, Children's Bureau. https://www.childwelfare.gov/topics/systemwide /laws-policies/statutes/safecare

Child Welfare Information Gateway. (2020d). *Responding to youth missing from foster care.* U.S. Department of Health and Human Services, Administration for Children and Families, Children's Bureau. https://www.childwelfare.gov/pubPDFs/missing_youth.pdf

Chung, R. C-Y. (2009). Cultural perspectives on child trafficking, human rights & social justice: A model for psychologists. *Counselling Psychology Quarterly, 22*(1), 85–96. https://doi.org/10.1080 /09515070902761230

Citrin, A., Martin, M., & Houshyar, S. (2018). Supporting youth at the intersection of immigration and child welfare systems. *Child Welfare, 96*(6), 69–85.

Crea, T. M., Evans, K., Lopez, A., Hasson, R. G., Palleschi, C., & Sittley, L. (2022). Unaccompanied immigrant children in long-term foster care: Identifying and operationalizing child welfare outcomes. *Child & Family Social Work, 27*(3), 500–512. https://doi.org/10.1111/cfs.12902

dePedro, K. T. (2015). Child maltreatment and military-connected youth: Developing protective school communities: School responses of referral and clinical interventions do not address needs of military families. *Child Abuse & Neglect, 47,* 124–131. https://doi.org/10.1016/j.chiabu .2015.06.004

Evans, K., Pardue-Kim, M., Crea, T. M., Coleman, L., Diebold, K., & Underwood, D. (2018). Outcomes for youth served by the Unaccompanied Refugee Minor Foster Care Program: A pilot study. *Child Welfare, 96*(6), 87–106.

Finigan-Carr, N., Steward, R., & Watson, C. (2018). Foster youth need sex ed, too!: Addressing the sexual risk behaviors of system-involved youth. *American Journal of Sexuality Education, 13*(3), 310–323. https://doi.org/10.1080/15546128.2018.1456385

Finno-Velasquez, M., & Dettlaff, A. J. (2018). The intersection of immigration and child welfare. *Child Welfare, 96*(5), ix–xv.

Fisher, P. A., & Chamberlain, P. (2000). Multidimensional treatment foster care: A program for intensive parenting, family support, and skill building. *Journal of Emotional and Behavioral Disorders, 8*(3), 155–164. https://doi.org/10.1177/106342660000800303

Font, S. A., Berger, L. M., Slepicka, J., & Cancian, M. (2021). Foster care, permanency, and risk of prison entry. *Journal of Research in Crime and Delinquency, 58*(6) 710–754. https://doi.org/10.1177/00224278211001566

Font, S. A., Cancian, M., & Berger, L. M. (2019). Prevalence and risk factors for early motherhood among low-income, maltreated, and foster youth. *Demography, 56*(1), 261–284. https://doi.org/10.1007/s13524-018-0744-x

Harp, K. L., & Bunting, A. M. (2020). The racialized nature of child welfare policies and the social control of Black bodies. *Social Politics: International Studies in Gender, State and Society, 27*(2), 258–281. https://doi.org/10.1093/sp/jxz039

Kravitz, E., Suh, M., Russell, M., Ojeda, A., Levison, J., & McKinney, J. (2021). Screening for substance use disorders during pregnancy: A decision at the intersection of racial and reproductive justice. *American Journal of Perinatology, 40*(6), 598–601. https://doi.org/10.1055/s-0041-1739433

Lipari, R. N., & Van Horn, S. L. (2017, August 24). *Children living with parents who have a substance use disorder*. The CBHSQ Report: Center for Behavioral Health Statistics and Quality, Substance Abuse and Mental Health Services Administration, Rockville, MD. https://www.samhsa.gov/data/sites/default/files/report_3223/ShortReport-3223.html

Lorthridge, J., Evans, M., Heaton, L., Stevens, A., & Phillips, L. (2018). Strengthening family connections and support for youth in foster care who identify as LGBTQ: Findings from the PII-RISE evaluation. *Child Welfare, 96*(1), 53–78.

National Child Traumatic Stress Network. (2014). *Children and domestic violence*. https://www.nctsn.org/sites/default/files/resources//children_domestic_violence_affect_children.pdf

Perlman, N. C., Cantonwine, D. E., & Smith, N. A. (2021). Toxicology screening in a newborn ICU: Does social profiling play a role? *Hospital Pediatrics, 11*(9), e179–e183. https://doi.org/10.1542/hpeds.2020-005765

Perlman, N. C., Cantonwine, D. E., & Smith, N. A. (2022). Racial differences in indications for obstetrical toxicology testing and relationship of indications to test results. *American Journal of Obstetrics & Gynecology MFM, 4*(1), 1–8. https://doi.org/10.1016/j.ajogmf.2021.100453

Phillips, S., & Bloom, B. (1998). In whose best interest? The impact of changing public policy on relatives caring for children with incarcerated parents. *Child Welfare, 77*(5), 531–541.

Porter, A. O. (2013). An examination of a case study with a military family and its involvement with child protective services. *Journal of Human Behavior in the Social Environment, 23*(6), 777–788. https://doi.org/10.1080/10911359.2013.795078

Price, J. M., Chamberlain, P., Landsverk, J., Reid, J. B., Leve, L. D., & Laurent, H. (2008). Effects of a foster parent training intervention on placement changes of children in foster care. *Child Maltreatment, 13*(1), 64–75. https://doi.org/10.1177/1077559507310612

Pullmann, M. D., Roberts, N., Parker, E. M., Mangairacina, K. J., Briner, L., Silverman, M., & Becker, J. R. (2020). Residential instability, running away, and juvenile detention characterizes commercially sexually exploited youth involved in Washington State's child welfare system. *Child Abuse & Neglect, 102*, 104423. https://doi.org/10.1016/j.chiabu.2020.104423

Roberts, D. (2017). Marginalized mothers and intersecting systems of surveillance: Prisons and foster care. In Y. Ergas, J. Jenson, & S. Michel (Eds.), *Motherhood: Procreation and care in a globalized world* (pp. 185–201). Columbia University Press.

Rouse, H. L., Hurt, T. R., Melby, J. N., Bartel, M., McCurdy, B., McKnight, E., Zhao, F., Behrer, C., & Weems, C. F. (2021). Pregnancy and parenting among youth transitioning from foster care: A mixed methods study. *Child & Youth Care Forum, 50*, 167–197. https://doi.org/10.1007/s10566-020-09567-0

Schoneich, S., Plegue, M., Waidley, V., McCabe, K., Wu, J., Chandanabhumma, P. P., Shetty, C., Frank, C. J., & Oshman, L. (2023). Incidence of newborn drug testing and variations by birthing parent race and ethnicity before and after recreational cannabis legalization. *JAMA Network Open, 6*(3), e232058. https://doi.org/10.1001/jamanetworkopen.2023.2058

Summersett Williams, F., Martinovich, Z., Kisiel, C., Griffin, G., Goldenthal, H., & Jordan, N. (2021). Can the development of protective factors help disrupt the foster care-to-prison pipeline? An examination of the association between justice system involvement and the development of youth protective factors. *Journal of Public Child Welfare, 15*(2), 223–250. https://doi.org/10.1080/15548732.2019.1696912

Travis, W. J., Heyman, R. E., & Smith Slep, A. M. (2015). Fighting the battle on the home front: Prevention and intervention of child maltreatment for the military family: The U.S. Air Force Family Advocacy Program seeks to provide safe and nurturing homes for children. *Child Abuse & Neglect, 47,* 114–123. https://doi.org/10.1016/j.chiabu.2015.05.015

Turner, W., & Macdonald, G. (2011). Treatment foster care for improving outcomes in children and young people: A systematic review. *Research on Social Work Practice, 21*(5), 501–527. https://doi.org/10.1177/1049731511400434

Turney, K., & Haskins, A. R. (2019). Parental incarceration and children's well-being: Findings from the Fragile Families and Child Well-being Study. In J. M. Eddy & J. Poehlmann-Tynan (Eds.), *Handbook on children with incarcerated parents* (pp. 53–64). Springer. https://doi.org/10.1007/978-3-030-16707-3_5

U.S. Department of Education. (2016, November 29). *Non-regulatory guidance: Ensuring educational stability for children in foster care.* https://www2.ed.gov/policy/elsec/leg/essa/edhhsfoster-carenonregulatorguide.pdf

U.S. Department of Health and Human Services, Administration for Children and Families, Administration on Children, Youth and Families, Children's Bureau. (2023). *Child maltreatment 2021.* https://www.acf.hhs.gov/cb/data-research/child-maltreatment

U.S. Department of Health and Human Services, Office of Disease Prevention and Health Promotion. (n.d.). *Healthy people 2030.* Retrieved January 13, 2023, from https://health.gov/healthypeople/objectives-and-data/social-determinants-health

U.S. Department of Health and Human Services, Office of Refugee Resettlement. (2022, March 13). *Unaccompanied refugee minors.* https://www.acf.hhs.gov/orr/grant-funding/unaccompanied-refugee-minors

U.S. Department of Health and Human Services, Office of Refugee Resettlement. (2023, July 5). *Fact sheet: Unaccompanied Children (UC) program.* https://www.hhs.gov/sites/default/files/uac-program-fact-sheet.pdf

U.S. Department of Health and Human Services, Office of Women's Health. (2021, February 15). *Effects of domestic violence on children.* https://www.womenshealth.gov/relationships-and-safety/domestic-violence/effects-domestic-violence-children

Weber, A., Miskle, B., Lynch, A., Arndt, S., & Acion, L. (2021). Substance use in pregnancy: Identifying stigma and improving care. *Substance Abuse and Rehabilitation, 12,* 105–121. https://doi.org/10.2147/SAR.S319180

youth.gov. (n.d.) *Homelessness and runaway.* https://youth.gov/youth-topics/homelessness-and-runaway

Zhang, S., Huang, H., Wu, Q., Li, Y., & Liu, M. (2019). The impacts of family treatment drug court on child welfare core outcomes: A meta-analysis. *Child Abuse & Neglect, 88,* 1–14. https://doi.org/10.1016/j.chiabu.2018.10.014

11 Trauma-Informed Practice for Child Welfare

DAVID A. SIMPSON AND VERÓNICA RODRÍGUEZ BAILEY

LEARNING OBJECTIVES

By the end of the chapter, you will be able to:

- Apply a trauma-informed lens to your work with youth in the child welfare system, their biological parents, foster parents, and other caregivers.
- Discuss the importance of assessment in understanding the impact of trauma exposure on youth.
- Discuss the different treatment models for addressing trauma exposure in youth.
- Demonstrate an understanding of the need for cognitive processing and exposure practices when treating youth with trauma exposure in the child welfare system.
- Discuss the importance of mindfulness-based treatments in working with trauma-exposure youth.

INTRODUCTION

Child Trends (2023) shows that at the end of 2021, there were 3.3 million maltreatment referrals in the United States, and 18% of these youth had *indicated* maltreatment cases. Additionally, at the end of fiscal year 2021, close to 400,000 youth were in foster care (Child Trends, 2023). Youth entered care for many reasons, including neglect (64% of those in care), parental substance abuse (40%), the inability of a parent to cope (13%), physical abuse (13%), and inadequate housing (9%; Child

Trends, 2023). Furthermore, Kisiel and colleagues (2009) suggested that additional traumatic experiences occur with the multiple placement disruptions experienced by youth in foster care.

While there are significant numbers of youth in care, not all youth with trauma exposure experience PTSD or suffer significant impairment from their symptoms. However, Betancourt and colleagues (2017) found that 60.3% of their sample of youth with trauma exposure had a diagnosis of PTSD. Early estimates (Dorsey et al., 2012; Stein et al., 2001) report that 80% to 90% of youth in foster care have experienced trauma exposure. Children and youth in foster care are most commonly diagnosed with PTSD, reactive attachment disorder (RAD), oppositional defiant disorder (ODD)/conduct disorder (CD), and major depressive disorder (MAD; Engler et al., 2022). Behavioral and mental health challenges often lead to placement disruptions for youth in foster care, compounding preexisting trauma. These statistics paint a dire picture of the experiences of youth and the subsequent symptoms of trauma exposure, and highlight the importance of treatment to cope with the symptoms associated with removal and trauma exposure these youth face. As such, this chapter addresses the treatment and assessment needs of youth in foster care, particularly surrounding the use of evidence-based treatments that address their needs. It also addresses the importance of training foster care workers, foster parents, and treatment providers on how to approach youth in care with trauma exposure.

TRAUMA AND POSTTRAUMATIC STRESS DISORDER

Trauma can lead to PTSD characterized by several responses, including four main symptoms following exposure to a traumatic event: intrusion, avoidance, cognitive, and hyperarousal symptoms.

Intrusion symptoms focus on the unwanted reminders or trauma triggers that someone with trauma exposure experiences. These reminders are often experienced from out of the blue and catch the person experiencing them off guard, leaving them to feel emotionally dysregulated. Symptoms can take the form of intrusive memories, dreams, or flashbacks that often lead to prolonged emotional distress (American Psychiatric Association [APA], 2013).

Avoidance symptoms include evading the experience of any event or emotion associated with past trauma. For example, people will avoid places, people, emotions, or any physiological arousal associated with the event.

Cognitive symptoms can take many forms in youth with trauma exposure. Youth may have irrational beliefs about the event (i.e., focused on what caused it or who is to blame, often believing they are to blame for the event, and thinking they are a bad person). They also believe the world is dangerous, have trouble learning or completing tasks, have problems with developing language (APA, 2013; Child Welfare Committee [CWC], National Child Traumatic Stress Network [NCTSN], 2013), or cannot remember certain aspects of the event. Affective symptoms of PTSD include intense fear, sadness, anger, anxiety, or affective dysregulation. Affective dysregulation can be viewed as an "impaired ability to regulate and/or tolerate negative emotional states" (Dvir et al., 2014, p. 149) and may be associated with underlying physiological arousal as the biology of trauma impacts the person's ability to regulate their emotions (NCTSN, n.d.).

Hyperarousal experienced by individuals following trauma exposure can take many forms. Irritability and angry outbursts may occur (APA, 2013). Due to hyper-arousal, individuals may also engage in sexualized behaviors, violent behaviors, bullying, substance use, or self-injury, or may have angry outbursts/temper tantrums to avoid the emotions associated with trauma reminders (NCTSN, n.d.). Individuals may also be hypervigilant about their surroundings, experience an exaggerated startle response, and have difficulty concentrating and sleeping (APA, 2013).

Other significant issues may arise in youth with trauma exposure. Disruption in the attachment to significant others in their lives occurs because the world is not predictable for them, leading to issues of boundaries, trust, and feeling isolated from others (CWC, NCTSN, 2013). Attachment issues may be of particular interest when working with youth in the child welfare system, particularly with youth with multiple placements, and thus be considered an essential part of the treatment process. Youth may also experience low self-esteem, limited sense of self, have problems with body image, and experience shame and guilt associated with their trauma exposure (CWC, NCTSN, 2013). Finally, in the short-term, individuals with trauma exposure may experience physical or somatic complaints such as headaches, other aches and pains, gastrointestinal problems, and increased illnesses. In the long term, these somatic complaints have been associated with many chronic diseases in adulthood (Felitti et al., 1998). While these additional considerations are not formal symptoms of PTSD, they must be addressed in the therapeutic work performed with youth with trauma exposure.

Effects of Trauma

Trauma can affect the youth in myriad ways, including attachments and relationships, physical health, emotional responses to trauma reminders/triggers, dissociation, behavior, cognition, self-concept, and future orientation (NCTSN, n.d.). These effects are discussed throughout this chapter (see Table 11.1 for a summary).

Trauma, Brain Development, and Neuroscience

Before providing information on how trauma exposure impacts brain development, a quick overview of the major brain centers is important. There are three major brain centers that have specific brain functions. The survival center of the brain is fully developed at birth and is designed to regulate breathing, digestion,

TABLE 11.1 TRAUMA EFFECTS ON YOUTH

CATEGORY	IMPACT
Attachment and Relationships	• Learn not to rely on others when they have unstable or insecure attachments and relationships. • Following the abuse, believe they are bad and the world is not safe. • May have difficulty developing healthy attachments with caregivers. • Without healthy attachments, are more vulnerable to stress. • Have difficulty controlling and expressing emotions. • May react more violently to stress. • Difficulty in romantic relationships, in friendships, and with authority figures.
Physical Health: Body and Brain	• In response to fear, developmental impact on the body's stress response, brain, and nervous system. • Exaggerated stress response, even if stress levels are out of proportion to the threat. • Lack of brain stimulation, which may cause limited brain development to be limited. • Recurrent, chronic physical complaints, which last into adulthood. • Because of changes to the brain and nervous system and their impact on regulating emotions, may over- or underrespond to sensory stimuli. Therefore, may be unaware of pain, touch, or other physical sensations and may engage in self-harm or be overly sensitive to internal sensations.
Emotional Responses	• Difficulty identifying, expressing, and managing emotions. • Limited emotional vocabulary. • Experience other mental health struggles such as stress, anxiety, or depression because of their inability to express their emotional states. • Difficulty regulating emotions following intense emotional responses and may be easily overwhelmed. • Because they may not have felt protected from caregivers in the past and/or believe the world is dangerous, may become more vigilant and "on guard" in their surroundings, even when such a response is not warranted. • May zone out to environmental threats.

CATEGORY	IMPACT
Dissociation	• Separate mentally from reminders of the event and feel detached from their bodies or in a dream. • Dissociate during a traumatic event and have no memory or experience of the event happening to them. • Dissociate in a way that may become a coping strategy when faced with reminders of the event. • Dissociate in a way that may interfere with being present in aspects of their lives (e.g., when dissociating at school, they may not pay attention to teacher instruction) and impact their learning, social interactions, and more.
Behavior	• React more intensely to trauma reminders and in ways that may impact their safety. • Struggle to self-regulate. • Lack impulse control and consider alternatives/consequences to their behaviors. • Act aggressively in response to a perceived threat and potentially enter the juvenile justice system. • Engage in more risk-taking behaviors such as smoking, substance use, diet and exercise, risky sexual behaviors.
Cognition: Thinking and Learning	• Difficulty problem solving and making rational decisions. • Difficulty planning ahead or for the future. • Difficulty acquiring new skills or learning new information. • Lower attention span. • Struggle to develop language and abstract reasoning.
Self-Concept and Future Orientation	• Feel worthless and despondent. • Blame self for trauma experience. • Have low self-esteem, shame, or guilt. • Believe they cannot change their situation. • Lower sense of competency. • Negative self-attributions impact ability to gain problem-solving skills or have a sense of agency in their own lives. • Difficulty feeling hope. • Living in survival mode does not allow planning or considering the future and what it might hold.

heart rate, and hunger. Thus, the survival center or primitive part of the brain is focused on behaviors that sustain life (CWC, NCTSN, 2013). The limbic system, or the *emotional center*, gives meaning to emotions and memory, guides the response to stressful events, and facilitates individuals' nurturing and caring responses (CWC, NCTSN, 2013). A significant development in the limbic system occurs between birth to age 5. The prefrontal cortex, or the executive center, controls one's ability to be logical and problem-solve, plan, be attentive, show self-awareness, creativity, and compassion, and, over time, the development of empathy (CWC, NCTSN, 2013). Major developmental changes occur around ages 5, 11, and 15; brain growth depends on stimulation and experiences and is particularly critical at major developmental milestones. Thus, trauma exposure during these critical periods can have long-standing effects on how traumatized individuals view their world.

Trauma exposure in childhood can have a negative impact on brain development. For example, trauma has been found to change the structure and chemical activity of the brain, decrease the size and connectivity in some parts of the brain, and impair the emotional and behavioral functioning in a child's life (Teicher, 2002). Furthermore, Teicher (2002) suggested that electroencephalogram (EEG) results look different in traumatized versus non traumatized youth: The fibers connecting the two hemispheres of the brain (the corpus callosum) are smaller in individuals with trauma exposure. This shrinkage of the corpus callosum may impair the ability of the two hemispheres to communicate with one another (CWC, NCTSN, 2013). People with trauma exposure have been found to have a smaller limbic system and amygdala (Karl et al., 2006); these parts of the brain are responsible for handling one's emotional responses.

The body is regulated through the collaboration of several organs and reactions in the body. One crucial regulatory system is the hypothalamic-pituitary-adrenal (HPA) axis, the central stress response system. Kuhlman and colleagues (2015) describe the HPA axis as a set of complex connections between the central nervous system (the neurotransmitters released from the brain and spinal cord throughout the nerves in the body to communicate and control reactions) and the endocrine system (the system that uses hormones to regulate functions in the body). Thus, the HPA coordinates the body's stress response throughout the nervous and endocrine systems, and when no threat is detected, bodily processes function normally. However, if a threat is detected, the body's stress response involves the hypothalamus (H) releasing corticotropin-releasing hormone (CRH). When CRH binds to receptors on the pituitary (P) gland, a hormone is released, which then binds to receptors on the adrenal cortex and stimulates the release of cortisol. Cortisol's main function is to release glucose in the bloodstream to facilitate the body's alarm system. When the body's alarm system is activated, cortisol will suppress and regulate the immune, digestive, and reproductive systems so the body can focus on survival, activating the fight, flight, freeze, and fawn response.

The fight, flight, freeze, or fawn (Taylor, 2022) response is how the body automatically informs us of a threat or danger in our environment. Cortisol and adrenaline provide the burst of energy the body needs to survive when faced with a threat. The brain determines if we can take on the threat (fight), run (flight), or freeze by playing dead or otherwise checking out. Finally, fawning is when someone experiences a threat and attempts to please someone to avoid harm (Taylor, 2022). When adrenaline and cortisol are released, and the fight, flight, freeze, or fawn response is activated, the individual may experience several physical feelings. A physical feeling that is often felt is an increased heart rate. Blood is pulled away from nonessential organs so that muscles can focus on survival, the fight response. Other physical feelings that are experienced include nausea, sweating, feeling cold, or alterations in vision (Taylor, 2022). Taylor (2022) described that someone would become overly agreeable, try to be overly helpful, or focus on making someone happy as examples of fawning behaviors. Past traumas influence how the brain interprets danger and, thus, the survival response (CWC, NCTSN, 2013). It is important to remember that when the HPA and fight, flight, freeze, or fawn response are activated, the individual is only focused on survival, and they do not have much time to problem solve possible solutions, as they are only focused on their safety. Because the HPA has suppressed other bodily functions, survival is the only thing that matters.

Adverse Childhood Experiences

Adverse childhood experiences (ACEs) were first described in the literature by Felitti and colleagues (1998) to offer an understanding of the connection between trauma exposure in youth and health outcomes in adulthood. Felitti and colleagues (1998) identified several trauma exposure types that their sample experienced during their youth: psychological, physical, or sexual abuse; neglect (emotional or physical); witnessing domestic violence against one's mother; living with an individual with substance use disorder; having a parent with a psychiatric illness (including being suicidal); or having a parent who was incarcerated. This study revealed associations between the number of ACEs and significant health risks. In addition to the significant associations on health, it was found that more than half of the participants (more than 17,000 individuals in their sample) experienced at least one ACE, and 25% experienced more than two ACEs. They also discovered that the more ACEs an individual had were associated with increasingly more severe outcomes. Thus, higher exposure to trauma leads to significant health risks in adulthood. The Philadelphia ACE Project (2021) expanded the types of trauma exposures to specifically include whether someone has ever lived in foster care as an ACE.

Turney and Wildeman (2017) found that youth in the foster care system are more likely to report multiple ACEs when compared to children in the general population. An earlier study found that youth with any exposure to an ACE were 69% more likely to experience another form of trauma within the following 12-month period and highlights how trauma exposure may be associated with high-risk environments (Finkelhor et al., 2005), something of particular interest when working with youth in the foster care system. As Liming and colleagues (2021) point out, foster youth with between six and nine ACEs and youth with over 10 ACEs were 28% and 42%, respectively, less likely to be reunified with their biological families than youth with one to five ACEs. Youth with multiple ACEs have been associated with starting drug use as an adolescent and continuing this use into adulthood (Dube et al., 2003). Furthermore, exposure to multiple ACEs has been associated with behavioral and learning problems (Liming & Grube, 2018) and worse education outcomes (Jimenez et al., 2016), and the accumulative effects of trauma exposure places youth at significant risk for suicide (Dube et al., 2001). While these studies did not include youth in the foster care system in their samples, system-involved youth share similar experiences and risks, higher rates of drug use (White et al., 2008), and more behavioral health problems than their peers (Simms et al., 2000). A systematic literature review also shows learning problems (Gypen et al., 2017). Youth in foster care have an increased risk of negative outcomes; therefore, child welfare professionals should employ evidence-based treatment options to support better outcomes. Understanding how to recognize ACEs in youth is the first step in finding much-needed support to overcome the psychosocial effects of trauma and ACE exposure. However, as Amaya-Jackson and colleagues (2021) point out, relying solely on an ACE score in the assessment process does not provide a complete picture of the experiences of the youth postexposure. The original ACE study narrowly defines childhood trauma (Amaya-Jackson et al., 2021). It excludes other significant sources of diverse trauma experiences such as community and mass violence, traumatic grief, medical trauma, chronic illnesses, natural or human-made disasters, racial and ethnic trauma, and racial, ethnic, or religious violence. Thus, a more systematic assessment is needed.

Reflection Box 11.1

TRAUMA AND CHILD WELFARE

There has been increasing recognition of how people experience trauma and the ongoing effects of trauma exposure in one's life. Coming from a strengths-based perspective, however, social workers do not diminish or minimize the experience of trauma but also recognize that trauma exposure is not the sole defining factor of someone's life.

1. How can you assist people in feeling heard about their painful life experiences while supporting their resiliency and coping strategies?

2. What steps can you take not to view children and youth in the system as victims or wounded individuals but rather as unique, complex persons with a wealth of skills and strengths?

3. The experience of trauma is highly individualized; it is not just the events themselves but how they are cognitively processed and understood by the individual. How can you help people process and make meaning from their experiences in a way that supports their growth?

4. Children and youth involved in the child welfare system, particularly those in out-of-home care, have likely experienced multiple traumas in their short lives. How can the increasing recognition of the role of trauma exposure on child development and social functioning assist child welfare professionals in providing more effective and meaningful support for children and youth?

Assessing Trauma Exposure

An ACE score, standardized measures/questionnaires, and semistructured interviews can all be used to assess trauma exposure and the intensity of the symptoms the youth experiences. Child welfare professionals are encouraged to discuss appropriate trauma exposure assessment measures with their colleagues and supervisors at their respective agencies. Sometimes, state agencies have standardized assessments, and other instruments/forms may be used to supplement what the state requires. Funding sources may also mandate the types of assessments that child welfare agencies (or agencies that contract with child welfare agencies) should use.

Briere and Scott (2015) stress the importance of assessing psychological stability and the youth's ability to tolerate stress, particularly if the youth has just recently experienced trauma exposure and the social worker is assessing the youth's current threat to safety. Once the social worker has ascertained that the youth is no longer at risk for further harm, they can begin to assess the trauma exposure. The components of the assessment include the *type*, *severity*, and *duration* of the trauma exposure(s); PTSD-related *symptoms* associated with trauma exposure; and other effects of the trauma, such as *activation* and *avoidant responses*, as well as *affective dysregulation*, and *difficulties in social, community, school*, and other areas of functioning (Briere & Scott, 2015).

Activation responses include reexperiencing physiological symptoms that remind the youth of the trauma or emotional responses, such as anxiety or fear, associated with triggers and reminders (Briere & Scott, 2015). Thus, assessing activation responses allows the social worker to learn when and where the youth may experience reminders or triggers of the traumatic event and if there are times when the activation responses are more or less intense (Briere & Scott, 2015). Having this additional understanding allows the social worker to explore coping strategies when the youth is activated, and if appropriate strategies are used, they can be incorporated into treatment. However, if these coping strategies are associated with avoidance, the social worker should recognize the function of this avoidance as a strength at the time of the reexperiencing; yet, over the long term, the strategy may be less productive in overcoming their trauma. Thus, the child welfare professional must be aware of the youth's avoidant behaviors to reduce this intensity, or what Briere and Scott (2015) call underactivation. Underactivation includes attempts the individual may make to reduce the intensity of the activation of emotional numbing, dissociative disengagement, denial, thought suppression, and anxiolysis without obvious intoxication (Briere & Scott, 2015). These behaviors attempt to minimize emotional and physiological activation of reminders and should initially be viewed as strengths; however, as treatment progresses, the child welfare professional will have them learn and use other coping strategies when they experience reminders, strategies that allow them to take mastery over their experiences. Avoiding places or situations that remind the youth of their trauma exposure should also be considered in the assessment phase. This behavioral avoidance protects the youth from experiencing any uncomfortable emotion or physiological activation and should initially be viewed as a strength and addressed with exposure as indicated.

The next area for assessment includes the youth's regulation of affect. Briere and Scott (2015) define *affect regulation* as "the individual's relative capacity to tolerate painful internal state (*affect tolerance*) and to internally reduce such distress without resorting to dissociation or other avoidance techniques (*affect modulation*)" (pp. 74–75). Therefore, assessing affect regulation allows the social work therapist to understand the ability for which the youth can tolerate trauma triggers and reminders in treatment (Briere & Scott, 2015). When assessing affect regulation, the social work therapist may ask the youth to describe their typical response to triggers and reminders to include when (or if) they notice any activation responses, including changes in emotions, what goes through their mind (cognitions), and if they engage in any avoidance (behaviors). The social work therapist should also assess how long it takes the youth to regulate their emotions (if at all). Remember, some youth experience a great deal of trauma and can never find relief from their heightened activation. When the youth struggle with affective regulation, a complete understanding of trauma exposure, including complex trauma and traumatic grief, is essential.

Other areas that are important to assess are how the symptoms of trauma exposure have interfered with (a) their family, friends, or community relationships; (b) their alertness to interpersonal danger (their ability to recognize harmful situations); (c) their issues of abandonment; (d) their sense of overall helplessness and how this helplessness relates to their need for control; and (e) their ability to maintain a clinical relationship with the social worker or therapist (Briere & Scott, 2015). Obtaining information in these areas allows the child welfare professional to understand the level of impairment and resources needed to manage symptoms. Treatment strategies listed in the following can be used to address these areas.

Finally, the social work therapist should remain mindful that assessment is a continuous process, and the more information that is shared/explained, the more the child trusts the worker. Additionally, the social worker should stay mindful that the trauma assessment will be a time of exposure to the trauma. Thus, they should be aware of the youth verbal and nonverbal communication to understand the comfort level and if the youth is becoming overwhelmed with the assessment. While obtaining the information is essential to the treatment process, solidifying the therapeutic relationship is crucial at this time in treatment.

TRAUMA-INFORMED PRACTICES FOR CHILDREN AND FAMILIES IN CHILD WELFARE

Following the appropriate screening and assessment of youth in the foster care system, treatments are available to address mental health needs, particularly for youth with trauma exposure. The treatments found to be effective in working with trauma-exposed youth include trauma focused-cognitive behavioral therapy (TF-CBT), trauma systems therapy (TST), trauma systems therapy-foster care (TST-FC), mindfulness-based stress reduction (MBSR), and mindfulness-based cognitive therapy (MBCT).

Case Scenario: Secondary Trauma: When Children Are Exposed to Intimate Partner Violence

Moe is a 14-year-old male living with his biological mother, Isabel (34), and his 17-year-old sister, Sofía. Moe and his sister were brought to the attention of their local child welfare agency following an event of intimate partner violence when their father, Marco (44), beat up their mother so severely that she required hospitalization. One of the paramedics who responded to the scene called child protective services (CPS) shortly after this incident out of concern for the safety of Moe and Sofía.

Following an investigation by CPS in which there was no evidence that either Moe or Sofía were physically or sexually abused or neglected and considering that Marco was arrested following the incident, the investigation was returned as unfounded. In her investigation, Lana, the CPS social worker, learned that Isabel and Marco had been married since she was 17 because Isabel was pregnant with Sofía. Isabel described a period when Marco was sweet and provided for her and their newborn, Sofía. However, when Sofía turned 1 or so, Marco lost his job, started drinking heavily, and began to verbally abuse Isabel. When Isabel became pregnant with Moe, Isabel was certain the abuse she was experiencing from Marco would stop. However, the abuse quickly turned from verbal to physical once Isabel shared the news that she was pregnant. During the investigation, Isabel stated that Marco became increasingly angry about the financial uncertainty a second child would bring the family.

When Marco had steady employment, he drank less, and the abuse happened less frequently. However, when Marco was unemployed for extended periods of time and drinking more, he would physically abuse Isabel. As Moe and Sofía grew, they witnessed more and more intimate partner violence toward their mother. When the abuse happened, Moe would hide in his bedroom and wait for his father to calm down. Over time, Moe became more aware of his father's actions, paying attention to warning signs, and made every attempt to appease him so that he would not get aggressive toward Isabel. Moe encouraged his mother and sister to do the same. Sometimes they could minimize Marco's abuse of their mother, doing everything right so Marco had everything he needed. Yet, at times, appeasing Marco did not work, and he would take his aggression out on Isabel.

(continued)

Case Scenario: Secondary Trauma: When Children Are Exposed to Intimate Partner Violence (continued)

As Moe grew older, he attempted to stick up for his mother, but Marco would only laugh at his efforts and continue to focus his abuse on Isabel. On the day that led to the CPS report, Marco came home intoxicated. Moe made unsuccessful attempts to interfere with Marco's aggressive behaviors, yet Marco was undeterred. Moe witnessed the entire event and was unable to help. Sofía called 9-1-1. When they heard sirens, Marco fled the house, only to be apprehended a short time later by the police. When the paramedics arrived, they quickly stabilized Isabel and transported her to a local hospital. Isabel suffered three fractured ribs, a black eye, and bruising; she was released from the hospital 2 days later. Moe and Sofía remained home with a neighbor, and soon, their Aunt Irma came to stay with them during Isabel's long recuperation period.

Isabel decided to press charges against Marco and filed for divorce. When Isabel was feeling better and Irma returned to her home, Isabel, Sofía, and Moe moved to a new city where they did not know anyone. Marco remained in jail and pled guilty to charges of domestic battery that led to a 6-year prison term.

The Department of Children and Family Services (DCFS) social worker, Lana, continued to be involved with this family. Recognizing they were both experiencing the effects of witnessing the long-standing history of abuse toward their mother, Lana referred Moe and Sofía for treatment. Following an initial assessment, Sofía decided that she did not want to receive treatment. However, Moe agreed to see the social worker, Tiara, to address issues related to his long-standing trauma exposure; Isabel supported this decision, and the DCFS case was then closed.

CASE SCENARIO DISCUSSION

During Tiara's work with Moe, he opened up about the fear he experienced that his father would murder his mother. He described feeling hopeless that things would ever get better and helpless because he could not do anything to prevent the abuse. Moe said that when he would make sure his father had a beer or a sandwich when he got home to make his father less angry overall. He said that sometimes, the more Marco drank and passed out, the less abusive he would be, but he knew this was not always true. He said that sometimes his dad would wake up and start yelling, even in the middle of the night. When this happened, he knew his mother was going to "get it."

Tiara asked Moe if he ever worried that his father would abuse him or his sister. Moe said that one time when he was about 8 years old and home alone with his dad, his dad got really mad at him because he spilled some cereal on the floor. As Moe was cleaning up the cereal, Marco got really angry and approached Moe with a raised hand. At this point, Moe screamed so loud and moved away from his father that Marco stopped in his tracks. Moe said that he

> **Case Scenario: Secondary Trauma: When Children Are Exposed to Intimate Partner Violence (*continued*)**
>
> screamed in a way he did not know he could, and it seemed to scare Marco. He said after this, Marco never approached him but still abused their mom. Moe thinks that if he did not scream like this, his father would have started to target him and not his mom. He wished sometimes that Marco took it out on him more because he thought he "could take it" better than his mom.
>
> **DISCUSSION QUESTIONS**
>
> 1. What are Moe's strengths?
> 2. What are some of Moe's negative cognitions associated with the abuse he witnessed?
> 3. What other negative cognitions does Moe describe?
> 4. How can Tiara challenge Moe's negative cognitions?
> 5. What other information would be helpful in understanding how to help Moe?

Trauma-Informed Care

Trauma-informed care (TIC) is a systematic approach to understanding how trauma impacts a person, including their behaviors and the impact trauma has on the brain. TIC also assumes a person-centered approach, focusing on what happened to the person versus thinking something is wrong with the person. TIC does not treat a diagnosis and heal others from trauma, yet when staff in the child welfare system learn about trauma and its impact, they approach youth differently, taking a solution or strengths-based approach, and not one focused on the person's deficits. A TIC approach can be understood within five principles (Purkey et al., 2018).

The *first principle* requires the professional to be aware of and *acknowledge the trauma* experienced by the youth. Here, the professional may recognize the trauma's impact on the child and how the coping strategies the child developed following the trauma exposure were adaptive to their survival (a strength). However, they may still be used long after the feared stimuli have passed. Understanding that these coping strategies may still be in use despite not being faced with the threat allows the child welfare professional or social work therapist to validate their usefulness at one point while remaining cognizant that the youth will learn more adaptive strategies in treatment to use when reexperiencing occurs. Purkey and colleagues (2018) remind us that youth should not feel responsible for their abuse and neglect. A *second principle* in TIC involves *ensuring that youths feel safe* with the professional (and at the office in general) and recognizing the need for both physical and emotional safety (Purkey et al., 2018) and stability (Briere & Scott, 2015). This principle can be viewed as the youth having predictable and consistent schedules and interactions with others, including child welfare professionals (Purkey et al., 2018). Thus, child protective services should offer experiences to the youth in their care that minimizes the chance they will reexperience their trauma or symptoms.

Youth and family need to be included in the *healing process* is the *third principle* defined by Purkey and colleagues (2018). Taking a collaborative approach to working with youths will allow them to feel a sense of agency in their recovery, particularly when these youth feel they have limited control in many aspects of their lives. *Hope*, the *fourth principle*, allows the youth to realize there is a possibility for recovery from trauma and that building on the youth's strength and resilience will lead to improved outcomes (Briere & Scott, 2015; Purkey et al., 2018). Briere and Scott (2015) and Purkey and colleagues (2018) espouse the importance of the *fifth principle*, a *culturally sensitive and historically accurate approach incorporating gender* issues in work with trauma-exposed youth. This *principle* specifically calls for the recognition that certain groups experience systematic abuse based on membership in historically nondominant groups (Purkey et al., 2018), that certain sexes experience different and more frequent traumas, and that sex role socialization impacts how trauma is experienced and expressed (Briere & Scott, 2015).

The five principles of TIC outlined here set the stage for the treatment interventions outlined in the following. These principles should be viewed as guides and reminders of the importance of an empathic approach that recognizes strengths and growth, not one guided solely by a diagnosis focusing on the child's deficits. Professionals who enter their work through a TIC lens not only approach it from a position of strength but, more importantly, the youth on their caseloads may have better outcomes with fewer placement disruptions simply by recognizing their symptoms and behaviors through this lens.

Trauma-Focused-Cognitive Behavioral Therapy

TF-CBT is one of the most studied interventions in treating any and multiple trauma exposures in youth. TF-CBT has been found effective with youth from diverse backgrounds and can be delivered effectively in outpatient and inpatient settings, educational settings, residential treatment facilities, and the youth's home. Studies have also shown its effectiveness in working with referred youth (Cohen et al., 2012; Weiner et al., 2009).

With TF-CBT (or other treatment strategies, for that matter), it is critical that all caregivers learn the treatment strategies and work in collaboration with the youth and their therapist; developing a partnership with caregivers is vital to treatment success. Caregivers will need to support the youth throughout the treatment process and often remind them to use their strategies when the youth is experiencing a trigger or reminder of their past trauma. Also, it is vital to help the caregiver to understand that when a child responds to a threat (either an actual threat or a false threat), the child's response is to ensure their survival or, as Saxe and colleagues (2016) define it, *survival-in-the-moment*. When caregivers see the youth's behavior through this lens, the caregiver can support the child in a more understanding and thoughtful manner. Additionally, the caregiver's thoughts and concerns about treatment should be assessed and addressed; understanding any barriers to treatment success should be handled directly from the beginning. Praise the caregiver (and other significant others) for bringing the youth to their appointments. Finally, the child welfare professional will want to work with the youth's clinician to coordinate discussions between the youth's biological family and foster family. Coordination and communication can limit the internal conflict the youth may be experiencing and potentially have a joint family meeting with everyone as necessary and appropriate.

All aspects of TF-CBT are designed to expose the youth to their trauma in one way or another; thus, it is important for people supporting the youth (including the treatment provider, the child welfare professional, and caregivers) to be cognizant of this reality and to be prepared to assist the child through their activation of the fight, flight, freeze, or fawn response following these exposures. Although avoidance is an important coping strategy at the moment when faced with trauma reminders or triggers, it is not an effective strategy for coping with the effects of trauma over the long term. For example, an exposure will happen when the youth is asked what brought them to treatment (even if they do not describe the traumatic event in detail, they are thinking about it), and when asked, the youth may experience intrusive thoughts about the event, physiological symptoms, or other reminders, and this is in the first meeting. Other exposures will occur throughout treatment, and discussing them gets easier over time.

An essential goal of TF-CBT is for the youth (and their caregiver) to learn new coping skills, and mastering components of the *PRACTICE model* early in treatment will allow them to feel more confident when completing more challenging elements of treatment (e.g., cognitive processing and the trauma narrative; Cohen et al., 2017). Youth deciding to avoid a (real or perceived) threat is a strength. The youth knew when to remove themselves from danger, to survive. Reinforcing that this was the best strategy at the time is important, as is letting the youth know that they will learn different strategies for coping with these reminders with TF-CBT. Using a subjective units of distress scale (SUDS) can be helpful throughout treatment, whereby the social work therapist can assess the anxiety level of the youth throughout their work together.

The PRACTICE components of TF-CBT include *psychoeducation, parenting skills, relaxation and stress management, affective modulation, cognitive coping and processing, trauma narrative, in vivo mastery of trauma triggers and reminders, conjoint parent–child sessions,* and *enhancing future safety* (Child Sexual Abuse Task Force and Research & Practice Core [CSATF], NCTSN, 2004; Cohen et al., 2012). Additionally, ensuring safety before starting treatment and implementing aspects of traumatic grief as necessary are components of TF-CBT (Cohen et al., 2012).

[P] Psychoeducation

Psychoeducation is the first component of TF-CBT. Psychoeducation includes an orientation to what treatment is, who goes to treatment, letting the youth and their caregivers know what to expect during treatment, the benefits of treatment, and, above all, instilling hope that the youth can have some symptom relief. For example, the treatment provider describes that the youth will work on addressing the thoughts, feelings, and behaviors associated with their past trauma exposures by developing new skills and engaging in various exposures. Psychoeducation also includes discussing the specific trauma(s) the youth experienced by naming the trauma(s). For example, if a child is in a car accident, psychoeducation includes collecting and discussing facts about car accidents (*an exposure*). If a child is sexually abused, psychoeducation includes discussing sexual abuse versus nonabusive relationships. When discussing traumatic events, it is essential to discuss the frequency of each trauma, how it happens, and who can experience the trauma.

Additionally, therapists and child welfare workers should discuss why the child was removed and other information about the perpetrator's experience after the disclosure that led to removal. For example, it is important to discuss why the perpetrator was arrested, issues related to *due process* of the perpetrator, and the perpetrator's rights. Finally, the therapist or child welfare professional needs to be informed about these topics to help dispel any myths associated with the trauma(s) experienced by youth.

[P] Parenting Skills

Parents and caregivers are central to treatment success as they are essential to healing. Youth in the foster care system must have a strong relationship with their caregivers, including foster parents, adoptive parents, residential treatment staff, child welfare professionals, other stakeholders (e.g., school personnel, extended family), and biological parents when appropriate. Caregivers are encouraged to be consistent, predictable, and follow through during treatment. Caregivers are encouraged not to blame the youth for their traumatic experiences but to set limits as they would with any youth without trauma exposure, as youth with trauma histories need structure and boundaries. Cohen and colleagues (2012) describe the importance of reframing the caregiver's thoughts that the child is "bad" to thoughts that "something bad happened to [them]" (p. 532); this removes any form of judgment about the youth's behavior and situates the caregiver's cognitions of the youth's acting out behaviors as a symptom of their trauma exposure instead. Caregivers are also encouraged to practice positive reinforcement and praise the youth when they witness the youth doing something positive or relying on their strengths.

In addition to positive reinforcement, several other parenting strategies should be covered and practiced with the caregiver, with follow-up with the therapist to discuss any issues related to their implementation. First, it is important to discuss ways the caregiver can ignore certain behaviors, such as mocking or mimicking the caregiver or when the child becomes verbally angry with the caregiver. Caregivers are encouraged to use time-outs with younger children to help manage any problem behavior that might occur. Time-outs will allow the child to practice self-regulation strategies. Contingency management plans can also assist youth with trauma exposure to increase desired behaviors. It is also important to find times when the youth and caregiver can come together to do activities they both enjoy. This time allows the caregiver to focus on positive behaviors that can be reinforced and rewarded. An important aspect of parenting skills is for the caregiver to use these skills consistently. While youth in foster care may not want to include foster parents in their treatment because they do not trust them (which is only exacerbated with multiple placements or residential treatment facilities; Cohen et al., 2012), including the foster parents will shape their understanding of treatment and allow foster parents to support any needs related to the youth in foster care (Dorsey et al., 2014).

[R] Relaxation and Stress Management

The goal of *relaxation and stress management* is so the youth can reduce the physiological experience of stress by learning new coping strategies when they become overwhelmed emotionally. The therapist should begin this phase with psychoeducation on how the body responds to stress and the connection to trauma triggers and reminders. The therapist will want to have an open conversation about what physiological symptoms the youth experiences when they encounter reminders. Physiological reactions may include shallow breathing, muscle tension, headaches, and nausea, to name a few. Once the therapist has identified the physiological symptoms, they can help the youth learn relaxation strategies for coping with these symptoms. These include deep breathing, mindfulness/meditation, and progressive muscle relaxation. A critical element of relaxation and stress management includes helping the youth understand the connection between trauma reminders and requisite physiological symptoms and recognizing the need to use these strategies when they become physiologically aroused. Relaxation strategies need to be practiced in the session to ensure mastery, and the therapist/child welfare professional should start and end each session with relaxation. Cohen and colleagues (2012) suggest that youth should learn relaxation strategies before psychoeducation discussions about the trauma type(s) the youth experienced. This way, they will have coping strategies to rely on when they become affectively dysregulated.

[A] Affective Expression and Modulation

This PRACTICE model component helps the youth develop their emotional intelligence by recognizing and identifying their emotional or affective expressions and then modulating them (Cohen et al., 2017). Social work therapists and child welfare professionals are encouraged to be as creative as possible in identifying affective expression. For example, the social work therapist may begin by asking the youth to describe/write down all the feeling words they know. Once the youth has done this, the social worker can ask the youth which feelings are *good* and *bad* and discuss the meaning behind these two attributes. In particular, if a youth says that being *mad* is a bad feeling, the social work therapist is encouraged to explore what the youth means by this. Through this discussion, the social work therapist will often learn of specific behaviors that accompany this feeling (e.g., slamming doors when mad) that lead the youth to be reprimanded, leading the social work therapist to discuss the connection between feelings and behaviors (see the cognitive triangle discussion that follows) and describe that the feeling is okay to experience; only the behavior is problematic. These types of discussions normalize talking about feelings and allow the youth to become more comfortable doing so. Discussions with caregivers in this phase of treatment include allowing them to become more comfortable discussing feelings and praising their child for appropriately expressing their emotions. For example, the caregiver is encouraged to praise their youth when the youth tells their caregivers that they are mad instead of slamming a door.

Affective modulation takes many forms. One way to modulate emotions is to help the youth learn ways to interrupt their thoughts and feelings as well as consider positive imagery; both are designed to have the youth recognize they may be experiencing a trauma reminder and focus on something more positive in the moment (Cohen et al., 2017). This strategy should be done only when the youth has yet to develop other strategies where exposure and desensitization can occur and not as a strategy for use in the long term. Another form of affective modulation is the use of positive self-talk, where the youth focuses more on their strengths and not on the negative aspects of the event. Ensuring safety is a meaningful way to manage emotions. For example, when a youth uses assertiveness skills to ensure their safety, they are less likely to focus on the negative aspect of the event. Thus, when the youth is focused on problem solving, they are less focused on negative reminders or triggers. Helping the youth develop problem-solving skills allows them to explore other avenues for coping with affective dysregulation associated with trauma reminders and triggers (Cohen et al., 2017).

[C] Cognitive Coping and Processing

The cognitive coping and processing step helps youth understand the connections between thoughts, feelings, and behaviors—the cognitive triangle—(Assigana et al., 2014) and differentiate between them. When youth understand the interconnectedness of these constructs, they become more equipped to cope when feeling physiological arousal. When the provider begins to describe the cognitive triangle, they should start with an example that would be easy for the youth to follow. For example, ask the youth *what feeling they have when they get to eat their favorite food* and ascertain a SUDS rating for this feeling. Once they share their feeling, the therapist or child welfare professional can also ask the youth what *thoughts* they have when eating their favorite food to directly connect the feeling of eating one's favorite food to a thought. Lastly, the child is asked to describe any *behaviors* that come to mind when eating their favorite food. Here, the youth might say they want to eat more or ask for seconds as behaviors. The goal in this sequence is to allow the youth to connect thoughts, feelings, and behaviors in a situation that is not threatening and, in fact, one that they enjoy. Once the worker is comfortable with the youth's understanding of the process with the cognitive triangle, they can move onto helping the youth identify thoughts, feelings, and behaviors that perpetuate their fear and anxiety, particularly thoughts associated with their trauma exposure. In doing so, youth learn strategies to challenge these negative thoughts and replace them with adaptive and rational thoughts. For example, in response to the negative cognition, *I hate thinking like I can't control what's going on*, the youth is encouraged to consider whether (a) this is true 100% of the time and (b) what they do have control over in the moment (e.g., using relaxation strategies). Once the youth looks for alternatives to their original negative thought, they are prompted to change their behavior with the goal of reducing the intensity of the feeling they experienced. The presumption is that their negative thoughts are not helpful and that finding alternatives will allow them to cope differently and have more successful outcomes.

Youth with trauma exposure often do not find alternatives to their negative cognitions and solely rely on this cognition as fact when there are several other ways to address their thoughts. Youth are encouraged to find alternatives to their thoughts and behaviors to lessen the impact of their current emotional state.

The following several elements of TF-CBT include exposing youth to various aspects of their trauma. The goal of exposure is to help youth develop mastery over their trauma reminders. Exposure reduces the power or intensity of the emotions associated with traumatic events and reduces avoidance of negative thoughts or feelings. When youth develop mastery over their thoughts, feelings, and behaviors, trauma reminders no longer create the same level of distress. When processed using the cognitive triangle, *exposure* also allows youth to challenge any distorted thoughts about their trauma exposure. For example, youth often feel guilty or blame themselves for the trauma. Challenging these distorted cognitions prepares youth to address them more rationally and cope differently when confronted with trauma reminders.

As one can imagine, exposing youth to traumatic thoughts, feelings, and behaviors is not an endeavor counselors, caregivers, or youth want to engage in because of their own discomfort. However, as the previous paragraph explains, exposure is critical to the successful outcomes of youth with trauma exposure. The following are strategies for exposing youth, which include developing a trauma narrative and in vivo mastery of trauma triggers and reminders.

[T] The Trauma Narrative

The trauma narrative is the most critical piece of TF-CBT because it allows the youth to describe their experiences as they remember them; it is their perspective of what happened. The goal of the trauma narrative is to desensitize the youth to their trauma reminders, both physiological and psychological arousal (Cohen et al., 2017). The trauma narrative should include the times when the trauma exposure was at its worst, and the social work therapist should encourage the child to provide as many details about the exposure as possible. These details include their thoughts, feelings, and behaviors during the event(s) to become desensitized to their thoughts and feelings rather than the specific details of the exposure. As such, the worker does not attempt to correct or challenge the youth as they prepare their narrative. Addressing the validity of thoughts, feelings, and behaviors occurs after the youth has completed their trauma narrative. Additionally, the trauma narrative allows the child to make meaning about what happened and to put the events behind them in a manner that says their trauma exposure is not all of who they are and that their trauma exposure does not define them; they possess other strengths.

Structure the trauma narrative into four chapters. The *first chapter* is designed for the worker to get to know their youth and their strengths. The social worker will ask the youth to write about their interests, favorite things about school, and what they like to do for fun. This chapter allows the youth to describe who they are away from their trauma exposure and reinforces that they are not only defined by their trauma.

The *second chapter* moves the youth closer to their trauma exposure. The youth begins to describe what they were doing just before the trauma exposure. For example, if the narrative is focused on witnessing domestic violence in the home, the social worker would ask the youth to describe what was happening before the event occurred. The social worker may ask who was present and what everyone was doing before it happened. The social worker would also want to focus on what the youth was doing (behaviors), their thoughts and feelings, as well as any physiological feelings they experienced before the event occurred. The social work therapist may want the narrative to include only the 10 to 15 minutes before the event occurred or longer, depending on the youth and events happening that led up to the trauma exposure.

In the *third chapter*, the youth describes the trauma exposure in detail. The social work therapist asks questions to prompt the youth to describe the event as the youth remembers the experience. It is vital for the social work therapist NOT to correct any inaccuracies in their experience. Furthermore, the social worker prompts the youth to describe their thoughts, feelings, behaviors, and any physiological experiences during the event, all of which are included in the trauma narrative. This level of detail allows the social work therapist to discuss any maladaptive cognitions associated with their experience later. If, in the same example, the youth indicates that they should have stopped the domestic violent event from happening, the social work therapist (a) is made aware of the youth's misperception of their control over the event and (b) can formulate challenges to this cognition when discussed later.

The *fourth chapter* is where the youth describes themselves following their treatment. Focusing on the future allows the youth to, once more, focus on being more than trauma exposure. In this chapter, the youth provides detail about what their life looks like, free of their negative cognitions and reminders, and focuses on how they handle reminders differently in the future and other successes they may see for themselves.

It is important to keep in mind that the trauma narrative should be written by the youth with the social worker's support. Further, the social worker should remain flexible when asking the youth to write the narrative (e.g., the social worker may write it for the youth, the youth may write a poem, or a song instead of a description of the four chapters that follows). As the youth and social work therapist collaboratively develop the trauma narrative, understanding the youth's fear or anxiety level throughout the development of the narrative is vital to progress. Awareness of the youth's anxiety level (SUDS) as they write the narrative allows the social work therapist to navigate how much to write (remember, completing the narrative is an exposure, and anxiety level should be monitored to avoid overwhelming the youth). Awareness of their SUDS level allows the social work therapist to navigate engagement in the exposure of writing the narrative. Typically, if the youth's SUDS level reaches half the feelings range (e.g., 4/8, 5/10), the social work therapist encourages the youth to perform relaxation strategies before continuing. By reducing the youth's SUDS level before moving forward, the youth will have a stronger chance for success, also reinforcing using relaxation strategies when feeling heightened anxiety outside of treatment sessions.

Once the youth has written the trauma narrative, Cohen and colleagues (2017) suggest the professional begin cognitive processing, which is to "identify, explore, and correct the child's trauma-related maladaptive cognitions (i.e., inaccurate or unhelpful thoughts)" (p. 193) as well as any emotions that are associated with these maladaptive cognitions. Maladaptive cognitions that are inaccurate include the youth inappropriately taking responsibility for the event or having thoughts that would be impossible for them to know about. For example, they may indicate that it is their fault they experienced physical abuse because they did not pick up their toys, or they believe that because they did not inform someone about the abuse they were experiencing, others were hurt (Cohen et al., 2017). Unhelpful thoughts, on the other hand, may still be inaccurate, or they may be unhelpful even though they are accurate. For example, the youth might state, *Someone will always drown every time it rains because it always floods.* While this may be accurate on some level, the thought ultimately perpetuates the youth's fear if left unchallenged.

The social work therapist begins to correct these inaccurate or unhelpful cognitions by challenging them, whereby the youth can explore alternatives. Progressive logical questioning (or Socratic questioning) is a strategy for challenging inaccurate or unhelpful thoughts that are woven through the trauma narrative (Cohen et al., 2017). In doing so, the youth is presented with information contrary to their beliefs to challenge their maladaptive cognitions. The child can explore alternatives to their original cognitions to remove unnecessary blame or responsibility for the trauma(s).

[I] In Vivo Mastery of Trauma Triggers and Reminders

In vivo mastery of trauma reminders and triggers includes exposure to feared stimuli associated with trauma exposure. It is a behavioral plan for overcoming their triggers and reminders. Cohen and colleagues (2017) indicate this is the only optional PRACTICE model step. In vivo mastery of trauma triggers and reminders is only needed in treatment if the youth continues to exhibit avoidance behaviors to innocuous or safe situations or cues so the youth can gain mastery over their emotions (Cohen et al., 2017). Once the trauma trigger or reminder is identified, the social work therapist develops a plan for exposure to the feared stimuli so that desensitization can occur. For example, suppose a youth who experienced sexual abuse in a particular room of their house continues to avoid that room. In that case, the social work therapist will develop an exposure plan to help the youth gain control through desensitization and cognitive processing and thus develop a sense of mastery over these fears. Additionally, caregivers need to participate in exposures here and support the youth during this mastery, where they can praise and reinforce the youth's work.

[C] Conjoint Parent–Child Sessions

These sessions are essential to the therapeutic work for youth with trauma exposure. Social work therapists engaged in TF-CBT with youth in the child welfare system should identify a caregiver or an adult early in the treatment process because finding a caregiver to participate may be difficult. The identified caregiver could be the child welfare professional, a foster parent, a teacher, an extended family member, or, if the youth is in a residential setting, one of the staff. It is important not to have a conjoint parent/caregiver session when the adult cannot provide support, the adult is overly emotional about learning about the trauma exposure, or the youth strongly opposes having the session (Cohen et al., 2017).

These conjoint sessions are intended for (a) the youth to share their trauma narrative, (b) the caregiver to learn more about the youth's progress in treatment, (c) the participants to have an open dialogue about the trauma, and (d) the participants to develop a plan should the youth experience trauma reminders or triggers in the future (Cohen et al., 2017). The social work therapist should meet individually with the youth before the conjoint session to discuss what the session will cover. At this time, the social work therapist should assist the youth in practicing relaxation strategies. Prior to the conjoint session, the social work therapist will also meet individually with the caregiver to inform them that the youth will read their trauma narrative in the session. It is important for the social work therapist not to share the contents of the trauma narrative with the caregiver; instead, the social work therapist should only prepare the caregiver for what they will hear. While caregivers may know some of what the child experienced during their trauma, they might not know the child's perspective, and thus, they may hear specific, distressing details they had not known previously. Thus, the social work therapist will also want to prepare the caregiver not to react to this new information in a manner that would lead the youth to believe that their trauma was too much for adults to handle. For example, the social work therapist would want to encourage the caregiver not to become too emotional when hearing elements of the trauma they did not know or are challenging to comprehend. Remember, the caregiver needs to support the youth, someone the youth can rely on when they need support and encouragement. Suppose the youth believes the caregiver cannot cope with their experiences appropriately (e.g., the caregiver becomes too emotional that their needs supersede the needs of the youth and interferes with the youth's belief that the caregiver is someone they can rely on for support). In that case, the youth will not seek them out for support. Of particular importance for youth in the child welfare system, the caregiver may be someone who knows nothing of the youth's trauma history and, thus, should be prepared using a trauma-informed practice lens as discussed. Finally, preparing both the youth and the caregiver for the trip back home is of utmost importance. As one can imagine, for the youth, sharing their narrative with another person will be overwhelming and yet therapeutic. However, for the caregiver, particularly one with no previous knowledge of the exposure, preparing them to praise the youth for being brave and reminding them that they are a source of support should take precedence over silence on the way home.

[E] Enhancing Future Safety

An essential component of the PRACTICE model is *enhancing future safety*. This is technically the "E" in the PRACTICE model; however, at the start of treatment, the social work therapist should also discuss issues of safety and trust (Cohen et al., 2017). This component is covered throughout treatment to enhance the youth's and caregiver's awareness of ways to ensure safety. It is also reviewed at the end of treatment to ensure safety moving forward. However, of critical importance is that TF-CBT should not be initiated until the youth is *safe and free* from additional trauma. If the social worker believes the youth continues to experience ongoing abuse or trauma, they must take all steps necessary to ensure the youth's safety (i.e., discussions with the child welfare professional and foster parents). The youth will be unable to focus on treatment if they are focused on their safety.

Enhancing future safety includes problem solving, assertiveness training, and body safety and should be reviewed thoroughly with youth. The six elements for safety planning include: (a) clearly and openly communicating feelings and desires to potential perpetrators, (b) relying on one's gut feelings in situations that may be threatening; (c) identifying people and places that are safe and can be supportive; (d) understanding appropriate touch and learning to say no, to leave certain situations, and tell others if they experience forms of abuse as well as discussing other elements of healthy sexuality; (e) learn that secrets are different from surprises and that both should be shared, particularly if an adult asks the youth to keep a secret regarding sexual abuse; and (f) keep sharing the secret until someone believes them (Cohen et al., 2017). Reviewing these elements is usually done in the conjoint family session so everyone involved can be aware of and take safety measures to protect the youth from further harm. Other practical elements should include whether the child knows how to call 9-1-1 and ensuring the youth knows their caregivers' names, numbers, and addresses (especially important for youth in foster care).

Trauma Systems Therapy

TST (Saxe et al., 2016) is an eco-systems approach (Bronfenbrenner, 1979; Bronfenbrenner & Morris, 2006) that addresses the emotional needs of trauma-exposed youth as well as the systems and social environments designed to care for these youth (e.g., caregivers, schools, community). TST assumes traumatized youth are behaving in a *survival-in-the-moment* state within social environments or systems of care that are not equipped to support the emotional regulation of these youth. Furthermore, TST assumes that (a) youth experience the *survival-in-the-moment* state even when their environment is relatively safe and (b) that the environments where these youth live are unsafe or these environments are full of trauma reminders (Saxe et al., 2016). TST seeks to intervene at the micro, mezzo, and macro levels of social work practice, thus treating the *trauma system* (Saxe et al., 2016) to improve the lives of trauma-exposed youth. Thus, by assessing the fit between a youth's coping skills and the support provided by their environment/ systems of care, TST seeks to intervene by teaching youth ways to regulate their emotions while supporting organizational and system-wide efforts to meet the needs of youth and families. Therefore, TST is a clinical treatment and organizational model designed to treat the entire trauma system. The child welfare professional must understand the principles of TST in treating youth involved in the child welfare system and their families and communities.

TST attempts to understand how the youth moves from an unaroused state to one of *survival-in-the-moment* within environments that may or may not be able to support the youth through this process (Saxe et al., 2016). Saxe and colleagues (2016) describe a usual state that transitions into the survival-in-the-moment state when exposed to trauma reminders and is based on the level of nervous system arousal. They suggest this transition begins with *regulating* their usual state with no arousal. In this phase, the youth can pay attention to what is happening in their environment without arousal (Suárez et al., 2006). As the youth moves into the survival-in-the-moment state, their nervous system becomes activated, thus *revving* their thoughts, feelings, and behaviors to perceive threats in their environment (Saxe et al., 2016). Critical to the revving phase, in the absence of a specific trauma reminder, the youth may be activated by other stimuli creating negative emotions similar to the traumatic event (Suárez et al., 2006). Once revving peaks, *reexperiencing* the traumatic event occurs where youth experience symptoms of physiological arousal, as well as thoughts and feelings in a manner where they believe the event is happening again (often in areas that are safe and free from threat; Saxe et al., 2016).

Finally, *reconstituting* occurs when the threat has passed and the youth has either regulated their emotions or removed themselves from the trauma-producing situation (Saxe et al., 2016). Suárez and colleagues (2006) suggest that youth in the reconstituting phase can pay attention to what is happening around them. These steps are accompanied by affect, action, and awareness that occur and change based on the environmental position of the youth during this pattern or arousal (Saxe et al., 2016).

Following a comprehensive assessment, treatment addresses maintaining safety for the youth in treatment (Saxe et al., 2016). Because TST is focused on an ecological approach, maintaining safe environments across systems needs to be addressed. As such, interventions may include working with school systems, foster families, community agencies, and child welfare agencies. Once safety has been addressed, Saxe and colleagues (2016) indicate that helping the youth regulate emotions when they experience survival-in-the-moment states is necessary for their improvement. In this phase, youth learn skills to address their emotional well-being and also, as discussed, learn to identify and address emotions and include family members (biological or foster families) in the process. Furthermore, as mentioned in the discussion of TIC, ensuring the agency and child welfare professionals know how to address dysregulated youth is essential.

Similar to cognitive coping and processing (Cohen et al., 2017), the next step in treatment for youth using a TST model includes challenging negative cognitions in a manner that helps them stop these thoughts, think more positively about their situation, and use other strategies to address these thoughts to minimize their negative impact on mood and behaviors (Saxe et al., 2016). Additionally, youth work on sharing their trauma story to "help children leave their trauma in the past" (Saxe et al., 2016, p. 309).

Bronfenbrenner's (1979) social-ecological model indicates that various social environments surround individuals and that these social environments directly impact the individual's lives. Social environments that surround youth in the foster care system include their biological parents (and families), foster parents, school, peer groups, neighborhood, culture, child welfare professionals, treatment providers, and the child welfare system itself. As described, self-regulation interventions support the youth's experience with trauma symptoms. However, the TST model suggests that social-environmental interventions are critical in addressing the needs of trauma-exposed youth, indicating that this is an important approach to meeting the needs of referred youth (Suárez et al., 2006).

Trauma Systems Therapy-Foster Care

Trauma systems therapy-foster care (TST-FC) seeks to develop trauma-informed child welfare systems, because when systems are trauma-informed, outcomes for youth improve. In a similar manner as discussed, TST-FC addresses both the emotional needs of trauma-exposed youth in foster care but extends its systems work to address the needs of the child welfare system itself, its staff, and resource/foster parents to ensure a more supportive response to these youth, ultimately leading to better outcomes (Bartlett & Rushovich, 2018). In doing so, TST-FC supports the development of systems that are present and influential in the child's life to support trauma-exposed youth in foster care to develop coping and self-regulation skills and use these skills when faced with reexperiencing a traumatic event. For example, TST-FC encourages child welfare systems to understand how trauma impacts youth, helps workers manage difficult behaviors, and teaches adults how to respond effectively when addressing difficult behaviors in youth (Bartlett & Rushovich, 2018). The importance of ongoing staff support and continued training allows providers to develop additional supervision and skills to engage in this work (Bunting et al., 2019).

Furthermore, a TST-FC approach includes ensuring foster parents receive trauma-informed training and support throughout their experiences as foster parents. This approach may also be associated with limiting the number of youth and families child welfare professionals have on their caseloads. Assuming this TIC approach, TST-FC can significantly impact the lives of youth, foster parents, biological parents, and child welfare professionals in a manner that protects the well-being and safety of some of this country's most vulnerable youth and its workforce.

Mindfulness-Based Stress Reduction and Mindfulness-Based Cognitive Therapy

While the treatments mentioned above help youth with trauma exposure understand and learn coping skills, other types of treatments can be used to cope with acute triggers of trauma exposures. As indicated, survival-in-the-moment states experienced by youth with trauma exposure often lead to inappropriate behaviors and behaviors that might lead to placement disruption for foster youth (Saxe et al., 2016). When youth can cope with the trauma reminders or triggers, they are able to engage in alternative behaviors that allow them to cope effectively with these reminders. Youth can also use MBSR and MBCT can be used for older youth.

Briere and Scott (2015) define *mindfulness* as the "capacity to maintain aware-ness of and openness to-current experience, including internal mental states and aspects of the external world, without judgment and with acceptance" (p. 216). Thus, people are encouraged to be alert to what is going on around them in an unbiased and accepting manner to minimize the distress experienced with emo-tional arousal. Because this is done without judgment, the individual is then able to view their symptoms as caused by an external force and not within themselves. Mindfulness-based strategies ground the person to focus on their immediate sur-roundings and sensations instead of being focused on their affect dysregulation in the *here-and-now* with acceptance of the reality of their experiences and without judgments (Briere & Scott, 2015). Individuals are then encouraged to focus on their breathing to minimize distress.

Mindfulness meditation is an important aspect of MBSR. When performing MBSR, the youth focuses their attention on their breathing (or a sensation in their body) and is encouraged to reengage their focus on this sensation when their mind inevitably begins to wander. The critical element here is to refocus one's mind in a nonjudgmental fashion. For example, a nonjudgmental response would be to simply recognize that one's mind has lost focus on their breathing or body sensa-tions and gently return that focus to breathing or the sensation without judging themselves for losing focus. To further ground the person, they are encouraged to focus on slow and controlled breathing and to complete a *body scan* that assesses muscle tension or stress. When tension has been identified, steps to address this tension are initiated (e.g., progressive muscle relaxation).

Incorporating several MBSR strategies, MBCT targets cognitive distortions, negative preoccupations, and other negative thought processes associated with trauma reminders (Briere & Scott, 2015). As such, youth are taught to understand that these negative thought patterns are merely thoughts and false alarms and not evidence that the person is in immediate danger. Additionally, these thoughts are not suppressed or avoided but rather considered as false alarms. While lim-ited research has been done solely on mindfulness-based therapies to treat trauma exposure overall, a study found that using MBCT effectively increased adoles-cents' ability (with trauma exposure and substance use disorders) to cope with stressors (Fortuna et al., 2018). Fortuna et al. (2018) also write that improved cop-ing strategies may have been brought on by incorporating cognitive restructuring activities to address negative thoughts. It is the combination of mindfulness-based activities and cognitive restructuring that was associated with a decrease in sub-stance use and a reduction in cravings (Fortuna et al., 2018).

Mindfulness-based strategies may not be the only strategy to use for youth with trauma exposure, and these techniques can be incorporated nicely into the treatments described previously. Additionally, the added cognitive component of MBCT can be effective in helping youth to challenge negative cognitions associ-ated with their trauma exposure that are already part of other forms of treatment (i.e., TF-CBT).

CHAPTER SUMMARY

This chapter described essential elements for working with youth and families involved in the child welfare system by focusing on treatment options designed to address trauma exposure in youth. This chapter serves as a resource for social workers engaged in child welfare work and provides suggestions for treatment and support for child welfare–involved youth. As indicated throughout this chapter, the work with youth and their families begins with everyone interacting with youth in the foster care system becoming trauma-informed, including the agencies themselves. When agencies are trauma-informed, they recognize the needs of the youth in their care, and their employees are charged with maintaining the care and safety of these vulnerable youth.

DISCUSSION QUESTIONS

1. What are the benefits of engaging in MBCT for youth in the foster care system?
2. How can MBSR and MBCT strategies be incorporated into TF-CBT or other therapies that may be used to treat youth in the foster care system?
3. Discuss the benefits of placing siblings together. What are ways a child welfare professional can support keeping siblings together? How can child welfare professionals advocate for these types of placements?
4. Discuss the benefits and barriers of having trauma-informed child welfare systems. What are ways you can address the barriers that you have identified?

RESOURCE

National Child Traumatic Stress Network (https://tfcbt2.musc.edu).

A robust set of instructor resources designed to supplement this text is located at http://connect.springerpub.com/content/book/978-0-8261-5285-5. Qualifying instructors may request access by emailing textbook@springerpub.com.

REFERENCES

Amaya-Jackson, L., Absher, L., Gerrity, E., Layne, C., & Halladay Goldman, J. (2021). *Beyond the ACE score: Perspectives from the NCTSN on child trauma and adversity screening and impact*. National Center for Child Traumatic Stress. https://www.nctsn.org/sites/default/files/resources/special-resource/beyond-the-ace-score-perspectives-from-the-nctsn-on-child-tauma-and-adversity-screening-and-impact.pdf

American Psychiatric Association. (2013). *Diagnostic and statistical manual of mental disorders* (5th ed.).

Assigana, E., Chang, E., Cho, S., Kotecha, V., Liu, B., Turner, H., Zhang, Y., Christel, M., & Stevens, S. (2014, October). TF-CBT triangle of life: A game to help with cognitive behavioral therapy. In

Proceedings of the First ACM SIGCHI Annual Symposium on Computer-human Interaction in Play (pp. 9–16). ACM. https://dl.acm.org/doi/10.1145/2658537.2658684

Bartlett, J., & Rushovich, B. (2018). Implementation of trauma systems therapy-foster care in child welfare. *Children and Youth Services Review, 91*, 30–38. https://doi.org/10.1016/j .childyouth.2018.05.021

Betancourt, T. S., Newnham, E. A., Birman, D., Lee, R., Ellis, B. H., & Layne, C. M. (2017). Comparing trauma exposure, mental health needs, and service utilization across clinical samples of refugee, immigrant, and U.S.-origin children. *Journal of Traumatic Stress, 30*, 209–218. https://doi. org/10.1002/jts.22186

Briere, J., & Scott, C. (2015). *Principles of trauma therapy: A guide to symptoms, evaluation, and treatment* (2nd ed.). Sage.

Bronfenbrenner, U. (1979). *The ecology of human development: Experiments by nature and design.* Harvard University Press.

Bronfenbrenner, U., & Morris, P. (2006). The bioecological model of human development. In W. Damon & R. Lerner (Eds.), *Handbook of child psychology: Theoretical model of human development* (pp. 793–828). John Wiley.

Bunting, L., Montgomery, L., Mooney, S., MacDonald, M., Coulter, S., Hayes, D., & Davidson, G. (2019). Trauma informed child welfare systems: A rapid evidence review. *International Journal of Environmental Research and Public Health, 16*, 2365. https://doi.org/10.3390/ijerph16132365

Child Sexual Abuse Task Force and Research & Practice Core, National Child Traumatic Stress Network. (2004). *How to implement trauma-focused cognitive behavioral therapy.* National Center for Child Traumatic Stress. https://www.nctsn.org/sites/default/files/resources//how_to _implement_tfcbt.pdf

Child Trends. (2023, March). *State-level data for understanding child welfare in the United States: Companion guide.* Child Trends. https://cms.childtrends.org/wp-content/uploads/2023/03 /CW-Companion-Guide-2023.pdf

Child Welfare Committee, National Child Traumatic Stress Network. (2013). *Child welfare trauma training toolkit: Comprehensive guide* (3rd ed.). National Center for Child Traumatic Stress.

Cohen, J., Mannarino, A., & Deblinger, E. (2017). *Treating trauma and traumatic grief in children and adolescents* (2nd ed.). The Guilford Press.

Cohen, J., Mannarino, A., Kliethermes, M., & Murray, L. (2012). Trauma-focused CBT for youth with complex trauma. *Child Abuse & Neglect, 36*, 528–541. https://doi.org/10.1016/j .chiabu.2012.03.007

Dorsey, S., Burns, B. J., Southerland, D. G., Cox, J. R., Wagner, H. R., & Farmer, E. M. (2012). Prior trauma exposure for youth in treatment foster care. *Journal of Child and Family Studies, 21*(5), 816–824. https://doi.org/10.1007/s10826-011-9542-4

Dorsey, S., Conover, K., & Revillion Cox, J. (2014). Improving foster parent engagement: Using qualitative methods to guide tailoring of evidence-based engagement strategies. *Journal of Clinical Child & Adolescent Psychology, 43*, 877–889. https://doi.org/10.1080/15374416.2013.876643

Dube, S., Anda., R., Felitti, V., Chapman, D., Williamson, D., & Giles, W. (2001). Childhood abuse, household dysfunction, and the risk of attempted suicide throughout the life span: Findings from the adverse childhood experiences Study. *JAMA, 285*, 3089–3096. https://doi.org/10.1001 /jama.286.24.3089

Dube, S., Felitti, V., Dong, M., Chapman, D., Giles, W., & Anda, R. (2003). Childhood abuse, neglect, and household dysfunction and the risk of illicit drug use: The adverse childhood experiences study. *Pediatrics, 111*, 564–572. https://doi.org/10.1542/peds.111.3.564

Dvir, Y., Ford, J., Hill, M., & Frazier, J. (2014). Childhood maltreatment, emotional dysregulation, and psychiatric comorbidities. *Harvard Review of Psychiatry, 23*, 149–161. https://doi.org/10.1097 /HRP.0000000000000014

Engler, A. D., Sarpong, K. O., Van Horne, B. S., Greeley, C. S., & Keefe, R. J. (2022). A systematic review of mental health disorders of children in foster care. *Trauma, Violence, & Abuse, 23*(1), 255–264. https://doi.org/10.1177/1524838020941197

Felitti, V., Anda., R., Nordenberg, D., Williamson, D., Spitz, A., Edwards, V., Koss, M., & Marks, J. (1998). Relationship of childhood abuse and household dysfunction to many of the leading causes of death in adults: The adverse childhood experiences (ACE) study. *American Journal of Preventive Medicine, 14*, 245–258. https://doi.org/10.1016/S0749-3797(98)00017-8

Finkelhor, D., Ormrod, R., Turner, H., & Hamby, S. (2005). The victimization of children and youth: A comprehensive, national survey. *Child Maltreatment, 10*, 5–25. https://doi.org/10.1177/1077559504271287

Fortuna, L., Porche, M., & Padilla, A. (2018). A treatment development study of a cognitive and mindfulness-based therapy for adolescents with co-occurring post-traumatic stress and substance use disorder. *Psychology and Psychotherapy: Theory, Research, and Practice, 91*, 42–62. https://doi.org/10.1111/papt.12143

Gypen, L., Vanderfaeillie, J., DeMaeyer, S., Belenger, L., & VanHolen, F. (2017). Outcomes of children who grew up in foster care: Systematic review. *Children and Youth Services Review, 76*, 74–83. https://doi.org/10.1016/j.childyouth.2017.02.035

Jimenez, M., Wade, R., Lin, Y., Morrow, L., & Reichman, N. (2016). Adverse experiences in early childhood and kindergarten outcomes. *Pediatrics, 137*, e20151839. https://doi.org/10.1542/peds.2015-1839

Karl, A., Schaefer, M., Malta, L., Dörfel, D., Rohleder, N., & Werner, A. (2006). A meta-analysis of structural brain abnormalities in PTSD. *Neuroscience and Biobehavioral Reviews, 30*(7), 1004–1031. https://doi.org/10.1016/j.neubiorev.2006.03.004

Kisiel, C., Fehrenbach, T., Small, L., & Lyons, J. (2009). Assessment of complex trauma exposure, responses and service needs among children and adolescents in child welfare. *Journal of Child and Adolescent Trauma, 2*, 143–160. https://doi.org/10.1080/19361520903120467

Kuhlman, K., Vargas, I., Geiss, E., & Lopez-Duran, N. (2015). Age of trauma onset and HPA axis dysregulation among trauma-exposed youth. *Journal of Traumatic Stress, 28*, 572–579. https://doi.org/10.1002/jts.22054

Liming, K., Brook, J., & Akin, B. (2021). Cumulative adverse childhood experiences among children in foster care and the association with reunification: A survival analysis. *Child Abuse & Neglect, 113*. https://doi.org/10.1016/j.chiabu.2020.104899

Liming, K., & Grube, W. (2018). Wellbeing outcomes for children exposed to multiple adverse experiences in early childhood: A systematic review. *Child and Adolescent Social Work Journal, 35*, 317–335. https://doi.org/10.1007/s10560-018-0532-x

National Child Traumatic Stress Network. (n.d.). *Effects*. https://www.nctsn.org/what-is-child-trauma/trauma-types/complex-trauma/effects

Philadelphia ACE Project. (2021). *Philadelphia ACE survey*. https://www.philadelphiaaces.org/philadelphia-ace-survey

Purkey, E., Patel, R., & Phillips, S. (2018). Trauma-informed care: Better care for everyone. *Canadian Family Physician, 63*, 170–172.

Saxe, G., Ellis, H., & Brown, A. (2016). *Trauma systems therapy for children and teens* (2nd ed.). Guilford Press.

Simms, M., Dubowitz, H., & Szilagyi, M. (2000). Health care needs of children in the foster care system. *Pediatrics, 106*, 909–918.

Stein, B., Zima, B., Elliott, M., Burnam, M., Shahinfar, A., Fox., N., & Leavitt, L. A. (2001). Violence exposure among school-age children in foster care: Relationship to distress symptoms. *Journal of the American Academy of Child and Adolescent Psychiatry, 40*, 588–594. https://doi.org/10.1097/00004583-200105000-00019

Suárez, L., Saxe, G., Ehrenreich, J., & Barlow, D. (2006). *Trauma systems therapy for adolescent substance abuse*. Center for Anxiety and Related Disorders and Boston University.

Taylor, M. (2022). *What does fight, flight, freeze, fawn mean?* WebMD. https://www.webmd.com/mental-health/what-does-fight-flight-freeze-fawn-mean#:~:text=The%20fight%20response%20is%20your,please%20someone%20to%20avoid%20conflict

Teicher, M. (2002). Scars that won't heal: The neurobiology of child abuse. *Scientific American, 286*, 68–75. https://www.scientificamerican.com/article/scars-that-wont-heal-the/

Turney, K., & Wildeman, C. (2017). Adverse childhood experiences among children placed in and adopted from foster care: Evidence from a nationally representative survey. *Child Abuse & Neglect, 64*, 117–129. https://doi.org/10.1016/j.chiabu.2016.12.009

Weiner, D., Schneider, A., & Lyons, J. (2009). Evidence-based treatments for trauma among culturally diverse foster care youth: Treatment retention and outcomes. *Children and Youth Services Review, 31*, 1199–1205. https://doi.org/10.1016/j.childyouth.2009.08.013

White, C., O'Brien, K., White, J., Pecora, P., & Phillips, C. (2008). Alcohol and drug use among alumni of foster care: Decreasing dependency throughout improvement of foster care experiences. *The Journal of Behavioral Health Services & Research, 35*, 419–434. https://doi.org/10.1007/s11414-007-9075-1

12 Secondary Traumatization and Self-Care for Child Welfare Professionals: Preventing Burnout

VERÓNICA RODRÍGUEZ BAILEY AND DAVID A. SIMPSON

LEARNING OBJECTIVES

By the end of the chapter, you will be able to:

- Apply trauma-informed self-care and trauma-informed care.
- Demonstrate the ability to conduct a wellness self-assessment.
- Understand different types of trauma and the signs and symptoms of trauma.
- Distinguish among burnout, secondary trauma stress (STS), and compassion fatigue (CF).
- Identify characteristics of child welfare work that can contribute to secondary trauma.
- Recognize the signs and symptoms of burnout, STS, and CF.
- Identify strategies for assessing and incorporating self-care.

INTRODUCTION

Child welfare work requires intervening and providing support and resources at a time when families are broken. They are at their worst. Although child welfare is a very rewarding and fulfilling career, it can also take a toll on a child welfare professional's body, mind, and spirit. Child welfare professionals impacted by stress and related conditions may experience a variety of symptoms that may affect all aspects of their daily lives, including negative changes in beliefs about themselves, others, and their work. The protocol on a plane is to always put the mask on first before helping others. That is good advice for airplane travelers, and it is relevant for child welfare professionals, too. In the context of a child welfare professional, putting on the oxygen mask first is to practice prevention and self-care. Intentional efforts to prevent burnout and minimize the negative impact of child welfare work are not only beneficial but necessary. In this chapter, we review the characteristics of child welfare work and explore the toll this type of work can have. We also present strategies to prevent or at least minimize burnout, secondary trauma stress (STS), and compassion fatigue (CF).

Case Scenario: Using Self-Care to Preserve the Professional Self

Valeria, a former child welfare professional, tells her story: I remember being in a case staffing meeting. The environment in the child welfare office at work felt both supportive and not. I worked in several child welfare offices throughout my child welfare work experience. The culture was determined by the leaders (i.e., the office administrator, the area managers, and the supervisors). Early on in my career, I don't remember it being a very nurturing environment where there was time to process lived experiences that created opportunities for self-care, growth, and development. I did learn lots, but it was not intentional. Ultimately, I was so burnt out that I decided to leave child welfare work after 17 years of service. It wasn't an easy decision but the right one for me. And it was not the families and children we served that did it. It was the *culture and nature of the work*. I felt it was a disservice to continue to practice in an environment where I didn't have the capacity to continue. This realization came to me after I lost my mother to cancer. Prior to this was the birth of my first grandchild.

Sitting in that case staffing meeting, hearing the details of an infant being brutally beaten and sustaining injuries for the first time in my child welfare career made me sick to my stomach. It's not that I didn't care about infants/children/teens being abused in the past. Previously, I was able to detach in a healthy way to maintain objectivity when thinking through and recommending case action/steps. The birth of my first grandchild made it harder to detach in a healthy way. The secondary trauma and burnout really impacted me. Not being equipped with healthy coping strategies or being encouraged to practice self-care led me to realize that I needed to leave child welfare altogether in order to give myself the time to grieve and heal. Had I known then what I know now about the importance of self-care and the office environment, my decision to leave child welfare might have gone differently.

DISCUSSION QUESTIONS

1. What can novice child welfare professionals do to maintain self-care and avoid burnout?

Case Scenario: Using Self-Care to Preserve the Professional Self (*continued*)

2. In child welfare practice, why is it important to incorporate strategies of self-care?
3. In particularly brutal cases, what could child welfare supervisors do to support their workers?
4. How did Valeria's private life and work become entangled?
5. What could have helped Valeria's cope better with the stress she experienced from her cases?

BURNOUT, SECONDARY TRAUMA STRESS, AND COMPASSION FATIGUE

If social workers are going to work with families to address child abuse and neglect, they need to understand how this type of social work impacts them. "If we are to do our work with suffering people and environments in a sustainable way, we must understand how our work affects us" (Van Dernoot Lipsky, 2009, p. 41). Child welfare practitioners should honestly assess potential bias that examines their feelings or behaviors in response to trauma (Van Dernoot Lipsky, 2009). Child welfare professionals need to remember their own humanity as well as the humanity of those they serve.

We often hear the term *burnout* to describe being tired of doing what we are doing. However, for professionals who work with people who have suffered traumatic experiences, the burnout they feel is likely also an *STS* response.

Child welfare professionals work with traumatized people all the time, whether it is the victim or the abuser, and their the lived experiences might include past exposure to trauma that still impacts them today. Child welfare work will expose one to trauma, and that is a fact. *Trauma* is an emotional response to an event or set of circumstances that cause physical or emotional harm, or a perceived life threat that has lasting adverse effects on daily functioning and mental, physical, social, emotional, or spiritual well-being. Shock and denial are typical responses right after a traumatic experience. Longer-term implications involve social/emotional functioning, such as experiencing flashbacks, relationship challenges, and physiological symptoms, including headaches or nausea. A traumatic experience for one person may not be a traumatic experience for another. It is a very personal experience depending on an individual's past lived experience and the coping strategies they use to deal with stressful situations.

There are three types of trauma:

- *Acute trauma* results from exposure to a single overwhelming event.
- *Chronic trauma* results from extended exposure to traumatizing situations.
- *Complex trauma* results from a traumatic event that is devastating enough to have long-lasting effects (Courtois, 2004; Wamser-Nanney, 2016; Wamser-Nanney et al., 2021).

In child welfare work, exposure to STS is inevitable (Armes et al., 2020). STS is also referred to as vicarious trauma. STS is when the child welfare professional experiences a range of symptoms after helping others who have been traumatized. Responding empathetically is normal; however, in doing so, the child welfare professional is exposed vicariously to the trauma of those they are serving. How do child welfare professionals protect themselves? How do they care for others while caring for their own needs? In order to answer these questions, one must first understand the difference between *burnout* and *STS*.

Burnout is defined as physical, emotional, or mental *exhaustion*, which decreases employee motivation and performance and leads to *cynicism* (or negative attitudes toward oneself, others, and the workplace; *APA Dictionary of Psychology*, n.d.; Maslach & Leiter, 2022). Many factors contribute to burnout in child welfare work (see Table 2.1).

CF is the combination of exposure to STS and burnout's cumulative effects. CF and burnout have similarities and differences in when and how they manifest. Burnout occurs over time and can cause a previously engaged person to disengage due to job stress and strain. CF can arise suddenly and with little warning. A single exposure to a traumatic incident can contribute to burnout (Conrad & Kellar-Guenther, 2006).

Suppose a child welfare professional has experienced trauma. In that case, it is important to acknowledge the past trauma exposure and assess whether it still impacts overall wellness in the present. Knowing how that *lived experience* shapes the professional's coping strategies is also essential. In responding to past trauma exposure, people may rely on learned coping strategies that helped them survive the traumatic experience, which is a survival response. Some of those coping strategies might still be the person's default coping mechanism in the present, and they may or may not work well. If a child welfare professional carries unresolved historical traumatic experiences in their body and mind, they might be operating in a survival and safety mode. What does this mean? It means that the coping strategies used are more likely to produce a stronger emotional, physiological, and behavioral response to present-day triggers (e.g., sights or sounds), and the person perceives those triggers as reality. In other words, the person thinks they are experiencing the traumatic event again in the present day. This understanding of trauma response is based on the seminal work of Cannon in the early 1900s (Cannon, 1927), which has been further developed by professionals treating stress

TABLE 12.1 TRAUMA AND BURNOUT

	DESCRIPTION	SIGNS AND SYMPTOMS	CONTRIBUTING FACTORS
Burnout (BO)	A state of emotional, physical, and mental exhaustion caused by excessive and prolonged stress	• Low motivation • Low energy • Not enough care • Feeling overwhelmed • Emotionally drained • Unable to meet constant demands • Negative attitudes to self and others	• Unmanageable workload • Role ambiguity • Negative work culture • Lack of support • High stress work tasks • Poor work–life balance
Secondary Trauma Stress (STS) (also known as Vicarious Trauma)	The indirect witnessing of or hearing about harm done to others	• Denial • Anger • Fear • Sadness • Shame • Confusion • Anxiety • Depression • Numbness • Guilt • Hopelessness • Irritability • Difficulty concentrating	Witnessing harm to others, reading about it, or hearing about it
Compassion Fatigue (CF)	The combination of having STS and the cumulative effects of BO, which is considered a state of physical and mental exhaustion caused by a depleted ability to cope with one's everyday environment	• Physical, emotional, or mental exhaustion • Physical symptoms such as headaches, stomachaches, and muscle tension • Detachment from work • Concentration and focus problems • Decreased motivation • Difficulty feeling positive emotions • Negative attitudes toward self and others • Difficulty caring for others • A draining of empathy toward others • Secretive addictions and self-medicating	• Having unreasonable job expectations and an inability to keep up • Being exposed to secondary trauma • Being new to the field • Having a history of personal trauma or burnout • Working long hours and/or having large caseloads • Having inadequate support systems

Source: (https://www.medicalnewstoday.com/articles/trauma)

(Quick & Spielberger, 1994). When our brain perceives a threat, we instantly react with one of four trauma responses: fight, flight, freeze, or fawn/feign. If one is thinking of a career in child welfare, one should acknowledge unresolved past trauma experiences and deal with them in order to learn healthy coping strategies and avoid being retriggered. In this way, one can proactively minimize the negative impact of further trauma-related exposure.

Some child welfare professionals/social workers choose child welfare work because of their own experience with child abuse or neglect and their desire to help others. In fact, Bride and colleagues (2007) collected web-based data surveys sent to 333 case managers and supervisors in Tennessee. Although their study focused on several variables, one of the variables was a personal history of trauma. Their findings suggest that child welfare professionals with personal histories of childhood trauma are at increased risk of STS. "More specifically, a combination of more than one type of childhood trauma presents the greatest risk for vulnerability to STS, with emotional abuse and neglect being the strongest predictors of STS" (Bride et al., 2007, p. 72). The same study found that younger workers may be more at risk, but this may be because they have less work experience and have not yet acquired coping skills.

CHARACTERISTICS OF WORKING IN THE CHILD WELFARE SYSTEM

Like other jobs, child welfare professionals have multiple tasks that are high priority and often time sensitive. The challenging part about child welfare work is that in responding to these types of tasks, failure to pay attention to detail and overlooking something might increase the risk of further child abuse and neglect. Here are some characteristics of stressful situations encountered by child welfare professionals.

Large Caseloads

High caseload size is the primary challenge for agencies to provide efficient and effective services to families. Cases are often assigned based on workload capacity and not often by their severity and level of complexity. Even if a supervisor does their best to assign by complexity, the case that might initially appear to be a lower-risk case may suddenly turn into a very high-risk, complex one. The median caseload size for child welfare professionals is 55 cases per year, and they typically remain on the job for less than 2 years (Child Welfare Information Gateway, 2022).

The consequences of the extremely high child welfare professional turnover rate are far reaching. The impact is spread to their coworkers, their supervisors, and the families being served. The increase in caseloads resulting from this high turnover rate significantly and negatively impacts the quality of service delivery and future child welfare professional retention. Cases need to be reassigned when a child welfare professional (a) resigns, (b) needs to take a leave of absence, or

(c) transfers to another role. Consequently, the cost for families is high because when their cases are reassigned, there is a delay in service delivery because the newly assigned child welfare professional needs to become familiar with the case. It is a smoother transfer when there is time to conduct a case staffing transfer meeting with the newly assigned child welfare professional before the current assigned child welfare professional leaves. Additional consequences of being unable to retain staff are time, money, and quality of service. Agencies need to take time to recruit, interview, and train new staff. Those child welfare professionals who assume responsibility for the additional cases are placed under additional stress. In fact, "turnover has increased in many fields in recent years as a record number of workers in the United States continue to quit their jobs . . . and high turnover continues to be a persistent challenge in the child welfare field" (Child Welfare Information Gateway, 2022, p. 3). Best practice recommends caseload sizes ranging from 12 to 35 children per caseworker, depending on the types of responsibilities assumed; however, one national report found some caseloads as high as 130 (Chen, 2019). That means that child welfare professionals, on average, handle approximately double the recommended caseload size. Of course, other factors contribute to high caseloads. For example, lack of funding contributes to an inability to hire new staff; legislative mandates and policy changes might increase expectations of child welfare professionals; and the complex needs of families make finding support and resources even more challenging. "When families cannot access the services they need, caseworkers often must do more work to fill in gaps, and it may take longer to resolve cases" (Child Welfare Information Gateway, 2022, p. 2).

Timely Response

A child welfare professional, especially a child protective services (CPS) investigator, does not have much control over their time when assigned an emergent case that needs to be responded to within 24 hours. A nonemergent case must be responded to within 72 hours, though these timelines may vary from state to state. The emergent cases are all-consuming and become the child welfare professional's exclusive focus for the next 24 to 48 hours, especially regarding a fatality or near fatality. Cases involving a fatality or near fatality are more intense and create an immense amount of work and stress. In child welfare work, the need to develop critical-thinking, problem-solving, detail-oriented, and task-prioritization skills is essential. So how does one manage all this? By having the ability to multitask? Is there such a thing as *multitasking*?

Brain Science: Can One Multitask?

We know so much more about how our brains work today. A human brain can only focus on one thing at a time. Jha (2020) has focused her research on understanding the science of *attention* at every level. In her research, she shows how there is no such thing as multitasking. Jha (2020) describes attention as a powerful brain function vulnerable to lived experiences like stress and feelings of threat. "Attention is, in some ways, your brain's superpower. But like many superpowers, it has kryptonite: threat, stress, and poor mood will rapidly degrade your capacities" (Jha, 2020, para. 8). Jha compares our attention to a flashlight in a dark room: Where the light shines, that is where our attention is at that moment. Child welfare professionals have many daily tasks that demand their attention. Deciding to place a child in care involves extensive information gathering and critical analysis to determine the best placement option.

In addition, there are a multitude of calls, consultations, and reports that need to be prepared. Meanwhile, the child welfare professional's remaining caseload is waiting for them once the immediate case is complete. The art of case management is not sequential; for instance, during a current urgent out-of-home placement case, the child welfare professional must diligently check in on their remaining caseload for fear of failing to respond in a timely manner to a nonurgent case that can suddenly become urgent. In short, a barrage of tasks comes to the child welfare professional at any time. They need to have the mental capacity to receive information and process it in a way that helps them prioritize those tasks with the mission of the child welfare agency always in mind—safety, well-being, and permanence. This example is not meant to scare potential child welfare professionals away from doing this incredible, meaningful, and vital work. It is merely a clear-eyed view of what the work looks like and why self-care is critical in helping child welfare professionals create physical and mental capacity, thus contributing to them becoming efficient and effective.

Reactive Versus Proactive Response

Because of the nature of child welfare work, the agency tends to operate under a reactive response. However, each child welfare professional must be as proactive as possible to minimize workload despite the challenges. Many child welfare professionals do great work. However, even the best child welfare professionals get caught up in the politics and reactive agency culture when a case does not go well. It takes extensive mental capacity to manage the scrutiny that comes with a case becoming one of those high-profile cases that has come to the media's attention. High-profile cases can be incredibly stressful and discouraging for the child welfare professional, their supervisor, and the whole team and office.

Working Under a Microscope

The public scrutiny of child welfare professionals can be incredibly stressful. Not only is the child welfare professional trying to navigate the judgment of others, but they may also begin questioning themselves about what they could have done differently to prevent the resulting negative impact on the child. Public opinion is quick to judge the child welfare professional's decision without understanding the facts of the case. The public will never fully understand the scope of the work, how complex the work is, the decision making involved, and all the many stakeholders, including law enforcement and investigators, who participated in the decision. In some cases, despite the incredible work a child welfare professional does, they may find themselves scrutinized for a case with unfortunate results. This cautionary tale emphasizes how important it is for child welfare professionals to make decisions in consultation with their supervisors and other stakeholders. The child welfare professional should also utilize their resources to collect and consider all relevant facts and document the decision-making process and the input of all stakeholders. Documentation is critical in one's professional life; it protects the client, the worker, and the agency. Doing this does not necessarily make the scrutiny and questioning of oneself go away. However, it helps highlight all the great work done and shows how and with whom decisions were made. Highlighting successes and how decisions are made takes it from an individual work performance view to a process/system view. Even if the child welfare professional does everything right, there may still be unforeseen circumstances that contribute to negative outcomes. It is important that child welfare professionals recognize this and not blame themselves. When child welfare professionals are fair-minded, social justice–oriented, highly skilled, ethical, dedicated to the field, and possess critical thinking, they operate with a strong professional ethic.

Self-Imposed Expectations

Self-imposed expectations can enhance a child welfare professional's capacity to fulfill their duties and their overall wellness. In addition to the high-stress work of child welfare, child welfare professionals bring their own work ethic and values into the mix. Their values, work ethic, and attitude influence how the child welfare professional shows up every day and how well they cope with the daily pressures. The expectation to work hard and long hours is often reinforced and rewarded by the direct supervisor or the organization of which the child welfare professional is a member. Understandably, the child welfare professional sometimes will add unrealistic self-imposed expectations to keep up with the work or prove their value to others. The reinforced work ethic and unrealistic self-imposed expectations are not sustainable over time. The combination of unrealistic expectations in a high-demand, trauma-exposed job and working unreasonable hours without opportunities to decompress, get supervision, or practice self-care is a recipe for experiencing burnout, STS, or CF.

SUPERVISOR SUPPORT AND ROLE

Brower (2023) notes supervisors' effect on their employees' mental health. Though not explicitly addressing child welfare supervisors, recommendations include

(a) modeling positive management of their own workloads, as supervisees are watching and learning from them; (b) recognizing the tremendous impact they can have, with an emphasis on showing empathy toward those they work with; (c) giving employees choice and autonomy, as that encourages innovation, well-being, and retention; (d) providing challenges, allowing opportunities for growth; (e) giving people a reason to care, helping them understand the importance of their work; and (f) connecting people by being responsive to their needs, connecting coworkers with each other, and making sure employees know how to reach the supervisor.

What is it like being a child welfare supervisor? Can they practice self-care while managing their teams effectively and ensuring high-quality service delivery to child welfare–involved children and families? Child welfare supervisors are accountable for monitoring their team's work and conducting the administrative work the job requires. Supervisors are held to certain standards, such as ensuring their team is fulfilling their duties and meeting performance expectations (e.g., responding to referrals within the designated timelines and conducting monthly child safety checks), assessing training needs, and setting the office work culture. Child welfare supervisors share the responsibility for case decisions, which requires paying close attention to detail. Supervisors need to assess the competency of each team member adequately and lean on that knowledge when discussing cases and making case decisions. For example, if caseworkers have about 15 cases each and there are 5 to 8 caseworkers on the team, that means the supervisor is responsible and accountable for knowing important case information for about 75 to 120 cases. In addition, when there is a child fatality or near fatality, it is the caseworker and the supervisor who are directly impacted, but for the supervisor, it is much harder to practice self-care. The supervisor needs to support their staff, perhaps even giving the child welfare professional time off, meaning they are left with managing the case temporarily while supporting the rest of the case-carrying staff. As a result, some child welfare supervisors work long hours to keep up with the pace of work. They are not immune to experiencing burnout, STS, or CF. They are exposed over and over to traumatic experiences of children. They learn, hear, and read detailed and sometimes tragic experiences of children in case files, court documents, and other records (Dill, 2007). Child welfare supervisors must be intentional about practicing self-care and model this for their workers. It is also imperative for supervisors to advocate for adequate support and staffing resources. Supervisors may provide peer support, consultation, and case coverage for one another.

POWER DYNAMICS IN CHILD WELFARE WORK

Power dynamics in this chapter refers to the relationships among participants in the child welfare system on multiple levels. Power and the awareness of power influence how decisions are made, how trust is built, how workers engage families, and overall case efficacy. Understanding and learning how to manage power dynamics and the power differential in the workplace are helpful. Failure to do so can cause a significant amount of stress. In child welfare work, this can be especially challenging. Supervisors are in a position of power, as are child welfare professionals. Power dynamics play out between the various participants in the process (e.g., child welfare professional and supervisor, child welfare professional and parents, parents and child welfare system).

The power dynamic between the child welfare professional and the family the child welfare professional is working with must be acknowledged and kept at the forefront when working with families involved in the child welfare system. Child welfare involved–families often feel targeted, angry, and powerless when they find themselves at the mercy of the system. This reaction can cause significant stress for the assigned child welfare professional. Bundy-Fazioli and colleagues (2009) highlight the struggle of sharing power and the dynamics between child welfare professionals and parent(s), which is further complicated by the power structures that govern how the child welfare professional does their job. According to their study, a child welfare professional needs to establish rapport and build a trusting, respectful, and nurturing relationship with the parent(s)/families to navigate the negotiation process. "Therefore, it is imperative that workers are cognizant of power dynamics and behaviors that foster rather than impede parent and familial openness and motivation to change" (Bundy-Fazioli et al., 2009, p. 1462).

The art of child welfare work is to care genuinely for the children and families being served, partner with families, and negotiate mutually agreed upon intervention plans that address child safety and create opportunities to promote lasting change to decrease future CPS involvement. A child welfare professional who is cognizant of the power dynamics and is open to sharing power with the families they work with will help decrease stress and enhance job satisfaction.

IMPLICIT BIAS IN CHILD WELFARE WORK

Implicit bias that is not understood and acknowledged can have profound negative implications for underrepresented groups involved in the child welfare system. The American Psychological Association (n.d.) describes implicit bias as "... a negative attitude, of which one is not consciously aware, against a specific social group" (para. 1). Implicit bias has contributed to racial disparities in the child welfare system. The child welfare system is not immune to the same racial bias that permeates other U.S. institutions because of the historic oppression of its Black, Indigenous, and People of Color (BIPOC) citizens. Child welfare professionals are conditioned to apply mainstream dominant group values, customs, and norms and use them to measure how families should be/look/act and make case decisions based on that (Beniwal, 2017). There are clear cases within the child welfare system where significant physical or sexual abuse or significant neglect manifested as abandonment or gross negligence warrants state intervention and removal of children from the home. However, Beniwal (2017) asserts that such cases are few and far between and that most decisions fall into a gray area, where implicit bias may be a factor.

One's life experiences, including personal ideas about parenting, family, and children, cannot help being a factor when making critical assessments and decisions about families encountered in the child welfare field.

When people are overwhelmed, stressed, distracted, or under immense pressure, their ability to process information fully is limited. As a result, they will more likely recall biased facts and information and make more stereotypical judgments (Murphy et al., 2023). Considering the pressure, ambiguity, and stress child welfare professionals face daily, it is not surprising that implicit bias may play a role in judgment and decision making. Therefore, the less stressed the child welfare professional is, the more likely they are to think clearly, conduct unbiased assessments, and convey unbiased facts and information to others. A child welfare professional's ability to think clearly is key and cannot be accomplished if self-care, self-reflection, and supervision are not regularly practiced professional habits.

Office Culture and BIPOC Child Welfare Professionals

Work cultures across child welfare agencies vary depending on the team's makeup. As stated, supervisors set the tone for their teams. Toxic work environments can take a toll on one's overall wellness. In addition, the global pandemic added another layer of stress for all. Furthermore, racial tension adds another layer of stress for Black social workers. In fact, in a study where social workers were assessed for symptoms of depression, anxiety, discrimination-related trauma, and quality of life in response to the pandemic and systemic racism, it was found that a significant increase in depression and anxiety was present among 113 Black social workers surveyed (Reese Foster et al., 2022). Black-identifying social workers are at higher risk of burnout and trauma exposure due to the White supremacy work culture they find themselves in and the racial tensions that exist.

ADVERSE CHILDHOOD EXPERIENCES IMPACT ON CURRENT-DAY COPING

Lee and colleagues (2017) studied adverse childhood experiences (ACEs) and coping strategies to mitigate work stress. The focus was on collecting survey data from 104 child welfare professionals in a midwestern state. The authors found higher stress levels in this group compared to the general population. Child welfare professionals who indicated choosing a career in child welfare due to their own childhood experiences reported even higher stress levels on the job. Furthermore, they found that many were using unhealthy coping strategies to deal with the stress, including alcohol, drugs, and denial. The study revealed that high caseloads, lack of time, inability to leave work at work, and lack of supervisors' support were some of the main stressors. This study was the first ACE study conducted exclusively focused on child welfare professionals, and it pointed out (or reinforced) the need for self-care (see Figure 12.1).

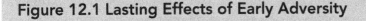

Figure 12.1 Lasting Effects of Early Adversity

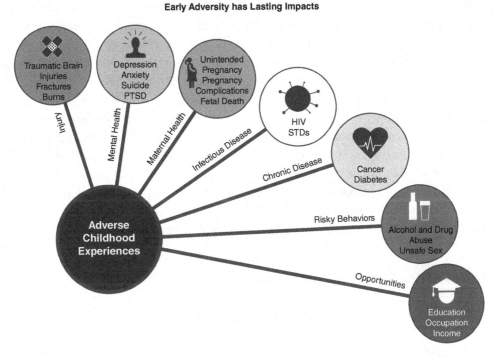

Source: https://www.cdc.gov/violenceprevention/communicationresources/infographics/preventchildhoodadversity
.html

The ACE study focused on child welfare professionals' ACEs and the implications of ACEs in their current personal and professional lives. A lack of awareness of how ACEs might contribute to feeling overwhelmed or stressed could negatively impact overall wellness and service delivery. This type of research has the potential to lead to early identification of risk for stress and, with the development of strategies, can help reduce the impact of ACEs, which ultimately improves overall wellness and services to families.

ORGANIZATIONS AND TRAUMA-INFORMED CARE

The culture and nature of child welfare work make it very challenging for child welfare agencies to implement self-care practices to increase productivity, reduce staff turnover, and promote employee well-being (Kanter & Sherman, 2017; Miller & Grise-Owens, 2020). Organizations should be responsible for addressing trauma regarding service delivery and workforce support and development. Both organizational factors and personal factors impact work performance. Ideally, employees should feel empowered to engage in self-care practices; however, while the organizational culture carries significant weight, the child welfare professional can engage in self-care practices that counteract the potentially damaging effects of unhealthy work environments (Miller et al., 2018). Regarding office culture, it is essential to remember that child welfare professionals have some control over how they cope and build capacity. However, child welfare organizations that do not embrace and engage in trauma-informed care or implement strategies to encourage self-care practices proactively will continue to experience workforce and service delivery challenges.

There are unexpected consequences of doing child welfare work. The nature of the work creates hazards for all engaged in this critical endeavor. It is complex and intense, with safety implications and competing priorities. It is also meaningful, necessary, and rewarding work. Not everyone is cut out for this type of employment. Those who determine this is the path for them should prioritize their overall wellness by learning healthy ways to decompress daily. Given that secondary trauma exposure is inevitable, the most critical self-preservation strategy a child welfare professional can employ is prioritizing self-care. Knowing this, acknowledging it, planning for it, and taking daily action to address it are key to preventing burnout and minimizing secondary trauma in child welfare work.

THE IMPORTANCE OF SELF-CARE

Self-care and wellness are receiving increasing attention. Self-care has gained momentum in the last few years, propelled by the global pandemic. In child welfare work, instances of child abuse and neglect do not stop when the world shuts down. Child welfare professionals keep working regardless of what is happening in the world; they are essential workers. As members of a helping profession, the tendency may be to be strong and tough it out even when one is not doing okay. For some, asking for help is not easy to do. Why is that? There are many reasons: maybe they were never taught to ask for help, or it is a value they learned, like pull yourself up by your bootstraps. Alternatively, they may have been let down in the past when they asked for help, and it is something they vowed not to do again as a way to protect themselves from further rejection, harm, or disappointment. Working in child welfare requires asking for help when needed.

Reflection Box 12.1: Self-Care

1. What is your definition of self-care?
2. How do you practice self-care?
3. What activities do others do for self-care?
4. How does the lack of self-care impact the quality of work?
5. Discuss with your classmates a plan of action for self-care.

No individual has perfect mental and physical health. Ongoing problems or challenges can take a toll on anyone's well-being. Taking time to be proactive with physical and mental well-being is worth the time and is necessary. Keeping the body healthy may be easier. Keeping the mind healthy is a bit more challenging due to the stigma related to mental health. It is important to understand that the same attention and care should be given to caring for the mind regardless of whether or not a mental illness exists. Mental health matters. Mental health includes:

- How one feels about oneself and the world around them.
- An ability to solve problems and overcome challenges.
- An ability to build relationships with others and contribute to the communities around them.
- An ability to achieve personal and professional goals.

Reflection Box 12.2: Self-Care Quick Check-in

What can be done now to begin focusing on overall self-care? You can:

- Become more self-aware of how you are doing in terms of your overall wellness (physical, mental, spiritual, cultural).
- Assess the level of your physical, mental, and spiritual health status.
- Seek help/support if you are feeling overwhelmed and are not doing well.

Self-care is much easier when one is aware of it, has the capacity to practice it, and is supported in doing so by others in both personal and professional contexts. Self-care, simply put, is being in good physical and mental health with the capacity to experience joy in one's life. However, how does one do that when one is a child welfare professional working in a high-stress work environment and when one regularly sees or hears the details of infants/children/teens being abused? The default for many is to not think about it, to suppress it, and maybe even to mask what they feel because they do not want others to know or see that they cannot handle it. Feelings are often not shared, much less acknowledged or processed. Child welfare professionals who demonstrate skill and efficiency are rewarded and given more cases because they can handle them. As stated, exposure to trauma directly or indirectly is inevitable in child welfare; therefore, acknowledging this and learning ways to develop and incorporate healthy coping strategies proactively is critical.

Self-Care: Essential for Child Welfare Professionals

Being proactive with self-care is vital to being effective and clear-minded on the job. Ideally, a self-care plan should be developed before starting a high-stress job, especially a child welfare job. However, at the very least, a self-care plan should be developed when child welfare professionals experience significant stress that is having a negative impact on their ability to do their job effectively or when they are not able to detach from the work in a healthy way in order to enjoy personal and family life, and when one or more of the following circumstances are contributing to the stress:

- High caseloads.
- Unsupportive supervisor/colleagues.
- Lack of clarity related to case direction.
- Lack of resources to offer families.
- Inadequate training.
- Expectation to work an excessive number of hours.
- Self-imposed expectations.

A good way to start is by evaluating current life stressors. There are competing priorities in both professional and personal lives. High ACEs, especially unresolved past traumatic experiences and failure to take self-care seriously, put one at higher risk for developing unhealthy coping strategies that might lead to stress, serious mental health challenges, or substance abuse. Self-care is a way of taking care of physical, emotional, mental, and spiritual health. Self-care, done right, helps with overall performance so that one can think clearly, focus, prioritize tasks, problem-solve, and do this very important, meaningful, and essential work for a long time. There are many ways that child welfare professionals can practice self-care. A self-care strategy that works for one person may not work for another. Table 12.2 lists some of the more common ones.

TABLE 12.2 SELF-CARE STRATEGIES

- **Getting enough sleep.** Sleep is essential for physical and mental health. When child welfare professionals are well rested, they are better able to cope with stress and make sound decisions.
- **Staying hydrated and eating healthy foods.** Eating healthy foods gives child welfare professionals the energy they need to get through the day and helps to improve their mood.
- **Exercising regularly.** Exercise is a great way to relieve stress and improve mood. It can also help to improve sleep quality and boost energy levels.
- **Taking breaks.** Child welfare professionals should take breaks throughout the day to relax and recharge. This could mean taking a walk, reading a book, or spending time with loved ones.
- **Seeking professional help.** If child welfare professionals are struggling with stress, burnout, or CF that is negatively impacting their daily functioning and mood, they should seek professional help. A therapist can provide support and guidance and help them develop coping skills.

Self-care is not selfish. Child welfare professionals must take care of themselves to continue doing this important work. When child welfare professionals are healthy and well-rested, they can better help the children and families they serve. Here are additional self care strategies.

Reflection Box 12.3: Additional Self-Care Strategies

For each of the strategies listed in the following, identify what you currently do. Are there any areas where you could develop stronger self-care strategies?

- Set boundaries and limits.
- Prioritize work; start the day by making a list of priorities to stay on track. Leave tasks that can wait for tomorrow for tomorrow. Checking tasks off the list and visually seeing this can produce a sense of accomplishment, which promotes a positive attitude.
- Develop strong organization and time-management skills.
- Take extra breaks when feeling overwhelmed.
- Say no to extra work.
- Find a support system.
- Talk to someone about your feelings. Do not suffer in silence!
- Seek professional help if you need it.

It is important to remember that burnout, secondary trauma exposure, and CF are real and serious conditions. A child welfare professional who is experiencing any of the symptoms should seek help. There are many resources available to help one cope with these conditions.

Trauma Prevention Strategies: Trauma-Informed Self-Care

Salloum and colleagues (2015) explored the relationship between trauma-informed self-care (TISC) and burnout, CF, and compassion satisfaction. They defined TISC as "being aware of one's own emotional experience in response to exposure to traumatized clients and planning/engaging in positive coping strategies, such as seeking supervision, attending trainings on secondary trauma, working within a team, balancing caseloads, and work–life balance" (p. 54). They found that higher levels of TISC were associated with lower levels of burnout and higher levels of compassion satisfaction, defined as pleasure in helping others, but not secondary trauma. Based on this study, TISC may help reduce the risk of burnout and preserve workers' positive experience of their job. Workers experiencing high levels of secondary trauma may need assistance to move toward recovery (Salloum et al., 2015).

For child welfare professionals who have lived experiences that include trauma exposure, raising awareness and assessing personal risk factors can help them begin to do some self-reflection about how those past lived experiences of trauma exposure impact them in the present day and influence the default coping strategies they are currently using. Past lived experiences, especially ones that include trauma exposure, resulted in developing coping strategies that served them well then. However, some of those learned coping strategies may not serve them well in the present. Reflection box 12.4 identifies some questions that might help them check whether past trauma exposure has an impact in the present day and gives strategies to enhance self-care.

Reflection Box 12.4: Emotional Check-in and Self-Care Strategies

SKILL DEVELOPMENT: AM I OKAY? QUICK EMOTIONAL CHECK-IN

- Are you having emotional experiences in response to exposure to traumatized clients that you are working with?
- Do you feel overwhelmed due to the amount of work you have to do each day?
- What are your default coping strategies? Do they help or hinder your ability to be effective at your job?

If one's responses to any of these questions are concerning, here are strategies to address this as soon as possible.

STRATEGIES TO HELP WITH COPING WITH STRESS

- Increase your knowledge and awareness of the signs and symptoms of burnout.
- Assess your current level of burnout, secondary trauma stress, and CF.
- Stay connected to other people. As human beings, we are wired to connect with others.
- Participate in training that helps you understand your self-care needs.
- Identify others that can empathize with your experience for support.
- Take care of your body (e.g., eating well, exercising, getting enough sleep).
- Create something; engaging in creative/expressive activities helps with processing trauma.

Reflection Box 12.4: Emotional Check-in and Self-Care Strategies (continued)

- Connect with nature (e.g., go on walks/sit outside/open a window and breathe in the fresh air).
- Do soothing things (breathwork, meditation, yoga, etc.)
- Experience your feelings. Be present in the moment so you can process and release feelings rather than suppressing/masking them.
- Identify and utilize specific self-care strategies in the form of a self-help support plan.
- Seek professional help if you are experiencing symptoms that negatively impact your daily functioning.

The following techniques are effective if one is busy and needs to incorporate some quick self-care strategies into their daily life:

I'M BUSY AND DON'T HAVE TIME: QUICK TRICKS TO ADDRESS SELF-CARE

- Move your body! Take a few minutes every day at your desk or in the break room to do a few exercises or stretches.
- Count down 5–4–3–2–1 . . . while using your senses to notice what's happening around you. This helps you to feel present in the moment.
- Practice breathwork techniques. Take deep, big, belly breaths. In hale through the nose as you feel your tummy expand, then slowly exhale through your mouth. Do this 3 to 5 times. Repeat as often as you need throughout the day.
- Notice how your body is feeling. Pay attention. Sit with the feeling and acknowledge it.

WHEN SHOULD ONE SEEK PROFESSIONAL HELP?

Seek Professional Help for Trauma When ...

- You are finding it hard to restore balance, and it affects social and work relationships.
- You feel overwhelmed and are easily triggered, finding it difficult to regulate your emotions; you cry and/or get angry and/or shut down.
- Fear, anxiety, or depression are present that are impacting daily functioning.

(continued)

Reflection Box 12.4: Emotional Check-in and Self-Care Strategies (Continued)

- You are unable to form close and satisfying relationships.
- Terrifying memories, nightmares, or flashbacks persist long after the traumatic event.
- You find yourself avoiding places that are a reminder of past traumatic experiences, and it is getting increasingly worse.
- You are increasingly using unhealthy coping strategies such as alcohol, drugs, and other addictive behaviors.

HELPING AND SUPPORTING OTHERS

There are several things one can do to help if concerned about a friend or colleague who may be experiencing burnout, secondary trauma exposure, or CF.

I'm Worried About My Colleague: What Do I Do?

- Talk to them about your concerns.
- Offer to be a support system.
- Help them to take breaks from work.
- Help them to find ways to relax and de-stress.
- Share supports and resources that might help them.
- Encourage them to seek professional help if warranted (see the preceding tips for when to consider for seeking professional help).

IS CHILD WELFARE THE RIGHT JOB?

When considering child welfare work, one might not intentionally ask themselves if it is indeed the right job for them. It is not often that one stops to evaluate their capacity to perform child welfare work while maintaining their own wellness. Other priorities might be present, such as paying back student loans and the need to find a job *now*! Finding the *why* is vitally important because it is the *why* that will help the child welfare professional during those times when the job becomes hard and overwhelming. It will also help to keep the following in mind when considering child welfare work.

Reflection Box 12.5: Is Child Welfare Work Right For Me?

- Reevaluate your ability to do child welfare work:
  - Why this type of work? Understand what motivation is driving this interest.
    - A sense of vocation, purpose, and duty?
    - A strong desire to protect children?
    - Will child welfare work be rewarding?
    - Will I enjoy child welfare work?
    - Will the job interfere with my personal life?
    - Will I use this experience to work on my own unresolved issues, or will I remain client-focused?

What to Look for in a Child Welfare-Related Job Offer

We are often excited to get that call for a job interview. When it is time for the interview, the interviewer may ask all the questions to determine if one has the skills and abilities to do child welfare work. Interviewing, however, is a two-way street. It is essential to ask questions that help assess what it might be like to work for that particular agency/organization. Here are some questions the interviewee can ask at a child welfare related interview.

Reflection Box 12.6: Job Interview Questions to Help Assess Fit and Work Culture

- What is the team culture like?
- In what ways does the agency support diversity among staff and in services to clients?
- Is the team culture/environment engaging and collaborative?
- Is the team culture supportive and flexible?
- Is there access to ongoing training and support to practice some of the skills learned?
- What are the average caseloads and turnover rate for the team?
- Does the hiring supervisor practice trauma-informed care?
- Is there ongoing support for consistent self-care?

If child welfare is the right career choice, attention to self-care and wellness is necessary to proactively address stress and trauma exposure on the job. To protect oneself, developing a self-care plan before starting a career in child welfare is important and a way to be proactive about addressing burnout, STS, and CF.

WORKPLACE WELLNESS

The COVID pandemic changed how many of us view the nature of our work and its impact on our overall wellness. Unfortunately, it took a pandemic to expedite a movement toward prioritizing wellness. As a result, the U.S. Surgeon General responded in 2022 by issuing a Framework for Workplace Mental Health and Well-Being (U. S. Department of Health & Human Services, 2022). The framework includes five essentials and their components for reimagining workplaces. Organizations that are able to create a plan to implement the practices presented in Figure 12.2 can promote and strengthen the essentials of workplace well-being. It is helpful to examine each dimension of workplace well-being to understand what the organization can do to support its employees.

Figure 12.2 The Surgeon General's Framework for Workplace Mental Health and Well-Being

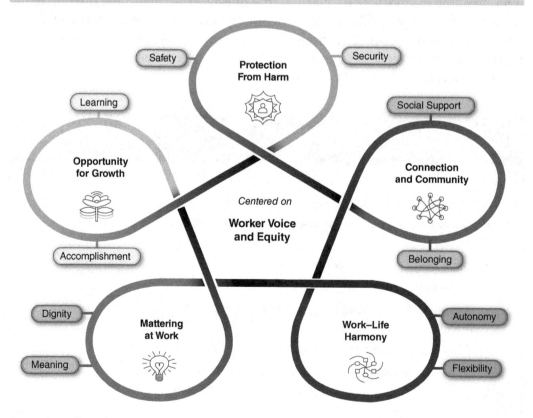

Source: https://www.hhs.gov/surgeongeneral/priorities/workplace-well-being/index.html

Organizational Trauma-Informed Care

Some organizations have embraced a culture that practices trauma-informed care. Agencies that are more reactive versus proactive have a more challenging time retaining their workforce. Although child welfare professionals are responsible for assessing and managing their own wellness, it is much more difficult to practice self-care when the organization one works for does not. Child welfare organizations can implement trauma-informed care. Leadership can take trauma-informed care seriously and develop initiatives to discover whether burnout, STS, or CF is present. Leaders within these organizations can be supportive and locate resources for their workers, thus avoiding a punitive approach.

A trauma-informed approach is not something to be done only once. It requires ongoing work with frequent assessment and quality improvement adjustments. The Substance Abuse and Mental Health Services Administration (SAMHSA, 2014) developed a framework that includes 10 implementation domains with accompanying questions that organizations can consider when implementing a trauma-informed approach. Under one of the domains, *Training and Workforce Development*, the agency can consider: (a) how the agency addresses emotional stress for people who have experienced trauma; (b) the ways the agency can support workforce training and development so staff can better understand trauma and interventions; (c) the support provided for training and workforce development for all staff, including clerical and maintenance employees; (d) processes to ensure that workforce development and staff training examine the ways in which culture, community, identity, oppression, and access to safe spaces affect experiences of trauma; (e) the ways that ongoing training helps staff to develop the foundation and the skills to work effectively with trauma survivors; (f) the types of training and resources for all staff so they can incorporate trauma-informed practice and supervision; and (g) the ways the agency can recognize and facilitate peer support.

> A trauma-informed approach seeks to resist retraumatization of clients as well as staff. Organizations often inadvertently create stressful or toxic environments that interfere with the recovery of clients, the well-being of staff, and the fulfillment of the organizational mission. Staff who work within a trauma-informed environment are taught to recognize how organizational practices may trigger painful memories and retraumatize clients with trauma histories. (SAMHSA, 2014, p. 10)

Shim (2010) explored how organizational culture and climate affect turnover rates in public child welfare. The study showed that child welfare agencies can decrease workforce turnover by creating a positive organizational culture and climate. Many strategies positively impact organizational culture, such as performance-based incentives/rewards, employee recognition, focusing on the overall goal of the organization (the greater good), decreasing worker exhaustion, promoting transparent organizational communication, and providing multiple forms of support and continued professional development (Shim, 2010). An organization implementing initiatives to reduce emotional exhaustion and enhance emotional wellness allows workers to develop coping skills critical to their work. The hope is to promote workforce retention and competence throughout the child welfare system (Shim, 2010). This approach is a win for everyone—the workers and the clients they serve.

Eight Dimensions of Health

SAMHSA adopted the eight dimensions of wellness as a holistic approach to addressing behavioral health to promote overall wellness. SAMHSA's eight dimensions of the health wellness wheel help one assess everything in their life that can positively or negatively impact overall wellness (see Figure 12.3).

Assessing overall wellness using SAMHSA's wellness wheel is easy to do. One should consider how one functions in each dimension. Effective functioning in the emotional dimension includes identifying and expressing feelings, adjusting to life's challenges, and enjoying life. When individuals have balance, they function well in all other dimensions. Balanced individuals can accept help when they need it, value routine and habits, and meet life's demands. SAMHSA's (2016) publication, *Creating a healthier life: A step-by-step wellness guide*, provides more information.

Figure 12.3 SAMHSA: Eight Dimensions of Wellness

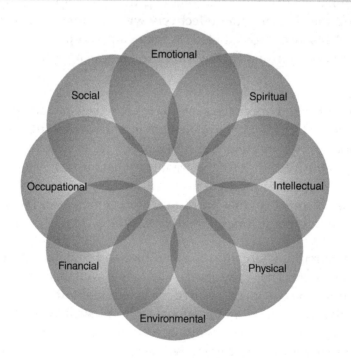

CHAPTER SUMMARY

Child welfare professionals are exposed to traumatic events in their daily work. They see and hear about children and youth who are neglected or abused. This harsh reality places them at risk for secondary trauma and accompanying stress. If not addressed, this can lead to burnout, CF, decreased employment satisfaction, and eventually leaving the field. Additionally, high levels of stress can increase the likelihood of implicit bias entering into critical decisions about the well-being of children and families. Self-care is essential in helping to mitigate this STS. Self-care can take many forms, as it is highly individualized. Supervisors can help staff recognize the signs and symptoms of STS. Supervisors can model appropriate self-care and encourage their staff to engage in proactive self-care strategies and support each other. The organization itself can incorporate trauma-informed practices and find meaningful ways to support staff. Child welfare professionals must become aware of their stress levels and overall wellness. Understanding one's stress levels and how to address them are critical for the well-being of child welfare professionals, their longevity in the field, and the quality of services provided to children and families.

DISCUSSION QUESTIONS

1. After reading this chapter, what are some of the questions that arise for you?

2. How effective do you think your self-care strategies have been in the past?

3. How will you recognize if secondary or vicarious trauma is affecting you (personally/professionally)?

4. How will you address secondary or vicarious trauma should this happen to you (personally/professionally)?

5. If you have past trauma experiences and want to do child welfare work, when will you know when you are ready to enter child welfare?

RESOURCES

Substance Abuse and Mental Health Services Administration (SAMHSA) National Helpline at **1-800-662-4357** for information on support and treatment facilities in your area. This resource is for those who are struggling with a trauma-related condition that is making it hard to get control of their life.

Substance Abuse and Mental Health Services Administration. (2016). *Creating a healthier life: A step-by-step guide to wellness.* https://store.samhsa.gov/sites/default/files/d7/priv/sma16-4958.pdf

Very Well Mind: How Social Support Contributes to Psychological Health. https://www.verywellmind.com/social-support-for-psychological-health-4119970

CAGE: https://pedagogyeducation.com/Resources/Correctional-Nursing/CAGE-AID-Substance-Abuse-Screening-Tool

Professional Quality of Life Scale (PROQO). PROQOL is a short instrument that has three subscales. It measures compassion satisfaction, burnout, and secondary traumatic stress (STS). https://img1.wsimg.com/blobby/go/dfc1e1a0-a1db-4456-9391-18746725179b/downloads/ProQOL_5_English_Self-Score.pdf?ver=1682438385713

Other trauma-informed assessment tools:

Brief Trauma Questionnaire (BTQ)

Combat Exposure Scale (CES)

COVID-19 Exposure Scale

Life Event Checklist for *DSM-5* (LEC-5)

Life Stressor Checklist-Revised (LSC-R)

Potential Stressful Events Interview (PSEI)

Stress Life Events Screening Questionnaire (SLESQ)

 SPRINGER PUBLISHING CONNECT™ | A robust set of instructor resources designed to supplement this text is located at **http://connect.springerpub.com/content/book/978-0-8261-5285-5.** Qualifying instructors may request access by emailing **textbook@springerpub.com.**

REFERENCES

American Psychological Association. (n.d.). *Implicit bias.* https://www.apa.org/topics/implicit-bias

APA Dictionary of Psychology. (n.d.). *Burnout.* https://dictionary.apa.org/burnout

Armes, S. E., Lee, J. J., Bride, B. E., & Seponski, D. M. (2020). Secondary trauma and impairment in clinical social workers. *Child Abuse & Neglect, 110*(3), 1–8. https://doi.org/10.1016/j.chiabu.2020.104540

Beniwal, R. (2017). Implicit bias in child welfare: Overcoming intent. *Connecticut Law Review, 49*(3), 1021–1067. https://opencommons.uconn.edu/law_review/365

Bride, B. E., Jones, J. L., & MacMaster, S. A. (2007). Correlates of secondary traumatic stress in child protective services workers. *Journal of Evidence-Based Social Work, 4*(3/4), 69–80. https://doi.org/10.1300/J394v04n03_05

Brower, T. (2023, January 29). Managers have major impact on mental health: How to lead for well-being. *Forbes.* https://www.forbes.com/sites/tracybrower/2023/01/29/managers-have-major-impact-on-mental-health-how-to-lead-for-wellbeing/?sh=2e1af06d2ec1

Bundy-Fazioli, K., Briar-Lawson, K., & Hardiman, E. R. (2009). A qualitative examination of power between child welfare workers and parents. *The British Journal of Social Work, 39*(8), 1447–1464. https://doi.org/10.1093/bjsw/bcn038

Cannon, W. B. (1927). The James-Lange theory of emotions: A critical examination and an alternative theory. *The American Journal of Psychology, 39*(1/4), 106–124. https://doi.org/10.2307/1415404

Chen, J. (2019). *Research summary: Caseload standards & weighting methodologies.* Academy for Professional Excellence. San Diego State University School of Social Work. https://theacademy.sdsu.edu/wp-content/uploads/2021/10/CWDS-Research-Summary_Caseload-Standards-and-Weighting.pdf

Child Welfare Information Gateway. (2022). *Caseload and workload management.* U.S. Department of Health and Human Services, Administration for Children and Families, Children's Bureau. https://www.childwelfare.gov/pubs/case-work-management/

Conrad, D., & Kellar-Guenther, Y. (2006). Compassion fatigue, burnout, and compassion satisfaction among Colorado child protection workers. *Child Abuse and Neglect, 30*(10), 1071–1080. https://doi.org/10.1016/j.chiabu.2006.03.009

Courtois, C. A. (2004). Complex trauma, complex reactions: Assessment and treatment. *Psychotherapy: Theory, Research, Practice, Training, 41*(4), 412–425. https://psycnet.apa.org/doi/10.1037/0033-3204.41.4.412

Dill, K. (2007). Impact of stressors on front-line child welfare supervisors. *The Clinical Supervisor, 26*(1/2), 177–193. https://doi.org/10.1300/J001v26n01_12

Jha, A. (2020). *The brain science of attention and overwhelm.* https://www.mindful.org/youre-overwhelmed-and-its-not-your-fault/

Kanter, B., & Sherman, A. (2017). *The happy, healthy nonprofit—Strategies for impact without burnout.* Wiley.

Lee, K., Pang, Y. C., Lee, J. L., & Melby, J. N. (2017) A study of adverse childhood experiences, coping strategies, work stress, and self-care in the child welfare profession. *Human Service Organizations: Management, Leadership & Governance, 41*(4), 389–402. https://doi.org/10.1080/23303131.2017.1302898

Maslach, C., & Leiter, M. P. (2022). *The burnout challenge: Managing people's relationships with their jobs.* Harvard University Press.

Miller, J., Donohue-Dioh, J., Niu, C., & Shalash, N. (2018). Exploring the self-care practices of child welfare workers: A research brief. *Children and Youth Services Review, 84*, 137–142. https://doi.org/10.1016/j.childyouth.2017.11.024

Miller, J., & Grise-Owens, E. (2020). Self-care: An imperative. *Social Work, 65*(1), 5–9. https://doi.org/10.1093/sw/swz049

Murphy, J., Farrell, K., Kealy, M. B., & Kristiniak, S. (2023). Mindfulness as a self-care strategy for healthcare professionals to reduce stress and implicit bias. *Journal of Interprofessional Education & Practice, 30*(10071), 100598. https://doi.org/10.1016/j.xjep.2022.100598

Quick, J. C., & Spielberger, C. D. (1994). Walter Bradford Cannon: Pioneer of stress research. *International Journal of Stress Management, 1*(2), 141–143. https://doi.org/10.1007/BF01857607

Reese Foster, C., Held, M., & Carter, A. (2022). Assessing the impact of COVID-19 and race-based trauma on the mental health of Black social work providers. *Journal of Ethnic & Cultural Diversity in Social Work, 33*(1), 1-16. https://doi.org/10.1080/15313204.2022.2155285

Salloum, A., Kondrat, D. C., Johnco, C., & Olson, K. R. (2015). The role of self-care on compassion satisfaction, burnout and secondary trauma among child welfare workers. *Children and Youth Services Review, 49*, 54–61. https://doi.org/10.1016/j.childyouth.2014.12.023

Shim, M. (2010). Factors influencing child welfare employee's turnover: Focusing on organizational culture and climate. *Children and Youth Services Review, 32*(6), 847–856. https://doi.org/10.1016/j.childyouth.2010.02.004

Substance Abuse and Mental Health Services Administration. (2014). *SAMHSA's concept of trauma and guidance for a trauma informed approach.* https://store.samhsa.gov/sites/default/files/d7/priv/sma14-4884.pdf

Substance Abuse and Mental Health Services Administration (2016). Creating a healthier life: A step-by-step guide to wellness. https://store.samhsa.gov/sites/default/files/d7/priv/sma16-4958.pdf

U.S. Department of Health and Human Services. (2022). *The surgeon general's framework for workplace mental health & well-being.* https://www.hhs.gov/surgeongeneral/priorities/workplace-well-being/index.html

Van Dernoot Lipsky, L. (2009). *Trauma stewardship, an everyday guide to caring for self while caring for others.* Berrett-Koehler Publishers.

Wamser-Nanney, R. (2016). Examining the complex trauma definition using children's self-reports. *Journal of Child & Adolescent Trauma, 9*, 295–304. https://doi.org/10.1007/s40653-016-0098-8

Wamser-Nanney, R., Cherry, K. E., Campbell, C., & Trombetta, E. (2021). Racial differences in children's trauma symptoms following complex trauma exposure. *Journal of Interpersonal Violence, 36*(5–6), 2498–2520. https://doi.org/10.1177/0886260518760019

IV

Visions for Transformation of the Child Welfare System: Putting Children and Families First

13

Looking Forward: Putting Children and Families First

LEARNING OBJECTIVES

By the end of the chapter, you will be able to:

- Apply a social justice lens to child welfare practice.
- Identify systemic issues that contribute to inequities in the child welfare system and ways to address them.
- Apply an understanding of antiracist and anti-oppressive practices, specifically as they relate to child welfare.
- Apply an understanding of diversity, equity, and inclusion in child welfare practice.
- Describe ways to reform the child welfare system to support children, youth, and families better.

INTRODUCTION

In the United States, the formal child welfare system emerged in response to the recognition that children's/youth's needs were not always adequately met in their home and family environment. Specifically, some children were abused, and some were not receiving the care and nurturing needed to thrive or were placed in situations where they were at risk of harm. Throughout history, informal arrangements have been made to care for children over the short or long term, including living with grandparents, other family members, close friends, or fictive kin. Over time, more formal interventions developed, first at local and state levels, some public and some private. The first attempts at the federal level include the White House Conferences on Children, the establishment of the Children's Bureau, the Social Security Act, and finally, the Child Abuse Prevention and Treatment Act. While child welfare programs and services have continued to develop, there is increasing recognition of the many inequities within the system, including the disproportionate overrepresentation of children of color, predominantly Black and Native American children. While there have been attempts to address disproportionality, others have called for the complete dismantling of the child welfare system, referred to by some as *family policing*. This critique recognizes how low-income families and families of color experience more surveillance and scrutiny than White families representing the dominant mainstream. At the same time, some children and youth from all racial and ethnic backgrounds are seriously abused or neglected, requiring a response from society.

The challenges facing the child welfare system are many. Undeniably, some children and youth need protection. Some families need additional support to meet the needs of their children. There are dedicated child welfare professionals with large caseloads and little support from the public, leading to high staff turnover. However, children of color experience disparate treatment at every stage of the process, from report to investigation to removal to termination of parental rights. Children and youth in foster care experience trauma that can last a lifetime and become a generational pattern. How can we support families and work at keeping families together while protecting children? How can we create a system where trauma is recognized, and children are only removed when absolutely necessary for their protection and safety? How can we protect children and youth who may be at risk of abuse or neglect? How can we ensure that all children are treated equitably, and that the child welfare system is not used to surveil and police families of color or low-income families? How can we provide social services in an integrated model so families get what they need to protect and nurture their children? This chapter explores these questions and envisions how the child welfare system can incorporate antiracist practices and be a model for diversity, equity, and inclusion in support of its mission of ensuring safety for all children. The chapter further identifies ways to strengthen and enhance services to support families and to ensure child well-being while addressing the inequities inherent in the current system.

Case Scenario: A Worker's Perspective

Emily was a new child welfare social worker. She recently completed her master's of social work and works in her state's public child welfare system. While a student, she completed a practicum at a private agency that contracted with the state agency to provide foster care. Emily clearly remembers one family served by the agency. There were two children, Becca, age 4, and Raymond, age 2. The children were removed from their home following a report from their pediatrician, who was concerned that they were

Case Scenario: A Worker's Perspective (*continued*)

not receiving adequate supervision, had unexplained bruises, and may be exposed to unsafe situations. There also were some reports from neighbors about the children being ignored or neglected and the mother seeming sometimes incapacitated due to alcohol or drugs. The mother, Elena, is 22, and the father, Micah, is 24. The parents' relationship is on and off again, and Micah is currently out of the home and has only infrequent, limited contact with Elena and Raymond.

The court ordered the children to be placed in foster care and the mother to attend substance use treatment and parenting classes. The children have been in foster care with James and Izzy for approximately 7 months. After 4 months, supervised visits began. Emily visited the children in their foster home. She also began supervising the visits between Elena and her children, first in an office setting, then in Elena's home. Emily remembers talking with the foster mother, Izzy, about how she seemed a steadying force for the children and provided them with needed care and structure.

Moreover, Emily wondered if the children would be better off remaining with the foster family, as Elena seemed less sure of herself, though she had been following the court's expectations. Izzy immediately replied, "I'm just the foster mother. I'm not perfect, either. It's not about people being perfect parents. If someone watched me all the time, they would see me make plenty of mistakes in parenting. It's about loving the children and making sure they know that they are loved and cared for. I am here to provide the kids with a temporary home and support and encourage Elena. The kids need that relationship with her, and she needs it with them. I don't want to undermine that relationship. I want to do all I can to care for the kids while they are here and support a move back home when deemed safe and appropriate."

Her words stuck with Emily—it is not about being a perfect parent; no one is perfect. But it is about trying to meet children's needs for safety and nurturing. This way of thinking has framed how Emily views the families she works with in her new position in child welfare. She recognizes that no parents are perfect, but they all possess strengths, and she can support them and their children on their path to reunification.

DISCUSSION QUESTIONS

1. How might the shift in Emily's thinking enhance her ability to identify strengths in all families?

2. There may be a tendency to apply one's own past experiences with parenting and being parented, judging other families by one's ethnocentric perspective. How might this disadvantage families that are different from the worker's in the child welfare system?

(continued)

Case Scenario: A Worker's Perspective (continued)

3. Ideally, foster parents work in tandem with biological parents, supporting the reunification of families. The foster parent in this scenario certainly had that mindset. However, families in the child welfare system often feel estranged from their children and feel like outsiders in the process. How can child welfare professionals encourage foster parents to collaborate more with biological parents?

4. What are some barriers to foster parents and biological parents working together for the well-being of the child(ren)?

5. The foster parent in this scenario made a point of stating that no one is a perfect parent and that if her own parenting were put under a microscope, many shortcomings would be identified. In what ways does this comment make you think differently about how families in the system may feel with their parenting under constant scrutiny?

BIAS AND THE CHILD WELFARE SYSTEM

We have seen how biases have affected the interventions for children and their families involved with the child welfare system and how trauma has been inflicted by the same services that should support and protect them. The decision to intervene in a family's life and the even more invasive step to separate children and youth from their caregivers should not be taken lightly. Since these weighty decisions are made by individuals, biases, even unconscious ones, can affect these decisions and other determinations made throughout the child welfare process, such as whether to remove a child from their home, what to require of parents for reunification, when to reunify, timing and frequency of visits, and other critical decisions. Biases can be explicit or implicit. They may occur at the system level as well as the individual level. As child welfare professionals, it is essential to consider and address personal and institutional biases and advocate for change.

Individual Biases

At the individual level, child welfare professionals and social workers in the child welfare field need to address personal biases. This requires the professional habit of self-reflection and introspection and the willingness to confront brutal truths about oneself, one's life experiences, the messages one has received over the lifetime about different populations, expectations of parenting, or understandings of the family. All of these can affect the types and quality of decisions that, in turn, have a tremendous impact on the lives of children and their families. Training on working with diverse populations is an essential first step. Diversity training can help individuals address personal biases they may hold and help them recognize and manage attitudes they may have. However, training can only go so far and is most effective when people apply the knowledge posttraining and find a way to put it into practice.

Reflection Box 13.1: Professional Habit of Self-Reflection

It is crucial to develop the professional habit of self-reflection. Self-reflection can help you process difficult situations, enhance practice, and confront biases. Self-reflection is an essential part of evaluating your practice. In evaluating practice, you attend to the client's progress toward goals and what you did that was effective or not. Do an honest reflection of what transpired and note your reactions and emotional responses: (a) Did you engage with the client? (b) Were you authentic? (c) Did you like the client? (d) Did the client's actions disgust you? (This may be especially relevant when thinking about harming children, but it can also apply in other settings.) (e) How aware were you of these emotions when working with the client? (f) Were you able to discuss your feelings in supervision or with consultation? (g) How do you believe your feelings affect the outcomes of your cases? (h) After examining your emotions and actions, how might your personal biases have influenced your decision making about cases?

Create a plan of action for developing the professional habit of self-reflection:

1. Name your action steps (e.g., *journaling, supervision, personal self-reflection, having crucially difficult conversations with an objective party and immersing yourself in experiences where you are the cultural other, followed by self-reflection*).
2. How often will you engage in the action steps?
3. To whom will you be accountable (e.g., *colleague, family member, friend, mentor*)?
4. How will you evaluate this practice of self-reflection to discern a difference both in your work with clients and within yourself?
5. How might you improve your practice based on what you learn?

We understand that bias is a natural part of the human experience. Biases grow from life experiences, observations, media communications, family messaging and values, and religious expectations about morality and socialized behaviors. Biases can be positive or negative, significantly influencing professionals' work with client systems. For instance, the child welfare professional could overidentify with clients, fail to realize something important about the case, or underestimate a client's ability based on negative stereotypes. It is vital to develop an awareness of one's unconscious bias and correct it to perform fairly, equitably, and ethically on the job. The professional habit of self-reflection can assist with this process of becoming aware of one's own biases.

In addition, child welfare workers need to confront their own racism. Given that 60% of social workers in the United States are White and many are in child welfare, issues of White privilege must be addressed. Ways to confront and explore the impact of privilege include professional training and education, conversations with colleagues, and ongoing self-reflection. It is easy to acknowledge that White privilege exists, but much harder to admit to one's own racist beliefs. When these biases, including racist reactions, are implicit and may go against one's outwardly stated beliefs, discovering and acknowledging them is even more challenging. However, it is essential to recognize racist practices at individual and systemic levels to challenge the status quo. Questioning why certain populations are disproportionately overrepresented within child welfare is an essential initial step in addressing this major issue of racism in the system, which contributes to gross inequities and harm done to families of color.

Role of Intersectionality

Williams-Butler and colleagues (2023) assert that the intersectionality of race, gender, and class is significant in understanding the overrepresentation of Black mothers reported to the child welfare system, as the child welfare labor force is mainly White and middle class. They argue that sexism also plays a role, as mothers are expected to be self-sacrificing, wise, and nearly perfect, carrying the responsibility for parenting, mostly absolving fathers of responsibility. Williams-Butler and colleagues (2023) further state that the complexity of Black motherhood, where mothers face stereotypes and biases directed against them while trying to raise children in a society where they are criminalized or ignored, is essential to remember. Additionally, parenting styles may differ, and Black mothers may be judged or misunderstood by someone from a different cultural background (Williams-Butler et al., 2023).

Beyond a sensitivity to the potential for social injustice imposed through individual biases and systemic racism, child welfare professionals are called to recognize the humanity in the clients they work with and to understand the life-altering effects of separating children and parents, even for the short term. Broadhurst and Mason (2020) conducted interviews with birth mothers who had repeated involvement with the family courts. They recognize that many families involved with the child welfare system have faced greater challenges but with fewer resources for parenting than their counterparts in the general population. Often, they are "women with long-standing histories of disadvantage who hold fragile and restricted social statuses" (Broadhurst & Mason, 2020, p. 15). Following involvement with child welfare, particularly when it involves the removal of child(ren), women often experience *grief, role loss, difficulties with extended family, social isolation, and stigma*. Without support, the circumstances that initially brought the family to the attention of child welfare, including substance use and mental health symptoms, may be exacerbated. If the decision is made to separate children from their families, Broadhurst and Mason (2020) note the need to acknowledge the potentially devastating effects of this decision and the increased support needed by mothers and families at this time. This additional support can also help prevent repeated contact with child welfare in the future. Knowing that families of color and low-income families are overrepresented in child welfare, such heavy decisions need to be made thoughtfully, cautiously, and with a sense of the potential impact on everyone involved.

Child welfare professionals must approach people from cultural backgrounds other than their own with a sense of humility and an openness to learning. While a complete understanding of another culture may not be possible, it is essential to take steps toward a greater understanding of diverse cultural values, including approaches to parenting. Familiarity comes from reading about and initiating friendships with various cultural groups. Child welfare professionals should, at minimum, extend *unconditional positive regard* to all children and families. It is not a matter of performing in a color-blind state but accepting people, acknowledging their humanity, and embracing difference. These are concepts that lead to cultural humility.

Cultural Humility

Ortega and Coulborn Faller (2011) cite cultural humility's importance in complementing cultural competence, noting that assumptions may not consider unique experiences and individual differences. They note the growth in training around cultural competence, including content on different cultural groups, developing practice knowledge and skills to work across cultures, valuing diversity, considering language differences, and knowing within-group differences. However, in child welfare, this may lead to overconfidence and may still leave the power with the child welfare worker, further reinforcing the power imbalance (Ortega & Coulborn Faller, 2011). In arguing for cultural humility, they describe three dimensions, to include:

1. *Self-awareness*, which includes an appreciation of who one is through a cultural lens and recognition of how that lens affects one's perceptions of the world;

2. *Openness*, recognizing that there is always more to know and not everything can ever be known; much of the world functions outside of one's level of awareness, and one should be open to learning from others; and

3. *Transcendence*, noting that the world is more complex than anyone can ever imagine; there is a vastness of cultural experience, much larger than any one individual. Keeping the worker in a learning mode is vital in child welfare work (Ortega & Coulborn Faller, 2011).

Considering Emily's experience presented in the case scenario, she has intentionally placed herself as a learner, recognizing that she does not know everything about parenting or caring for children. She has much to learn from the families with whom she works. She sees herself as a partner with them, working toward the common goal of providing safe, nurturing care for children.

Ortega and Coulborn Faller (2011) further suggest a series of practical strategies and skills for practicing in a culturally humble way: (a) active listening, (b) reflecting, (c) reserving judgment, and (d) entering the client's world. While these may be characteristic of good professional practice in general, they are especially critical in connecting with families and working collaboratively toward positive outcomes in child welfare work.

The National Child Welfare Workforce Institute (2017) has built upon the work of Ortega and Coulborn Faller (2011) to further develop a series of 10 practice principles related to cultural humility specifically applied to child welfare practice:

1. *Embrace the complexity of diversity*, recognizing that each person holds multiple identities.

2. *Be open to individual differences* and the ways these differences affect one's expectations, quality of life, and capacities as parents.

3. *Reserve judgment*, as there is much that one does not and cannot know about another person's experience. In child welfare, this means not prejudging families based on culture alone but valuing their cultural expressions and strengths.

4. *Utilize, as much as possible, culturally appropriate communication* and interaction skills.

5. Think of *cultural humility as an ongoing process* rather than an end product.

6. *Encourage collaboration* among colleagues that promote nonpaternalistic and respectful relationships with others, both clients and workers.

7. *Become familiar with the living environments of children and families* to build upon strengths and break down barriers.

8. *Develop self-awareness* and the ability to address one's own biases.

9. *Challenge assumptions* about one's openness to learning from others, recognizing that attitudes can create barriers to learning from others.

10. Work to *create organizational supports* demonstrating the importance of cultural humility to the agency and its work; these include policies, practices, environmental factors, knowledge, and skills.

Cultural humility is an ongoing professional goal, and practitioners must expand their cultural awareness, acceptance, and appropriateness to fully appreciate client strengths. While essential to all practice, this is critical to child welfare work, as so many culturally linked values and assumptions are connected with families, parenting, and children.

Societal and Institutional Factors Contributing to Bias

Societal factors also play a role in the inequitable delivery of services. Historically as well as in the present day, policies and services have disadvantaged populations of color and lower-income communities. Judgments have been made about families and what a *good home* and *good parenting* look like, often elevating a Eurocentric perspective while demeaning other approaches. The lack of access to resources and paths out of poverty have disadvantaged large swaths of the population. In terms of services, programs, and funds, benefits have been offered to White populations while excluding or making it more difficult to access by populations of color. Accumulation of wealth to benefit subsequent generations has been undermined, particularly for African American, Native American, and Latinx populations. Access to education and employment advantages the White population. These factors perpetuate disparities based on race, ethnicity, national origin, and citizenship. The social work profession has engaged in practices that have historically been harmful to families and communities.

It is essential to acknowledge that aspect of historical and current practices and to seek ways to address any injustice that has come at the hands of the profession. Child welfare is stressful; plans and progress toward goals do not transpire as smoothly as expected. There may be a tendency to want to blame someone, often the parent or caregiver, when something goes wrong. Child welfare professionals must be able to suspend judgment, reflect on the situation's complexity, and consider ways to proceed fairly.

How to Combat Oppression and Discrimination in Social Work

Social work is a profession that is committed to helping and advocating for oppressed and disadvantaged people and fighting injustice in society. According to the National Association of Social Workers (NASW, 2020), "Social workers have an ethical duty to dismantle racism, both personally and professionally, and to demonstrate what it means to be antiracist" (para. 6). Historically, however, the social work profession has played a role in maintaining the existing power structure, thereby upholding racism and oppression in American society. It is critically important to acknowledge social work's complicity in practices that perpetuated harm on families across generations. In child welfare, this includes the separation of families of color (specifically Native American, African American, and Latinx families). NASW has issued a statement of apology in acknowledgment of the role the profession has played in maintaining structural racism and in engaging in policies and practices that were blatantly racist and have harmed individuals and communities:

> Although social workers strive to improve the lives of others, we must also face some uncomfortable truths in the history of social work. For these grave mistakes, we apologize to the clients, colleagues, and communities of color who were harmed by our profession. (NASW, 2021, p. 2)

Concerning child welfare, NASW (2021, 2022) identifies the disproportionate removal of children of color from their homes and families, the criminalization of poverty, and inadequate cultural awareness, which can lead to the application of a deficit model in assessing families in crisis.

Antiracism is one way of acknowledging that racism exists in our institutions, systems, and other structures (Ladhani & Sitter, 2020) that vulnerable families encounter. As Corneau and Stergiopoulos (2012) assert, antiracism can take the form of movements, practice, knowledge, and thoughts and give rise to power dynamics. Antiracism in child welfare can take many forms. It is critical to engage in antiracist practices to be equity minded when social work practitioners work with children, youth, and families. Having adequate knowledge about differences aids in curtailing misinformation that emanates from a lack of exposure and appreciation of differences. Ladhani and Sitter (2020) remind their readers that antiracism without action is insufficient, as action is an integral part of antiracist practice. Nelson and colleagues (2011) write, "Racism can be broadly defined as a phenomenon that maintains or exacerbates avoidable and unfair inequalities in power, resources, or opportunities across racial, ethnic, cultural, or religious groups in society" (p. 263). They argue that racism is expressed through our beliefs. When our beliefs encompass negative and inaccurate thoughts about groups of people, these beliefs result in stereotypes. Racism is also caused by emotions such as fear or hatred and can lead to behaviors and practices that cause unfair treatment of the *othered* individual or group. Racism in this way is indiscriminate, callous, and unaware.

In addition, gender-based oppression is present in the child welfare field. Some of this is reflective of the traditional roles played by mothers and the expectations around mothering. Also, social structures may treat women involved in intimate partner violence as partly to blame for their situation. They may be viewed negatively for getting into an abusive relationship in the first place, for contributing to the dysfunctional relationship, and for remaining with an abusive partner. Women in abusive relationships may be blamed for leaving children in a potentially risky situation, while there may be few alternatives or the alternatives may create an even greater risk to the mother's and her children's lives and well-being. It is essential to see the social context, understand the other factors, including poverty and mental health concerns, and understand the experience from the *battered woman's* perspective.

Working to Support Children and Families of Color

Soni and colleagues (2022) recommend a dramatic change in how our society responds to children and families in challenging situations. They note that to develop and promote policies and programs that specifically enhance the well-being and safety of youth of color as well as their families and communities, "we must turn to practices and strategies that deconstruct traditional power hierarchies and address the complex contexts in which lives are led" (Soni et al., 2022, p. 105).

To this end, they suggest a series of principles to guide community-driven antiracist design for service delivery:

1. *Redefine success*: Ensure that the community is involved in determining measures and definitions of successful outcomes.

2. *Move from human-centered to situation-centered design*: This allows for the social structural factors related to family well-being in the context of child welfare, such as racism, classism, and political influences currently and historically, to be considered in designing programs and practices.

3. *Prioritize healing-centered* over trauma-informed approaches: Though less well known, healing-centered approaches build upon strengths rather than deficits, advocating for community and political action rather than only clinical interventions.

4. *Prioritize the needs of children and families* over child welfare and policy designs: While incorporating the input of children and youth, be sure to respect their boundaries around how and how much of their story is shared, with whom, and for which purposes.

5. *Shift power to communities*: This occurs through information-sharing, decision making, allyship, and deliberate steps to unpack how existing power structures benefit the organization. Community members should be official participants in governing and advisory bodies with compensation for their service.

6. *Develop bidirectional feedback loops*: In this way, community members retain a voice. Input is gathered from youth, families, and communities, but the organization must also inform the community on how their contributions are being implemented.

These strategies have the potential to shift power dynamics, enhancing community input, buy-in, and cooperation. Prevention then becomes the responsibility of everyone, including the community.

More Approaches to Combat Racism

Racism may be best addressed in training, supervisory sessions, and in assessing one's practices. Ladhani and Sitter (2020) describe three ways of combating racism: *racial storytelling, critical ethnography,* and *racial identity caucusing*. We focus on only two as critical autoethnography, which they cite, is used in research. For racial storytelling, the authors draw on the work of Johnson (2017), who describes this as a way to connect the past with the present while reimagining our future: "This entails assessing the intricacies of our social identities and the way in which we are all involved in the complexity" (Ladhani & Sitter, 2020, p. 61). Racial storytelling can be used as a tool to assist child welfare professionals in coming to terms with their own experiences or lack thereof. "The process of racial storytelling must include everyone to ensure that the stories of racialized peoples are not shared for the consumption of others" (Ladhani & Sitter, 2020, p. 62). Antiracism training can assist in uncovering hidden biases and helping child welfare professionals understand the origins of their beliefs in others. Child welfare is a difficult job, but when one commits to a larger purpose, one realizes there are things one can do to manage the stress without inadvertently punishing others by acting in grossly misguided ways (e.g., ignorance of difference).

Ladhani and Sitter (2020) also refer to racial identity caucusing as a strategy allowing participants to examine, confront, and dismantle institutional and cultural racism. Additionally, racial identity caucusing will enable participants to explore internalized beliefs of racist superiority from the dominant culture. Caucusing allows participants to explore how racism operates in institutions and affects the people we serve. Groups with shared experiences can gain greater clarity about how power and privilege shape identity; the goal is to collectively attend to how it manifests and build collective accountability (Ladhani & Sitter, 2020) to reduce or eliminate it. Ladhani and Sitter assert that this strategy can facilitate an authentic antiracist partnership between racialized and nonracialized groups. This approach allows for critical and honest dialogue about the dynamics of racism from a lens that opposes it (antiracism; Ladhani & Sitter, 2020). Child welfare systems can think of innovative ways to use either approach in training and supervision. It should be consistent and provide a safe space for such transformative conversations. Expanding and exploring child welfare professionals' cultural ethos may have lasting implications and empower them to work toward policy and practice changes.

ADDRESSING POVERTY

There is a complex relationship between child welfare involvement and poverty. There is no simple explanation for the overrepresentation of low-income families in the system.

> In the past, prevention strategies have often focused on family-level issues and dynamics, but the role of poverty, and the systemic factors that make escaping poverty difficult for families, cannot be ignored. Research tells us that families who are experiencing poverty are far more likely to be reported to child protective services (CPS) than families with more resources, but it does not tell us *why* this is the case. (Child Welfare Information Gateway, 2023, p. 2)

Although there are programs to address poverty, they do not work in a coherent, integrated fashion to help families move out of poverty (Feely et al., 2020).

Further, we have not, as a society nor as child welfare professionals, viewed economic hardships as a variable perpetuating neglect (Feely et al., 2020).

However, some data suggest that poverty plays a role in child neglect, though we may not understand the mechanisms nor the actual causal factors; additionally, data indicate that programs to support families, such as Earned Income Tax Credit (EITC), increased minimum wage, and child support enforcement can decrease rates of child neglect (Feely et al., 2020). These factors suggest that macrosystem policies can play a significant role in preventing or causing child maltreatment (Feely et al., 2020). Circumstances such as low wages, inadequate transportation that can affect employment, and unsafe or unstable housing contribute to child neglect but are not typically assessed in child welfare screenings.

Feely and colleagues (2020) assert that CAPTA was never designed to prevent or address neglect. Because it was passed during the Nixon administration, the legislation was watered down, and any connection of addressing poverty as a way of addressing neglect was removed because of a fear that Nixon would not sign the legislation. Because abuse was more connected to mental health rather than environmental systems, funding went to mental health and other related services (Feely et al., 2020) with a focus on changing parents and the home environment. This approach continues, even with the Family First Prevention Services Act, which is supposed to radically transform child welfare. Concerning neglect, "siloed systems effectively capture families in a CPS system that is not designed to respond to their needs" (Feely et al., 2020, p. 145).

Feely and colleagues (2020) recommend that neglect not be the sole responsibility of the child welfare system but that it extend to housing agencies, agriculture, and other entities. Similarly, Lenz-Rashid (2017) recommends collaboration among child welfare, public housing authorities (PHAs), and private housing agencies.

Housing and Child Well-Being

Safe and stable housing is essential for a child's well-being. Parents and caregivers want the best for their children and want to provide them with adequate housing. Imagine trying to raise a family in a shelter or a car. Beyond being stressful, inadequate housing has been cited as a reason for the removal of children for 9% of the cases, or 19,406 children and youth, in fiscal year 2021 (Children's Bureau, 2022). Housing may be a factor in even more cases, as child abuse investigators may not list all of the reasons for concern beyond abuse or neglect (Pergamit et al., 2017). Lack of stable housing also can create challenges for parents seeking to engage in services to secure their children's return. Even if parents and caregivers comply with the court's requirements, their children's return may be delayed if they are not in secure housing. While it may be difficult to establish causality, because many of the factors that contribute to housing instability, including deep and chronic poverty, substance use, mental health challenges, and domestic violence, are also found in many families involved with child welfare, it still is clear that a connection exists between child welfare and housing stability.

Logically, then, helping families access safe, affordable housing would be essential in maintaining children in their homes and in returning, as quickly as possible, children who have been removed from their homes. The Family Unification Program (FUP) was implemented in 1990 and is currently designed to provide housing choice vouchers (HCV) to those families for whom lack of stable housing is the primary reason for child removal or for foster youth, ages 18 to 24, who left the child welfare system after age 16 and have inadequate housing (youth .gov, n.d.). The program requires a partnership between public housing agencies (PHAs) and public child welfare agencies (PCWAs; U.S. Department of Housing and Urban Development [HUD], 2022). Pergamit and colleagues (2017) found only minor reductions in out-of-home placements in FUP families and no effect on the likelihood of reunification. However, they did find that FUP cases were closed more quickly. They also found that FUP reduced the likelihood of new reports of abuse or neglect in participating families. While there are some positive outcomes, they suggest that child welfare agencies do not target the families at greatest risk and who may benefit most from the program.

Though FUP has been around since 1990, there does not seem to be a high level of awareness nor coordination between PHAs and child welfare. Child welfare professionals also may feel that they are not housing agencies and do not have control over those resources (Cunningham & Pergamit, 2015). The program also requires a Memorandum of Understanding between the PHA and the PCWA, which may create an extra layer of complication. There may be differences in the orientations of employees in both programs. Child welfare professionals view child safety as the priority and, without training about the benefits and structure of the program, view *housing first* as a challenge to this priority. PHAs, on the other hand, tend to have a screen-out approach, setting up criteria for exclusion from housing. Cunningham and Pergamit recommend a screen-in approach, noting that many families in the child welfare system have poor rent histories, evictions, and leaving without notice. However, these are the families who need housing stability the most. Cunningham and Pergamit (2015) also believe that child welfare agencies do not have the assessment tools to collect adequate data on housing needs. Additionally, they recommend that housing needs should be met first and suggest that what typically happens is that these limited housing resources are offered to families who are meeting the service plan and are nearing the end of their work. Instead of housing used as a reward for compliance when families are moving out of crisis stages, it might be offered as a resource earlier in the process, potentially shortening the time a family would need services (Cunningham & Pergamit, 2015).

Housing stability is essential for families. While child welfare professionals are not expected to be housing specialists, it is crucial to explore resources and options to best meet the needs of families. FUP is one program; nonprofit housing agencies also may be leveraged to meet this foundational need so that families can work on the other steps for reunification or prevention of child removal.

Looking to the Future: Reimagining a Stronger System

Innovation begins with unbridled imagination. It helps to brainstorm ideas freely without constraints from judgment, rules, concerns of money, or other limitations. To begin a brainstorming activity like this, we often ask participants to think of solutions as if money were no object. In the case of child welfare, it would be to think of ways to improve the child welfare system if money, time, and politics were of no consequence. Once uncensored ideas are generated, the group can sort them based on no-cost, low-cost, and feasible ideas. The more difficult-to-reach solutions can be reimagined to mitigate whatever barriers exist. Child welfare leaders should use an array of strategies to reimagine the system. It would be essential to bring in ideas from children and families who have been involved in the child welfare system, foster parents, academic scholars, child welfare professionals, and perhaps even legislators. This type of project should create a true sense of collaboration, ownership, and incentive for the group to move forward.

One example of reimagining the system comes from *Powerful Families, Powerful Communities* (PFPC) in New Jersey, which " . . . is a collaboration to design a family and community-driven model that will transform child welfare by creating a bold, new, child and family well-being system for New Jersey, and obsolete the need for nonkin foster care" (Powerful Families, Powerful Communities, n.d., para 1). Their advisory board comprises diverse community members, including the Annie E. Casey Foundation, public and private partners, and philanthropists. Their goal is to make sure parents/families have what they need so children can remain safely in the home. They identified three specific communities where they would pilot their powerful families' ideas, making it into a movement. PFPC works with teams of parents (i.e., a mixture who have and have not experienced the system) to design prototype interventions. New Jersey's child welfare commissioner states they are trying things they have not tried before, "some things that are completely unique to the field of child welfare, and even go beyond child welfare" (Burke Foundation, 2021, para. 8). It is important to track the progress of these interventions to understand their effectiveness. Moreover, they emphasize that child welfare includes many service delivery systems to support families adequately.

PFPC works with a nonprofit design and an innovation organization to develop its intentional approach to codesigning interventions. As PFPC notes, they work with their partners to create accountability and, in turn, empower their partners toward active participation. They create tangible solutions that are feasible through a system of shared power. PFPC combines human-centered design methodologies, equity-centered community design, and liberatory design (see Figure 13.1).

- *Human-centered design* is an innovative technique for solving problems that places people at the center of the development process, making design relevant to their lived experiences (Van der Bijl-Brouwer & Dorst, 2017).

- *Equity-centered design* emphasizes inclusive approaches and considers the history of oppression, power dynamics, and the lived experiences of people and communities. It centers on multiple voices (Green et al., 2021) and examines injustices.

- *Liberatory design* is a process and practice approach to address equity issues. The liberatory design assumes that (a) racism and inequity have been intentionally designed; hence they can be redesigned; (b) design requires partnership with the end user who is impacted by inequity; and (c) the use of an equity-centered design process, requires fair-mindedness, and the inclusion of complex multicultural voices (Harper & Kezar, 2023).

These equitable and inclusive approaches generate cocreative processes and programs relevant to end users (see Figure 13.1).

Another innovative program is *Thriving Families, Safer Children*, developed through a partnership among the Annie E. Casey Foundation, the Children's Bureau, Casey Family Programs, and Prevent Child Abuse America (Administration for Children and Families [ACF], 2020; Casey Family Programs, 2021; Children's Bureau, 2020; Prevent Child Abuse America, 2020). This initiative began in 2020, was piloted in four jurisdictions, and has expanded to over 20 states and tribal communities. "The effort aims to help select jurisdictions move from traditional, reactive child protection systems to systems designed to proactively support child and family well-being and prevent child maltreatment and unnecessary family separation" (Casey Family Programs, 2021, para. 6). The organizations are committed to collaborating with one another and partnering "with families, communities, and jurisdictions in new, highly intentional ways that are driven by the lived expertise of parents and young people to bring child and family well-being systems to life"

Figure 13.1 Innovative Design

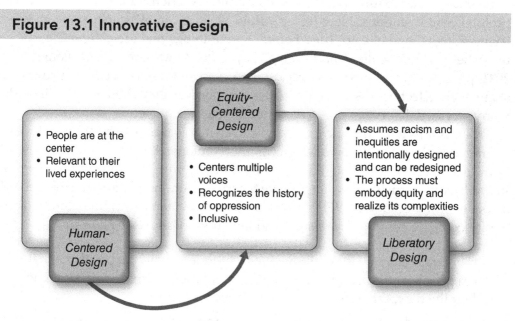

Source: Adapted from Powerful Families, Powerful Communities.

(Children's Bureau, 2020, para. 1). The purpose of this initiative is to fundamentally rethink child welfare and move from a reactive approach to a preventive one.

When the child welfare system considers new solutions, it may be better equipped to lift the constraints parents experience when trying to comply with mandated services. The system requires parents to adhere to expectations without regard for their working-class employment status, leaving little room for flexibility. Without work flexibility, parents do not have the option to adjust their schedules in order to make mandated appointments without the risk of losing their jobs. In addition, the system removes children and pays foster parents when those funds could be used to bolster a family's need for income. One example Beyer provided from an interview with a parent is, "You took my child, and you placed them with a foster parent, and then you started paying that foster parent $800 a month. If you gave me the $800 a month, I'd be able to take care of my child because I could get to work, and I would be able to pay for childcare" (Burke Foundation, 2021, para. 11). Beyer indicates that they hear these comments from parents, prompting them to think differently about solutions. "It's not just the Child Protection Division; it's public health, it's our medical community, it's our schools, it's law enforcement. Everybody has a role to play in changing the way we support families or how we intervene in their lives" (Burke Foundation, 2021, para. 11).

Beyer also discusses the importance of recognizing work-related stress and secondary trauma staff experience. She noted that staff observe humanity's raw and painful moments, which take a toll on them and their families (Burke Foundation, 2021). The authors believe the child welfare system is responsible for caring for their employees, addressing the issue of traumatic stress, making their caseloads manageable, and creating ways to strengthen families whenever possible. It is a tremendous responsibility, so much so that in New Jersey, they worked toward transformation in this area and created an Office of Staff Health and Wellness.

Reimagining Child Welfare: Addressing Family Poverty

Recognizing the importance of families in the well-being of children, communities can be more responsive and provide resources that support families. That requires listening to families and paying attention to their needs (Casey Family Programs, 2022).

Attempts to reform the child welfare system will not be effective unless they involve former and current consumers or participants in the child welfare system (Casey Family Programs, 2022; Soni et al., 2022). Too often, suggestions for reform are made by professionals without consideration of the needs and desires of the participants (Soni et al., 2022). The PFPC program seeks to implement full inclusion of key stakeholders (especially families involved in the system). Other systems may include the voices of youth and families.

Previous prevention and intervention approaches have been focused on family dynamics and issues. However, little attention has been paid to systemic issues that keep families impoverished and interventions that may address those larger system issues (Child Welfare Information Gateway, 2023). Feely and colleagues (2020) have suggested that we have created federal policies to explicitly omit strategies that ease financial hardships from any interventions to address neglect. These omissions have been a long-standing, contentious, and possibly divisive political topic that continues to be avoided.

Pelton (2015) argues, "If we really intend child safety and child protection to be our goals, we should be concerned about protecting children from harm, no matter what the presumed source" (p. 34). However, he asserts that rather than looking broadly at environmental threats to safety, we have defined child protection as protection from the parent. That mindset often leads to removing the child rather than addressing the environmental or systemic hazards for children.

Soni and colleagues (2022) call for a move toward antiracist policies and processes in redesigning child welfare and other systems. They describe a continuum of approaches to program design focusing on the dimension of power, moving from concentration of power to redistribution of power. They assert that such approaches to program design as *exclusion* (decision makers creating the design) and *tokenism* (limited representation from the community) perpetuate racist practices. Even *consultation* and *codesign* do not go far enough. The only antiracist designs are *community-driven* (where community members have the voice and skills to address equity and power) and *community ownership* (where community members design and operate programs without outside involvement). The healing-centered engagement recommended by Soni and colleagues (2022) includes political action and clinical interventions.

Grüber (2020), a former foster youth, asserts that the child welfare system "is led primarily by well-intentioned advocates who have never experienced foster care, and who advocate for incremental change that will never deliver the type of bold reform that it so desperately needs" (para. 5), suggesting that changes are made, but not in a way that significantly addresses the flaws in the system. Soni and colleagues (2022) assert that as long as changes are made to child welfare—directed by professionals already in power—without full inclusion of participants in the system, the changes will make sense only to those holding power and will maintain the existing power dynamics.

Ortega and Coulborn Faller (2011) recommend that workers demonstrate cultural humility, not assuming they are experts in cultural competence, and work to truly engage families as active participants in the process. They also note intersectionality and the many identities clients and families may hold, including but not limited to race.

RETENTION OF CHILD WELFARE WORKERS

Another challenge of the child welfare system is the retention of child welfare workers. In many departments, they are overworked and underpaid. There are high rates of staff turnover, as workers may feel underappreciated or have to deal with repeated difficult and painful situations. The late poet Maya Angelou was credited for saying, "People will forget what you said, people will forget what you did, but people will never forget how you made them feel" at Bill Clinton's inauguration in 1993 (Shende, 2023, p. 2201). If professional child welfare workers do not receive the support they need to process and cope with the difficult circumstances they encounter regularly, they will not feel valued, seen, or heard. Feeling underappreciated and overwhelmed by high caseloads does not bode well for staff morale. In addition, the child welfare system handles exceptionally complex cases laden with some of humanity's worst problems, and solutions are not always easily obtained. Unfortunately, the lack of supervision, systemwide support, or incentives adds to worker burnout and fatigue. More importantly, employer emphasis on self-care is sorely needed within the child welfare system to maintain employee morale and well-being and to curtail vicarious trauma.

Other factors contributing to high employee turnover are changing viewpoints on careers, stigma caused by blame, and lack of autonomy. Younger employees may have a different view of their jobs and careers and are not afraid to walk away from a job they believe is unfulfilling or too stressful. The days of entry-level workers identifying career paths as *callings* or lifelong commitments are long gone. Today's entry-level workers are well indoctrinated by the gig economy and frequently blaze their own trails. Generally speaking, people want to feel pride about the time they spend at work. Societal factors such as *blaming the system* may bring about stigma and a desire to distance oneself from the child welfare system. Employees may not feel they have a sense of autonomy in their jobs. "Flexible and autonomous work styles are considered to improve worker productivity and work engagement" (Yokoyama et al., 2022, p. 296). When employees have less flexibility on the job, they are at an increased risk of burnout. To avoid losing valuable workers, leaders within child welfare agencies must advocate for their workers, implement systemwide self-care strategies, show employee appreciation, and elevate employee status by inculcating messages about the importance of child welfare work that resonates with employee perspectives of what they value.

LOOKING FORWARD

The well-being of children and families is foundational to a just and caring society. Some children have experienced significant abuse; others have been neglected and are at risk of harm. However, children at the greatest risk may be overidentified in the system.

Critics call for overhauling the child welfare system, even to the point of abolishing it, starting over, and even challenging the assumptions of the benefits of mandated reporting (Gruber, 2023). The authors make several suggestions for changing this very important system. Improvement requires comprehensive structural changes to societal perspectives on families and changes within the child welfare system:

1. Address poverty to better support children and families.
2. Address systemic racism, which requires acknowledgment and action.
3. Improve collaboration and integration of services and supports to benefit families (Feely et al., 2021).
4. Ensure that family's and children's/youth's voices are central to reimagining child welfare (Chambers et al., 2020).
5. Provide support and supervision for those who do the work; this includes promoting trauma-informed workplaces and self-care.
6. Restructure the way we think about interventions with families. How might child welfare professionals build on the strengths of families?
7. Understand the persistence of neglect allegations. The child welfare system must consider the potential for bias and the role that poverty and structural racism play.
8. Provide ample support for families after a child is removed (Broadhurst & Mason, 2020).

If there were no child welfare system, what protection would children have? Are there other systems that could fill the gap? How would society protect children from harm and fatalities in caregiver spaces? Conversely, imagine being a parent whose children are removed, which would not happen if resources had been provided. There are no easy answers—the system must be transformed, but children still need to be protected.

CHAPTER SUMMARY

This chapter identified and explored topics in child welfare practice from an antiracist lens. Topics included addressing individual and structural racism, the role of cultural humility and intersectionality in understanding families, training, and support for staff to encourage retention and equitable service delivery, addressing poverty and housing needs, collaboration among programs to address family needs, and reimaging a system that elevates the voices of children and families while incorporating antiracism, diversity, equity, and inclusion.

DISCUSSION QUESTIONS

1. What ideas do you believe would help to transform the child welfare system?
2. Which examples in this chapter show promise and why?

3. How might liberatory, equity-centered, or human-centered design promote true transformation within the child welfare system?

4. What are the pros and cons of system abolishment?

5. What does the saying "the measure of a society is how it treats its most vulnerable members" mean in the context of child welfare?

RESOURCES

Burke Foundation
https://burkefoundation.org/
Child Welfare Information Gateway. Episode 49: A Guide to Implementing Family First. Podcast.
    https://www.childwelfare.gov/more-tools-resources/podcast/episode-49/
Human Rights Watch (2022). "If I wasn't poor, I wouldn't be unfit": The family separation crisis in the U.S. child welfare system. https://www.hrw.org/sites/default/files/media_2022/11/us_crd1122web_3.pdf
Powerful Families, Powerful Communities NJ
https://www.powerfulfamiliesnj.org/

 A robust set of instructor resources designed to supplement this text is located at **http://connect.springerpub.com/content/book/978-0-8261-5285-5.** Qualifying instructors may request access by emailing **textbook@springerpub.com.**

REFERENCES

Administration for Children and Families. (2020). *First-of-its-kind national partnership aims to redesign child welfare into child and family well-being systems.* Department of Health and Human Services. https://www.acf.hhs.gov/media/press/2020/first-its-kind-national-partnership-aims-redesign-child-welfare-child-and-family

Broadhurst, K., & Mason, C. (2020). Child removal as the gateway to further adversity: Birth mother accounts of the immediate and enduring collateral consequences of child removal. *Qualitative Social Work, 19*(1), 15–37. https://doi.org/10.1177/1473325019893412

Burke Foundation. (2021). *Dispatches from the field: Re-imagining our child welfare system.* https://burke-foundation.org/interviews/dispatches-from-the-field-re-imagining-our-child-welfare-system/

Casey Family Programs. (2021, April 21). *News and updates. National partnership to reinvent child welfare expands.* https://www.casey.org/thriving-families-safer-children-expands/

Casey Family Programs. (2022). *Investing in equity: Sustaining hope for children and families.* 2022 Signature report. https://www.casey.org/media/2022-Signature-Report-Web.pdf

Chambers, R. M., Crutchfield, R. M., Willis, T. Y., Cuza, H. A., Otero, A., Goddu Harper, S. G., & Carmichael, H. (2020). "Be supportive and understanding of the stress that youth are going through:" Foster care alumni recommendations for youth, caregivers and caseworkers on placement transitions. *Children and Youth Services Review, 108,* 104644. https://doi.org/10.1016/j.childyouth.2019.104644

Children's Bureau. (2020, October). *Thriving families, safer children.* Children's Bureau Express, 21(7). https://cbexpress.acf.hhs.gov/previous_issues/e86e6d5d1bdec910517620efe54bcb17

Children's Bureau. (2022, June). *The AFCARS report.* Department of Health and Human Services, Administration for Children, Youth, and Families. https://www.acf.hhs.gov/sites/default/files/documents/cb/afcars-report-29.pdf

Child Welfare Information Gateway. (2023). *Separating poverty from neglect in child welfare*. U.S. Department of Health and Human Services, Administration for Children and Families, Children's Bureau. https://www.childwelfare.gov/pubPDFs/bulletins-povertyneglect.pdf

Corneau, S., & Stergiopoulos, V. (2012). More than being against it: Anti-racism and antioppression in mental health services. *Transcultural Psychiatry, 49*(2), 261–282. https://doi.org/10.1177/1363461512441594

Cunningham, M., & Pergamit, M. (2015). Housing matters for families: Promising practices from child welfare agencies. *Child Welfare, 94*(1), 123–140.

Feely, M., Raissian, K. M., Schneider, W., & Bullinger, L. R. (2020). The social welfare policy landscape and child protective services: Opportunities for and barriers to creating systems synergy. *The Annals of the American Academy of Political and Social Science, 692*(1), 140–161. https://doi.org/10.1177/0002716220973566

Feely, M., Raissian, K. M., Schneider, W., & Bullinger, L. R. (2021). Creating systems synergy across the social welfare policy landscape. *Focus on Poverty, 37*(2), 21–28. https://www.irp.wisc.edu/wp/wp-content/uploads/2021/09/Focus-on-Poverty-37-2.pdf

Green, P. M., Bergen, D. J., Stewart, C. P., & Nayve, C. (2021). An engagement of hope: A framework and equity-centered theory of action for community engagement. *Metropolitan Universities, 32*(2), 129–157. https://doi.org/10.18060/25527

Grüber, L. (2020). Child welfare policymakers need to learn user centered design. *The Imprint.* https://imprintnews.org/opinion/child-welfare-policymakers-need-to-learn-user-centered-design/43938

Gruber, T. (2023). Beyond mandated reporting: Debunking assumptions to support children and families. *Abolitionist Perspectives in Social Work, 1*(1), 1–26. https://doi.org/10.52713/apsw.v1i1.12

Harper, J., & Kezar, A. (2023). Designing with, not for students: Prioritizing student voice using liberatory design thinking. *About Campus, 27*(6), 31–39. https://doi.org/10.1177/10864822231151876

Johnson, L. L. (2017). The racial hauntings of one Black male professor and the disturbance of the self(ves): Self-actualization and racial storytelling as pedagogical practices. *Journal of Literacy Research, 49*(4), 476–502. https://doi.org/10.1177/1086296X17733779

Ladhani, S., & Sitter, K. C. (2020). The revival of anti-racism: Considerations for social work education. *Critical Social Work, 21*(1), 54–65. https://doi.org/10.22329/csw.v21i1.6227

Lenz-Rashid, S. (2017). Supportive housing program for homeless families: Foster care outcomes and best practices. *Children & Youth Services Review, 79*, 558–563. https://doi.org/10.1016/j.childyouth.2017.07.012

National Association of Social Workers. (2020, August 21). *Social workers must help dismantle systems of oppression and fight racism within social work profession* [Press release]. https://www.socialworkers.org/News/News-Releases/ID/2219/Social-Workers-Must-Help-Dismantle-Systems-of-Oppression-and-Fight-Racism-Within-Social-Work-Profession

National Association of Social Workers. (2021, June). *Undoing racism through social work: NASW report to the profession on racial justice priorities and action.* https://www.socialworkers.org/LinkClick.aspx?fileticket=29AYH9qAdXc%3d&portalid=0

National Association of Social Workers. (2022). *Undoing racism through social work: A collaborative vision for an antiracist future*, Vol 2. https://www.socialworkers.org/LinkClick.aspx?fileticket=QsNmikJGKj0%3d&portalid=0

National Child Welfare Workforce Institute. (2017). *Cultural humility practice principles.* https://ncwwi-dms.org/resourcemenu/resource-library/inclusivity-racial-equity/cultural-responsiveness/1415-cultural-humility-practice-principles/file

Nelson, J. K., Dunn, K. M., & Paradies, Y. (2011). Bystander anti-racism: A review of the literature. *Analyses of Social Issues and Public Policy, 11*(1), 263–284. https://doi.org/10.1111/j.1530-2415.2011.01274.x

Ortega, R. M., & Coulborn Faller, K. (2011). Training child welfare workers from an intersectional cultural humility perspective: A paradigm shift. *Child Welfare, 90*(5), 27–49. https://pubmed.ncbi.nlm.nih.gov/22533053/

Pelton, L. H. (2015). The continuing role of material factors in child maltreatment and placement. *Child Abuse and Neglect, 41*, 30–39. https://doi.org/10.1016/j.chiabu.2014.08.001

Pergamit, M., Cunningham, M., & Hanson, D. (2017). The impact of family unification housing vouchers on child welfare outcomes. *American Journal of Community Psychology, 60*, 103–113. https://doi.org/10.1002/ajcp.12136

Powerful Families, Powerful Communities NJ. (n.d.). *A collaboration in which families and communities design their future.* https://www.powerfulfamiliesnj.org/

Shende, A. M. (2023). Culture in the novels of Maya Angelou. *Culture, 52*(4), 2200–2203. http://www.journal-iiie-india.com/1_apr_23/257_online.pdf

Soni, S., Mason, J., & Sherman, J. (2022). Beyond human-centered design: The promise of anti-racist community-centered approaches in child welfare program and policy design. *Child Welfare, 100*(1), 81–109. https://www.proquest.com/docview/2725348465/fulltextPDF/ED132615D1A84AA3PQ/1?accountid=2130

U.S. Department of Housing and Urban Development. (2022). *FY 2022 family unification program.* https://www.hud.gov/program_offices/spm/gmomgmt/grantsinfo/fundingopps/fy2022_fup

Van der Bijl-Brouwer, M., & Dorst, K. (2017). Advancing the strategic impact of human-centred design. *Design Studies, 53*, 1–23. https://doi.org/10.1016/j.destud.2017.06.003

Williams-Butler, A., Boyd, R., & Slack, K. (2023). Parenting strengths and distress among Black mothers reported to the child welfare system: The role of social network quality. *Social Service Review, 97*(2), 231–269. https://doi.org/10.1086/724564

Yokoyama, K., Nakata, A., Kannari, Y., Nickel, F., Deci, N., Krause, A., & Dettmers, J. (2022). Burnout and poor perceived health in flexible working time in Japanese employees: The role of self-endangering behavior in relation to workaholism, work engagement, and job stressors. *Industrial Health, 60*(4), 295–306. https://doi.org/10.2486/indhealth.2022-0063

Youth.gov. (n.d.). *Family Unification Program.* https://youth.gov/content/family-unification-program-fup

Index

African Americans (*cont'd*)
  housing patterns in colonies, 24
  and kinship care, 72
  police presence at home visits, 170
  racial injustices faced by, 135–136, 139
  social injustices faced by, 130, 131
  and War on Drugs, 118
aging out, 111, 130
  of foster care, 78, 212, 229–233, 277
  risks in, 265
  as single mothers, 264–265
AHT. *See* abusive head trauma
Aid to Dependent Children/Aid to Families
  with Dependent Children (ADC/
  AFDC), 19, 92, 95–96, 97, 105, 112, 116
Ainsworth, Mary Slater, 190, 191
algorithmic justice, 144–145
American Psychiatric Association, 268–269
American Psychological Association, 335
American Society for the Prevention of Cruelty
  to Animals (ASPCA), 17–18, 22, 38
amplification of listening, 174
amygdala, 41, 298
Anti-Drug Abuse Act, 118, 280
anti-oppression, 134, 363–365
antiracism, 147, 148, 177, 363, 364, 365, 366,
  372
Armstrong Association of Philadelphia, 24
Arnold, Mildred, 37
ASFA. *See* Adoption and Safe Families Act
  1997
Asian Americans and Pacific Islanders
  and child welfare, 27–28
  racial injustices faced by, 140–141
ASPCA. *See* American Society for the
  Prevention of Cruelty to Animals
assessment, 157–158, 188, 192
  interviewing children, 175–177
  interviewing parents/family, 173–175
  tools, 177–184
  of trauma exposure, 301–302
Association for American Indian Affairs
  (AAIA), 16
attachment, 53–54, 295
  disruption, 187, 192
  and family disruptions, 193–195
  and neurodevelopment, 195–198
  stages of, 191
  theory, 190–192
  types of, 190–191
attention, 331–332
autonomy, sense of, 267, 373

avoidance, 294, 301–302, 303
avoidant attachment, 191

BACW. *See* Black Administrators in Child
  Welfare
barriers to engagement, 163–168
battered-child syndrome, 22
behavior(s), 48, 50, 73, 173, 187, 189, 193, 197,
  247, 251, 252, 297, 308–309, 311
  behavioral health, 73, 113, 215–216, 219,
  284, 285, 287, 294, 348
  challenges, 196–197, 241, 244–245
  foster child, and placement disruption, 199
  needs, of children, 189
  parental interpretation of, 191
  and placement disruption, 196–197, 199
  traumatized, 241, 244–245, 246–247
Benjamin, Syrene Elizabeth Thompson, 24
BIA. *See* Bureau of Indian Affairs
bias, 52, 133, 145, 170, 358
  assessment of own biases, 171–172
  combating oppression and discrimination,
  363–365
  and drug testing, 271, 272
  implicit, 120, 335–336, 360
  individual, 358–362
  and intersectionality, 360–361
  positive, 166
  racial, 150, 222, 271, 272
  self-reflection, 358, 359, 360
  societal and institutional factors
  contributing to, 363
Biden, Joseph, 26
big data, 144, 145
bio-power, 170
bite marks, 43
Black Administrators in Child Welfare
  (BACW), 25
blame, 65, 145, 163–164, 311, 364
boarding schools, 14–15, 16, 26, 119, 141, 142
bonding of youth, 251, 252
Bowlby, John, 190, 193
Brace, Charles Loring, 13–14
brain, 40, 241, 331–332
  centers of, 295, 297–298
  development, 195, 241, 298
  neurobiology, and child abuse/neglect,
  39–42
  plasticity, 41
brainstem, 195
bruises, 43